Horses of the World

Also published by W.H. Allen

DOGS OF THE WORLD
Maurizio Bongianni and Concetta Mori

GREAT HORSES
Maurizio Bongianni

Horses of the World

Maurizio Bongianni and Concetta Mori

Illustrations by Piero Cozzaglio

Translated by Simon Pleasance

W.H. ALLEN · LONDON
1986

Abbreviations used on pages 121–133 of this volume:
b. – bay; bl. – black; ch. – chestnut; dk.b. – dark bay; g. – gelding; gr. – grey; h. – horse; m. – mare; ro. – roan

Produced by ERVIN s.r.l., Rome, under the supervision of Adriano Zannino
Editorial assistant Serenella Genoese Zerbi

Copyright © 1985 Arnoldo Mondadori Editore S.p.A., Milan
English translation copyright © 1986 Arnoldo Mondadori Editore S.p.A., Milan
First British edition 1986

Translated by Simon Pleasance

Drawings by Mario Pedrazzi

This book is sold subject to the condition that it shall not, by way of trade or otherwise, be lent, re-sold, hired out or otherwise circulated without the publisher's prior consent in any form of binding or cover other than that in which it is published and without a similar condition including this condition being imposed upon the subsequent purchaser.

Printed and bound in Italy by
Officine Grafiche di Arnoldo Mondadori Editore, Verona
for the Publishers, W.H. Allen & Co. Plc
44 Hill Street, London W1X 8LB

ISBN 0–491–03035–5

CONTENTS

PREFACE	7
CONFORMATION OF THE HORSE	9
Qualities and defects	10
Stance	12
Natural and artificial gaits	14
Shoes	15
Teeth and determining the age of a horse	16
Senses	18
Psychology and behaviour	20
Coats – Individual markings	23
ORIGINS AND EVOLUTION	30
Domestication	31
Breed formation and classification	34
European breeds	34
American breeds	38
Asian breeds	38
African breeds	39
Breeds from Australia and New Zealand	39
Breeds which have played an important part in the formation of other significant breeds	39
WARS AND WAR GAMES	46
Tourneys and jousts	50
TRANSPORT	55
Driving and carriages	56
Stagecoaches	65
AGRICULTURE	67
Forestry work	67
Herding	70
Light draught and farm work	72
Heavy draught work and agriculture	77
PONIES	
Origins and geographical distribution; Uses and usefulness	90
The Pony Express	92
FLAT RACING	121
TROTTING RACING	126
HORSEMANSHIP	135
Classical equitation	136
French schools	137
German and Spanish schools	137
The Spanish school of Vienna	137
Dressage	140
The three-day event	146
Show jumping	152
Fox hunting	168
Polo	171
Rodeos	172
Circus horses	173
Riding schools	175
Riding holidays	175
Parades	175
Horse shows	175
Breeds that have reverted to the wild	191
Bibliography	195
Index	196

PREFACE

More has probably been written about the horse than any other animal, and this comparative importance is more than justified by the significant role that this noble and versatile animal has played in the history and development of mankind. This book takes a close look at this role and by outlining the many different ways in which the horse has been used by man through the ages, it has been possible to examine the individual breeds, grouping them according to their particular aptitudes for certain types of work and a whole range of equestrian sports.

Unlike most other books on the subject, which generally classify breeds according to factors such as conformation and country of origin, this unique volume also presents the reader with a valuable insight into the important historical and social events that have affected their creation and development. Breeds are also frequently categorized under the three main headings of ponies, warm-bloods and cold-bloods but, it is our opinion that although the group of ponies has a valid significance, this system is the most artificial of all, since the distinction between warm- and cold-blood breeds is based only on the extent to which they have been influenced by the Arab.

Organizing a book on horses in this way has not proved an easy task. Horses are exceptionally adaptable animals and since most breeds prove themselves reasonably well-suited to a variety of tasks we have had to try and group them according to their most marked aptitudes. Some breeds have been categorized according to their modern role, even if this differs from the role they played in the past. In other cases, however, history has not allowed us to concentrate solely on the present-day uses of the breed, and, in fact, one breed made such an impact in two different periods of history and in two entirely different roles that we have had to present two of its three types in separate sections of the book: while the massive Draught Breton represents an heir to the medieval war horse, the Bidet d'Allure, a smaller version of the breed, the Postier-Breton, is remembered for the important part it played in the development of intercity postal services.

In writing this book we hope to have at least partly succeeded in achieving our goal, of bringing to life the image of this magnificent animal, emphasizing the significance and importance that it has had in the history of human progress.

THE AUTHORS

CONFORMATION OF THE HORSE

1—neck; 2—poll; 3—ear; 4—forelock; 5—forehead; 6—temple; 7—eye; 8—nose; 9—cheek; 10—muzzle (upper lip); 11—lower lip; 12—chin; 13—fontanelle; 14—jaw; 15—parotid region; 16—throat; 17—jugular groove; 18—shoulder; 19—breast; 20—elbow; 21—forearm; 22—knee; 23—cannon; 24—fetlock; 25—pastern; 26—hoof wall; 27—hoof; 28—chest; 29—ribs; 30—abdomen; 31—flank; 32—stifle; 33—shin; 34—hock; 35—buttock; 36—tail; 37—thigh; 38—haunch; 39—croup; 40—loins; 41—back; 42—withers.

QUALITIES AND DEFECTS

The conformation of a horse is its shape and form and is largely concerned with the proportions of the individual parts of the body in relation to each other. A horse that has good conformation, for instance, will be noticeably free of defects, well balanced, with elegant lines and bearing, and the overall impression will be pleasing to the eye. The conformation of a horse can also tell us a great deal about it. By looking closely at the way a horse is built and examining any qualities and defects present, it is possible to make a reasonably accurate assessment of the animal, its appearance, general disposition and its suitability for a specific task or role. It is, however, wrong to generalize too much about what constitutes good conformation, since points such as a light frame and long slender bones, which would be considered perfect qualities in a race horse, would be defects of conformation in a draught horse, where the emphasis should be on a heavy frame and shorter, thicker bones. To be able to analyze the potential of a particular horse both accurately and fully, it is important, therefore, to be able to recognize and understand the functions of the parts of the body and to be familiar with the various qualities and defects that may affect them.

HEAD

Qualities
Small and light, clean-cut, lean and covered with fine, delicate skin, allowing the tiny superficial veins to show through from beneath; in proportion with the body and set well onto the neck, from which it should be clearly separated by a line running down from the parotid region, parallel to the rear edge of the lower jaw.

Defects
Bulky and heavy (heavy-headed) or long and thin (due to old age); poorly set on the neck, out of proportion with the body.

EARS

Qualities: not too far apart; small and pointed, mobile, not inclined to lop

Defects: too thick, broad and drooping; too small and short (fox-like); too long and close together (hare-like)

FORELOCK

Qualities: not too wide at the base; long and fine

Defects: thin and short

TEMPLES

Qualities: clean-cut and prominent, with skin intact

Defects: presence of scars, or bald patches

FOREHEAD

Qualities: fairly wide

Defects: too wide or too narrow

EYES

Qualities: full, with a soft but lively expression; the eyelids should have long lashes

Defects: small and sunken (pig eye); large and protruding (buck eye); pale grey in colour

NOSE

Qualities: broad and straight; the nostrils should be large and after a gallop should flare out, showing the red lining membrane

Defects: showing grazing; small nostrils

CHEEKS

Qualities: muscular and clean-cut, covered with fine, delicate skin

Defects: fat and too muscular, or too lean or skinny

LIPS AND MUZZLE

Qualities: fine, with the presence of long tactile hairs

Defects: too wide or narrow; covered in coarse hair

CHIN

Qualities: rounded and prominent

Defects: loose and not clearly distinct from the lower lip

FONTANELLES

Qualities: shallow, full

Defects: deep and sunken

JAWS

Qualities: not too fleshy on the outside; the lower jaw should be lean and strong with a wide space between the two jawbones

Defects: jawbone too large (heavy-jawed)

PAROTID REGION (bilateral)

Qualities: clean-cut

Defects: swollen

POLL

Qualities: fairly wide

Defects: too narrow or too wide; scarred

NECK

Qualities
Well proportioned, long, clean and muscular; the upper edge or crest should be straight and have a full mane of straight, fine hair

Defects
Short and thick (bull neck); small, narrow and concave (ewe neck); markedly convex (swan neck)

CREST

Qualities: slender with a slightly convex profile and a mane of straight, fine hair

Defects: mane too thick or full with coarse or wavy hair

JUGULAR GROOVE (bilateral)

Qualities: well defined

Defects: inconspicuous

THROAT

Qualities: well developed and rounded

Defects: covered with loose, drooping skin

BODY

Qualities
Well proportioned; well built with elegant lines

Defects
Lines lacking harmony and proportion

WITHERS

Qualities: high, prominent and well formed; should be level with the croup

Defects: low, fleshy and flat; presence of scars or grazes

BACK

Qualities: strong, straight, broad and not too long, blending well with the loins and in line with them

Defects: sunken (hollow back) or convex (roach back); long

LOINS

Qualities: strong and muscular; short and wide; neatly joined to the croup

Defects: weak and poorly developed or long and too pronounced

CROUP

Qualities: flat or slightly rounded; well proportioned; level with the withers

Defects: too broad, sunken on either side (mule-like) or too fleshy and crossed by a furrow

HAUNCHES

Qualities: long, well rounded and giving an impression of strength

Defects: weak, short and sloping; too prominent

TAIL

Qualities: well set-on, full and carried clear of the buttocks; strong and muscular at the root

Defects: low-set, with thin sparse hair; carried close to the body

FLANKS

Qualities: full and well shaped; not too wide

Defects: wide and hollow

BELLY
Qualities: full and rounded, firm and well held

Defects: large and pendulous (cow belly)

CHEST

Qualities: full and muscular; high and moderately wide

Defects: narrow and poorly developed, or too broad and protruding forwards

RIBS

Qualities: rounded and well sprung; long and carried well back into the loins

Defects: short, flat and poorly developed; bulging ("barrelly")

LIMBS

Qualities
Long and muscular; joints broad and clean; tendons set well apart, tense and hard

Defects
Flawed stance; poorly built

SHOULDER

Qualities: long and sloping, well muscled, flat, broad and giving a free-flowing movement

Defects: straight or too fleshy and bulky (loaded shoulders)

ARM BONE (HUMERUS)

Qualities: a good length and well muscled, sloping, with a flowing movement

Defects: too short or too long

ELBOW

Qualities: prominent and separate from the trunk

Defects: showing swelling, turning in or out

FOREARM

Qualities: long, good and straight, muscular

Defects: short and thin

KNEE

Qualities: large, well defined and wide; low-set

Defects: slender and poorly shaped, throwing the lower leg out of line

CANNON

Qualities: quite long, broad and rounded; tendons at the back should stand out, be well defined, tense and hard

Defects: too long or too slender

FETLOCK

Qualities: flat and well rounded

Defects: narrow and poorly shaped

PASTERN

Qualities: nicely sloping; its length should be in proportion to the size of horse

Defects: thin and too sloping; upright

CORONET

Qualities: even and clean

Defects: presence of hollows or protuberances

FOOT

Qualities: well proportioned pointing straight to the front, sole concave, heels open, hoof supple and strong

Defects: too small or too large, turning out or in, dropped sole, poorly shaped and weak, brittle hooves

THIGH

Qualities: muscular and well rounded; sloping

Defects: too straight; heavy; poorly developed and flat

BUTTOCK

Qualities: prominent and well muscled

Defects: poorly developed

STIFLE

Qualities: well shaped and rounded

Defects: presence of any inflammation or unusual swelling

SHIN (TIBIA)

Qualities: long, good and straight, and with well-developed muscles

Defects: too short in relation to the cannon

HOCK

Qualities: wide and flat, straight and strong

Defects: poorly shaped, throwing the lower leg out of line; weak

STANCE

Before attempting to assess whether or not the proportions between the various parts of the body constitute good conformation, it is first important to take a close look at the "natural" or "true" stance of the animal. A horse's stance is thus described when the weight of the body can be seen to be evenly distributed over all four limbs, placed squarely on the ground. Having positioned the animal in its natural stance it is then possible to begin to examine the four limbs, observing them from the side, the front (forelimbs) and the back (hind limbs). This will instantly reveal any defects or deviations from the perpendicular. To facilitate this examination a system has been devised using four imaginary vertical lines, running at right angles to the ground. These start respectively from the point of the shoulder, the point of the elbow, the point of the buttock (seat bone) and the stifle. The examination should be made from both sides which means, in effect, using eight such imaginary lines. Any deviation from the normal ratios existing between these four vertical lines and the position of the limbs represents a defect of stance.

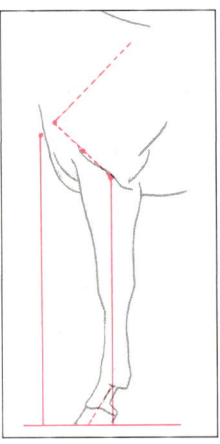

FORELIMBS
Side view

Correct natural stance
The vertical line dropping from the point of the shoulder meets the ground about 4 in (10 cm) in front of the point of the toe. The second vertical line running from the point of the elbow divides the knee, the cannon and the fetlock into two equal parts and touches the ground slightly behind the heel.

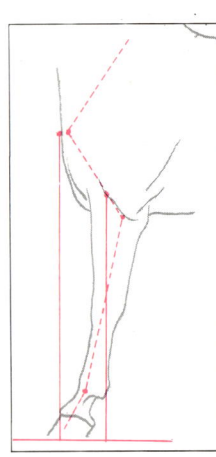

Thrust forward
The vertical line from the point of the shoulder meets the ground closer to the foot, or even passes through the hoof.
Adverse consequences: the horse lacks speed because it covers less ground in its action; the weight has to be supported by the heels, causing a greater strain to be put on the flexor tendons.

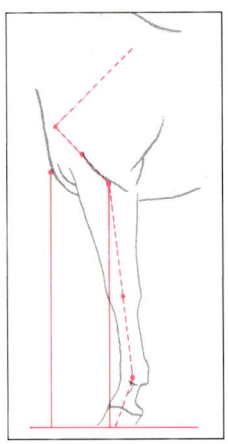

Under in front
The vertical line from the point of the shoulder drops to well in front of the toe. The second vertical line from the point of the elbow touches the side wall of the hoof, near the toe.
Adverse consequences: the horse lacks balance and tends to stumble due to its legs knocking into each other (brushing).

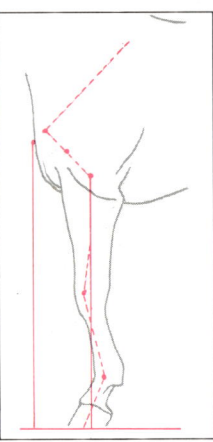

Over at the knee
The deviation of the limb from the perpendicular is caused by a curving of the forearm and cannon making the leg bow forwards. The vertical line from the point of the elbow does not divide the knee, cannon and fetlock into two equal parts but drops to a point on the hoof in front of the heel.
Adverse consequences: a tendency to trip and bend involuntarily at the knee.

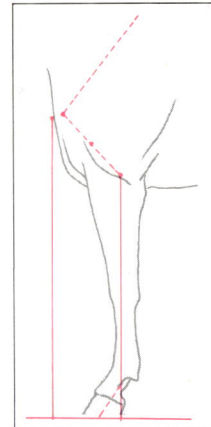

Back at the knee
The deviation of the limb is caused by a curving of the forearm and cannon making the leg bow backwards. The vertical line running from the point of the elbow does not divide the knee, cannon and fetlock into two equal parts, but passes to the front of the cannon, dropping to the heel.
Adverse consequences: the tendons of the flexor muscles of the phalanges are unduly stressed.

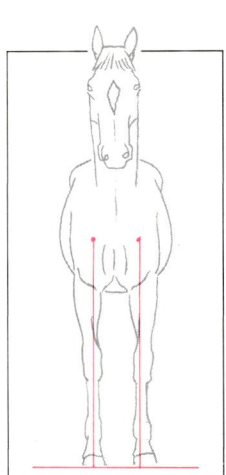

FORELIMBS
Front view

Correct natural stance
The vertical line dropping from the point of the shoulder divides the knee, the cannon, the fetlock and the foot into two equal halves.

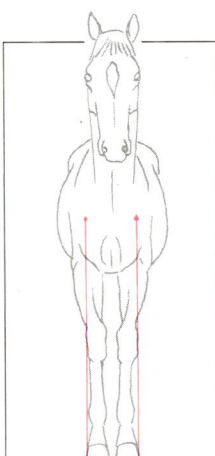

Close or narrow forward
The feet are too close together and the vertical lines dropping from the point of the shoulders fall laterally to meet the ground on the outer side of each foot.
Adverse consequences: poor balance; tendency for the legs to touch each other in action (brushing).

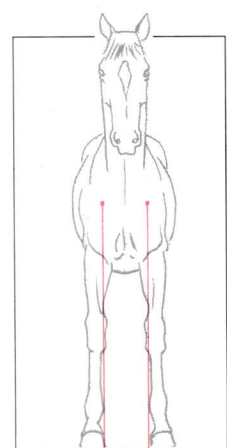

Too open forward
The feet are too far apart; the vertical lines dropping from the points of the shoulders meet the ground on the inner side of each foot.
Adverse consequences: rolling gait; tendency to bruise the soles of the feet.

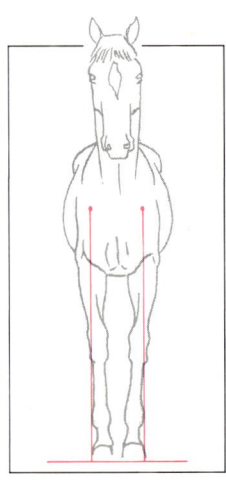

Pigeon-toed
The point of the toe is turned inwards; the two vertical lines dropping from the points of the shoulders fall to the outer quarters (sides) of the hoof. This defect may sometimes apply to just one foreleg.
Adverse consequences: tendency to trip or for the legs to touch each other in action (brushing).

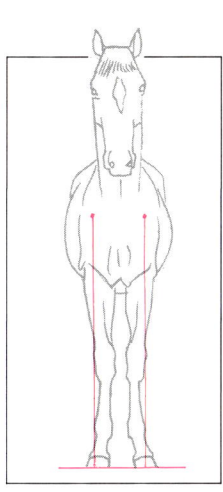

Splayed or turned out
The point of the toe tends to be turned outwards; the two vertical lines dropping from the points of the shoulders fall to the inner quarters of the hoof. This defect may sometimes apply to only one foreleg.
Adverse consequences: tendency to trip due to "dishing," where, during action, the limb is carried outwards in a circular fashion.

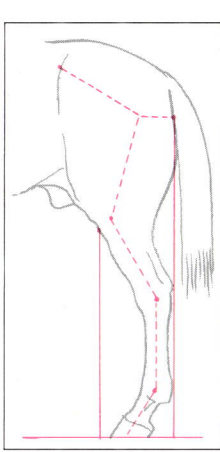

HINDQUARTERS
Side view

Correct natural stance
The vertical line dropping from the point of the buttock just touches the point of the hock and continues down the back of the cannon; the vertical line from the stifle meets the ground slightly in front of the point of the toe.

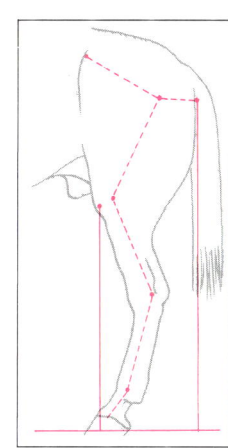

Under at the back
The hind leg slopes forward from the hock downwards and as a result is carried in front of the vertical line that drops from the point of the buttock; the vertical line dropping from the stifle falls to the side of the hoof.
Adverse consequences: the horse loses balance and tends to slip; in action the hind limbs tend to knock into the forelimbs.

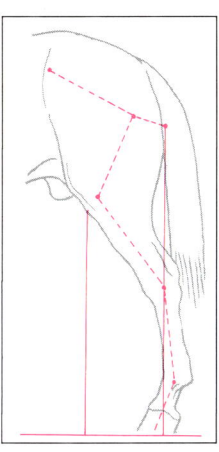

Straight hocks
The vertical line dropping from the point of the buttock touches the side of the hoof due to the backwards deviation of the axis of the cannon.
Adverse consequences: the horse is slower since the muscles of the back and the lumbar region are put under greater strain, which shortens the stride; the horse tends to slip.

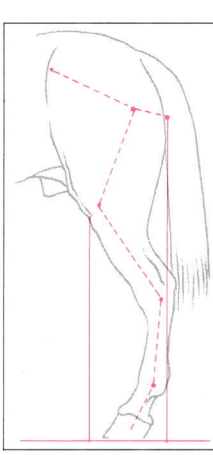

Sickle hocks
The hock falls behind the vertical line that drops from the point of the buttock; the vertical line running from the stifle meets the ground closer than normal to the point of the toe.
Adverse consequences: too much strain is placed on the hocks, the tendons of the flexor muscles of the phalanges and the suspensory ligament of the fetlock.

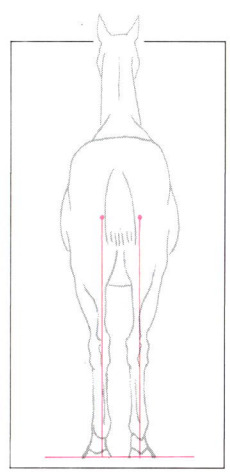

HINDQUARTERS
Rear view

Correct natural stance
The vertical line dropping from the point of the buttock divides the hock, the cannon, the fetlock and the foot into two equal parts.

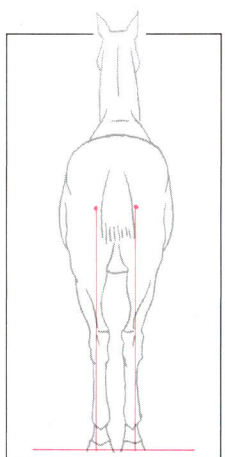

Narrow at the back
The hind feet are too close together; on each side the vertical line dropping from the point of the buttock touches the outer side of the heel.
Adverse consequences: the horse's balance is less steady; tendency for the legs to knock into each other (brushing).

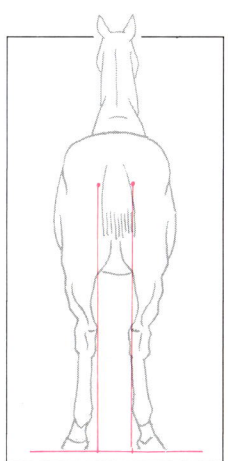

Open at the back
The hind feet are too far apart; on each side the vertical line dropping from the point of the buttock touches the inner side of the heel.
Adverse consequences: too much strain is placed on the inside of the hock.

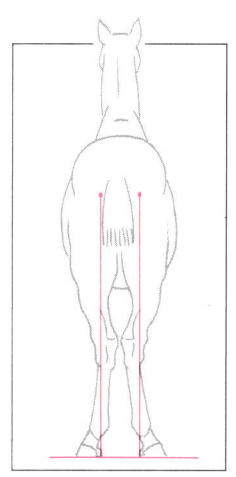

Cow hocks
The hocks are turned inwards causing the feet to splay or turn out; on each side the vertical line dropping from the point of the buttock touches the outer side of the heel.
Adverse consequences: even though the horse's balance is still good, its action is somewhat clumsy.

DEFECTS IN THE INCLINATION OF THE PASTERN IN THE FRONT AND HIND LIMBS

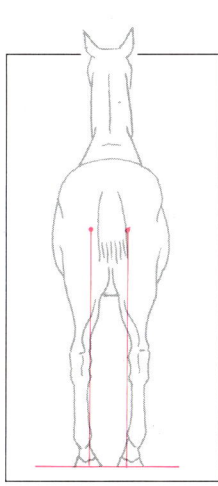

Bow hocks
The hocks are turned outwards causing the feet to turn in; on each side the vertical line dropping from the point of the buttock touches the inner side of the heel.
Adverse consequences: too much tension on the lateral ligaments and poor overall distribution of pressure resulting in damage to the bones.

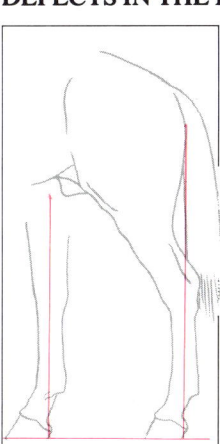

Upright and short
The angle of the fetlock joint tends to open out and increase resulting in a short, upright pastern. This is desirable in a trotting horse.
Adverse consequences: when the foot is placed on the ground in action, the short, upright pastern does not sufficiently absorb the concussion.

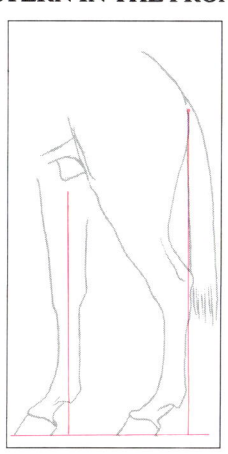

Long and sloping
The pastern is excessively sloping and the angle formed by the cannon with the fetlock tends to diminish.
Adverse consequences: the horse will tend to have a springy action as the pastern is more flexible, but too much strain is liable to be thrown on the tendons of the flexor muscles of the phalanges and the suspensory ligament of the fetlock.

NATURAL AND ARTIFICIAL GAITS

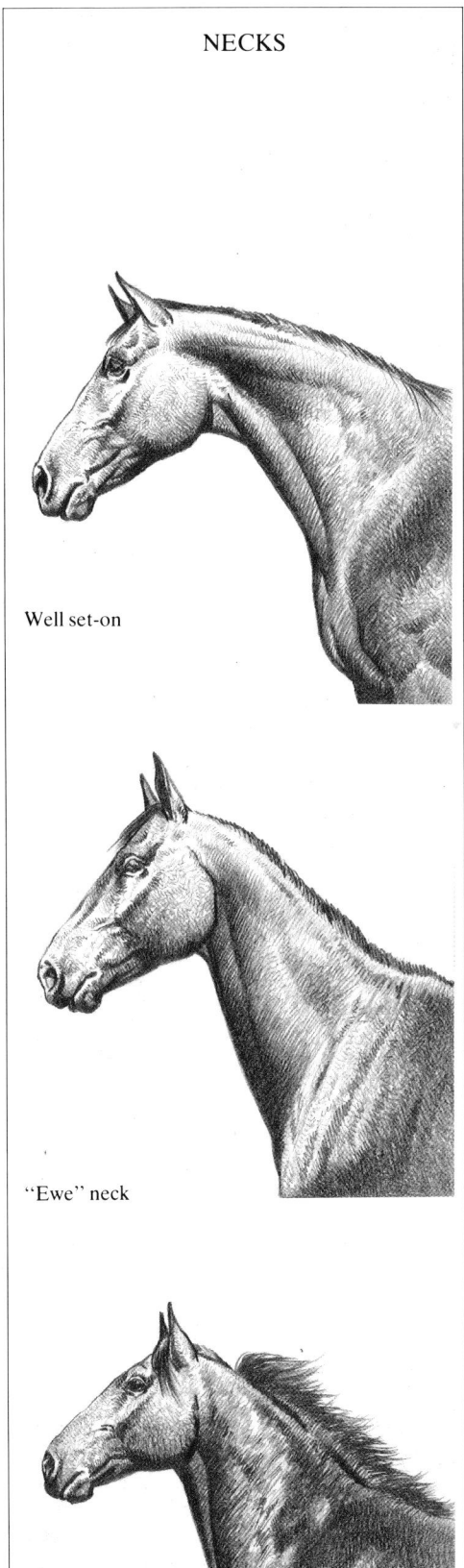

NECKS

Well set-on

"Ewe" neck

"Bull" neck (short and thick)

The natural gaits or paces of a horse are the walk, the trot, the canter and the gallop. In all these gaits the basic movements of each leg are the same: the foot is raised, giving the necessary propulsion to move the body forward, and then placed on the ground again, first with the point of the toe and then fractionally later with the heels.

The walk is a regular gait of four distinct beats, in which the limbs are moved one at a time and in the following order: right foreleg, left hind leg, left foreleg, right hind leg. At the walk the horse always has three feet on the ground, forming a triangle within which the center of gravity of the animal's body remains to make this gait extremely stable and comfortable for the rider. This moderately slow pace does not require any major output of energy, enabling the horse to keep going steadily over long distances at a speed of approximately 3½ mph (6 kmh).

At the trot, the horse's legs move in diagonal pairs making a regular pace of two beats: the right fore with the left hind, then the left fore with the right hind. Each pair of limbs is raised before the preceding pair has touched down, thus creating a brief moment of total suspension before there is contact with the ground again. This gives rise to continual vertical shifts of the center of gravity (twice for each stride completed) and the animal will be seen to move up and down. Although this phenomenon tends to reduce the horse's stability it does not affect the overall balance and increases its speed. In a horse of average size the length of one trotting stride can range from 8–10 feet (2.4–3 m) and the speed varies from 9 mph (15 kmh) at a working trot to as much as 28 mph (45 kmh) achieved in trotting races.

The canter is a fast pace of three beats which always leads off from one of the hind legs. Depending on which foreleg is the last to leave the ground, the canter is described as being left or right. In the right canter, for example, the sequence is as follows: left hind leg, right hind leg and left foreleg together, right foreleg followed by a brief moment of suspension when all four legs are in the air, before beginning the next stride. Because it is a diagonal pace and also due to the considerable speeds developed, varying from 12 mph (20 kmh) to 40 mph (60 kmh), the horse's center of gravity continually moves up and down in this pace, causing the animal to lose a certain amount of stability. At the canter, unlike the other gaits, the propulsion is given almost entirely by the limbs, while the back remains relatively rigid.

The full gallop is the fastest and most exhausting pace. Like the walk it has four beats although the legs move in a different order: left hind leg, right hind leg, left foreleg, right foreleg. The length of stride at the gallop is variable and the marks left by the same hoof may be as much as 25 feet (7.5 m) apart—four times the length of the horse itself.

Although for the sake of convenience the different paces are defined as having two, three or four beats, each individual movement can be split into several phases with at least 16 different positions. Technology was first applied to the scientific study of animal movement by the American photographer, Edward Muybridge (1839–1904). In 1872, using 24 synchronized cameras placed in position along a track, he produced a chronophotograph or motion analysis of the successive phases of a running horse, thus predating present-day stroboscopic techniques. His extremely interesting observations are compiled in an eleven-volume encyclopedia published in 1887 under the title *An Electrophotographic Investigation on Consecutive Phases of Animal Movements*.

The natural "amble" of the camel, the dromedary and the giraffe is a pace of two beats, in which the two legs on the same side of the body move simultaneously. This pace can also be acquired by the horse and has the advantage of being less tiring for the animal, and more comfortable for the rider. The speed of the amble is halfway between walking and cantering. A natural tendency towards ambling can be passed on genetically as is shown by the American Standardbred racing "pacers." One variant of ambling is the "stepping pace," defined in the United States as the "rack." This pace is quite spectacular and is brisk with four equally spaced beats: right foreleg with right hind leg, right foreleg with left hind leg, left foreleg with left hind leg, left foreleg with right hind leg. Another typical American gait, also acquired, is the slow trot, slow gait or fox trot, which is in fact a trot in which the two usual beats are broken by a longer interval between the foreleg and opposite hind leg touching the ground. This pace is halfway between the walk and the trot and is reasonably restful. The horses best suited to these gaits are the Missouri Fox Trotting Horse and the American Saddle Horse. Another gait which is not natural in the horse is the "broken trot" in which the horse trots with its forelegs and gallops with its hind legs.

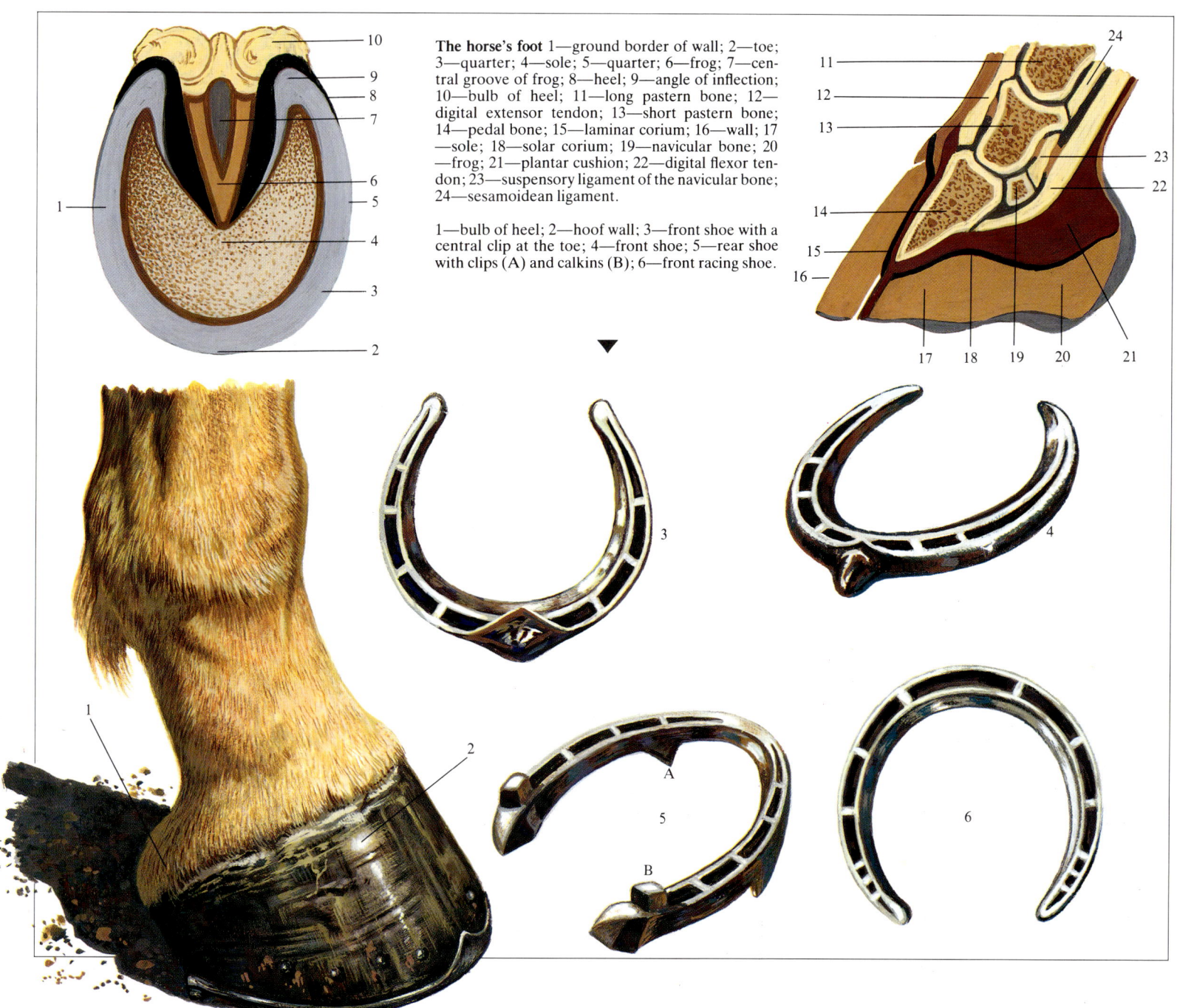

The horse's foot 1—ground border of wall; 2—toe; 3—quarter; 4—sole; 5—quarter; 6—frog; 7—central groove of frog; 8—heel; 9—angle of inflection; 10—bulb of heel; 11—long pastern bone; 12—digital extensor tendon; 13—short pastern bone; 14—pedal bone; 15—laminar corium; 16—wall; 17—sole; 18—solar corium; 19—navicular bone; 20—frog; 21—plantar cushion; 22—digital flexor tendon; 23—suspensory ligament of the navicular bone; 24—sesamoidean ligament.

1—bulb of heel; 2—hoof wall; 3—front shoe with a central clip at the toe; 4—front shoe; 5—rear shoe with clips (A) and calkins (B); 6—front racing shoe.

SHOES

It is difficult to determine exactly when the practice of shoeing began. There is no doubt that the Romans shod their horses, but with shoes that differed a great deal from their modern counterparts. Their nailless horseshoe or *solea* consisted, in fact, of a metal plate that was attached to the underside of the hoof by means of two "clamps" at the front and one or more extensions at the rear. These were bound to the hoof with leather straps. At the tip there was a hooked piece to improve the grip on the ground.

It would appear that peoples predating the Romans had also adopted some form of horseshoe, but less for everyday use than for a specific purpose, such as to correct a defective hoof or to prevent the horse slipping on icy ground. Some authorities, however, maintain that the use of iron shoes to protect the hoof wall, and thus prevent it from wearing down too quickly, can be traced to as far back as the Cimbrians (an ancient Germanic tribe) in 1600 B.C. They may have been used in even more remote times by Oriental peoples, including the Chinese, but despite these conflicting views it seems certain that the modern horseshoe, which is attached to the horse's hoof by means of nails, dates back to the Middle Ages.

In the wild a horse does not need shoeing, because on pasture land and natural terrain there is a perfect balance between the rate at which the hoof wears down, and the rate at which it regrows. In captivity, both as pack animals and during times of war, the horse has been forced to walk on very hard surfaces, such as roads and rough dirt tracks, often carrying extremely heavy loads. Extreme examples were the medieval chargers which, themselves heavily laden with armour, were made to bear the additional weight of their riders, also clad in armour. All these factors subject the hoof to an excessive rate of wear that is not naturally compensated for, and this has serious consequences for the animal. Shoeing gets around this problem, but because a shod hoof is not liable to any wear and tear, the farrier or blacksmith must also make sure that the hoof, which is growing constantly, is trimmed down to its original size every time the shoes are replaced (on average every 30–40 days). Shoeing is an extremely skilled operation which must be carefully executed so as not to affect the natural stance of the animal, nor should it interfere adversely with its action.

Shoeing may also have corrective or therapeutic purposes, if, for example, a horse's natural stance is defective, or if there is damage to the tendons. Obviously in such cases the fitting of special shoes will follow consultation with, and approval by, a veterinary surgeon. A good shoe must fit the hoof perfectly, and should not be too heavy. For this reason, race horses are usually shod with aluminium, which is lighter, though less durable than iron. The shoe is attached to the lower edge of the hoof wall by means of nails, the number and positioning of which will vary from the front shoe, which is more rounded, to the back shoe, which has a more oval shape. The shoe may also have projecting elements at the heels, bent downwards and slightly forward, called calkins, which give a better grip on the ground, or extensions on the upper outer edge, turned upwards, called clips, which ensure a more secure fit to the hoof wall.

The popular belief that horseshoes bring good luck dates back to former times when, as a mark of their benevolence, certain wealthy noblemen would have their personal charger loosely shod with a gold horseshoe, so that as he rode through towns and villages, it would fall off, bringing good luck and prosperity to whoever found it.

TEETH AND DETERMINING THE AGE OF A HORSE

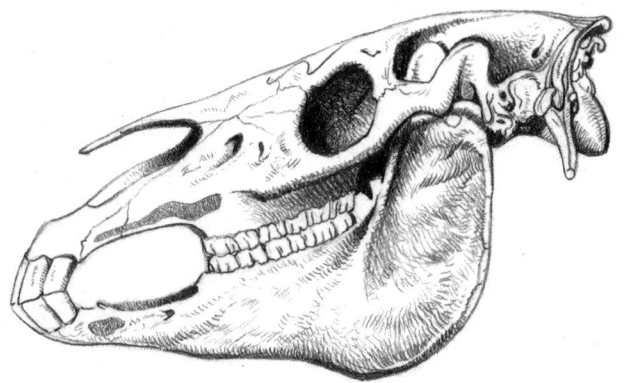

The average life of a horse is between 20 and 25 years. For much of this span an experienced horseman will be able to determine the age with reasonable accuracy, by examining the teeth. This is possible, not only because the teeth, like the hooves, are continually growing to compensate for the general rate of wear of about 1/6 in (2 mm) per year, but also due to their particular structure.

In a horse each tooth is made up of a specific substance called ivory or dentine, and covered on the outside by a layer of cement and enamel. Inside the tooth there is a cavity, containing the dental pulp, rich in nerves and blood vessels. The outer, exposed part of the tooth is called the crown and the part hidden below the gum, and fixed into the sockets of the dental arches on the jawbone, is called the root. The area between the two is the neck and is surrounded on all sides by the gum. The crown has the following surfaces: the anterior (vestibular or labial), the posterior (lingual), the cutting or grinding surface, and the surfaces in contact with adjacent teeth. According to their particular function the teeth are divided into incisors (nippers), which have a reduced cutting surface; canines (tushes) with a sharp cutting surface; and premolars and molars (grinders) with a large, rough grinding surface. Like other mammals, young horses have temporary or milk teeth (incisors and premolars), which are replaced by the permanent teeth by the time they are five years old. The canines and molars, however, are permanent from birth. In comparison with the permanent incisors, the milk incisors are smaller and whiter, there are no distinct lengthways grooves on the anterior surface and the neck is more pronounced in that it is constricted. The permanent incisors are pale yellow with grooves running down the anterior surface and the neck is not very evident.

The complete, permanent dentition of an adult horse consists of 40 teeth in the male and 36 in the female, since mares do not generally have canine teeth. The teeth are arranged as follows: in each right and left, upper and lower jaw, there are three molars, three premolars, one canine and three incisors. The front two incisors are called the centrals, the next two the laterals and the last two, the corner teeth.

Over the years the cutting surface of the incisors goes through a series of modifications in shape, corresponding to the various cross sections of the tooth. As the surface wears down, the tooth continues to grow, constantly pushing the lower sections to the top. Thus the tooth is initially oval, becoming round, then triangular and eventually taking on the shape of a flattened quadrilateral. To begin with there is a comparatively deep, transversely elongated hollow between the anterior and the posterior surfaces of the tooth, in the center of which is a raised part called the infundibulum or mark. As the tooth is progressively worn down the cross section of the infundibulum is revealed. This is dark in colour surrounded by a lighter circle formed by the enamel. As soon as this mark has disappeared from all the incisors, at about eight years, the horse is said to be "out of the mark," or "aged." After this point the cutting surface of the tooth is referred to as the table. As the mark becomes less evident, the "dental star" will begin to appear. This is formed by the dentine which continues to build up inside the pulp cavity as the tooth grows. The "hook," or "dovetail," is a projection of enamel at the back of the upper corner incisors that has not worn down as quickly as the surrounding parts of the tooth. This appears at the age of seven and persists until the eighth year. It then disappears and reappears at 14 years and again after 20 years.

One last indication of the age of the horse is "Galvaynes's groove." This is a conspicuous black groove, formed by the presence of cement on the anterior surface of the upper corner teeth. Gradually, as the tooth grows, this will move down from the gum. Galvayne's groove generally appears at ten years, is apparent down the whole length of the tooth at the age of 20 and disappears altogether at 30.

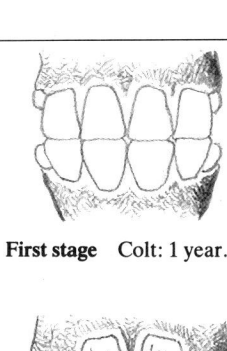 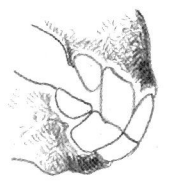 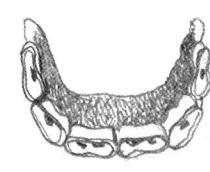 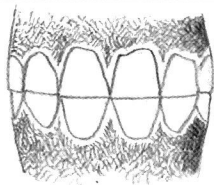 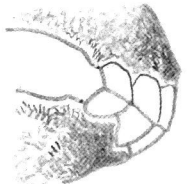 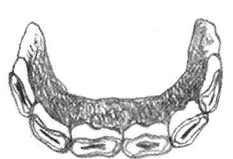

First stage Colt: 1 year. Wearing down of temporary central incisors   2 years Wearing down of temporary corner teeth

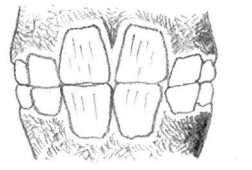 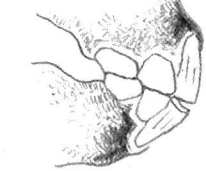 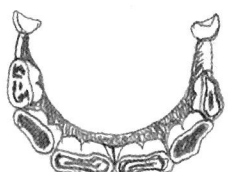 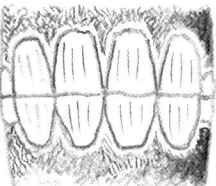 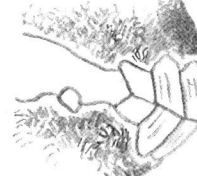 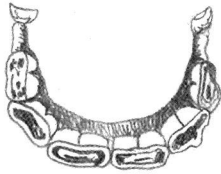

3 years Appearance of permanent centrals   4 years Appearance of permanent laterals

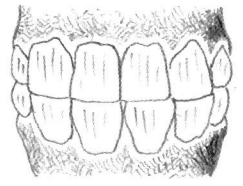  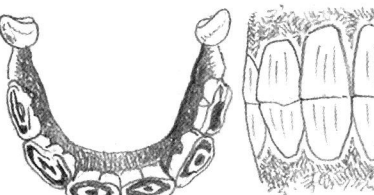 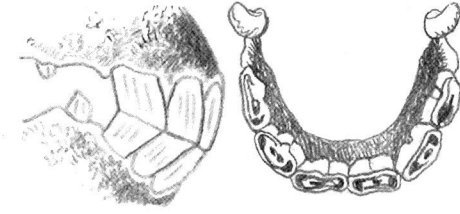

5 years Appearance of permanent corner teeth   **Second stage** Adult male: 6 years. Wearing down of lower centrals—oval cutting surface

7 years Wearing down of lower laterals   8 years Wearing down of lower corner teeth

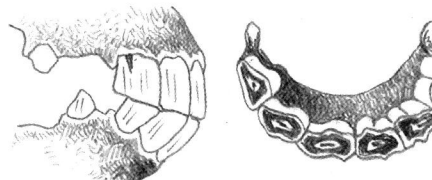 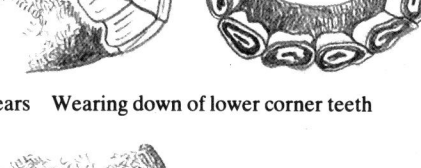

9 years Dental star appears on centrals—round table 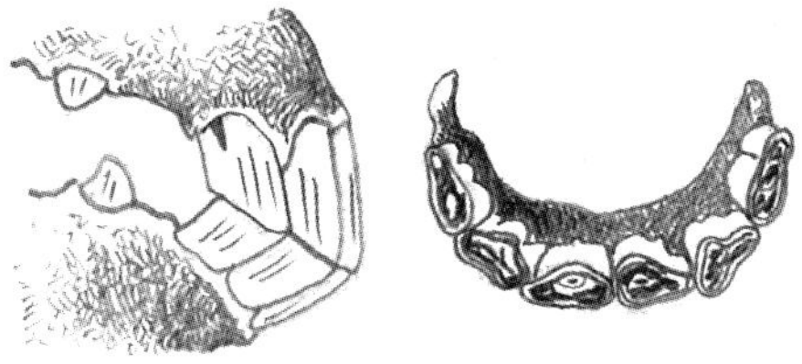   10 years Dental star appears on laterals—Galvayne's groove

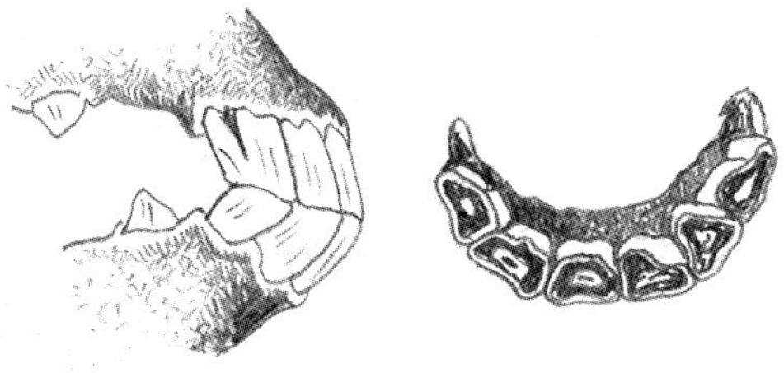

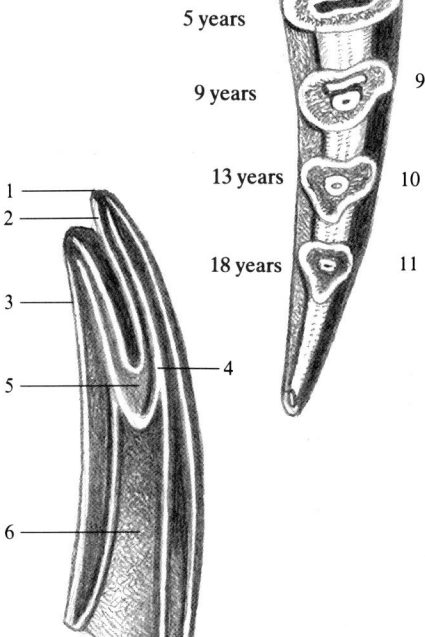

Third stage (Old horse)
12–13 years Dental star on centrals becomes central, Galvayne's groove   15 years Table of laterals becomes triangular—Galvayne's groove

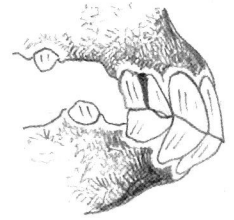 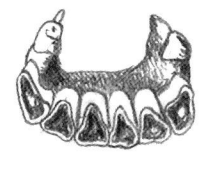 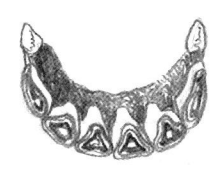

19–20 years Table of corner teeth becomes quadrilateral—Galvayne's groove   20–25 years Galvayne's groove tends to disappear from the upper part of the tooth

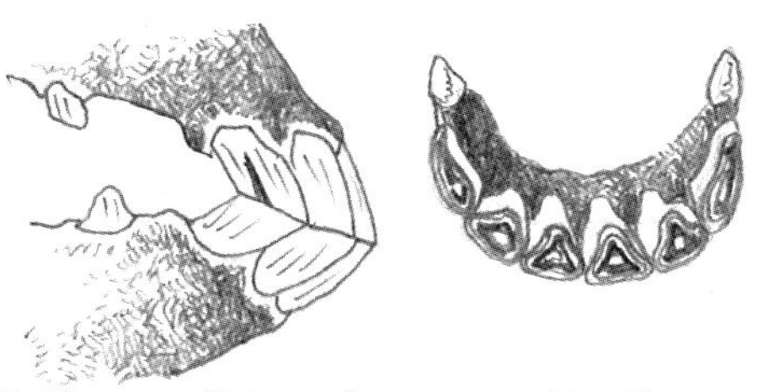

Vertical and horizontal cross sections of a new lower central incisor
1—enamel on crown; 2—infundibulum; 3—enamel; 4—dentine; 5—central enamel; 6—pulp cavity; 7—elongated table; 8—oval table; 9—round table; 10—triangular table; 11—quadrilateral table.

SENSES

In all living creatures the sense organs represent the means by which the individual relates to the outside world, receiving from it messages that are then elaborated on by nervous structures. In higher animals these structures make up the central nervous system. Since the horse is a vertebrate mammal, it belongs on the highest level of the evolutionary scale and therefore possesses highly developed sense organs. These organs are capable of supplying the animal with extremely detailed information about an object such as its distance, size, colour and shape. Besides the "general" sense organs present throughout the body (the skin is sensitive over its whole area to pressure, temperature and pain) there are also "special" sense organs, formed by a great number of nerve cells. These cells are sensitive only to the appropriate stimulus and are grouped together to form characteristic structures, situated in specific regions of the body. It is no accident that all these organs are situated in the head, firstly because this occupies the highest position of the body, thus permitting a wider field of reception, and secondly because their proximity to the brain permits a more rapid response to stimuli. This is because the nerve impulses have to reach the corresponding areas of the brain in which they are recognized and the appropriate response formulated. This means that for the animal to function properly the sense organs must be wholly integrated with the central nervous system.

Although the general structure of the nervous system is much the same in all vetebrates, including man, the senses have developed in different proportions according to the needs and habits of a particular species. In man, for example, the cerebral hemispheres are larger, since he has had to use the thinking part of his brain to survive. His other senses, however, such as that of smell, have "regressed" in comparison with those of animals such as the dog which, in order to survive, relies on being able to smell the scent of its prey.

The sense of taste, combined with the sense of smell, with which it is closely associated, enables a horse to distinguish and choose between the different types of food offered to it. The prime receptors for taste are the taste buds, situated on the tongue, although there are also some less sensitive areas on the palate and the pharynx.

A horse's sense of smell is acute and approximately 10,000 times more sensitive than its sense of taste. The receptors for smell are the olfactory nerves, located on a moist mucous membrane that lines the innermost part of the nasal cavities. If this membrane is irritated or damaged, the sense of taste, as well as that of smell will be seriously impaired. Since a horse will often be seen to sniff its food before tasting and subsequently eating it, it is not always advisable to mix unpleasant tasting medicines in with the feed, since they may put off the animal. Horses have remarkably retentive memories and an animal may continue to refuse a certain type of food even when it no longer contains the medicine, because in its mind it will still associate the appearance with the unpleasant taste and smell.

The sense of touch enables a horse to examine more closely the texture and physical nature of an object. Although every part of the skin is sensitive to external impressions such as temperature and pressure, touch such as we possess in our fingertips is localized to the animal's lips, the tip of its tongue and to a lesser extent its feet, all of which parts of the body are liberally supplied with sensory nerves. Thus a horse will often examine the physical nature of an object on the ground first with its hoof and then by touching it with its lips. Obviously the sensitivity of the feet also helps the animal determine the nature and condition of the ground. Long, tactile hairs on the lips and eyebrows also act as feelers, warning the horse of the presence of an object and thus protecting it from possible injury.

The ear is a particularly important sense organ in the horse. Not only does it enable the animal to hear, but it also contains other specialized structures which permit it to maintain its balance during movement, for example when changing from one pace to another. This highly developed sense of balance, aided by sight, also enables the horse to make the magnificent jumps that arouse so much admiration at show jumping events and to execute those fantastic balancing acts that attract circus crowds. The external parts of the ear (auricles) are exceptionally mobile and can move independently of each other to catch a sound and direct the vibrations into the inner ear. This is clearly demonstrated by the fact that unless a sound is produced from a source directly in front of

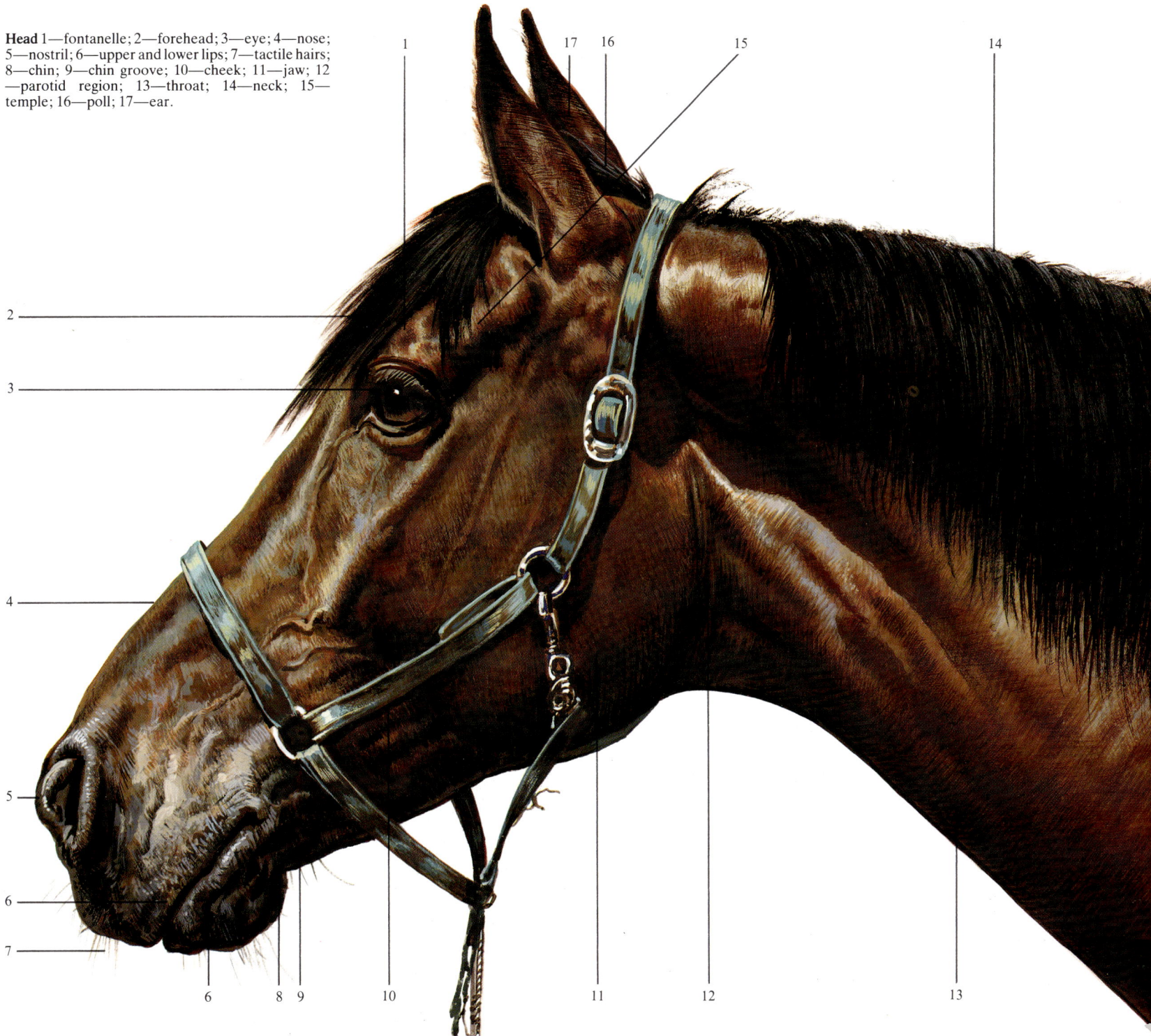

Head 1—fontanelle; 2—forehead; 3—eye; 4—nose; 5—nostril; 6—upper and lower lips; 7—tactile hairs; 8—chin; 9—chin groove; 10—cheek; 11—jaw; 12—parotid region; 13—throat; 14—neck; 15—temple; 16—poll; 17—ear.

the animal, it will be received with greater intensity and in advance by one ear rather than the other. The difference between the differing intensities and the time lapse are in effect the basic data required for identifying the direction of the sound. The efficiency of the horse's hearing apparatus is much greater than in man.

For example it has been proven that if 32 sources of sound are set in a circle, the horse, in the middle of the circle, will manage to identify the direction of almost all, whereas man can only pinpoint eight. If a sudden and unfamiliar sound reaches the horse's ears, the horse may display nonoriented reactions of fright (phobotaxis) followed, or not followed, by reactions oriented towards the source of the stimulus (topotaxis). This shows the result of the successive reactions to stimuli coming from other sense organs, for example, that of sight. The external parts of the ear are of great value to the horseman, since they offer the best, fastest and most visible indication of the horse's state of mind and his intentions. A grazing horse moves its ears in all directions, but without displaying any kind of excitement or agitation. If these movements become quicker and more intense, this indicates nervousness and should the head start to move about at the same time with a forward motion this may mean that the animal is afraid of something or feels insecure or threatened. When the ears are pinned back this indicates hostility or aggression. When the animal is on the move and in a calm mood, the ears should be turned to the front and tipped slightly forwards.

The horse does not have exceptionally good vision. When stationary it is able to see objects up to a distance of about 300 yards (300 m) and up to 150 yards (150 m) when it is moving. A horse's eyes are set on either side of the head, consequently its vision is predominantly monocular as opposed to

19

binocular. Although this has the advantage of allowing very considerable all-round vision, it does, however, make it more difficult for the horse to judge depth and distance. The horse calculates distance partly by considering the apparent size of an object and partly by making it seem to move in relation to recognized immobile objects in the distance, by moving its head from side to side. The horse's vision is thus essentially involved with movement, rather than precise observation, a feature that it shares in common with other mammals (with the exception of the primates). The underlying reason is in the animal's need to get away quickly at the first sign of danger, its safety being dependent on its speed of movement. The lateral position of the eyes also gives the horse a very wide field of vision, by enabling it to see to the rear, leaving a "blind" spot of only 3°. Another blind spot, which extends about 3 ft (1 m) in front of the forelegs when the head is in its normal position, is created by the elongated shape of the muzzle, which prevents the horse from seeing objects situated beneath its body. As a result, if the horse is to have a good all-round view of things, it must be able to move its head about freely. It is therefore a good rule to use the reins with care and caution, especially when the animal is being ridden over rough or uneven ground, or must negotiate fences, as is often the case with show jumpers.

The horse's eye is able to distinguish colours, but this factor is of secondary importance to the animal, which primarily needs to know the shape of things and the way they move. A horse's reactions towards certain objects can often be affected by the familiarity of its shape. This helps to explain why a frightened horse will invariably take refuge in its box, even if the box is wrapped in flames, because the sight of familiar surroundings and objects helps to calm it down.

An interesting point worth mentioning regarding the horse's monocular vision is that the two eyes appear to jog two independent visual memories. Very often an object, already familiar to the right eye, may not be recognized by the left eye and would consequently lead to two successive reactions, for example, assurance followed by fright.

In conclusion, it is true to say that the horse's sensory equilibrium depends entirely on the perfect efficiency and functioning of all its sensory organs, which must work together as a whole. For example, the acute hearing and finely attuned sense of smell, more than compensate for the mediocre eyesight, with the result that the horse is a highly developed animal, capable of making very precise identifications of people, animals and things, and of reacting in a positive way, avoiding improper responses and incoherent reactions, which in the long term, could cause psychological damage.

PSYCHOLOGY AND BEHAVIOUR

The horse is considered by many to be an intelligent animal, in so far as he can be trained to carry out a number of tasks for his master. This capacity to learn certain procedures is, however, based on reflex and should not be equated with human intelligence, based on reason. Unlike all humans, a horse, however educated he were, would never be capable of fully understanding and coping with new and awkward situations. He cannot think in abstract forms, nor can he create patterns of behaviour or solve problems that go beyond simple association, or beyond a choice between a limited number of possibilities. This lack of initiative should not, however, lead to the conclusion that the horse is stupid, but rather that his mental ability relies almost totally on instinct and a considerable capacity to learn. The horse learns from experiences gained from a variety of different situations such as trial and error, suitable training exercises and imitating other horses. Equipped with extremely acute senses, finely tuned hearing and an exceptionally good memory, the horse learns essentially from repetition, duly adapting his behaviour to the various situations he encounters, and once he has learnt exactly what man requires of him, he is then capable of using this acquired ability to cope with similar situations. The horse's prodigiously retentive memory has been scientifically examined, by comparing it with that of other animal species. After one particular training programme was interrupted for a year, it was observed that the horse was still capable of successfully completing 19 out of 20 exercises, a score matched only by the elephant.

The visual learning tests used involved the simultaneous recognition of pairs of figures and graphic symbols; the identification of one object from a series of similar objects (concept of disparity); the ability to distinguish between similar objects (concept of similarity); the capacity to retain the image of an object that gradually undergoes a certain degree of alteration over a period of time; training in the "use of numbers" by means of series that follow a precise pattern. It is important to realize that before a horse can be expected satisfactorily to complete tests of this nature, he must have some motivation. Also, not all animals lend themselves to being tested. During the tests it is important that the horse be kept calm and any form of distraction must be avoided. There is little or no point in basing your analysis on only one test and ideally the horse should undergo several tests carried out, where possible, at the same time and under the same conditions. Lastly, it would be wrong to carry out any tests on a horse without first taking into consideration its temperament and natural aptitudes. Failure to take these factors into account will produce imprecise results: the most gifted horses will not be given a chance to improve, and the less gifted will be helped along by the repetitive nature of the programme. Great care should be taken to ensure that a training programme is started in the correct way, since a horse will always remember the first impressions he receives, and any subsequent change in method will disorient him, making him less willing and less receptive. Horses are particularly sensitive to rewards and punishments: the anticipation of a reward will help him to achieve results more quickly, whereas although a punishment will prevent him from repeating a mistake, it may increase the length of time required to carry out a certain test or trial.

A great deal of time and effort is required to train a horse, and it is futile to become impatient. Studies carried out in the United States have proved that better results can be obtained by decreasing the frequency of the "lessons," even to as little as once a week. This goes to show that the horse requires a period of consolidation, during which time he establishes in his mind the patterns of a particular exercise.

The concept of imitation, briefly mentioned above, is also a very important factor in the learning process and one that is typically found among higher animals. A horse will learn better if he imitates another horse that has already been trained, in the same way that a child will learn how to talk by repeating the sounds made by adults. In order to assess the intellectual capacity of the horse, horse psychologists, mainly Americans, have devised a series of tests for the animal, which provide comparable re-

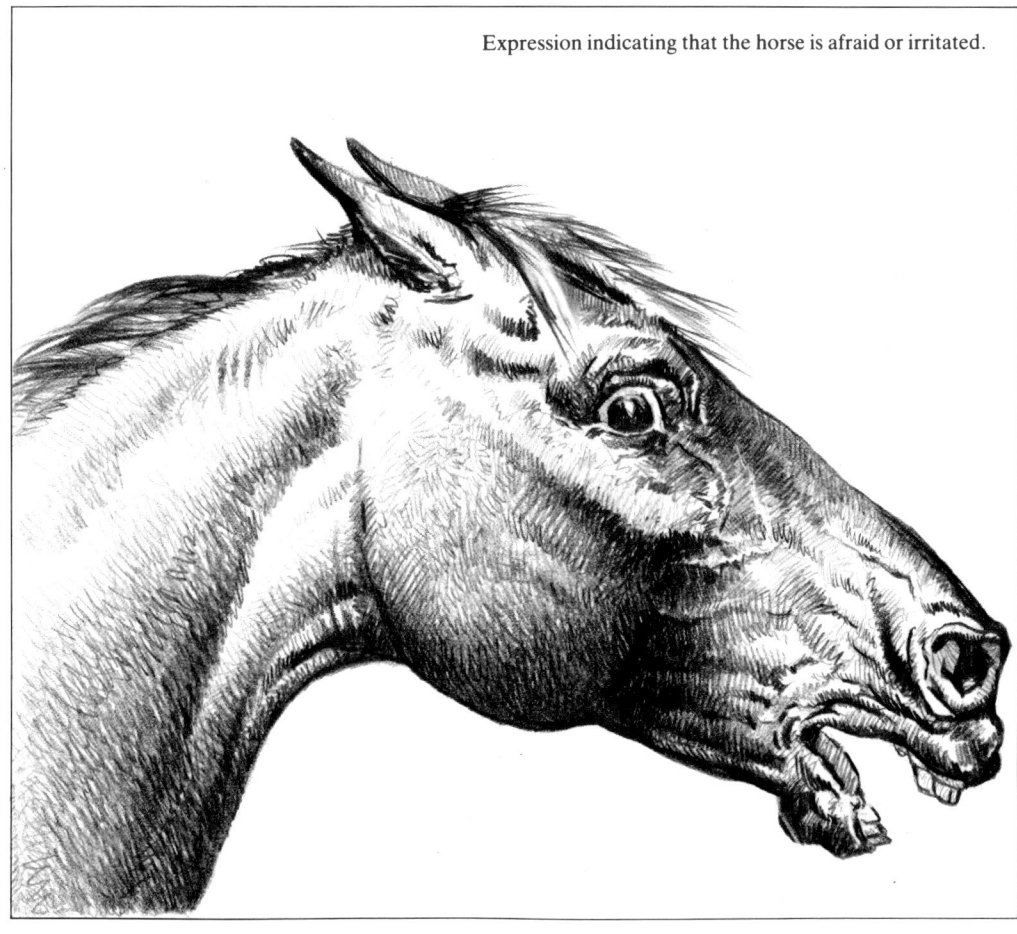

Expression indicating that the horse is afraid or irritated.

sults. The tests are formulated to allow the horse to memorize previous experiences and utilize the data to solve the next test, which will be slightly harder. By accurately analyzing the times taken and methods used by the horse to complete the tests, an overall result is then calculated, which provides a useful point of reference for assessing the intelligence of other animals. Generally, a young horse is more prepared to learn than an old one, but in certain unexpected situations, in which it is necessary to learn very quickly, the store of experience of an older horse will more than make up for the greater receptivity of the younger one. The speed at which a horse learns depends also on how well domesticated he is. The more accustomed to people, the friendlier and subsequently the more easy to train a horse will be. It is sometimes mistakenly believed that horses in the wild state are stupid. In reality their intelligence is differently oriented, because of the difference in their way of life.

The prime concern of a wild horse is survival against the natural hazards of the environment, consequently his mentality is oriented towards the search for food and shelter, the identification of predators and the need to escape when danger threatens. A wild horse is not required to learn how to live side by side with man in the way a domestic horse is. However, although a domestic horse is much better suited to understanding and learning from his owner, he would find it difficult to survive if he were abandoned in the wild.

The horse is frequently considered to be courageous and bold, but as a general rule he is a timid, non-aggressive animal, often nervous and apprehensive. His main defense mechanism is not to attack, but to run away. By nature he is not a hard-working creature either, and will try to avoid overexerting himself whenever he possibly can. His relationship with man can be defined as based, above all, on his desire to lead a quiet life, with daily food guaranteed and protection assured. If at times he shows a recalcitrant streak, or unseats his rider, he does so not so much out of a desire for freedom, but rather because he feels insecure, and in poor hands. The horse's long span of domestication has over the years moulded his character, rendering him docile and patient with man, although this is a generalization. To attempt to classify a horse by his characteristics, it is once again necessary to turn to studies made by American psychologists who have worked out various behavioural tests based on the reactions shown by a horse in ordinary, everyday situations such as feeding in the stable, grazing outdoors or being groomed and harnessed. The way in which a horse behaves gives a valuable insight into his natural tendencies, making it possible to categorize him into a particular character type. It must, however, be said that, since all classification is necessarily based on patterns and models, these results should not be taken too literally. Some horses are defined as being "sensitive," and are quick to learn and react, even to slight variations in the tone of voice. Such horses, however, are easily distracted, are prone to depression, and need to have contact with people who will understand and soothe them, and who will never raise their voice or make brusque movements, that might provoke sudden uncontrolled reactions. Then there are "hypersensitive" horses who are incapable of controlling even their slightest reactions to things and often display nervous twitches that become most acute in moments of tension. Their relationship with man is difficult as a result of this excessive feeling of insecurity. At the opposite end of the spectrum there are "insensitive" horses who show little reaction to things, are difficult to ruffle or surprise and are concerned only with their own gratification. These animals will tend to put up a passive resistance to learning programmes, and as such they are difficult subjects, with little hope of improvement. Fourthly there are "intolerant" horses who at the very first opportunity, will try to compete with man for supremacy, sometimes even resorting to kicking and biting to achieve their end. Only a firm and confident hand will enable an individual to establish a good relationship with such horses. This will rarely be possible with "obstinate" horses, who will on principle oppose all human designs and demands, unless they happen to suit them. Finally, horses with a more easy-going nature are described as "tolerant" and "cooperative" and make ideal companions. They are good-hearted and understanding, allow themselves to be mounted and ridden even by children and beginners without any complaint; they have a natural desire to subordinate themselves to man's wishes and to please their owner and will also carry out repetitive and often unpleasant tasks with good grace. These horses are therefore particularly suitable for riding schools. This general list of characteristics is only intended as a guideline and does not imply that each and every horse should fit neatly into a particular category.

Defining a horse's character is a much more complex matter, since in many instances the different character traits will be so subtly interrelated as to be virtually indistinguishable. Before categorizing a horse under a certain character type, for example as "hypersensitive" or "insensitive," it is important to remember that his behaviour will have been considerably conditioned by factors such as habitat and the way in which he has been treated. A horse who is free to move about as he pleases will clearly be less prone to a "fit of nerves" than a Thoroughbred who is cooped up in his box for 23 hours out of 24. Similarly, a horse who spends much of the day engaged in very tiring work will be less likely to react nervously than a horse carrying out relatively undemanding tasks. It is interesting to note that even the most highly-strung, obstinate and ill-natured horse will rarely display such negative characteristics with small children and other animals. In fact particularly highly-strung race horses are often given a kid goat, a cat or a dog to keep them company. A horse may have feelings of fairly marked sympathy or antipathy towards other horses. One well-known case is that of the race horse Ribot, who had developed such a strong attachment towards one of his stablemates that he would not be moved unless his friend went too.

The causes of bad temper in a horse may be physiological (problems with vision or hearing, defective stance, or excessive sensitivity in some part of the body); psychological (due to the trauma of being beaten or disorientation at the end of a particular method of training) or hereditary. Of the three, bad habits that have been inherited will be the most difficult, probably impossible, to correct. Character disorders damage not only the horse, but its owner as well in that they will entail a considerable drop in the animal's commercial value.

Horses are capable of communicating both with other horses and with man, by making sounds, or assuming specific positions with certain parts of their body. The distinctive sound made by the horse is the neigh or whinny. If this is long and drawn out and ends on a high note it conveys a sense of well-being and contentment; if on the other hand it is long, but rather solemn, it can indicate that the horse wants something; if it is very short and high-pitched, it can express anger; and if it is short, low-pitched and almost forced, it denotes fear. As a general rule pain does not cause a horse to neigh loudly; instead he will tend to bellow, making a short, light, low-pitched sound, that almost seems like a plea for help. When a horse is afraid, or victim of some unexpected agitation, he will abruptly breathe in a large amount of air, which makes the membranes in the nasal cavities vibrate, producing a distinctive noise known as "snorting," followed by another short, dull noise produced by the rapid exhalation of air. These sounds also serve to alert the rider to some unseen danger. Alarm in the horse is also expressed with the eyes, which are kept wide open with the eyelids raised, and by the ears, which prick up and turn in the direction of the possible danger. The combined use of the lips and the nostrils is very frequent, both to display aggression, in which case the horse raises his upper lip and clenches his teeth, and to show affection, when he moves his upper lip about at the same time as dilating his nostrils. Displaying or grinding the teeth, biting in midair, and raising the head at the same time are all indications that the horse has noticed something of interest, perhaps a mare on heat. If a horse shows his teeth,

Typical attitude indicating that the horse's front left leg is hurting.

stretches his neck forwards and at the same time lays back his ears and whisks his tail, this is a sign that he is very annoyed, or about to bolt. In such cases the best advice is to keep well away from the animal, because his subsequent actions may well be extremely rapid and violent. To indicate that a certain part of his body is giving him pain, a horse will swing his neck and head towards the area that is hurting. Pain can also be expressed by a movement of the loins, accompanied by the horse veering away from anyone who tries to approach him. These are only the most conspicuously visible ways in which a horse may express his feelings. Beyond this, it is up to the owner to learn the art of patient observation so as to be able to interpret the numerous messages that the horse will transmit to him. In this way a sound basis of affection, trust and mutual dependency will be built up between man and animal, leading to an untroubled and lasting relationship.

VICES AND BEHAVIOURAL DEFECTS

Some horses may display quite obvious character disorders or fairly conspicuous defects in their behaviour, both of which will considerably affect their commercial value.

As a general rule, such horses are defined as being "unsound" and only in a few cases will it be possible to correct such habits or defects. More often than not any attempt will be in vain.

Vices involving the protracted use of natural defense mechanisms
Bucking
Biting
Bolting

Vices involving abnormal and unnatural defense mechanisms
Running at people
Not answering to the reins
Shying
Rearing
Difficult to mount or presenting awkward behaviour once mounted
Touchy
Backing away
Restless and obstinate
Trying to crush rider against a wall or fence

Vices resulting from chronic bad habits
Boring: the horse bows his head low so that the neck is carried in a high curve
Tossing the head, shaking it constantly up and down with a brisk rhythmical movement
Star-gazing: holding the head and muzzle too high

Inherent vices
Expanding the girth
Pawing the ground
Untying the halter
Rubbing the tail

Vices caused by nervous disorders
Blowing the lips
Lying down like a cow
Lying down in water
Lying down as soon as the harness is on
Throwing the food to the ground
Eating too much straw
Taking the bit between the teeth
Chewing the rug
Unshoeing the hooves
Resting one foot on the other
Nervous twitches

COATS—INDIVIDUAL MARKINGS

The hair that covers the horse's body, protecting it from the adverse effects of the climate, is collectively described as the coat. This coat, which once served to camouflage the horse in its wild state, may come in a variety of different colours and shades and may be uniform or variegated. The various coats are divided into two basic groups: simple and compound. Simple coats (black, white and chestnut) consist of hairs of the same colour, although there may be slight variations in shade in different parts of the body, whereas compound coats are made up of hairs of different colours, either in separate areas, or mixed. Consequently, in addition to coats consisting of two separate colours (bay, brown and the various shades of dun), there are also coats with two colours interspersed (grey and red roan) and others with three interspersed colours (roan). Then there are part-coloured coats with patches of two or more distinct colours (skewbald, or piebald), which are conspicuous but not common. All these different types of coat offer a huge range of colours, which come in a whole series of shades.

A horse's coat is also affected by the seasons. During the summer months, when the animal moults, the coat becomes less thick and is made up of shorter hairs, often causing it to change colour slightly. Particular importance is attached to the individual peculiarities of a horse's coat because these differing features make it possible to distinguish between two horses of the same breed with almost total accuracy. It is precisely for this reason that horses are always identified by these markings rather than just by colour. While the colour of the coat may be subject to variations after a foal is born (in many cases the colour of a foal's coat will be different from its adult coat, although it is usually possible to see what the adult colouring will eventually be from the colour of the head), the markings on the coat are more permanent and less likely to alter.

Perhaps the most distinctive marks are those known as whorls, since their character and position vary in every animal. These peculiar whirlpool-like formations of hair are invaluable when attempting to distinguish between two horses of the same colour, and without any other form of distinctive marking. Other factors such as breed, sex and age help towards the identification of a horse, but it is quite possible to be confronted by two horses of the same breed, sex and age with exactly the same colour coat, which clearly illustrates the importance of a horse's markings.

Besides whorls a horse will often have white markings of varying sizes, situated on the limbs or head. When these occur on the lower part of the leg they are popularly described as "socks" or "stockings." On the head, depending on the exact positioning, as well as the shape and size, such markings are called blazes, stars and stripes. The star is a white irregularly shaped marking on the horse's forehead and varies greatly in size and shape. The stripe is a narrow white marking down the face extending as far as the nostrils. The blaze is a wide, white band that covers almost all the forehead and extends down the nose to beyond the muzzle. When the white marking covers large areas of the face, both lengthwise and crosswise, the horse is described as having a "white face." A horse is described as having a white muzzle when it has white markings on one or both lips, extending up to the nostrils. A snip is a downy pink or white marking between the nostrils. Other special features of the coat include occasional patches of skin that are devoid of pigment. These are called flesh marks and are found in parts that are not covered with hair, such as the lips and nostrils. Some horses may also have a list or eel stripe, which is a black line extending along the spine from the withers to the croup.

The white markings on the legs, can vary considerably from a narrow band just above the coronet to an area of white extending as high up as the hocks. When describing the markings it is very important to state exactly how high they reach, such as halfway up the pastern, to the fetlock, or halfway up the cannon, and to note the number of legs affected. Horses may have markings on one, two, three or four legs.

The colour of a coat is defined as whole or solid when it is uniform and devoid of any white markings; roan when it is bay, chestnut, brown, dun or black but flecked throughout with white hair; and dappled when it has a background colouring dotted with circular markings of different shades, but all of the same colour. Zebra markings are black stripes that run crosswise, especially on the legs, and grey-ticked indicates the presence of sparse groups of white hairs on the coat.

Other individual details used to help identify horses are "acquired" markings. These are not congenital and occur as groups of white hair or scars resulting from an injury, bruise or graze; pressure from the saddle or other parts of the harness; firing or branding; surgery or tattoos. Another distinctive mark, which, although not technically concerned with the coat is nevertheless interesting to look out for, is the "prophet's thumb mark." This is a muscular depression usually seen in the shoulders and at the base of the neck and occasionally in the hindquarters. This mark is more common in Arabs and Thoroughbreds.

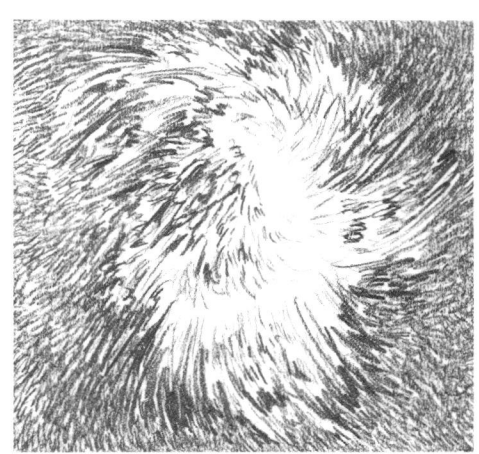

Whorl

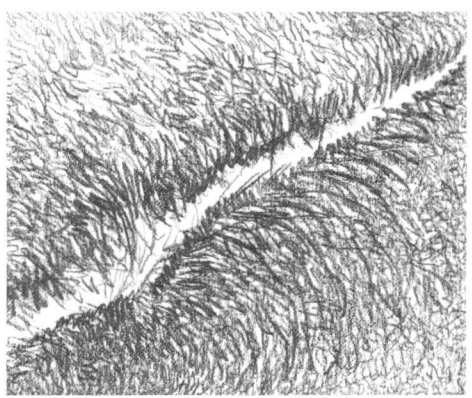

Herring-bone whorl

SIMPLE COATS OF ONE COLOUR

White: white hair on a pink skin
a) silver (metallic tinge)
b) porcelain (bluish tinge)
c) dirty (tending to cream)

Black: black hairs
a) dull (slightly reddish)
b) coal (dark and glossy)

Chestnut: Yellow to red hair; chestnut or flaxen mane and tail
a) light (red tending towards yellow)
b) golden (gold coloured hair)
c) liver (tending towards brown)
d) bloodstone (tending towards maroon)
e) bronze (bronze coloured)
g) mealy (pale and washed out)

COATS COMPOSED OF TWO COLOURS INTERSPERSED

Red roan: white and red or yellow hairs
a) light (predominantly white)
b) dark (predominantly red or yellow)

Grey: white and black hairs; occasional admixture of red
a) light (predominantly white hairs)
b) dark (predominantly black hairs)
c) steel (glossy with a predominance of black hairs)
d) silver (glossy with a predominance of white hairs)
e) flecked (predominantly black hairs with occasional small clusters of white
f) dappled (with clearly-defined patches of white hair)
g) flea-bitten (small clusters of darker or reddish-brown hair)
h) pinkish (admixture of red hairs)
i) white (white hairs on black skin)

COATS COMPOSED OF TWO SEPARATE COLOURS

Yellow or mouse dun: dark yellow hairs, black at the tips; black mane and tail

Dun: yellow hair down to the knees and hocks; black hairs below the knees and hocks; black mane and tail
a) light (tending towards white)
b) cream (pale sandy colour)
c) golden (more glossy yellow)

Blue dun: lead-coloured hairs, black at the tips; black mane and tail

Bay: reddish hairs, black at the tips; black mane and tail
a) brown (almost black)
b) dark (brownish red)
c) chestnut (brownish chestnut)
d) light chestnut
e) golden
f) light (almost white at the muzzle, the underbelly, the flanks and on the inside of the thighs)

COATS COMPOSED OF THREE COLOURS

Roan: white, red and black hairs
a) bay or red (bay with an admixture of white giving a reddish tinge)
b) blue (predominantly black hairs)
c) chestnut (predominantly red hairs)

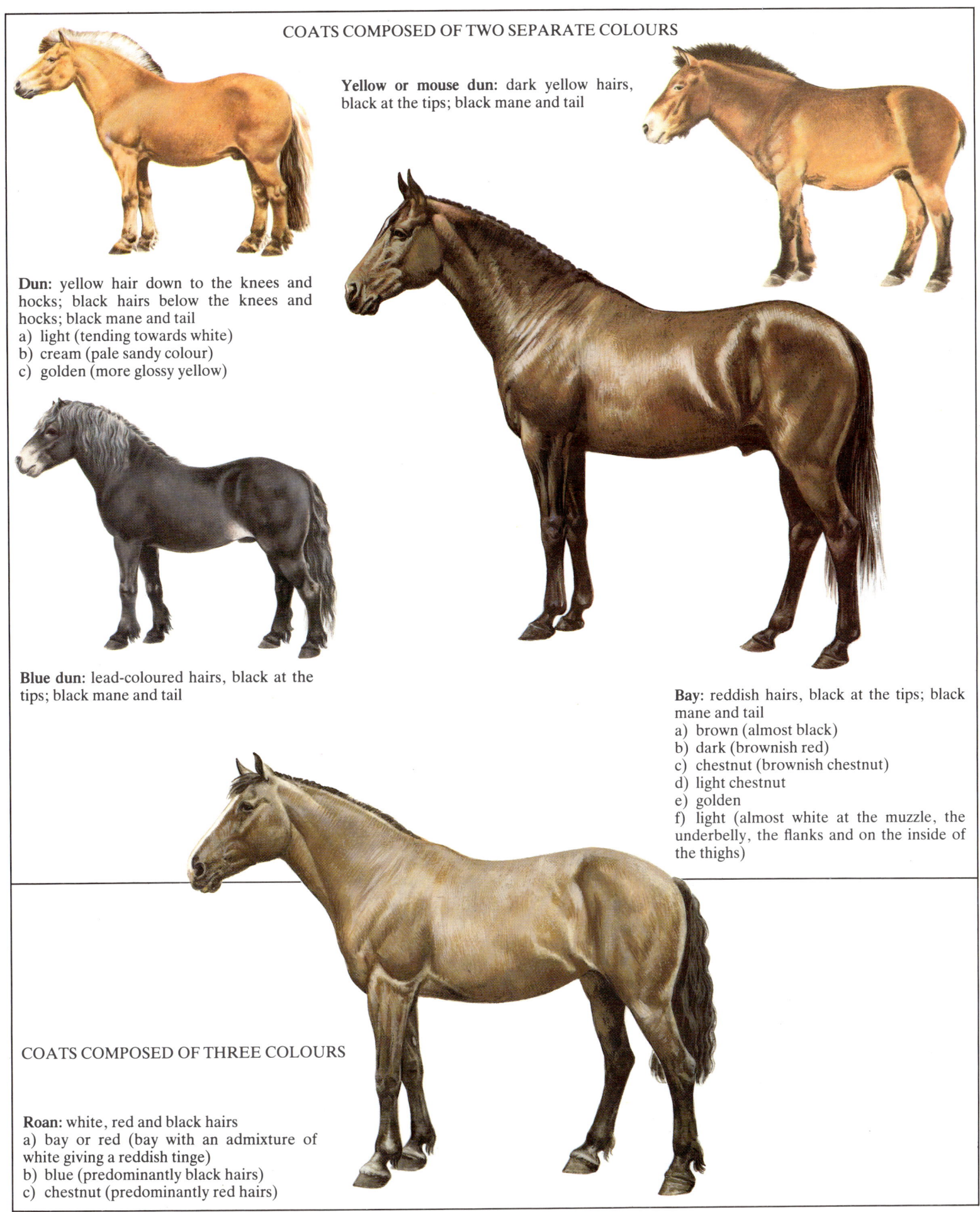

25

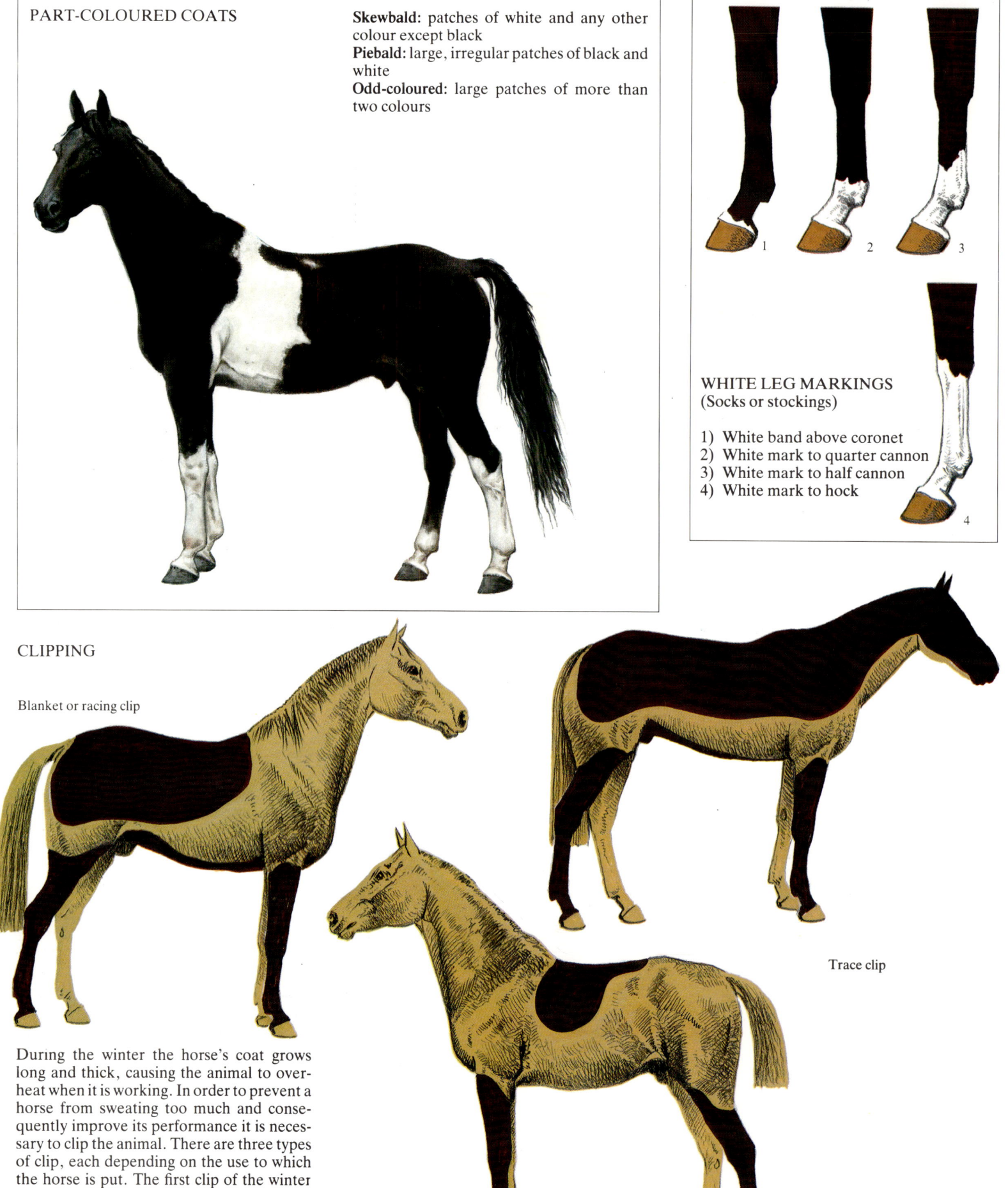

PART-COLOURED COATS

Skewbald: patches of white and any other colour except black
Piebald: large, irregular patches of black and white
Odd-coloured: large patches of more than two colours

WHITE LEG MARKINGS
(Socks or stockings)

1) White band above coronet
2) White mark to quarter cannon
3) White mark to half cannon
4) White mark to hock

CLIPPING

Blanket or racing clip

Trace clip

Hunter clip

During the winter the horse's coat grows long and thick, causing the animal to overheat when it is working. In order to prevent a horse from sweating too much and consequently improve its performance it is necessary to clip the animal. There are three types of clip, each depending on the use to which the horse is put. The first clip of the winter should never be given before mid-October.

MARKINGS

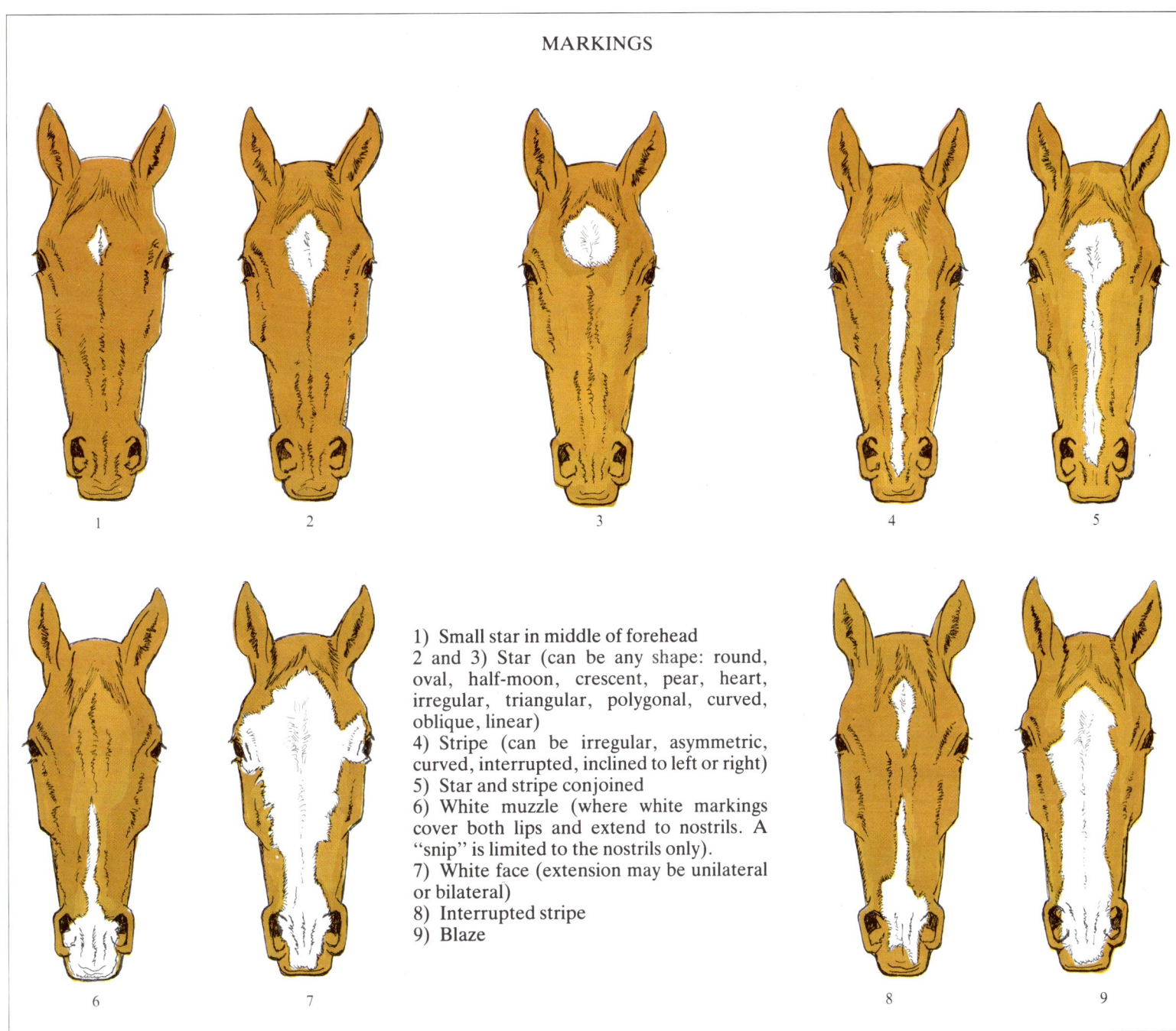

1) Small star in middle of forehead
2 and 3) Star (can be any shape: round, oval, half-moon, crescent, pear, heart, irregular, triangular, polygonal, curved, oblique, linear)
4) Stripe (can be irregular, asymmetric, curved, interrupted, inclined to left or right)
5) Star and stripe conjoined
6) White muzzle (where white markings cover both lips and extend to nostrils. A "snip" is limited to the nostrils only).
7) White face (extension may be unilateral or bilateral)
8) Interrupted stripe
9) Blaze

NAMES FOR COLOURS IN VARIOUS OTHER LANGUAGES										
Colour	Italy	France Belgium	Germany Austria	Spain	Venezuela	Argentina	Brazil	Chile	Peru	Uruguay
CHESTNUT	Sauro	Alézan	Fuchs	Alazán	Alazán	Alazán	Alazao	Alazán	Alazán	Alazán
BAY	Baio	Bai	Braun	Castaño	Castaño	Zaino colorado	Castanho	Zaino (or colorado)	Castaño	Zaino
BLACK	Morello	Noir	Schwarz	Negro	Negro	Oscuro	Preto	Negro	Negro	Oscuro
GREY	Grigio	Gris	Schimmel	Tordo	Tordillo	Tordillo	Tordilho	Tordillo	Tordillo	Tordillo
ROAN	Roano	Rouan	Rotschimmel	Ruano (or Rosillo)	Tordillo vinoso	Rosillo	Rosilho	Rosillo	Rosillo	Tordillo vinoso
BROWN	Baio oscuro	Bai brun	Schwarzbraun	Castaño oscuro	Zaino	Zaino negro	Zaino	Mulato	Zaino (or Mulato)	Zaino negro

ORIGINS AND EVOLUTION

Even today the genealogical tree of the horse (*Equus caballus*) is probably the most widely known evolutionary example. From its beginnings in the Upper Tertiary, some 55 million years ago, it has followed a steady course through the entire Quaternary Period and into the present day. The diagram on the opposite page, although simplified, shows how the phylogenetic tree of the horse is represented by a number of branches, some of which are termed as sterile since they have given rise to forms that are now extinct, or for which no fossil remains have ever been unearthed and others, which are undoubtedly fertile. By looking specifically at these latter, fertile branches it has been possible to reconstruct the evolution of the species with a reasonable degree of certainty. It is still very difficult, however, to establish a uniform line that accurately traces the evolution of the essential modifications to the feet, teeth and shape of the head, and it is these very modifications that have led to the physical form and appearance of the modern horse. Nevertheless, by closely examining the fossil series available, the fundamental stages through which this evolutionary process has moved have been satisfactorily established.

It is now generally accepted that the various changes, produced by genetic mutation and natural selection, led to the contemporary formation of several genera of ancestral horses. In the Pliocene, in particular, the genus *Merychippus* divided into several genera and species, with the result that 13 species of herbivorous equids were all in existence in the North American continent at the same time. It is here, in fact, that the crucial chapters in the history of the horse began to unfold. The first horses were primitive ungulates, closely resembling carnivores in appearance, with pointed teeth and very well-developed canines, but with five-toed limbs, each toe bearing a small nail or hoof. *Phenacodus*, which was omnivorous and about the size of a sheep, is considered to be the most remote forbear of all the ungulates, and thus of the horse as well. It belonged to the order of Condylarthra. These are fossil mammals characterized by a type of movable joint (specifically known as a diarthrosis) permitting movements of bending, extension, adduction (bringing forward), abduction (bringing backward) and circumduction (rotation).

The principal evolutionary phases of the modern horse can be summarized and described as follows:

Eohippus This genus of which there were many species had short legs, an arched back, and a long, bushy tail. The front feet had four toes, the rear three. All the toes had small hooves, but *Eohippus* did not actually stand on these. Instead it stood on small pads situated behind them, rather like dogs. The small head had a short nose, and the eyes were set centrally between the ears and the tip of the nose. The teeth, numbering 44 in all, were represented by well-developed incisors, and primitive premolars and molars, with a flat, uncemented crown and a chewing surface with three or four cusps. *Eohippus* lived in woodland, feeding on leaves and young plants. The contemporary genus *Hyracotherium*, which lived in Europe and was very similar to *Eohippus*, did not produce any fertile branches, and became extinct at the end of the Eocene. For many years it was hypothesized that *Hyracotherium* was the "founding father" of the horse, with a line passing by way of *Anchitherium* and *Hipparion*, but towards the end of the nineteenth century, research carried out in the Mississippi Basin and in the Rocky Mountains by the University of Columbia led to the discovery of more than 800 fossils of equids. Some of these were complete and very well preserved, and close study of them has made it possible systematically to retrace the evolutionary processes of the horse.

Orohippus and Epihippus These genera made their respective appearances in the middle of and towards the end of the Eocene. Both were larger than *Eohippus*, and about the size of a fox. In addition their dentition showed a series of gradual modifications.

Mesohippus and Miohippus These two forms were also extremely similar. They stood about 2 ft (60 cm) at the withers. The feet were three-toed, the central toe being more powerful than the others. The dentition was even more specialized, with the dental tubercles connected by ridges. The back was straight, the head elongated and the eyes set at the sides. These genera lived at the beginning and towards the middle of the Oligocene.

Parahippus This form appeared in the Lower Miocene, and stood 2 ft 6 in (75 cm) at the withers. Its dentition was already starting to take on the structure and arrangement of the teeth of animals whose specialized feeding habit was grazing. Its actual phylogenetic placement is still a matter of controversy, in view of the fact that some scholars maintain that the subsequent evolutionary phases pass through this genus, whereas others maintain that they come directly from *Miohippus*.

Merychippus This genus displayed important changes of various sorts, first and foremost in the teeth, which had a high crown and were cemented, with enamelled ridges running through the chewing surface (molars and premolars). These ridges or crests enabled *Merychippus* to chew on very hard grasses with a high silica content. In addition, the central toe was much more highly developed than the others, and was fitted with a large hoof designed to support the animal. This form made its appearance towards the middle of the Miocene.

Pliohippus This genus, which appeared in the Lower Pliocene, also signified a major leap forward, because this was the first horse to have just one "toe." The molars had a high crown and were in a permanent state of growth, like the modern horse. However, this growing process was faster in the outer part, which is why the teeth curved inwards, whereas the teeth of the modern horse are almost straight.

Equus This genus first made its appearance about one million years ago. In height and structure it closely resembled the modern horse: the back was straight, and the legs long and lightly built. Only the head was slightly more crudely structured, due to the heavier lower jaw and the slightly receding muzzle. *Equus* was highly specialized for both running and grazing, with chisel-like incisors, and molars and premolars with a high crown, and very grooved masticatory surfaces, of the lophoselenodont type, i.e. a cross between the lophodont, which has very irregular ridges running crosswise, and the selenodont, in which the regular ridges are crescentic (as in the ungulate artiodactyls).

Equus underwent various developments in North America, and then migrated to Asia, Europe and, later on, South America. Fossil remains of *Equus* have been found all over the world, with the exception of Australia. At a later stage, during the Pleistocene, which ended some ten thousand years ago, the species living in the Americas became extinct, for reasons that have still not been satisfactorily explained.

Eras	Years	Periods	Epochs	Evolutionary forms
Neozoic or Quaternary	8,150	Olocene	Neolithic	Equus caballus
	1.5–2 million	Pleistocene	Paleolithic upper / middle / lower	Equus, Hippidion
Cenozoic or Tertiary	26 million		Pliocene	Hypohippus, Megahippus, Hipparion, Pliohippus
			Miocene	Anchitherium, Archaeohippus, Parahippus, Merychippus
	37 million	Paleogene	Oligocene	Miohippus, Mesohippus
	53 million		Eocene	Epihippus, Orohippus
	65 million		Paleocene	Hyracotherium, Eohippus

Eohippus

Mesohippus

Merychippus

DOMESTICATION

Whilst the evolutionary history of the horse took its course essentially in North America, the processes of domestication and refinement of the horse's features, took place in Europe. Once the ancient genus *Equus* had successfully migrated to the Old World, it gave rise in due course to the large family of *Equidae* (the equids). The most important of these, now regarded as the original ancestors of all modern horses, are *Equus (caballus) przewalskii* or Przewalski's horse, from Mongolia, with only a very small population now in existence, and *Equus (caballus) gmelini*, the Tarpan (now extinct); *Equus onager*, the onager or Asiatic wild ass, that lives in herds in Asia Minor; *Equus hemionus*, the kiang, that also lives in herds in the steppes and semi-desert regions of central Asia, and which cannot be domesticated, even though it has been crossed with other members of the *Equidae*, including the common horse; *Equus africanus*, which, together with the onager, is the original ancestor of all domestic asses and donkeys; and the three currently existing species of zebra, *Equus zebra*.

It is not known exactly when the horse was first domesticated but it was an extremely important step, since it meant that man was no longer daunted by long distances. It encouraged and promoted contact between people, and gave rise to the whole network of social relations that lies at the root of any modern society. Some scholars consider that the horse was first domesticated at the end of the Paleolithic epoch, while others maintain it came about at the hands of the Chinese around 3500 B.C. Others still claim that it was the Ancient Egyptians who tamed the horse, a belief supported by biblical references in the books of Genesis and Exodus. It is thought that in primitive times the horse would have been used for riding and as a pack animal and it was only later that man found ways of using the horse as a draught animal that could also be adapted for various other forms of work. The delay was due to the fact that this entailed the development of forms of harness very different from those used for heavy oxen. Once all these difficulties had been surmounted, the increase in popularity of the horse was both rapid and worldwide, contributing greatly to the progress of humankind. Eventually, man was able to concentrate on breeding different types of horse for an extensive range of roles and functions.

TARPAN

The Tarpan is regarded as the progenitor of all breeds of lightly-built horses (warm bloods) currently in existence. Unfortunately, the Tarpan itself has now been extinct for almost a century. The last specimen living in the wild died in 1879, as it tried desperately to avoid being captured. It was a mare, and on it rested great hopes for saving the breed. Then the last Tarpan in captivity died in 1887 in Munich zoo. For centuries the Tarpan was extensively hunted by peasants for its meat, and local farmers would catch and domesticate the wild ponies to use them for working the fields. This led to the eventual extinction of the breed due, as in so many other cases, to man's greed and sheer lack of common sense. It appears that there were two distinct strains of Tarpan, one living in the steppes, and the other in forested areas. Both strains, however, were to be found in the wild in eastern Europe, from Poland to the Ukraine. After the last members of the breed had vanished, the Polish authorities did take a certain initiative, inspecting all the farms in the country and comandeering any horses that displayed features similar to those of the Tarpan, with a view to restoring the breed as best they could. These animals were introduced to nature reserves, and it is here that the present-day breed has developed. However, although these presumed heirs of the Tarpan, living in the forests of Popielno and Bialowieza clearly display the same exceptional resistance to the diseases and ailments that affected their ancestors from the steppes, there is still some confusion regarding their true link to the original breed.

Breed: Tarpan (*Equus przewalskii gmelini* Antonius)
Place of origin: Poland
Height at withers: approx. 13 hands
Structure: mesomorphic
Colour: grey—yellow dun—mouse dun—brown—(black mane and tail—black eel stripe—legs black or with zebra markings)
Temperament: brave—independent—unmanageable
Aptitude: life in the wild
Qualities: resistant to disease and bad weather conditions—prolific
Head: slightly on the heavy side with straight or convex profile and a bulge around the nostrils—ears long, pointing forward and slightly to the side—eyes small and almond-shaped—thick forelock
Neck: short and thick—with a thick mane
Body: withers not prominent—back long—quarters weak and sloping—tail set low and flowing—deep chest
Legs: slender but strong—sloping shoulder

ASIATIC WILD HORSE

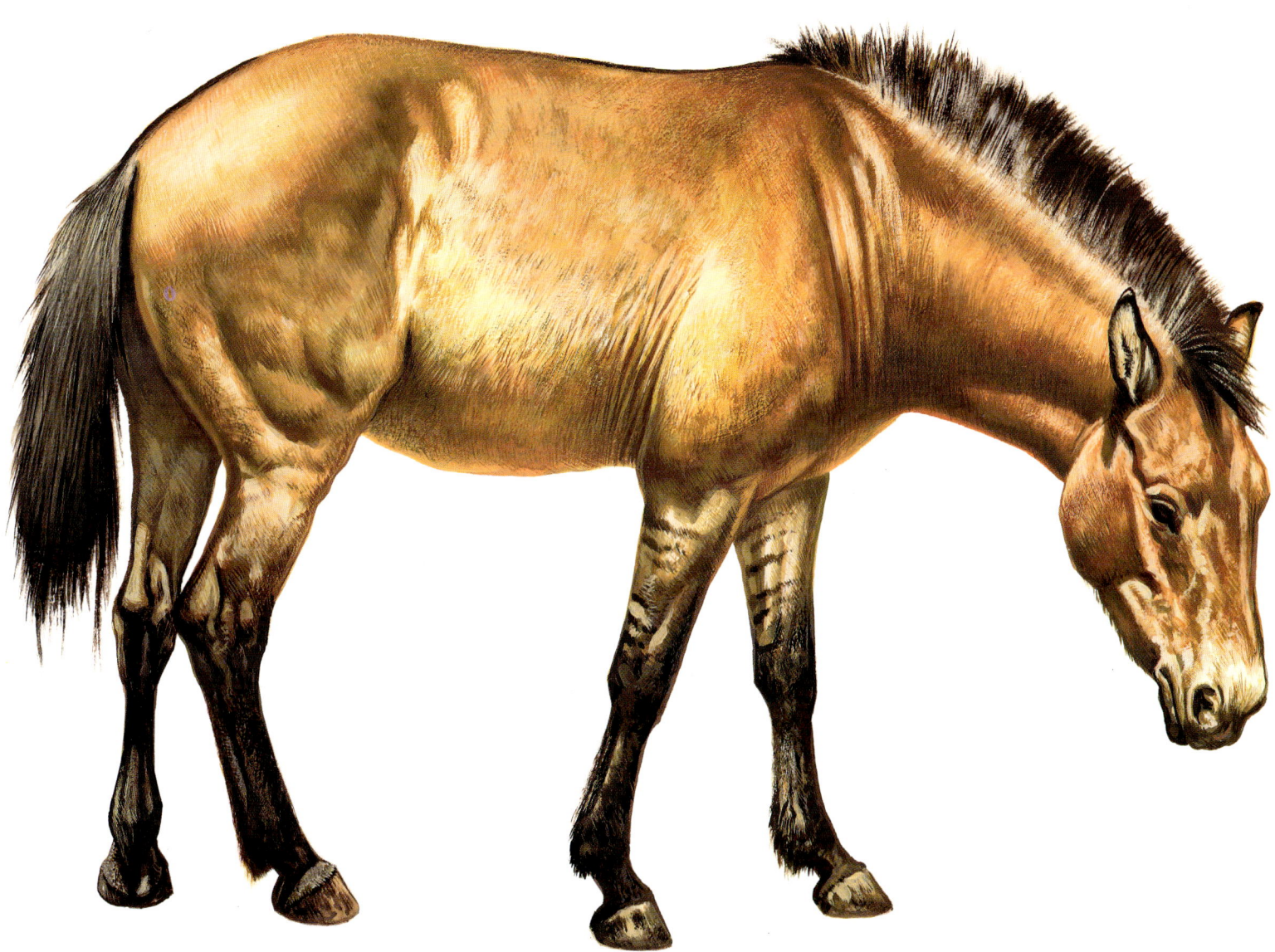

Most authorities and zoologists agree that the place of origin of this last, truly wild horse is in the region of the Daqin Shan Mountains (literally, the "mountains of the yellow horse"). This range is situated at the edge of the Gobi desert, and today the few surviving members of the breed, which was discovered as late as 1881 by Colonel N. M. Przewalski, still roam wild in this area. After being ruthlessly hunted, and with its numbers drastically reduced as a result, the breed is currently protected by the governments of the Soviet Union, Mongolia and China. There would appear to be about 50 surviving wild horses living in the wild, plus an additional 200 or so specimens which are in the careful hands of zoos in various parts of the world. These horses were probably once used as mounts by the Huns and the Chinese, before the latter managed to enlist the services of those famous horses from the Fergana Basin. It seems very likely that the appearance of this horse, one of the basic types from which most modern breeds probably descend, has changed very little since the Ice Age. This ability of the breed to remain physically unaltered over thousands of years is easily explained by the inhospitable environment which has always been its habitat, and perhaps even more importantly, by its natural aversion and aggression towards horses belonging to other breeds. The overall aspect of this animal reveals a certain discrepancy between the anterior parts of the body, which are characterized by good muscular development, and the hindquarters, which are rather poorly developed.

Breed: Asiatic Wild Horse, or Mongolian Wild Horse (*Equus przewalskii przewalskii* Poliakov)
Place of origin: Mongolia
Height at withers: 12–14 hands
Structure: mesomorphic
Colour: dun (varying from reddish bay to sandy)—mane and tail black—black eel stripe—legs black with possible zebra markings
Temperament: brave—energetic
Aptitude: life in the wild
Qualities: strong and resistant
Head: large and heavy with a straight or convex profile—wide forehead—long ears—eyes small and almond-shaped—mealy markings on muzzle
Neck: large and thick (tendency towards a "ewe" neck—mane bristly and very short with no forelock
Body: withers not prominent—back straight and short—back and loins powerful—quarters underdeveloped and quite sloping—tail set low—deep chest
Legs: short and sturdy—shoulder straight—good skeletal and articular development—pasterns short—hoof shallow and very elongated

BREED FORMATION AND CLASSIFICATION

Before going on to discuss the various breeds in more detail, it would seem appropriate to give a clear definition of the concept of species, since this is regarded as the basis of all biological classification. As far as the higher animal forms are concerned, a species indicates a group of related individuals, that are able to breed among themselves but not with members of another species. The breed, or sub-species, represents a group of individuals that have in common the basic characteristics of the species, but differ from each other in certain secondary features. Although all breeds are necessarily affected by environmental factors, there are no precise guidelines as to exactly how the many different breeds should be differentiated and classified. The difficulty is increased by the fact that the traits which differ from breed to breed are, for the most part, concerned with physical modifications (phenotypical) and are not generally inherited (genotypical). The definition of a sub-breed is even more delicate, for here the variations are limited to one, or very few, features which are of secondary importance.

One of the horse's most conspicuous characteristics is undoubtedly its coat, the colour and structure of which form an integral part of the basic features of a particular breed. However, there are also exceptional cases, such as the group of horses that have the distinctive Palomino coat, the colour of a newly minted gold coin. It is extremely difficult to breed this delicate colour, since crosses between a Palomino mare and a Palomino stallion do not always guarantee its continuation. The Palomino is, in fact, regarded as a colour type and is not a breed in its own right; only careful and accurate crossing is likely to produce a correct colour.

Similarly, the American Appaloosa cannot, strictly speaking, be considered a proper breed. The Appaloosa's coat varies considerably from one horse to the next and the only commonly shared feature is that this colouring becomes paler in certain parts of the body, which are generally covered with irregular dark markings. For this reason there is considerable controversy over whether it is more correct to talk in terms of the Appaloosa coat, or the Appaloosa breed.

There are various methods of classifying horses, all based on different parameters. One of these involves the principal use that is made of a particular animal, such as saddle horses or race horses, like the Arab, the American Saddle Horse and the English Thoroughbred; heavy draught horses, like the Belgian horse, the Percheron, the Shire, the Suffolk and the Clydesdale; light draught horses, or horses used for trotting races, like the Hackney, the Morgan and the Standardbred; ponies, like the Welsh pony, the Shetland pony and the Highland pony. Another use to which horses are put, primarily in England and Ireland, is hunting. In these countries, therefore, particular emphasis is placed on the hunter, the typical hunting horse, with the aim of improving its suitability for the job. The ideal hunter should be gentle and very docile and its structure should be powerful, especially in the hindquarters. In addition, a good specimen should be capable of keeping up a sustained brisk pace.

As far as the basic size and appearance of the body of a horse are concerned, the various breeds can be divided into three very general categories: brachymorphic (compact, with predominantly short, strong lines and particularly suitable for heavy draught and agricultural work); mesomorphic (sturdy, with harmonious lines, and a powerful and rapid action making them good riding horses, suitable for light agricultural work); dolichomorphic (long-limbed, and particularly well suited to running and racing).

A further way of distinguishing between the various breeds is to refer back to the geographical region of origin, since a particular environment has a decisive effect on breed characteristics such as size and appearance. A mountain-bred pony, for example, will tend to be small, stocky and resilient to rough terrain and extremes of temperature, whereas a horse living in an ideal, temperate climate will achieve larger proportions but will be less resistant to adverse climatic conditions.

Today, due to the increase in international travel, horse breeds that have originated in specific countries and regions have gradually become widespread in other parts of the world. One cannot, for example, regard the English, the French and the American Thoroughbred as different breeds as all three types belong to the same breed that has been taken to different countries where it has been bred and reared with equal success.

There are many different classified breeds in existence today, most of which can be found in Europe and western Asia.

EUROPEAN BREEDS

Icelandic pony

Iceland The only native breed is the attractive Icelandic pony, which has existed on this island for a very long time, and in large numbers.

Fjord

Norway and Sweden There are few breeds whose origins can be traced back to these two countries, but among them are the Norwegian Fjord pony, also known as the Westlands pony, the Swedish Ardennes and the North Swedish, all of which are used as heavy draught horses; the Gotland or Skogsruss pony, which is very similar to and closely related to the Norwegian Døle pony, and bred in Sweden; the Swedish Warm Blood, a good light draught and saddle horse. In both these countries trotting races are very popular and this has led, via careful selection involving an input of English bloodstock, to the development of the Døle Gudbrandsdal in Norway, and the North Swedish Trotter in Sweden.

Finnish horse

Irish hunter

Finland This country does not have a great tradition of horse breeding and in fact the only officially recognized, classified breed is the Finnish horse. Descended from two closely related breeds, the Finnish Universal and the Finnish Draught, the Finnish horse is a good all-rounder and can be used for a wide variety of purposes.

Great Britain and Ireland The enthusiasm, careful selection, and high-quality breeding techniques in these two countries have produced the most beautiful of the ponies (the Welsh pony), the largest horse (the mighty Shire), the fastest horse at the gallop (the English Thoroughbred) and the most spectacular jumper (the Irish hunter).

Most modern breeds have at some stage been influenced by the English Thoroughbred, which claims an ability to improve any other breed with which it is crossed. Another very important English breed, is the Hackney, an elegant, strong and swift horse, with a natural aptitude for trotting. Even though as a breed the Hackney has not itself been trained to compete, it has played an important part in the development of other important breeds which are used for competitive trotting events.

A place of honour must rightly be accorded the Cleveland Bay horse, a tall and majestic animal whose particular aesthetic qualities and elegance of movement have ensured it the qualification of high-class carriage horse. This breed has played an important role in the development not only of other carriage horses, such as the Yorkshire Coach horse, but also of the English hunter.

Another very interesting group is represented by the large heavy draught horses, distinctive for their stature that reaches its maximum height in the Shire. These mighty horses can weigh up to 1 tonne. It seems very likely that this group of horses is descended from the Great Horse, a large medieval charger used as a fighting steed in tourneys and jousts. Its powerful physique was vital for it to be able to support the combined weight of the elaborate harness and the rider's armour and weaponry. As well as the Shire horse, other heavy draught horses are the slightly smaller Clydesdale, and the Suffolk Punch. All these horses are still used today in some parts of Britain, for pulling brewer's drays, and in days gone by they were used for pulling coaches and omnibuses. Despite their bulk these horses display a certain harmony, partly due to the stateliness of their movements, which are by no means clumsy. This brief summary of English horses would not be complete without mentioning the numerous breeds of pony—Dartmoor, Exmoor, Dales, New Forest, Highland, Hackney, Shetland, Fell, Welsh and Welsh Mountain.

Among the typically Irish breeds, in addition to the Irish hunter, there are the Irish cob, a fairly tall, compact and sturdy breed which is an excellent draught horse, and docile by nature; the Connemara, which is reared in the wild state for its remarkable endurance in bad weather conditions, and used as a riding horse, as well as for young and inexperienced riders; and the Irish Draught horse which, despite its massive bulk and its stout skeletal structure, often shows a natural aptitude for jumping.

Denmark The most widely known Danish breed is the Jutland, a heavy draught horse whose origins date back over a thousand years. This massive breed was used by the Vikings as a saddle horse, and by the heavily-armoured knights of the Middle Ages as a charger in jousts and tourneys. But the pride of Danish horse breeding is the Frederiksborg, which is nowadays considered one of the most sought-after European saddle horses, both because of its elegance, and its flowing but powerful action.

Belgium. The rearing of heavy draught horses goes back a very long way in various parts of Belgium, and has given rise to

Medium Belgian

breeds which essentially differ only in terms of their size. The massive Brabant or Belgian Heavy Draught Horse, originally called the Flanders horse, weighs up to a tonne and is an excellent, slow, steady draught horse, as is the Condroz, or Medium Belgian. In the Ardennes there is the Belgian Ardennes, not to be confused with the French Ardennais, compared with which it is lighter and more slender in build. It is used for brisk draught duties, but often displays good trotting qualities as well.

Holland Dutch horse breeding is not renowned for its variety. Nowadays there are only two indisputably native breeds: the Friesian and the Gelderland, both of which are used essentially as draught horses and for agricultural purposes, although their physical build makes them particularly suitable as saddle horses. The Friesian, which is one of Europe's oldest breeds, boasts an illustrious past, being used in the Middle Ages as a war horse.

English Thoroughbred

Connemara

As far as saddle horses for sport are concerned, a recent arrival on the scene is the Dutch Saddle horse. This modern breed, which derives from the old Groningen and the Gelderland, has benefited from the influence of the English Thoroughbred.

Germany For the most part the native German breeds are large, and solidly built, with a majestic and often elegant action. How-

Friesian

Hanoverian

ever, changes in requirements have encouraged breeders to introduce gradual variations to these particular characteristics, in order to develop more versatile horses—both saddle horses, and horses that will perform well in various equestrian sports. Consequently, while heavy draught breeds such as the Rhineland (Rhenish) and the Schleswig are in a state of evident decline, greater importance is now being attached to these "new" breeds which, by means of crossbreeding (in particular with the English Thoroughbred), have undergone certain modifications. Although these breeds still tend to be quite large, they display a marked aptitude for trotting and jumping, and are thus used with spectacular results for eventing, show jumping, dressage, horse shows and hunting. The most important of these are the Hanoverian, which is one of the oldest breeds; the Oldenburg, the largest, with a noble history as a good, strong carriage horse; the Holstein, which produces good all-round riding horses; and the Mecklenburg, the Trakehner and the Württemberg, which all produce good and very versatile horses.

France France has had a long history of horse breeding due to the important role of the horse in society, in agriculture, for pulling vehicles and nowadays for sport. Through the ages, often due to historical events most French breeds, some of which are extremely ancient, have been altered by the introduction of bloodstock from other breeds. In the Pyrenees, the breeds known as Tarbes and Limousin (now extinct) were developed as a result of crossbreeding with Arab and Berber horses. The most impressive modern-day example of this breeding is the French Anglo-Arabian, an excellent saddle horse and a good, natural jumper. In Normandy, in addition to the old Anglo-Norman or Norman breed, now known as the Selle Français or French Saddle Horse, there is the French Trotter (Demi-Sang) whose origins partly overlap with those of the Selle Français. The French Trotter is the only trotting horse which is a match for the American Standardbred. In Brittany, in past times, the breeding and rearing of the Breton was of great importance. This horse, which dates back a very long way, is of medium height, compactly built, very sturdy and with good endurance. It was extremely popular in the Middle Ages on account of its particular gait which did not tire the horseman, making it well suited to long journeys. In Picardy and the Artois region the Boulonnais is bred. This is a large heavy draught horse, which is generally regarded as the most harmonious and elegant in its category. Among the various other draught horses are the Percheron, a huge animal that reaches a remarkable height at the withers and weighs up to one tonne, and the Ardennais. In France there is also a horse called the Camargue that lives wild in the region of the same name, at the mouth of the river Rhône. In this wild and marshy nature reserve, this sturdy, strong horse has found its ideal habitat. When domesticated it is used by the local Camargue cowboys (gardiens) who herd the bulls in this area.

Ardennais

Franches-Montagnes

Switzerland Due largely to its limited territory and geographical situation, Switzerland has never really developed its own national history of horse breeding but has tended to be influenced by neighbouring countries, and by France in particular. The two native breeds, the Freiberger and the Einsiedler, are often so like their French cousins, the old Anglo-Normans, that it is hard to tell them apart.

Lipizzaner

Austria The equestrian pride of place in this country is associated mainly with the creation of the Lipizzaner breed (named after the small, once Austrian town of Lipizza, now in northwest Yugoslavia). These horses are small and compact and tend to live to a good age. They have a stately bearing, and with their elegant gait, are still the pride of the Spanish Riding School in Vienna. Nowadays they are also used for leisure riding, and are excellent carriage horses because of their docile nature and considerable intelligence. In addition, in the province of Salzburg, in the Tyrol, in Styria and in Carinthia, draught horses such as the Pinzgauer and the Noriker are bred.

Poland, Czechoslovakia, Hungary, Yugoslavia, Bulgaria and Greece These countries share a strong agricultural tradition, which has led essentially to the development of working breeds, the importance of which has waned over the years. In addition, the geographical position of these countries and the historical events that have beset them (in

Kladruber

Hucul

Avelignese

East Bulgarian

Furioso-North Star

Peneia

this century. Yugoslavia produces good and sturdy horses, usually small in size, in Slovenia, Croatia, and the Drava valley, while in Bosnia-Herzegovina and Dalmatia two small and sturdy ponies, the Bosnian and the Dalmatian, have been bred since very early times. Poland similarly produces only a few breeds. In addition to the now extinct Tarpan, are the Sokolsky, a recently developed breed, the Hucul and the Konik. These horses are of medium or small stature, sturdy, with good endurance, and are good working horses, suitable for both light and heavy draught duties, as well as being good saddle horses. More recently, two relatively new breeds have been developed, the Malapolski and the Wielkopolski. Both breeds display the aptitudes mentioned above, although they are predominantly used as riding horses. Hungary boasts a greater number of native breeds, mainly as a legacy of the Austro-Hungarian Empire. The Hungarian breeds, which are generally lightly built, have been obtained by crossing native horses with Arabians, English Thoroughbreds, Andalusians, Anglo-Arabs and Anglo-Normans. The most important of these are the Shagya, Furioso, Nonius and Gidran breeds, among the medium-heavyweight to light builds, and the Murakoz among the heavyweight types. Greece has never had a proper horse-breeding programme and although there are several resident horse populations, these are not always easy to define. The term "native breed" can only really be applied to the Peneia, Pindos and Skyros ponies.

Italy In the past, particularly in the fifteenth and sixteenth centuries, great importance was attached to horse breeding in this country, which represented an international market for both draught and saddle horses, and for the outstanding stallions and mares that were in demand all over Europe. After a period of decline, Italy is now witnessing a renewed interest in horses, which has brought about the rediscovery and reutilization of Italian stud farms in many parts of the country, such as the Po Valley, where stout draught horses are reared, Alto Adige, the home of the Aveglinese, and the Tuscan

region of the Maremma which extends into the Roman plain, where we find the Maremmana, a tough, sturdy horse with good endurance, quite capable of living contentedly in the wild if necessary. Other important Italian breeds are the Bardigiano, a well-built pony, the Murgese, from the region of Murge in Puglia, the Sicilian horse (Siciliano), the San Fratello, and the Salerno, which are all saddle horses and light draught horses, together with the Sardinian horse, with marked Oriental characteristics.

Spain and Portugal The most famous Spanish breed is the extremely noble Andalusian horse, which played a role of great historical importance over a long period, from the

Andalusian

Lusitano

particular foreign domination), have both hampered and in terms of numbers all but prevented the creation of native breeds. It is for this reason, therefore, that the only breed classified as Czechoslovakian is the Kladruber, while in Bulgaria there are the Danubian horse, the East Bulgarian horse and the very recent Pleven, only developed

Middle Ages until the seventeenth century. In addition to its strong and distinguished appearance, this breed has great presence, combining agility and fire with docility and intelligence. It also owes its renown to its ability to improve the stock of other breeds.

Nowadays the purebred Andalusian is much less common, and has been outstripped by the elegant Hispano, or Spanish Anglo-Arab, which makes an excellent saddle and light draught horse. In the northern parts of the country, and in Catalonia, heavy draught horses are bred, obtained by crossing local horses with the Percheron, the Breton, the Ardennais and the Boulonnais: these include the Aragonese horse, obtained by crossbreeding with the Percheron; the Catalan horse, a descendant of the ancient Cerdaña horse, and a result of crossing with the Breton, the Ardennais and the Boulonnais; and the Burguete horse, which is bred in Navarre and obtained by crossing with the Breton. Neighbouring Portugal has been greatly influenced by Spanish horse breeding, with the result that there are only two classified native breeds: the Lusitano and the Altér Real.

Orlov

Soviet Union The vast area and the immensely varied nature of this country are reflected in the horses bred there. In fact the number of breeds is truly remarkable, and embraces horses with every conceivable aptitude. In the group of saddle horses that perform well in competitive events, pride of place goes to the Akhal-Teké, a strain of the ancient Turkmene horse. Other saddle horses and light draught horses include the Tersky, the Kustanair, the Don and the Budyonny; work horses are the Kirghiz, the Karabair, the Latvian horse, the Karabakh, the Kabardin, the Lokai, and the Zemaituka. The Soviet Union also produces two very good trotting horses, the Métis and the Orlov, and two small and distinctive ponies, the Viatka and the Kazakh. Lastly, for heavy farming work there are the Russian Heavy Draught, the Soviet Heavy Draught, the Lithuanian Heavy Draught and the Vladimir Heavy Draught all of which have excellent endurance.

AMERICAN BREEDS

Even though horse breeding in America has a relatively recent tradition, it is nowadays regarded by many as the most developed in the world because of the extremely modern techniques it employs.

Most American breeds are developed in North America. Breeds produced in South and Central America include the Mexican Galiceño, a saddle and light draught pony, the Paso Fino, an excellent saddle horse, and the Criollo, by far the most important and widespread breed, which is agile, docile, very tough, sturdy, and a typical horse of the pampas, where it is used by the gauchos. Argentina produces the smallest pony in the world, the Falabella, which derives from the Shetland pony. Other North American ponies, include the Chincoteague and the Assateague, which are named after two small islands off the coast of Virginia, and the Pony of the Americas. Included among the saddle and light draught horses are the Morgan, the Pinto and the American Saddle Horse; among the breeds used more specifically as saddle horses are the Albino, the Tennessee Walking Horse, with its distinctive gait, and the Quarter Horse, which is used by cowboys, and is nowadays a fierce rival of the English Thoroughbred in races over very short distances. The jewel of American horse breeding, however, is undoubtedly the Standardbred, which has produced the best trotting horses in the world.

Morgan

ASIAN BREEDS

Mongolian pony

Any discussion of Asian breeds must necessarily include the Przewalski and the Arab horse. The first is the undisputed forerunner of all modern horses, and the second is one of the breeds that has made notable contributions to the creation or improvement of a great many other breeds. The Arab is the forbear of two excellent saddle horses, the Syrian and the Persian Arab; and the two small Indian horses, the Kathiawari and the Marwari, are the result of crossing the Arab with native ponies. In Asia, and Indonesia there are many breeds of small pony. These include in Asia, the Spiti, Manipuri, Tibetan or Nanfan, Mongolian Wild Horse and Caspian; in Indonesia we find the Timor, Java, Batak, Bali, Sumba, Sumbawa and Sandalwood.

Criollo

Galiceño

AFRICAN BREEDS

Africa's contribution to horse breeding comes in the form of the Berber, which shares with the Arab and the Andalusian the prize for having contributed to both the creation and the improvement of a great many other breeds. The Berber, known today as the Barb, is bred and reared in Morocco and Algeria. In the rest of Africa, horses are poorly represented, partly due to long term poverty and poor breeding techniques, and partly also because of the scourge of the tse-tse fly. The bite from this fly, which injects *Tripanosoma gambiense* (sleeping sickness), causes severe nervous disorders which in due course lead to the deterioration and eventual death of the affected animal. A few other breeds do exist, however, and these include the Basuto pony from Lesotho, the Malagasy pony from Madagascar, and the Dongolo horse from Eritrea and Ethiopia.

BREEDS FROM AUSTRALIA AND NEW ZEALAND

Horse breeding in these two countries goes back only as far as the late eighteenth century when European settlers imported the first horses. These animals soon became naturalized and are now considered native Australian breeds. They are the Waler, which is now renamed as the Australian Stock Horse, a fine saddle and light draught horse; the Brumby, a wild pony, and the Australian pony. However, many breeds have since been introduced into both Australia and New Zealand from their countries of origin, particularly from England. In both these countries, where the environment is ideally suited to horse rearing, successful steps have already been taken to breed various imported types of horse, with a clear preference being shown for race horses.

BREEDS WHICH HAVE PLAYED AN IMPORTANT PART IN THE FORMATION OF OTHER SIGNIFICANT BREEDS

At first glance it might seem strange that the age-old Przewalski horse has retained its physical characteristics for such a very long period, and at the same time given rise to such a varied lineage. In addition to the Przewalski, however, there are other breeds such as the Arab, the Barb, the Andalusian and the Friesian, which have also played a decisive role in the creation of many highly important breeds, but which have, at the same time, also retained their own distinctive features. To understand properly how this can be the case, it is necessary to take a close look at the factors governing evolution, and in particular at natural selection.

Natural selection, which occurs as a result of the climatic and geographical effects of the environment, ensures the survival of a particular group of animals by improving or reducing the reproductive efficiency of the individual members. Strong, robust animals will consequently reproduce and their healthy strain will be continued through successive generations, whereas weaker, less suitable animals will be rejected as mating partners and die out. In nature, therefore, it is not just the reproductive efficiency of the individual that is important but the reproductive efficiency of the whole population, as the individual is only valuable as part of a group with which it shares common, hereditary characteristics. From this it is possible to see that the physical preservation of the group is infinitely more important than the preservation of the individual. This explains the way in which the various natural breeds, homogenous racial groups, have been formed in nature, and how these breeds have retained their particular acquired characteristics over very long periods of time.

Artificial selection on the other hand, tends to modify the characteristics of a horse, not with a view to improving its reproductive efficiency, but according to the way in which it could be used by man. Today, artificial selection has assumed a role of considerable importance, due to the continual increase in demand for horses for work and sport, and also due to the need to improve natural aptitudes, such as speed, in the case of race horses. In order to create new breeds, or even just to improve existing breeds, it is necessary to know how characteristics are both manifested and transmitted. Only in this way is it possible to work out the correct programmes and then scientifically assess the results. Successful breeding depends, first and foremost, on a precise understanding of the genetic basis of the characteristic that is to be modified in some way; secondly it implies the use of a sufficiently broad population of horses; and thirdly it must entail suitable mating programmes.

Man has made concerted efforts since the earliest times to produce new breeds, long before the study of genetics became an accepted discipline. As a result he had no option but to proceed by trial and error, and the process was invariably lengthy and often fruitless, but nevertheless it frequently produced very good results. Although there was no sound scientific basis, native breeds of horses were instinctively used which, as a result of natural selection, had developed a high degree of reproductive efficiency, suitability and uniformity. These breeds were able to pass on to their progeny the particular characteristics, by now consolidated in the genes and chromosomes, that had become distinct from those of other breeds. Even now that genetics is a widespread science not all the obstacles have been surmounted, and often the theoretical principles behind the selection of a given characteristic subsequently produce in reality either a different result from the one planned, or an actual step backwards in relation to the desired goal. This happens because it is not always possible to quantify the correlations existing between the various characteristics, or the interactions between genes. It is therefore difficult to establish precisely which characteristics will be modified, and to what extent, and whether this potential modification will be temporary in nature (such as the example of the Palomino), or permanent. Even today therefore a good and successful horse breeder must have not only a sound scientific basis, but he must also be endowed with patience, intuition and determination.

ARAB

The Arab or Arabian horse is the oldest and purest breed still in existence today. Its origins would seem to go back to more than 3000 years B.C., and evidence of this is given by archeological finds that have come to light in the deserts of Arabia. As a result the origins of this breed are literally lost in the tide of time, and this superb creature is shrouded in a web of legends, lending it a certain aura of magic and mystery.

According to one legend this horse is descended from seven original ancestors selected by King Solomon from the 40,000 chariot horses and 12,000 saddle horses that he owned. From these seven original steeds, so the legend goes, seven breeds were subsequently produced, called Kokeilan (with eyelids that look coloured), Manaki (with a superb neck), Hedregi (an energetic and tireless animal), Saklaui (brave and intelligent), Gilfi (swift and powerful), Hedban (noble and valiant), and Trefi (proud)—all qualities that are to be found in the modern-day Arab. Popular tradition claims that the Arab descends from the five mares of Mahomet which were the first to reach Mecca out of a total of 85 sent by the Prophet to bring news of victory. These two tales clearly illustrate why, for the Arabs, the horse is a sacred animal, a true gift offered by God to man, for his greater happiness. This concept is backed up by holy books, and the Koran, which contain advice, instructions and directions to ensure that this animal be well looked after and loved.

According to the Raswaan, one of the leading authorities on the subject, there are three basic types of Arab: the Assil or Kocklani, the purebred Arab and the Arab breed. The Assil, which was also called Kohuail, Koheil, Khamsa or Kamsat by the various different tribes that reared it, is the true Bedouin Arab and can be classified into three sub-breeds: the Kuhailan, a perfect example of endurance, the Siglavy, which symbolizes beauty and elegance and the Muniqi, which represents swiftness and speed. The Kuhailan (Kehylan) and Siglavy (Seglawi) also represent the male and the female type respectively. In comparison with these two, the Muniqi (Munighi or even Managhi) tends to be more elegant in appearance and has longer limbs, a longer neck and back, and a straight profile. The purebred Arab is essentially the result of crossing these three main sub-breeds. Finally the Arab breed includes all animals whose pedigree includes one or more ancestors of dubious or obscure origin, or records the influence of Barb, Persian, Syrian, Egyptian Arab or related blood. Most Arabs bred in Europe belong to this last group. According to Guarmani (1824–1884) another famous horse expert, the Assil type can be divided into two basic types which have each, in turn, given rise to five sub-breeds or strains: the Kamsat el Ressul type and the Kamsat el Mascecur type. The former can be divided into the strains of Gilfi, Manaki, Makladi, Saklani and Koheilan and the second includes the Obeyan, Gedran, Sueti, Daageni and Heabescian lines.

The Arab is swift and strong, good-natured and generous with well-proportioned and elegant lines and an undemanding temperament. On average it lives to an age of 21, but it is in its prime between seven and 14, which would explain an Arab saying: "Seven years for my brother, seven years for me, and seven years for my enemy"—which gives a fairly accurate description of the Arab horse's range of performance throughout its life.

This breed is now widespread throughout the world and it has been widely used to create or improve other breeds in particular the English Thoroughbred. The introduction of the Arab horse into Europe seems to date back to the time of the Moorish invasions of western Europe.

Breed: Arab or Arabian horse
Place of origin: Arabia
Height at withers: 14–15 hands (average)
Weight: 855–970 lbs (380–430 kg)
Structure: mesomorphic
Colour: grey—bay—chestnut—occasionally black
Temperament: highly-strung but gentle
Aptitude: light draught-horse
Qualities: speed and endurance
Geographical distribution: worldwide
Head: small with a broad forehead—straight or dished profile—ears small and pricked—eyes large and expressive—nostrils large and flared—lips fine
Neck: long and clearly curved—elegant and well set into the jaws—broad at the lower end—with a long thick mane
Body: withers prominent and clearly defined—back straight and short (17 vertebrae instead of the usual 18)—loins short (5 lumbar vertebrae instead of 6) and broad—croup broad and flat—tail attached, on a level with the back, full and carried high—chest broad and deep, body well ribbed up—abdomen somewhat drawn in
Legs: muscular—shoulder long and sloping—joints big and flat—tendons clearly defined and set well apart—hoof small with very tough horn—natural stance perfect
Skin: thin and elastic, covered with short silky hairs

BARB

The origins of this horse, also known as the Berber, date back to time immemorial and become confused with those of the North African Berber people themselves, who dedicated a great deal of care and attention to the development of the breed. Some authorities maintain that the Barb was introduced into Europe back in Roman times, since it seems likely that the Romans used this breed in their chariot races. However the other theory, which sets the introduction into Europe at the time of the Moslem invasion of Spain in the eighth century, would seem more probable. In Spain, by being crossed with local horses, the Barb contributed greatly to the development of the Andalusian horse. Since then, the Barb, like the Arab, has continued, as if predestined, to have a considerable influence on the formation of some of the world's most famous and important breeds. In fact the Godolphin Arabian (1724), the horse which almost a thousand years later played such an important part in the creation of the English Thoroughbred, was claimed to be a Barb and not an Arab, as his name would suggest. In the late seventeenth century the Barb horse was widely renowned and was widespread not only in England, but throughout the rest of Europe—particularly in the north. However, it should not be forgotten that as early as the fifteenth century Pope Paul II was the patron of the famous Berber horse races which took place in Rome along the Via del Corso, (literally the "street of the race") and finished in the present-day Piazza Venezia. Here the pontiff built the Palazzo di Venezia, and took pleasure in watching these wild competitions from its windows. Today the true, purebred Barb is only to be found in very reduced numbers among the nomadic peoples of North Africa, who have a traditional respect for this horse's swiftness and extraordinary endurance. In general, however, the breed has been subject to crossing with the English Thoroughbred, or the Arab, as is the case with the Libyan Barb.

Breed: Barb (Berber)
Place of origin: North Africa (Algeria and Morocco)
Height at withers: 14–15 hands (average)
Structure: mesomorphic
Colour: bay—brown—black—chestnut—grey
Temperament: docile—courageous
Aptitude: all-purpose riding horse
Qualities: fast and resistant—very undemanding
Geographical distribution: Algeria, Tunisia and Morocco
Head: quite long—profile straight or slightly convex—eyes lively—nostrils wide—jaws pronounced
Neck: medium length—muscular and arched
Body: high withers—back short and straight—quarters sloping—tail low-set and flowing—chest broad and deep
Legs: slender and solid—shoulder long and sloping—joints broad and well defined—tendons set well apart and well defined—feet small, but with tough hoof

ANDALUSIAN

Many theories have been put forward regarding the origins of this breed. Some experts maintain that it descends from Barbs and Arabs that were introduced into Spain in the eighth century at the time of the Moslem conquest and crossed time and again with native breeds. Others are convinced that it is a descendant of the *Equus ibericus* encountered by Julius Caesar's legions in Roman times. Here, the theory is that, in prehistoric times, this horse made its way across the isthmus which then linked Africa with Europe (the present-day Straits of Gibraltar), crossing from Spain into North Africa where, conversely, it developed as the Barb. Lastly, there are those who claim that it is descended from the 2,000 Numidian mares that were shipped across the Mediterranean to Spain by the Carthaginian general, Hasdrubal. Of all these hypotheses the most likely would appear to be the first.

The Andalusian dominated horse breeding in Spain from the twelfth to the seventeenth century, and was only seriously rivalled by the Arab. On his second voyage of discovery across the Atlantic, Christopher Columbus included a number of Andalusian and Neapolitan horses in his cargo. Thus, in addition to their already considerable influence in Europe, these two breeds, the Neapolitan itself a descendant of the Andalusian, also contributed to the formation and development of almost all American breeds. The most important European breeds to have been affected by the direct or indirect inclusion of Spanish blood are the Lipizzaner, the Friesian, the Hackney, the Kladruber, the Frederiksborg, the Oldenburg, the Holstein, the old Norman horse, and the Orlov; of the American breeds it is the Criollo that has been most markedly influenced.

Historically the breeding of the Andalusian can be traced back to the reign of Philip II of Spain who, in 1571, established the royal stables at Cordoba. This horse, with its somewhat compact, gathered lines, is still very much in demand today for its swift and elegant action. A characteristic gait is the *paso de andatura*, a frisky, high-stepping movement that is most effective in processions, where it used to play an important part. Another breed considered to descend from the Andalusian are the so-called jennets. These small horses which were reared in the province of Granada by Berber peoples who had settled in upland areas of Andalucía, were extremely popular in the Middle Ages. More recently, organized breeding of this horse has enjoyed a considerable expansion and it now has an enthusiastic following not only in Spain, but also in South America. In Mexico, for example, there is an association of "Criadores de Caballos de Pura Raza Española" (Breeders of Purebred Spanish Horses). In fact, what is commonly known as the "Andalusian" should properly be called the "Spanish Horse," since the true Andalusian differs from the latter in various features: the back is more gathered, the quarters are more developed, the hoof is smaller, the height at the withers does not exceed 15.2 hands, it does not include grey or chestnut among its range of coats, and its morphological type is meso-brachymorphic.

Despite the fact that this breed itself is no longer so revered as it once was, it is still of considerable importance on account of the distinctive mark it has left on many modern breeds of horses.

Today the Andalusian still performs in the bull-ring or *corrida* where, with its high-stepping gait, it is very much a part of Spanish tradition.

Breed: Andalusian
Place of origin: Spain (Seville and Jérez de la Frontera)
Height at withers: approx. 15.2 hands
Weight: approx. 1,300 lb (570 kg)
Structure: mesomorphic
Colour: bay—black—grey—roan
Temperament: balanced and energetic
Aptitude: riding horse
Qualities: good jumper
Head: handsome with a straight or sometimes hawk-like profile—ears small with the tips facing outwards—eyes large and expressive
Neck: well proportioned—curved—well set-on
Body: withers prominent—back straight and short—quarters broad and rounded—tail attached low down, thick, flowing and often wavy—chest broad and deep with well-curved ribs—abdomen roundish
Legs: strong—shoulder broad and sloping—joints broad—cannons and pasterns long—hoof well formed

FRIESIAN

The Friesian, which takes its name from Friesland, in northern Holland, is one of Europe's oldest breeds, In fact, in Friesland, relics dating back to 1000 B.C. reveal the remains of a horse which was very similar in build to the present-day Friesian, and from the evidence available it would appear that even in those remote days this breed had already been domesticated.

The Friesian was greatly sought after in the Middle Ages as a war horse, not least because of its considerable prowess as a trotting horse. It is also portrayed in the works of many Flemish masters as the mount of noblemen. In medieval times it was being continually improved by the addition of Andalusian and Oriental blood (this latter deriving from horses brought back to Europe by returning Crusaders), but for all this, the modern breed has not lost the appearance and aptitudes of its ancestor.

The Friesian is a horse that is well suited to the duties of both a heavy and light draught horse, and during the winter months in Holland it would often be harnessed to sleds that it pulled along frozen canals. In the not too distant past it was also used as a carriage horse. Once known as the Harddraver, which in Dutch means "good trotter," it has contributed to the development of the various competitive trotting breeds, both directly and via the Hackney, itself greatly influenced by the Friesian. Early this century the breed was in danger of becoming extinct and in 1913 only three registered stallions remained in Friesland. However a group of breeders set up a consortium and averted this demise by introducing measures to preserve the breed. During the Second World War the Friesian played an important role, being widely used for heavy farm work and transport, due to the shortage of both fuel and vehicles. This is a horse with distinctive compact and solidly built lines, a superb bearing, and with a smooth and supple action that includes a beautiful and eye-catching trot similar to that of the Andalusian—a breed which has over the years influenced the development of the Friesian.

Breed: Friesian (Harddraver—Dutch horse)
Place of origin: Holland (Friesland)
Height at withers: approx. 15 hands
Structure: meso-brachymorphic
Colour: black (very rarely with white markings on the head only)
Temperament: docile and sensitive
Aptitude: heavy and light draught horse—farm work—weight-bearing saddle horse
Qualities: an excellent trotting horse
Head: elongated and narrow with a straight profile—ears short and pointed—eyes gentle but lively—full forelock
Neck: quite short—arched—muscular—well set-on—with a flowing mane
Body: withers wide and not very prominent, merging with the line of the neck—back short and straight—loins broad—flanks rounded—quarters muscular and sloping—tail full, flowing and well set-on—chest broad, muscular, wide and deep
Legs: muscular with feathering (long hair) on the backs of the cannons downwards—shoulder muscular, long and sloping—joints prominent—foot broad

WARS AND WAR GAMES

Evidence of the horse being used to pull chariots of war dates back to the Assyrians, the Babylonians, the Persians and the Greeks of the Mycenaean period. The use of these war chariots spread rapidly to many other parts of the world, both east and west. The war chariot was a fearsome contraption: it was fast and easy to handle, and was catapulted into the ranks of the enemy where it spread panic and terror, not least because its wheels were often fitted with extremely sharp blades. Once victory had been secured, the chariot was transformed into a triumphal carriage, bearing the victorious commanders and the spoils of the conquered, who were often dragged along in chains behind the carriage.

The widespread use of cavalry, on the other hand, has evolved more recently and its development closely follows the history of successive changes in military techniques.

Bronze horse from the Geometric period (Greece, 8th century B.C.)

It was already being widely used by the Assyrians and the Persians from 900 B.C. onwards, but in the western world its development was less rapid. In fact, while in the west the horse remained in the hands of the privileged few, Oriental peoples had very wide access to this animal, and whole populations were able to move about over long distances with its help. In Greece, between 620–480 B.C. (the Archaic era) the aristocracy was made up from a very small class of wealthy knights who owned horses, yet the battles were in fact fought and won by the hoplites (heavily-armed foot soldiers). The title of knight or cavalier (from the Latin *caballus* for horse) had essentially political and social overtones. In Rome, too, from the eighth century B.C. onwards, there was a huge cavalry divided up into centuries (*centuriae*), which were squads of 100 mounted soldiers. The Roman legions,

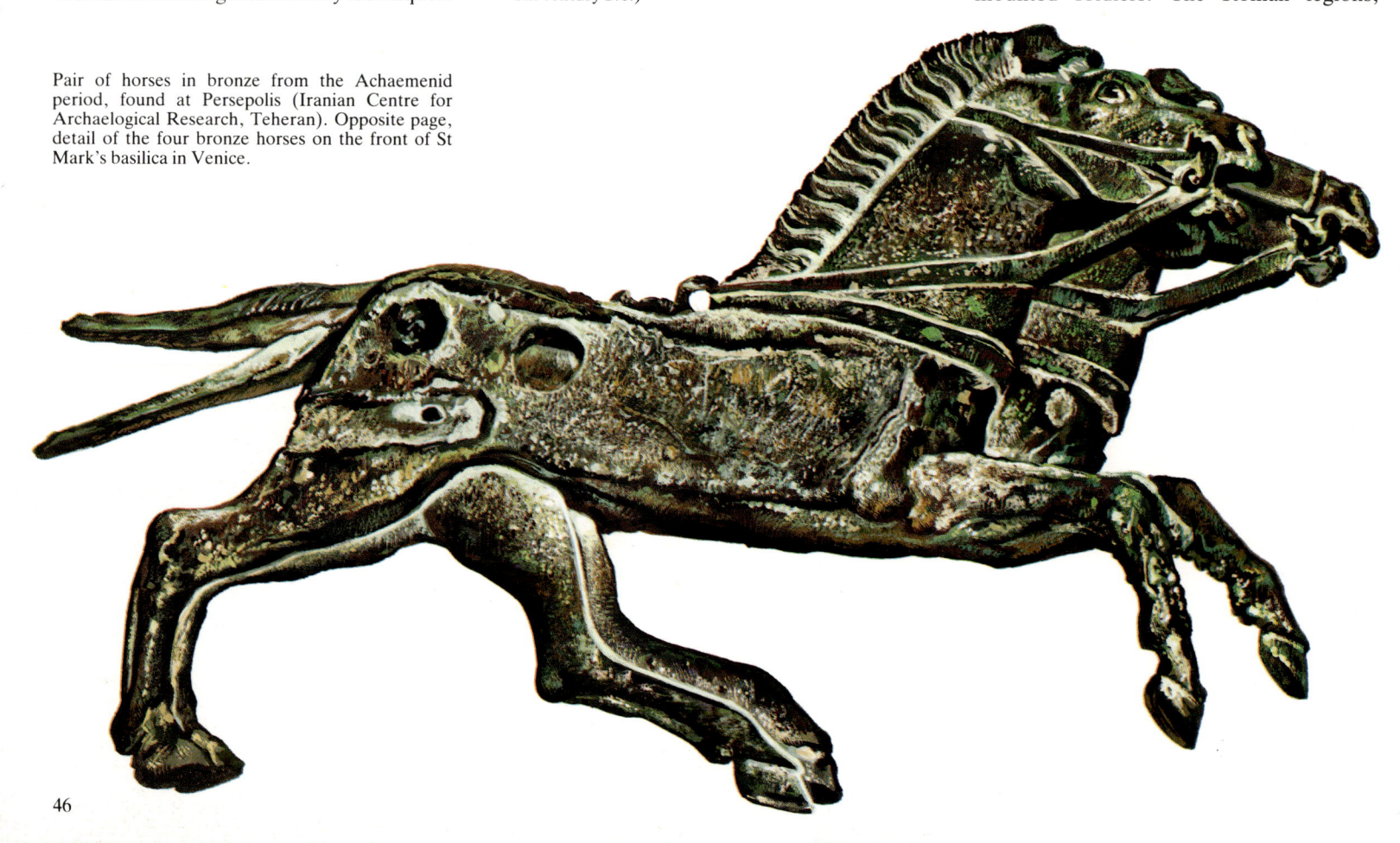

Pair of horses in bronze from the Achaemenid period, found at Persepolis (Iranian Centre for Archaeological Research, Teheran). Opposite page, detail of the four bronze horses on the front of St Mark's basilica in Venice.

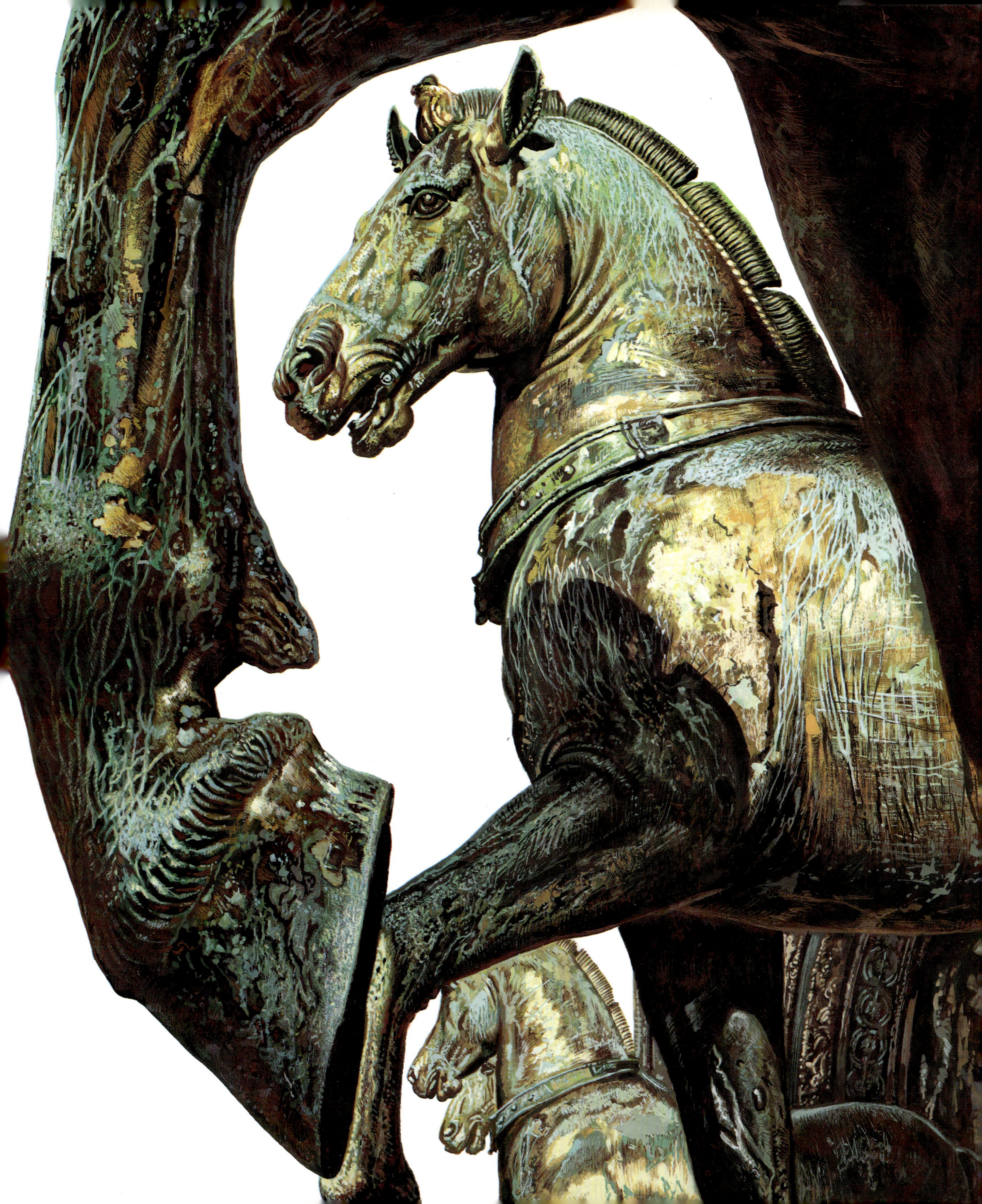

however, fought on foot, and the élite group of knights, drawn from the moneyed circles of merchants and financiers, was, as in Greece, of political and social importance. In fact this élite eventually formed the "equestrian order" as opposed to the "senatorial order," formed by the old landed aristocracy.

Alexander the Great, who died in 323 B.C. was largely responsible for the organization of cavalry as a "war machine" and divided this fighting force into the cataphract or heavy cavalry, in which both horse and knight were armoured and the knight wielded a lance and sword, and the light cavalry, in which the knight was armed with a javelin and a sword. The task of the heavy cavalry was to attack and breach the enemy lines; the light cavalry would then swiftly penetrate the breach in order to chase and scatter the enemy. Julius Caesar, who lived from 100–44 B.C. and was undoubtedly one of the greatest military commanders of all time, did not greatly favour the use of mounted troops. He deployed his centuries essentially for reconnaissance duties, flanking maneuvers, cover, and, only in exceptional circumstances, as an attacking formation. It was only towards the end of the Roman Empire in 476 A.D. that the invasions by Asian hordes made greater use of cavalry obligatory, firstly to confront the enemy, and then to back up the infantry. This marked the beginning of what has become known as the "golden age" of cavalry, which lasted throughout the Middle Ages.

As early as the eighth century A.D. the warmongering peoples of central Europe—the Frankish and Germanic tribes—already had a very efficient cavalry. The ever-increasing spread and rise of the cavalry also had far-reaching social repercussions. In fact, while the foot soldiers changed their status from peasant to soldier with relative ease and little expense, becoming a knight necessarily implied the acquisition of a horse, and the skills required to use it. Clearly only the prosperous and well-to-do classes could afford this. This in turn laid the foundations for a more clearly defined social hierarchy and resulted in the formation of an aristocratic caste of highly specialized warriors. The horse thus became a symbol of social supremacy, and admission to the ranks of the cavalry, which until the eleventh century had been free for all wealthy persons, irrespective of background, gradually became more and more exclusive. Finally it became restricted to the sons of the nobility, or even, as was the case in England, only to the eldest son of a nobleman. Membership of the cavalry entailed a considerable financial outlay and burden, and this was in turn increased by the need for the horseman to display his own might with sumptuous trappings, weaponry and armour, and with a large following of retainers. Indeed a knight usually owned more than one horse, and would use his various steeds for different purposes: he would thus have a battle horse or charger, a heavy, sturdy mount, capable of carrying loads of 700–900 lb (300–400 kg); a light mount that was quick, agile and easy to handle, and was used in jousts and tourneys; and one or more horses used for transporting provisions and equipment. The most important of these was the battle horse—the legendary charger.

The charger had to have specific physical qualities and be thoroughly trained. It had to be capable of stopping very quickly and making swift changes of direction, despite the load it was bearing. The loss or death of a charger was thus a serious matter for the knight, not only financially, but also emotionally and the relationship of affection and mutual understanding between man and animal was often so deep that among the Teutons and other ancient peoples, it was the custom to bury a knight slain in battle together with his steed.

The knight's suit of armour completely covered his body and consisted of a cuirass (protecting the torso), made of cloth or leather to which plates of metal were attached. Later the cuirass or breastplate was replaced by a knee-length coat of chain mail, complete with a hood. On his head the knight wore a helmet, which was sometimes fitted with an extension at the back to protect the nape and often had a projection at the front to cover the nose. The legs were protected by high greaves or shin guards and the feet by pointed iron sabatons, which could also be used as weapons. Lastly, there was the shield, which came in various shapes and sizes, and was long enough to protect the left leg. The attacking weapons included, the long double-edged sword, the heavy-tipped lance shaped in such a way as to prevent too deep a penetration of the target, the dagger and the mace.

Weapons were frequently lost or rendered unusable in the course of a battle, so in such cases they had to be replaced, which involved further expenditure. In addition the knight had in his service a retinue. This could be limited to just one man, but in most cases it consisted of a total of five grooms and pages. These servants would not only help the knight to arm himself, to carry his colours, and assist him to mount the horse, but they were also permitted to fight along-

The importance of the horse in China is reflected in numerous legends. The horse illustrated below dates from the T'ang dynasty (British Museum, London).

Cheekpiece from a bronze bit from Luristan (Colléction Jean Fribourg, Paris).

side him. The value of the knight's complete equipment would have been roughly equivalent to the money required to buy between 20 and 30 oxen, that is, enough to maintain a great many peasant families.

As the cavalry grew in importance a complex ritual of preparation developed simultaneously. During this time of "apprenticeship," the aspiring knight had to learn how to wield the various weapons, and acquire particular war skills. At the same time he had to display incontestable proof of his valour. Appointment to the status of knight then involved a lengthy ceremonial procedure, which took place in the lavish surroundings of the court, and often became an occasion for public feasting. A code of conduct had also been elaborated, which included, precepts of a religious nature. The knight, who was noble and wealthy, shunned all manual activities, which he regarded as beneath his dignity. Instead he would devote all his time and energy to jousts and tourneys, hunting and war. Some knights became great experts in the joust, travelling from court to court, and seeking every opportunity to display their considerable skills. As well as being endowed with great courage, the perfect knight had to be loyal, generous of spirit, and compassionate towards the defeated. He often drew inspiration from religious ideals and took upon himself the task of defending the weak, the oppressed and womenfolk, sometimes even considering himself to be sent by God to restore divine justice on earth. For this reason, many knights, known as errant knights, travelled around their countries looking for wrongs to be righted, or needy people to protect.

The mystical aspect of the knight reached its highest point with the Crusades. There were eight such campaigns, which lasted from 1195 to the latter years of the thirteenth century. A number of religious and military orders were formed, such as the Knights Templars and the Knights Hospitallers, which sprang up in Palestine between 1110 and 1120, with the task of defending the holy places. The figure of the knight triumphed throughout the fourteenth century, but the

Bronze bit from Luristan; the cheekpieces depict mythical figures (Musée de Louvre, Paris).

Bronze horse from Gallic-Roman epoch, dedicated to Mars, found in Neuvy-en-Sullias (Musée Historique et Archéologique de l'Orléanais).

Miniature depicting Sir Geoffrey Luttrel, lord of Irnham (Lincolnshire) who is preparing for the tourney (Luttrel Psalter, England, 1340).

original spirit of the cavalry was progressively contaminated by the laxity of the courts which, in some instances, degenerated into decadent centers of immorality.

The advent of firearms delivered a severe blow to the cavalry, not only as far as fighting techniques were concerned, but also because the very ideals that inspired the knight and the cavalryman were being questioned. Once the mystical and romantic aspect of the cavalry had faded away, the knights had to learn new ways of waging war, no longer based on displays of personal valour or skill, but now founded on efficient military organization in which every individual soldier had a clearly defined role. In the first half of the seventeenth century, Gustavus Adolphus of Sweden devised a new method of attack based on several ranks of cavalrymen, each one of which was preceded by a rank of musketeers on foot. These musketeers would open fire on the enemy, and thus create breaches through which the mounted troops were quickly able to advance and penetrate the enemy lines. This technique, which was improved and somewhat modified by Frederick the Great, and also adopted by Napoleon Bonaparte, is known as the "cavalry charge," and was, in due course, to become the central action of many a valiant battle. However, the unceasing improvement of the firearm and the ease with which it was possible to check advancing cavalry charges with barbed wire and other obstacles quickly marked the conclusive decline of the cavalry as a "war machine," relegating it to the past, often idealized out of all proportion with reality.

TOURNEYS AND JOUSTS

The emergence of war games such as the tourney and the joust can be explained by the need to keep abreast of the arts of war even in times of peace. The tourney gave the knight a chance to put to the test both his valour and his courage, and at the same time offered the public a stirring and colourful spectacle—just like any other form of competitive event. In about 1000 A.D. tourneys were governed by various rules and regulations to do with both the type of weapon and armour admissible, and the number of strikes or blows which should be scored to ensure victory. In an attempt to prevent serious injuries tourneys were also contested with "courtly" weapons: daggers with blunted tips and dulled blades, and maces with no spikes.

Tourneys and jousts were sumptuous and carefully choreographed spectacles, with a precise ceremonial structure. They were very costly to stage, so could only be organized for special occasions, and then only by wealthy feudal lords and landowners. These occasions might be to celebrate victories, or important moments in the life of the court. The first stage of the typical tourney consisted of the jousts, in which two knights at a time did battle with each other to display their skill at arms. There then followed the main attraction where large numbers of knights and horsemen enacted an actual battle, blows included, in a spectacle in which the rider and his mount vied fiercely for the leading role, and often sorely tried their respective physical and mental capacities. Even if the weapons used were less dangerous than in a real battle, the clash of the knights as they hurtled towards each other was nevertheless very violent because of the heavy armour being worn. The keen urge to win was closely linked not only with public acknowledgement of the knight's particular skill and courage, but also with the aim of pleasing and impressing the beautiful ladies attending the tourney. Defeat was not only dishonourable but financially damaging, since the victor had the right to relieve the vanquished of his horse and armour, although the defeated could reclaim his belongings against payment of a sizable sum. In fact certain rules and regulations went as far as to establish that the vanquished knight could even become the "property" of the victor, and could only regain his freedom once he had paid the victor an adequate sum in compensation. Inevitably, despite all the precautions that were taken, tourneys often ended in bloodshed and in 1559, no less a contestant than Henry II of France died after being wounded in such a competition. The frequency with which these lavish contests were organized soon stirred up an indignant reaction from governments and the Church alike. From 1139 onwards the Church enacted a special provision, denying religious burial to anyone who died in a tourney.

The gradual and progressive decline of the ideals of knighthood and of the feudal world finally resulted in the disappearance of the warring aspects of the tourney, which retained only its spectacular side. Nevertheless, tourneys continued to be organized in different forms right up to the end of the seventeenth century, usually as a way for princes and noblemen to display their wealth and power, but still offering the knights a chance of glory, to the delight of the ladies present. Poets and writers of all kinds naturally found considerable inspiration in these colourful events.

It is interesting to note how this love of competition, and the desire to display one's own physical abilities was not only confined to aristocratic circles: it was very much a thing of the people too. In Italy, towards the middle of the thirteenth century, the humbler sections of society, dissatisfied with continually being mere spectators, but equally, without the means to organize their own tourneys because of the cost of horses and equipment, introduced an event known as the *Palio*. This consisted of races on foot to see who could be the first to seize a standard or banner. These races were held in various towns and cities, such as Siena, Arezzo, Leghorn, Asti, Ferrara and Verona. In due course these foot races turned into buffalo races, with the buffalo mounted by "jockeys," and finally horses were used. The most famous *Palio* in Siena has been held in its current form since 1656.

THE SUFFOLK PUNCH

Heir to the Great Horse

As the name of this breed would suggest its place of origin is the English county of Suffolk. There can be no doubt that this immense horse is one of the descendants of the Great Horse, a type of medieval charger used in tourneys, and bred in the Netherlands for military purposes by crossing the largest and most powerful draught horses in northern Europe with the valuable qualities of eastern bloodstock, probably developed by the Romans. According to references made by William Camden in his historical and geographical work entitled *Britannia* (1586), the origins of the Suffolk Punch appear to date back to the year 1506. Its further development has been assisted, in more recent times, by the Norfolk Trotter and the Norfolk Cob, and it seems likely that the English Thoroughbred has also made a contribution, though not one of great significance. The typical chestnut coat of the breed would appear to derive from Blakes Farmer (1760), a smallish trotting horse, that handed down its particular colouring to all its heirs.

The Suffolk Punch was used in the past for farm work and hauling forms of urban transport, and for these reasons it was also exported to the United States. In fact it is still occasionally used today as a brewery dray horse. In times of war it was also used for hauling pieces of heavy artillery, and was even exported to Russia and Germany up until the First World War. Numerous members of this breed were sent to the various British colonies, where they adapted well to the warm, tropical climate. Among the distinctive features of this horse are its early development and its longevity. The Suffolk Punch can be put to work at the early age of two or three years. This breed would appear to be endowed with an exceptionally robust physique, if there is truth behind the tale of one stallion working uninterruptedly for 25 years, and another of a mare giving birth for 16 years in succession. In 1877 the Suffolk Horse Society was founded, and this has greatly contributed to the continued purity of the breed, by perfectly preserving those particular characteristics established back in the eighteenth century.

Breed: Suffolk Punch
Place of origin: England
Height at withers: 16–16.2 hands
Weight: about 1 tonne
Structure: brachymorphic
Colour: chestnut of seven shades (without white markings)
Temperament: gentle and sociable
Aptitude: heavy draught work
Qualities: strong, economical feeder, long-lived
Head: short and with a handsome shape—profile straight—forehead broad—eyes expressive
Neck: short with a broad base—muscular—arched
Body: withers low and broad—back straight, short and broad—loins full and powerful—quarters muscular, full and rounded, slightly elongated—chest wide, deep and muscular
Legs: quite short but strong, almost hairless—well muscled—shoulder long, sloping and muscular—joints broad—cannons and pasterns short—foot sound

DRAUGHT BRETON

Heir to the *Bidet d'Allure*

The Grand Breton is the largest of the three distinct morphological types into which this breed is divided. The other two are the Postier, a fast heavy draught horse, and the Cheval de Corlay, or Corlay, the lighter type, suitable for use as a riding horse and for light draught work. Although the Corlay was at one time a popular choice for use in equestrian sports, it is now very rare if not actually extinct due to limited breeding. The origins of the Draught Breton seem to date back to earlier than 2000 B.C., to the time when the Aryans were embarking on their emigration from Asia towards Europe, bringing with them the horses that were the very symbols of their civilization. Perhaps the most glorious period in the long history of this horse came during the Middle Ages, when it was particularly sought after by military leaders because its gait did not tax the rider, and it was thus ideal for long journeys and tiring marches. This alluring gait, a cross between a brisk trot and an amble, caused the Breton to become known as the *Bidet d'Allure*. In the Middle Ages its stature tended to be smaller than that of its modern counterpart, with the height at the withers not exceeding 14 hands. Important contributions to the development of the Grand Breton have been made by the Boulonnais, the Ardennais and the Percheron.

Breed: Draught Breton
Place of origin: France (Brittany)
Height at withers: approx. 16 hands
Weight: 1,200–1,300 lb (550–600 kg)
Structure: meso-brachymorphic
Colour: chestnut—bay—roan—grey—red roan
Temperament: energetic
Aptitude: heavy draught work
Qualities: long endurance
Head: well proportioned—profile straight or slightly snub—forehead broad—ears short—jaws heavy
Neck: broad and muscular—arched—quite short—solidly attached
Body: withers broad and muscular, not very prominent—back short, straight and broad—loins muscular and broad—quarters sloping, full and muscular—chest wide, deep and muscular—abdomen firm
Legs: short and powerful—shoulder sloping, long and muscular—joints broad and strong—forearm, gaskin, thigh and leg muscular—cannons sometimes slender but solid—pasterns short, covered with hair—hoof well shaped and tough

Draught Breton

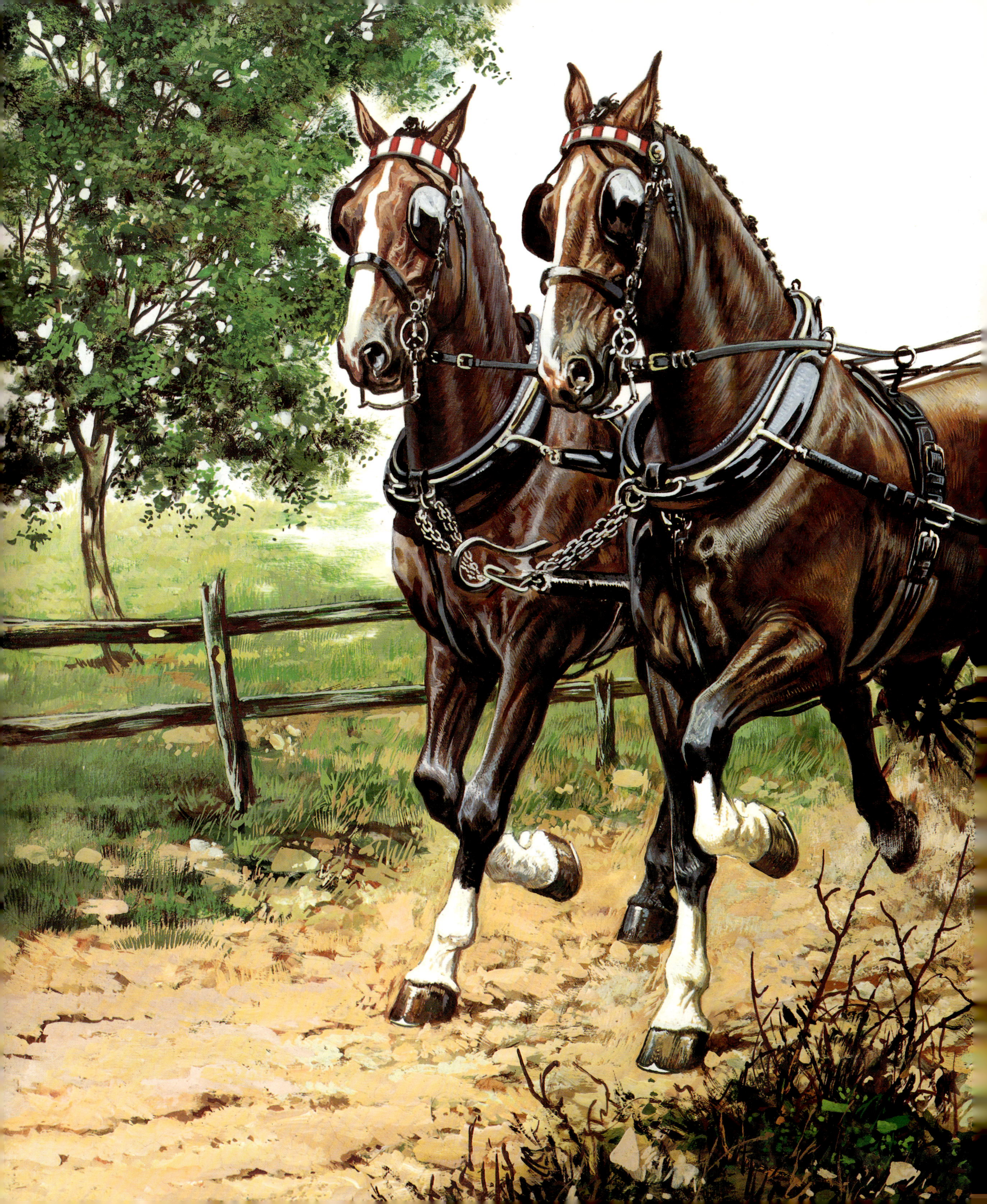

TRANSPORT

In about 3000 B.C., while the ancient Egyptians were still making wide use of slave labour for transport, elsewhere animals were already being used: donkeys, oxen and camels in the Middle East, yaks in the Himalayas, reindeer in the Arctic region, llamas in Peru, and elephants in India. However, in the steppes of Asia, where large numbers of horses were roaming wild, the local peoples had already learnt how to use this animal both for riding and transportation; they had also invented the bit, the bridle and reins, and this had enabled them to gain perfect mastery of the horse. The bit, which is nowadays of metal, was probably made of woven, twisted leather, and was kept taut by pivots made of horn, examples of which have been found, together with other tools and implements. But although those ancient people had learnt how to ride, it was only during the Roman Empire, with the invention of the stirrup, that this art really came to the fore. Numerous stirrups have been discovered, dating back to 400–100 B.C., and it was the Huns who first taught the Romans how to use them. A great deal of time then passed before man realized that he would never be able fully to exploit the muscular strength of the horse for pulling loads if he did not have the right kind of harness. This is why oxen had been used for this task from very early times. A team of oxen required less complicated harnesses and tended to be easier to handle since their pace rarely exceeded a steady plod. The horse, on the other hand, was used mainly as a pack animal being heavily laden with equal loads on both sides, just as happens with donkeys and mules today. A further, but not less important invention, was the horseshoe, that seems to have appeared for the first time in Gaul, at the time of Julius Caesar. Thus the horse was finally ready to make its triumphant entry into the history of transportation. It is, of course, impossible to establish who exactly was the first to attach a horse to a cart, and it seems likely that this came about simultaneously in different parts of the world. Inevitably this led to the emergence of the various skills and trades associated with the building of carts and wagons. Some of these early carts, usually with two wheels, but sometimes four, are extremely ancient, and there is evidence of Chinese carts existing as far back as the fifteenth century B.C. These carts, however, would have been rather uncomfortable and awkward for the horse since the harnesses used were fastened around the animal's neck and thus there was the risk of suffocation from excessively heavy loads. In addition, if the road or track ran downhill, it was more than likely that the cart would career into the horse's hocks, since there was nothing to protect its hindquarters. There were also various problems inherent in the actual construction of carts. These involved the strength and elasticity of the materials, the statics and dynamics of the cart (for example the position of the center of gravity), analyzing the relative proportions between the radius of the wheels and the dimensions of the body, the way it would be supported on the shafts and the suspension, making the actual cart independent of the wheels to prevent the slightest bump being felt by passengers. This latter problem was particularly important, firstly because it made journeys tiring to undertake, and, secondly, it had various adverse effects on the structure of the cart or coach. Therefore various solutions were tried, such as the use of flexible materials, for example interwoven bamboo canes, or wood used in sheets rather than blocks, but these were short-lived, and for a long time the problem remained unsolved. The existence of carts with two or four wheels (the wheels being either rough or well finished) is documented throughout the world by carvings, paintings, statuettes and bas-reliefs. These are important not only from an artistic viewpoint, but also for understanding the level of cultural development reached by the different peoples in antiquity. The Romans tackled and resolved the problem of transportation by employing their considerable technical and organizational abilities, showing themselves to be constantly receptive to new ideas whether from remote provinces of the Empire, or from foreign parts. They then put these ideas into practice adapting them to their own particular requirements.

The Romans were accustomed to using large numbers of horses for pulling even very light weights such as the *biga* and the *quadriga*. These were both forms of light chariot, drawn by teams of either two or four horses. Then there was the *rheda*, a sort of stagecoach that was drawn by eight or ten horses, even though this vehicle only weighed around 700–750 lb (320 kg). Another vehicle used in Rome, although it was originally Celtic, was the *carrum* that had four iron-rimmed wheels, and was used for carrying heavy loads, such as large weapons of war. These various functional vehicles, all of which could be described as "carts" of sorts, were gradually joined by other types, used for conveying people. This latter type can be better defined as "carriage" or "coach." One example was the light and elegant two-wheeled *carpentum*, that was often finely decorated, and fitted with a canvas awning. Because of its elegance it soon became a favourite means of transport among well-born ladies of the day. Other carts and carriages had their specific uses, such as the *tensa*, which was used only for religious rituals, or the *plaustrum*, which was used for transporting farm produce.

One important use of coaches was for communication. Even though there are earlier references to similar services, there is no doubt that the first regular and safe postal service dates back to the Roman Empire, where there was an impressive road network that was constantly being improved. The fall of the Roman Empire brought the construction of carts and carriages to a virtual halt. In the confusion, destruction and indiscriminate plundering that followed this historical catastrophe, the use of more refined carriages dwindled fast. The only vehicles to be seen in circulation were the cruder forms used by peasants and merchants. As order was gradually restored, private carriages started to be built once again, on a limited scale, but the styling was for the most part very simple. The most important development, however, was the gradual increase in trade and commerce which spread further and further afield along new trade routes. Because transportation in the Middle Ages was primarily for cargo rather than passengers, this period marked a decline in the skills of coach building, and it was not until the end of the thirteenth century that luxury carriages made their reappearance. The major revolution that was to affect the construction of carts and coaches for evermore did not occur until the fifteenth century: this involved the suspension of the body of the cart or coach on large, strong straps or belts made of leather or iron, instead of fixing it directly to the wheel axles. With its body now cradle-shaped instead of flat-bottomed, the carriage became a comfortable, well-sprung form of conveyance. It was better suited to long journeys and less prone to breakdowns, since the body itself no longer directly absorbed or was affected by the roughness of the highway, now that this was minimized by the new system of suspension. Thus, little by little, the coach and the carriage became status symbols, resulting in a great deal of rivalry when it came to lavish decoration, elegant fabrics and materials for the interior, and eye-catching liveries for the drivers. This ostentatious taste became "bad" taste, descending to the level of pure exhibitionism. Victorian England set the fashion of accompanying carriages, particularly those of wealthy ladies, with packs of Dalmatian dogs, whose elegance was intended simply to enhance the prestige of the owner. The first public services were set up in the first half of the seventeenth century, initially with coaches with limited seating capacity, but before long with actual stagecoaches or diligences, whose speed, which started out at a stately 4 mph (6 kmh), increased progressively, until it had almost tripled by the mid-nineteenth century.

DRIVING AND CARRIAGES

Today, as a means of transport, horsedrawn coaches and carriages are not compatible with the hectic pace of modern life. Despite this, however, they are still used in certain countries for official functions and important ceremonies (such as royal weddings or state visits) and in some countries where there is little industrialization, or where the road system is still relatively undeveloped, they are also used for everyday purposes. Elsewhere the carriage survives as a romantic symbol in the midst of chaotic city traffic, for example, in Rome, Seville or even New York, offering tourists the momentary illusion of a city brought back to human dimensions. The fascination for carriages also occurs in specialized races and competitive performance trials. These competitions for carts and carriages drawn by varying numbers of horses may be either national or international, and never fail to attract large audiences. The masters in these equestrian events are undoubtedly the Hungarians. These driving competitions involve different types of test: in the Presentation Test the jury is called upon to assess the elegance of the coach itself, and the costume or livery of the driver, the groom and any passengers in the carriage, all of which factors should be in keeping with the type of harness being used. The driven dressage tests, on the other hand, involve the execution of obligatory movements or "figures," and are held in an arena measuring 100 × 40m (110 × 44 yards). Another test takes the form of a "marathon," where the judges are looking for a smooth ride at a specified pace. In the marathon there are also prescribed times, and along the course there are various natural obstacles which are by no means easy to negotiate. The final test consists of an "obstacle course:" this is a form of gymkhana where the accent is placed firmly on the skills of the driver and the fitness of the team of horses after having completed the demanding earlier tests. In Canada there is a coach race in which the competitors drive wagons like those used by the pioneers heading west in the nineteenth century; they are drawn by a team of four horses, and it is the team that covers the course in the fastest time that wins. This is a daredevil and thrilling spectacle, and in it horses frequently break free of the reins and carry on galloping around the course, obstructing the other wagons taking part in the race.

In many cities, such as Leningrad, London (Victoria and Albert Museum), Versailles, and Florence (Pitti Palace), there are carriage museums, in which visitors can admire actual examples of coaches and carriages from different historical periods, and learn how man's imagination and ingenuity has been put to use in the past to produce vehicles designed for the most varied occasions and requirements.

After a long and chequered history, the most dramatic developments in coach building came about in the sixteenth century and after. It was in this century that many towns and cities started to see the emergence of coach and carriage building works, where craftsmen tried in their different ways to instil some sense of order into the wide variety of models whose shape and size had been dictated by local custom and tradition. The resulting trend was towards fairly uniform lines, and a European style. At the same time, with the advances being made in science, technology was progressing in leaps and bounds: the suspension system of the body of the coach was greatly improved; the body itself became lower, and shaped in such a way that it offered less wind resistance; the size of the wheels was calculated by making careful studies of the type of load and terrain; the front wheels were often smaller, so as to improve the handling and maneuverability of the carriage; and the various fabric decorations on the outside of coaches and carriages were gradually replaced by decorations made of wood and brass, and paintings on the sides of the body.

Increasingly the carriage became a symbol of pomp and social prestige, and the decorative work involved was often entrusted to worthy artists and skilled craftsmen. In Italy the art of coach-building became highly developed in Milan in the sixteenth century and, in France too, it was an important trade, starting in earnest during the reign of Louis XIV and continuing right through to the end of the eighteenth century, which signalled the beginning of English predominance in this field. This marked an important turning point in the construction of coaches and carriages, which now became characterized not by their grandeur and lavishness, but by their functional aspect and the ease with which they could be handled. Thus they became nimbler and lighter, and as a result, faster, their increased speed being due to the demands of continually expanding trade and industry. At the beginning of the nineteenth century Germany, too, became internationally recognized for the ability of her highly skilled carriage builders.

The logical consequence of the development of the coach and carriage was a great expansion in road networks making it possible to set up regular mail and passenger services to any destination. In order to meet extremely demanding requirements, horse breeders devoted much of their attention to the selection of a wide range of draught horses: heavy draught horses like the Breton, the Percheron and the Swedish Ardennes; slow, heavy draught horses like the Suffolk, the Shire and the Poitevin; and fast draught horses like the Cleveland Bay and the Freiberger.

Driving a coach or carriage is not as simple and straightforward as it might appear. In fact, in addition to requiring a perfectly trained team of horses, it demands a great deal of skill on the part of the driver, who must know precisely how tightly to rein his team, how to use the whip, and measure his tone of voice in such a way that the horses will obey his commands quickly and accurately. This becomes particularly difficult when the coach or carriage involved is a large one, drawn by several horses that must pick their way over rough unmetalled highways, as they had to do in the last century, when roads were often left in a state of disrepair.

The driver of a troika must have a particular set of skills. The troika is a distinctive type of Russian vehicle drawn by three horses abreast, the central one being a good trotting horse (usually an Orlov Trotter), and those on either side of it, which are somewhat smaller in size, being sound gallopers. Clearly the major difficulty here involves coordinating the different paces of the three horses. The three-horse team can be harnessed either three abreast (the traditional Russian way) or with the trotter in the center, and in front of the two gallopers. There is a typical Hungarian team involving five horses, three in the front formation, and two behind. Then there is a whole series of teams with even numbers of horses, from two to eight, harnessed in pairs one behind the other. One particular team formation is known as the "Daumont:" this involves anything from two to four pairs of horses. There is no coachman as such, and the driving is in the hands of mounted postillions—one per pair of horses. Originally, this type of team was used for military purposes, for hauling pieces of artillery, and for drawing heavy vehicles over awkward terrain. With this arrangement, driving is not the responsibility of one man, and the horsemen also have a much better view of the terrain. Nowadays this type of team is used only for official ceremonies, as in Great Britain, for example, for coronations, or royal weddings. On such occasions the crowds lining the way can admire not only the opulence and splendour of the carriages, but also the perfect training of the horses belonging to the stables of the English royal family, which are justifiably regarded as the best in the world.

Personal coaches and carriages
(see page 58)

Tilbury

Hansom cab

Tilbury phaeton

Victoria

Clarence

Berlin

Dorsay

57

PERSONAL COACHES AND CARRIAGES

The **calèche** (or **calash**), from the Czech word "kolesa," may or may not have a fold down top and is drawn by a single horse.

The **cabriolet**, which is a sophisticated version of the calèche, is a light two-wheeled carriage. It is drawn by a single horse, and was often used for elegant drives in the country.

The **tilbury** is a typically English gig. It seats two persons, has two large wheels, and is light and elegant.

The **stanhope** is a light, open vehicle with one seat.

The **clarence**, named after the English Duke of Clarence, is a closed, four-wheeled vehicle with one seat inside and one outside for the coachman.

The **tonneau** is an open vehicle drawn by one medium-build horse, making it easy to handle and popular with ladies.

The **spider phaeton** or **tilbury phaeton** is a light and elegant four-wheeled vehicle with a folding top over the front seat and a rear seat for the footman.

The **buggy** or **bouguet** is a small, light, one-horse carriage, with or without a hood, four wheeled in the US and two-wheeled in the UK, with no seat for the coachman. It is suitable for country use.

The **hansom cab**, named after the English inventor Hansom, is a low, two-wheeled carriage with the coachman's seat placed behind the passenger seat. The body is enclosed by windows at the front, thus enabling the passenger to have a good all-round view. It was usually drawn by a single horse.

The **victoria** is a small four-wheeled carriage with a low seat and a folding top, designed for two persons plus the coachman. It was usually drawn by one horse, and was designed for negotiating narrow city streets. It was often used for hire.

The **berlin** is a carriage for two persons with four wheels and the body suspended.

The **dorsay** is a typically English covered carriage for two persons; it has four wheels and is very softly sprung on long springs. The coachman's seat is outside and open.

The **whiskey** is an open carriage with very high wheels, for two persons.

Personal carriages for several passengers

Vis-à-vis

Duc

Break

Mylord

Britzka

Berlin

Phaeton

Brougham

Coupé

Fiacre

PERSONAL CARRIAGES FOR SEVERAL PASSENGERS

The **landau** is a four-wheeled carriage drawn by a pair of horses, with two folding tops, one for each seat. It is named after the German town of the same name. The Landau is designed to carry four persons.

The **break** is an open four-wheeled sprung coach with two facing seats for the passengers, a front seat for the coachman and an auxiliary rear seat for the footman. It can carry six or more people, and has a team of four or six horses. The light version, known as the gentleman break, would be driven by the owner himself, sitting on a raised front seat, with two footmen sitting at the rear.

The **vis-à-vis** is an open four-wheeled carriage with facing seats for four passengers.

The **duc**, like the vis-à-vis which it resembles, came into being in the mid-nineteenth century.

The **mylord** is an elegant four-wheeled carriage with a folding top, designed to carry two persons plus a coachman.

Sporting carriages

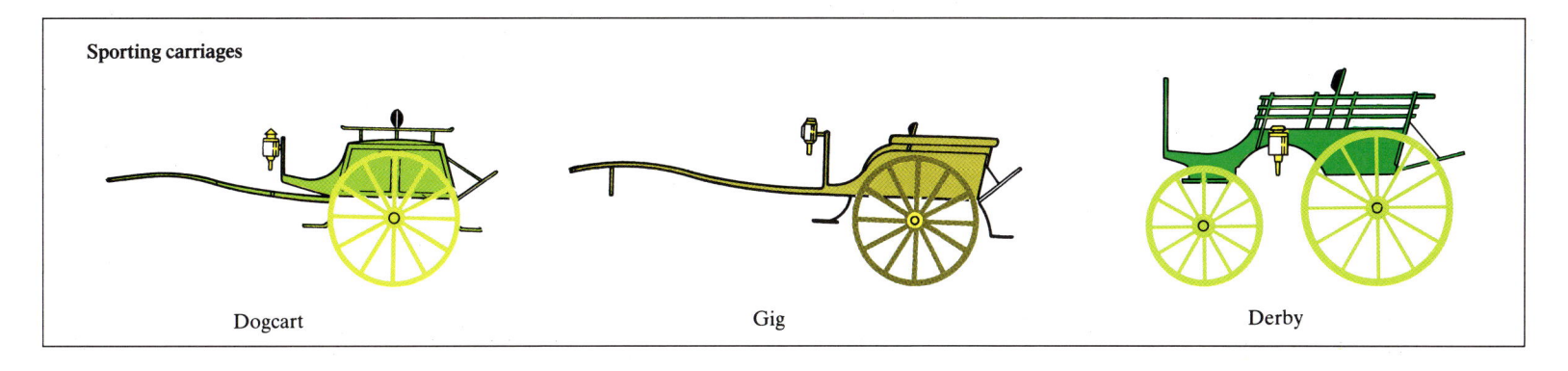

Dogcart — Gig — Derby

The **phaeton** is a country carriage, drawn by a pair of horses, with four wheels, a high front seat and a low rear seat. Only the front seat is protected by a hood.

The **berlin**, named after the city, is a formal four-wheeled covered carriage with two facing seats and a seat outside for the coachman. It is drawn by four or six horses.

The **brougham**, named after an English lord, is an elegant closed carriage with two or four wheels, designed for city use. It started out as a private vehicle, but was in due course used for hire, as it still is in certain parts of the world. It is drawn by one horse.

The **britzka** is a Polish carriage, originally open, but later fitted with a top. It used to be widely used for hire. The front wheels are much smaller than the rear pair, and the "travelling" version has an extra rear seat.

The **coupé** is a closed, four-wheeled carriage for two or three persons, with a front seat outside for the coachman.

The **fiacre** is a carriage which a certain Nicolas Sauvage had built for himself in 1640. It is so-called after the Hotel St Fiacre, outside which these carriages were parked. The fiacre was in fact the first carriage used for public service.

PUBLIC COACHES

The **charabanc** or **char à bancs** is a long, light, four-wheeled vehicle, completely open, and with seats arranged in parallel rows. Drawn by pairs of horses, it was originally used for hunting.

The **wagonette** was a coach used for public services between towns. It has a low body with two lengthwise facing seats, and a rear entrance.

The **drag** is the classic covered berlin, drawn by at least four horses, and designed to carry passengers and their luggage.

The **stage coach** or **diligence** is a large, four-wheeled coach drawn by up to eight horses.

The **omnibus** is another name for the horse-drawn tram. It is a covered, four-wheeled public coach, drawn by two or more horses. The body is long, with the seating arranged lengthwise. There is a rear entrance.

The **mail coach** is a large closed vehicle with four wheels and two facing seats, used for carrying both mail and travellers. The mail coach would travel at speeds of around 11 mph (18 kmh), and was drawn by two or four horses.

SPORTING CARRIAGES

The **tandem** is a covered carriage with two large wheels, designed for country use, and drawn by two horses, harnessed one behind the other. A typically English model, it was used by huntsmen. In fact the horse at the front was used for riding with the hunt, and was saddled.

The **sulky** is a small cart with two rubber-covered wheels, designed for one person, and used for trotting races.

The **cart** is an open, long-shafted vehicle with two large wheels. It is drawn by one horse and can carry four people on seats running lengthwise.

The **dogcart** is a two-wheeled vehicle drawn by a single horse (often a pony) with a low, closed body.

The **gig** is a two-wheeled vehicle designed for country use, usually used for attending fox hunts in the old days.

The **derby**, so-called because it was originally built for Lord Derby, is an open, four-wheeled carriage, designed for carrying four passengers. In its day it was used as a private carriage and for hire.

Public coaches

Stagecoach-Diligence — Charabanc — Omnibus — Wagonette — Mail coach

GRONINGEN

This horse was probably produced by crossing the Friesian, the East Friesian and the Oldenburg. In the past it was much sought after as a carriage horse, although it was also often relegated to the more menial task of farm work. Although it has its own Stud Book, as a breed it has often been associated with the Gelderland, which it resembles quite closely, and the Oldenburg, from which it is partly descended. Sadly, this breed is now considered to be very rare, if not extinct, in as much as there are no longer any stallions registered in its Stud Book.

Breed: Groningen
Place of origin: Holland (Groningen)
Height at withers: 15.2–16 hands
Structure: mesomorphic
Colour: bay—dark brown—black
Temperament: quiet
Aptitude: fast heavy draught horse—farm work
Qualities: endurance
Head: well proportioned—profile usually straight—ears quite long—eyes lively—full forelock
Neck: average length—arched—muscular—with full mane
Body: withers broad and fairly pronounced—back long and straight—quarters broad, short and flat—low-set, flowing tail—chest broad and deep
Legs: muscular—quite long—shoulder long, sloping and well muscled—foot broad

Groningen

FREDERIKSBORG

It was in 1562 that King Frederik of Denmark set up the Royal Frederiksborg Stud, after which the breed is named. This is the oldest Danish horse of the mesomorphic type, and its development has included contributions from Neapolitan and Andalusian stallions. At one time it was highly prized by the European courts as a good school horse for beginners, because of its particularly calm nature. Its elegant looks also made it suitable for military parades and for use as a high-class carriage horse. Its principal merit, however, lies in the important role it has played in the formation of other breeds, including the Orlov Trotter and the Lipizzaner. After a rather unclear period of decline during which the continuity of the breed was interrupted, the Frederiksborg surfaced once again in 1939 and further developments took place first with the addition of Friesian and Oldenburg blood, and later of Arab and English blood. Nowadays it is much sought after as a riding horse, and is one of the most popular breeds in Europe, because of its elegance, and its powerful, flowing action. The characteristics of the modern breed, however, have changed considerably since its origins in the sixteenth century.

A particular strain known as the Knabstrup issued from a Frederiksborg stallion and a mare named Flaebehoppen left behind in Denmark in 1808 by the Spanish army. This animal was characterized by a spotted grey coat, identical to that of the mare. Today, however, the Knabstrup no longer displays the particular features that had enabled it to become a separate breed, and it is not known whether the spotted horses, still in existence in Denmark, are in fact direct descendants.

Breed: Frederiksborg
Place of origin: Denmark
Height at withers: approx. 15.3 hands
Structure: mesomorphic
Colour: chestnut
Temperament: docile and lively
Aptitude: fast heavy draught horse—light draught work—riding horse
Qualities: strong and agile
Head: well proportioned—profile usually straight—ears straight—eyes expressive
Neck: well proportioned—slightly arched—muscular—well set-on
Body: withers broad and muscular but quite pronounced—back straight—quarters wide and rounded—tail well-set-on—chest high, full and fairly deep—ribs rounded—abdomen well held
Legs: well muscled and strong—shoulder muscular and sloping—joints broad—foot small with tough horn

Frederiksborg

OLDENBURG

The origins of this breed can be traced back to the Friesian, with blood from Spanish, Neapolitan, Anglo-Arab and English Thoroughbred stallions, followed by an important contribution from the Cleveland Bay, towards the end of the nineteenth century. The first enthusiastic breeder of this horse was Count Anton Gunther (1603–1667), owner of the famous stallion Kranich. It therefore took the best part of three centuries to develop the impressive carriage horse that appeared at the beginning of the twentieth century. This horse, like many others, was forced to undergo a series of changes to meet modern requirements, with the emphasis clearly on an all-round saddle horse for use in equestrian sports. To achieve this the Oldenburg was crossed with Hanoverian, Anglo-Norman and English Thoroughbred stallions. The breed also benefited enormously from the importation, in 1950, of the stallion Condor, an Anglo-Norman horse, but in whose pedigree there is a high percentage of English Thoroughbred. With its calm but bold temperament, the Oldenburg matures early and can live a long time, although it is not particularly resilient.

In Bavaria the lighter Rottaler variety is bred with a distinctive chestnut coat.

Breed: Oldenburg
Place of origin: West Germany
Height at withers: 16.2–17.2 hands
Structure: meso-dolichomorphic
Colour: bay—brown—black—grey—chestnut
Temperament: calm and bold, energetic
Aptitude: riding and light draught horse
Qualities: a good jumper
Head: of average proportions—profile usually straight—ears straight—nostrils flared
Neck: of average length—muscular—carried with elegance and well set-on
Body: withers quite pronounced—back straight—quarters broad and flat, well muscled—tail set high—chest wide and deep
Legs: good skeletal and muscular development—shoulder sloping and muscular—joints broad—tendons clearly separated—hoof strong—good natural stance

KLADRUBER

The Kladruber takes its name from the royal stud at Kladruby in Bohemia, established in the sixteenth century by Emperor Maximilian II, where it has been bred since 1572. With the exception of blood from Andalusian or Neapolitan horses, both of which made a direct contribution to the formation of this breed, the Kladruber has remained a horse of great purity. The royal stud at Kladruby also had the privilege of producing not only parade horses, but also the famous carriage horses of the Viennese court, where only the Emperor had the right to have his own carriage drawn by white horses (which were in fact grey) on festive occasions. For funerals black horses were used, and these made their last appearance in 1916, following the death of Emperor Franz Josef. Grey and black are the two distinctive colours of this breed, and can be traced back to the two foundation sires, Pepoli (grey, 1764) and Sacromoso (black, 1799), both of Neapolitan origin. After the fall of the Austrian Empire, the breed suffered a series of setbacks, although these were quickly overcome and now it is possible to distinguish four distinct bloodlines descending from Generale, Generalissimus, Sacromoso and Favory. Favory is also one of the foundation sires of one of the most important present-day families of another famous breed, the Lipizzaner. This breed has been markedly influenced by the Kladruber and presents the same characteristics of late development and longevity as well as a certain similarity in its action that can be traced back to their common Andalusian origins.

It is worth noting that in the past the Kladruber was somewhat taller than its modern counterpart, sometimes reaching a height of more than 18 hands.

Breed: Kladruber
Place of origin: Czechoslovakia (Bohemia)
Height at withers: 16.2–17 hands
Structure: mesomorphic
Colour: grey—black
Temperament: calm but lively
Aptitude: light draught—fast heavy draught—saddle horse
Qualities: strong and generous
Head: elongated—profile convex—forehead broad—eyes large—nostrils wide—jaws pronounced
Neck: well proportioned—muscular—slightly arched
Body: withers broad and not very pronounced—back long and straight—loins full—quarters short and broad, rounded—tail well set-on, flowing and fine—chest full and deep
Legs: strong—well muscled—shoulder nicely sloping and muscular—forearm and leg quite long—knee and hock broad and clean—cannons slender but solid—tendons strong, clearly defined and set well apart—pasterns rather long—feet well shaped with tough horn on the hoof

CLYDESDALE

This breed originates in the Clyde valley, at one time known as Clydesdale, in the Scottish county of Lanarkshire. The horse is said to date back to the beginning of the eighteenth century when a local farmer, spurred on by the improved condition of the roads in the area and the need for a heavier horse, decided to import a black stallion from Flanders. If the story is true it is to this stallion that much of the credit for the subsequent formation and development of the breed should be attributed. However, over a century was to pass between those early days and the first appearance of the Clydesdale bearing its official breed name, at the Glasgow Fair of 1826. The breed benefited greatly from the attentions of the Highland and Agricultural Society of Scotland, founded in 1784, which showed great interest in the production of a heavier type of horse, and, from 1816 onwards, offered prizes to breeders to encourage the improvement of the various existing breeds. At the beginning of the nineteenth century the characteristics of the breed could be considered firmly established, largely as a result of contributions from Flemish and Friesian horses, that had been crossed with local breeds. Initially this horse was used for the arduous task of transporting coal from the mines as well as for equally tiring farm duties. However, with the progressive improvement of the roads, requiring swifter horses, the Clydesdale took on the role of coach horse, replacing the Shire, with which there had, incidentally, been more than a few reciprocal exchanges. The Clydesdale Horse Society was founded in 1877 and a year later the first Stud Book was published. One of the most important criteria used for judging the quality of this breed is concerned with the shape of the foot, which must be open and round, with the hoof heads set wide apart and the frog well developed. The Clydesdale is a very active animal, and must have regular daily exercise. With the disappearance of coaches and carriages this breed has suffered a drastic but forseeable decline, even though a few Clydesdales are still used in some parts of Britain for hauling brewery drays. In the north of England and in Scotland they are still occasionally used for transporting timber, and for traditional farm work. Despite their decline, however, they are still in demand and exported to certain European countries, as well as to the United States, Canada, South Africa and Australasia.

Breed: Clydesdale
Place of origin: Scotland (Lanarkshire)
Height at withers: 16.2 hands (mare); 17 hands (stallion)
Weight: up to 1 tonne
Structure: brachymorphic
Colour: bay—dark brown—black—chestnut and roan (rare); white markings very frequent, occasionally extending to some parts of the body
Temperament: docile and friendly
Aptitude: heavy draught—farm work
Qualities: strong and sturdy
Geographical distribution: Great Britain—United States—Australia—New Zealand—South Africa
Head: not large, but the face is wide—profile usually straight—large nostrils
Neck: fairly long—broad at the base—muscular—arched
Body: withers prominent—back slightly hollow and short—loins full—quarters long, full and muscular, fairly sloping—chest broad and deep
Legs: "feathered" below the knee and the hock—sturdy—shoulder sloping and muscular—joints broad and firm—pasterns long—feet round and open with tough hoof (often pale in colour)—good natural stance with front legs—hind legs slightly cow-hocked

HACKNEY

Some controversy surrounds the etymological origins of this breed in as much as its name might derive from the verb "to hack" (meaning to hire out) or from the English town of Hackney (now a London borough). Whatever the true answer, in 1883, with the establishment of the Stud Book Society, the breed was officially given its present name. The Hackney is descended from the old Norfolk Roadster, that was in turn descended from a group of Danish horses which had been introduced into England in the eleventh century at the time of King Canute. This original nucleus of horses was crossed and recrossed first with native and Arab horses and later with English Thoroughbred or halfbred horses deriving from it. Finally with the undoubtedly decisive contribution of Dutch and Danish Harddraver blood, this breed gradually developed in the county of Norfolk, from which it takes its name. Its most famous examples include Norfolk Phenomenon, who sired Niger (1896), one of the foundation sires of the French Trotter. A notable contribution to the development of the breed was made by the halfbred stallion Old Shales, sired by the Thoroughbred, Blaze (by Flying Childers), as was Sampson, a horse that played an important part in the formation of the American Trotter and the French Trotter.

The present-day Hackney is a descendant of Old Shales, Gold Farmer and Foxhunter, the latter two being sired by Sampson, and is a sturdy, elegant horse, of a good size, and enjoying a long life span. Its trot is fairly pronounced with a high-stepping action. The hind legs give the horse a remarkable thrust, whereas, in the upward action the front legs are carried with the knee thrown well forward and the hoof almost brushing against the knee, and then thrust forward, thus giving it the flat, far-reaching action, typical of all high-stepping horses. The Hackney has good endurance and moves quite fast. As well as being a good light trotter, it is also well suited for use as a riding horse. It is also bred in the United States, where it is somewhat taller, reaching a height of 16.3 hands.

Breed: Hackney
Place of origin: Great Britain
Height at withers: approx. 15 hands
Structure: mesomorphic
Colour: bay—brown—black—chestnut—roan (rare); frequent white markings on the head and limbs
Temperament: spirited
Aptitude: light draught—saddle horse
Qualities: good speed—excellent endurance
Geographical distribution: Great Britain—United States
Head: small and well set—profile straight or convex—forehead broad—ears well proportioned and straight—eyes large
Neck: long and muscular—well shaped, slightly arched—well set-on
Body: withers quite low—back straight and short (sometimes slightly concave)—quarters long, broad and rounded—tail carried high and well set-on—chest wide and deep—ribs rounded—belly drawn in
Legs: not too long—slender but strong—shoulder sloping but not long, quite flat but powerful—cannons very long—joints clean and solid—foot well shaped with tough horn on hoof—hind legs carried somewhat behind

STAGECOACHES

The stagecoach had its heyday in the nineteenth century, when the development of trade and commerce created the need for regular mail and passenger services. These large four-wheeled coaches, which could easily weigh a tonne or more, consisted of three parts: the front or *coupé*, the central section or *intérieur* and the rear section, or *rotonde*. They could carry between 15 and 20 people, with their luggage stacked in the upper part, above the roof, called the imperial. The drivers of these impressive vehicles—the fastest and heaviest on nineteenth-century roads—had to be extremely strong and agile, capable of enduring long and tiring journeys, often fraught with danger. One of the most famous stagecoach routes was the Overland Mail that crossed the various mountain ranges in the western United States, travelling without respite for three to four weeks, and managing to cover an average daily distance of 85–95 miles (140–150 km). Another famous service was run between London and Brighton at an average speed of 11 mph (18 kmh), which was quite remarkable for those days.

The continual development of the stagecoach was made possible by the use of horses that were particularly well suited to heavy draught duties. Such horses included the Breton, which was called the Postier-Breton because of its connection with the postal services, followed by the Boulonnais, the Swedish Ardennes, the North Swedish, the Percheron, the Cleveland Bay, and many others, all of them large and sturdy breeds capable of working continually for anything up to five hours at a time. The use of large teams of horses, ranging from four to eight depending on the size of the coach, distributed the work load among them, and at the same time increased the speed of the vehicle. It was important that the overall load and the number of horses were suited to the nature and gradient of the route to be covered. The uncertain nature of the roads and the real possibility of accidents befalling both the coach and the horses made such journeys not only long and tiring, but also dangerous and unpredictable.

POSTIER-BRETON

This is the medium-size form of the Breton and unlike its larger brother, the Draught Breton, it has been markedly influenced by the Norfolk Trotter and more recently by its modern counterpart, the Hackney. It consequently has a particular aptitude when it comes to fast draught duties, a quality which has in the past made this horse the ideal choice for drawing mail coaches. It is this connection with the post that gave it the name "postier." The breed is supervised by the Syndicat des Eléveurs du Cheval Breton. The Stud Book was started in 1909 and it may only be used to register horses born in the four departments of Brittany, and in the Loire-Atlantique. Registered foals are given the breed's distinctive brand, which is a cross surmounting a splayed, upturned V.

Breed: Postier-Breton
Place of origin: France
Height at withers: approx. 15.2 hands
Weight: 1,100–1,320 lb (500–600 kg)
Structure: meso-brachymorphic
Colour: chestnut—bay—roan—red roan—grey—black (rare)
Temperament: energetic and lively
Aptitude: fast heavy draught—farm work
Qualities: excellent endurance
Head: well proportioned—profile straight or slightly snub—forehead broad—ears short—jaws powerful
Neck: broad and muscular—arched—quite short and well set-on
Body: withers broad and muscular, not pronounced—back short and straight—loins broad—quarters sloping, full and muscular—chest broad, muscular, full and deep
Legs: short and powerful—shoulder nicely sloping, long and muscular—joints broad and strong—forearm and shin well muscled—cannons sometimes slender but solid—pasterns short and "feathered"—hoof well formed and strong

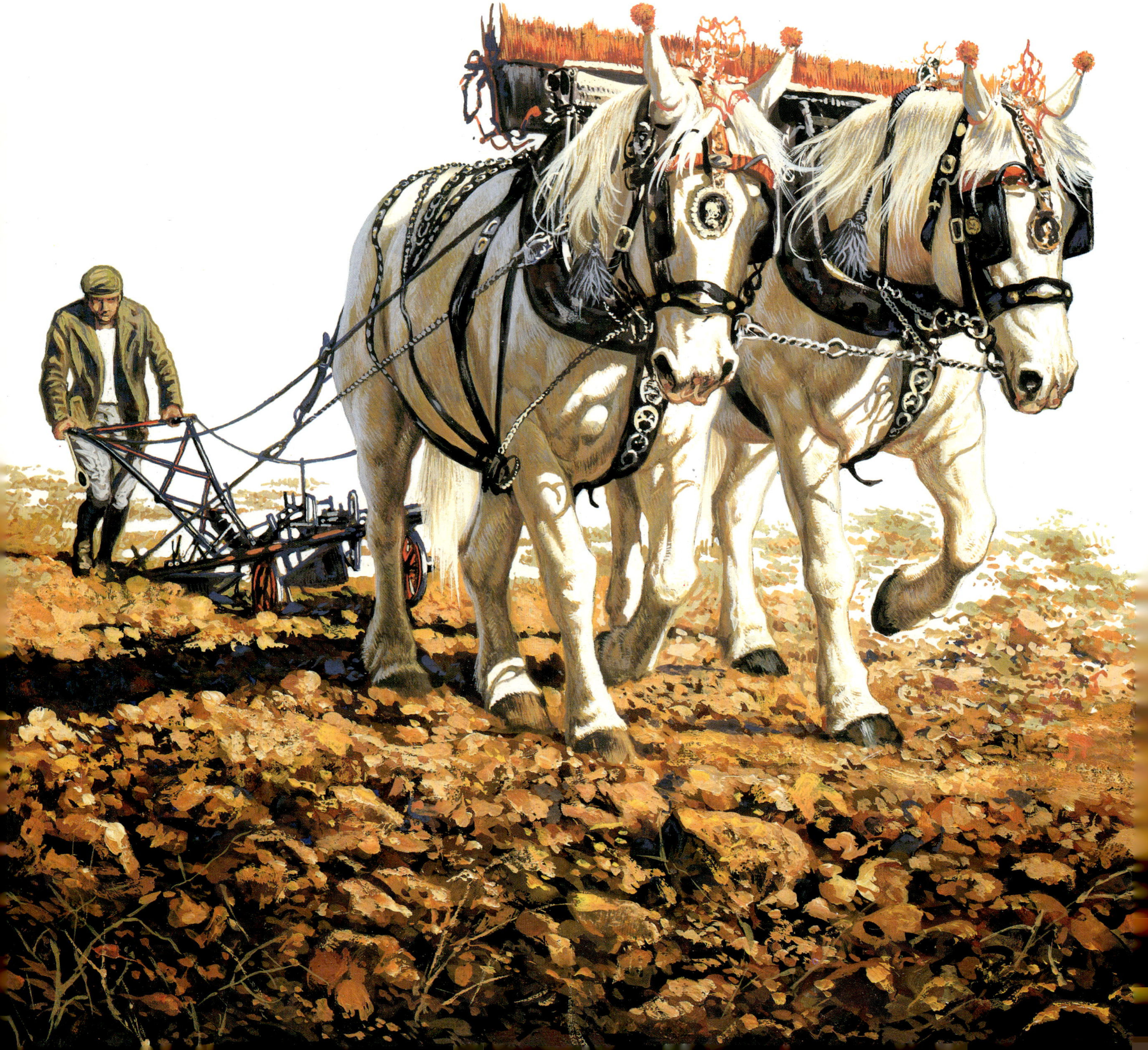

AGRICULTURE

From very earliest times man has relied on the muscle power and strength of animals to help him with heavy jobs of work, one of which, of course, has been tilling and breaking up the ground. Ploughing and tilling are essential operations for preparing ground to sow crops and in fact by turning the earth the richer subsoil, which contains more mineral salts, is brought up to the surface. Turning also improves the aeration of the soil, improves drainage and enables manure and other fertilizers to find their way into the ground. Because of its agility and relatively low weight, the horse was better suited to these tasks than the slow and heavy ox that had previously been used, and its powerful build enabled it to withstand lengthy periods of physical exertion. The muscle power provided by the horse was indispensable to man for heavy agricultural work until the early nineteenth century, when the Scottish engineer James Watt developed and improved the steam engine, by increasing its performance and output and reducing its running costs. Over the years, Watt's steam engine gradually replaced muscle power, eventually bringing about an industrial revolution that was soon to affect the rest of the world. However, those sturdy English draught horses, once used for transporting coal from the mines, have nevertheless lent their name to a universally used and now standard unit of power—horsepower. Even today, in many countries with a traditional rural and agricultural economy, or on very steep or inaccessible land where the use of farm machinery would be impossible, horses are still used for transport and farm work.

In order to make working the land more profitable, man has had to study closely the best way of harnessing or yoking animals, to make the most of their muscle power, without injuring or putting too much physical strain on them. From the ninth century A.D. onwards, the efficiency of horses employed in draught work greatly improved, due to the growing practice of shoeing and the invention of a new type of harness. This had a rigid collar that lay across the shoulders, and it replaced the old type of harness with the double bridle. When a horse fitted with this latter type was under strain, there was a real risk of the animal choking, because the resistance of the load being drawn was concentrated at the top of the neck tending therefore to pull the collar upwards. In the new type of harness the point at which the resistance of the load was concentrated, moved to a lower position that corresponded with the shoulder, thus preventing any adverse consequences and making possible the full use of the horse's muscle power. In addition to drawing ploughs, harrows and carts, the horse was also used in other ways to help farmers work their land. In the vast cotton plantations in the United States, man found an invaluable helper in the Tennessee Walking Horse whose regular and well-balanced gait was extremely comfortable for the rider who often had to stay in the saddle for many hours at a time. Another way in which horses have helped man is in leading and rounding up livestock. Even if many of these uses now belong to days gone by, man will still owe a debt of gratitude to this noble animal for many years to come.

FORESTRY WORK

In times when muscles provided the major source of power for tree felling, the horse was invaluable for forestry work. Man would fell trees with an axe and then, saw them up into lengths, according to the type of wood and the use required of it. The horse would then help him to transport the sawn lumber out of the wood (timber haulage). On the flat a horse is capable of hauling a load equivalent to five or six times its own weight. This explains why heavy horses, weighing up to a tonne were chosen for the job, and these animals, although slow, could work uninterruptedly for eight or nine hours a day. This is why, in some countries, including the Soviet Union, farms where draught horses are reared are still important, in spite of ever-increasing mechanization. Wherever there were plenty of water courses, timber would be floated downstream, using both the current and the force of gravity. In stretches where the river flowed more slowly, or where timber was transported by means of man-made canals, the lumber would be moved on its way more quickly by horses hauling it from both banks. However, those countries with the largest areas of forest, such as the United States, Canada, the Soviet Union, Sweden, Finland and Romania, have now abandoned such old-fashioned working methods. In the United States they now use a colossal machine mounted on a tractor, which grabs the whole tree, removes all the branches, lops the trunk at the base and loads it automatically onto the vehicle. However, the sheer size and weight of these new and increasingly more sophisticated techniques have also made selective tree felling impossible. With this type of heavy machinery it is always necessary to level vast areas of forest or woodland, and this destroys the delicate balance of the surface soil. It also means replanting the deforested area, often for the wrong reasons, with trees that are not indigenous. The disappearance of the old, time-honoured systems has led not only to the progressive decline of certain breeds of horses, but also to the disappearance of large numbers of small or medium sized wooded areas where the price of felling and transporting the trees by traditional methods, generally exceeds the value of the timber.

NORTH SWEDISH HORSE

The origins of this horse are somewhat vague and confused. The only certain fact is that from 1890 onwards the possibility of crossbreeding has been restricted to the Døle Gudbrandsdal, to which it is closely related. Because of its marked aptitude as a trotting horse it has been subjected to careful, selective breeding with the aim of improving its racing performance. The outcome has been the North Swedish Trotter, also known as the North-Hestur, which can be regarded as a lighter strain of the North Swedish Horse, and is bred and selected with the sole purpose of participating in competitive trotting races. However, its recorded times do not better 1′30″ per kilometer. The Stud Book for this breed was established in 1924. The North Swedish Horse is undemanding, long-lived and exceptionally resistant to disease, displaying both surprising energy and speed in relation to its physical build, which is solid and sturdy, with rather elongated lines.

Breed: North Swedish Horse (North Swedish Trotter—North-Hestur)
Place of origin: Sweden
Height at withers: 15.1–15.3 hands
Structure: meso-brachymorphic
Colour: bay—brown—black—chestnut—dun
Temperament: calm and energetic
Aptitude: heavy draught duties—farm work—trotting races
Head: of average proportions but fairly heavy—profile straight—face broad (squared)—ears long—eyes small but expressive
Neck: quite short—muscular—broad at the base—mane full and flowing
Body: withers broad and quite pronounced—back long and straight—loins wide—croup broad and quite sloping—tail low-set, full and flowing—chest full and deep—belly rounded and large
Legs: quite short with good bone—shoulder muscular and sloping—joints broad—tendons strong—hooves large, round and solid—"feathering" behind fetlock

Breed: Swedish Ardennes
Place of origin: Sweden
Height at withers: 15.2–16 hands
Weight: 1,100–1,540 lb (500–700 kg)
Structure: brachymorphic
Colour: bay—brown—black—chestnut
Temperament: calm and docile, but energetic
Aptitude: heavy draught work—farm work
Qualities: strong, with good endurance
Head: heavy—profile straight—forehead broad—eyes small—full forelock
Neck: short and muscular—mane full
Body: withers not very pronounced, broad and muscular—back short—croup muscular and broad, rounded and often double—chest full and deep
Legs: short, without much feather—strong and muscular—shoulder sloping and muscular—joints broad and strong—hoof broad and round, with strong horn

SWEDISH ARDENNES

This breed was developed during the nineteenth century with blood from the Belgian Heavy Draught Horse and the Ardennais, two important heavy breeds that have left their mark both in terms of temperament and physical appearance. The Swedish Ardennes is a strong animal with a compact, massive build and a long life expectancy; it is extremely undemanding, versatile and has good endurance in cold conditions and under strain. There is no doubt that the arrival of mechanization has considerably restricted the development of this breed, but in spite of everything it is still occasionally used in agriculture, particularly for transporting timber in inaccessible areas.

DØLE GUDBRANDSDAL

The Døle Gudbrandsdal bears a marked resemblance to the Dales pony and apart from the fact that the English pony is smaller it would seem likely that both breeds come from similar if not identical strains. The development of the Døle Gudbrandsdal has been varied and in more recent times important contributions have been made by the English Thoroughbred, various breeds of trotting horses, as well as some breeds of heavy horses that helped to increase the girth. One particular horse that greatly influenced the Døle Gudbrandsdal is the Norfolk Trotter called Partisan (later changed to Odin)—although some authorities maintain that this stallion was an English Thoroughbred. Another important horse was the purebred Arab Mazarin, imported to Norway in 1934.

This is undoubtedly the commonest native Norwegian breed but it has also achieved popularity beyond its birthplace and been an important factor in the development of the North Swedish Horse, which it closely resembles. The Døle Gudbrandsdal displays a natural aptitude for trotting, which is why a lighter version of it has been selected with the specific aim of improving this outstanding ability. The result has been the Døle Trotter, which is generally regarded as a separate strain of this breed. In effect there are no very obvious differences between the two, even though the latter has had its own Stud Book since 1941, marked with the letter "T" to make it distinct from the original breed marked with a "G." In the period between 1840 and 1860 three stallions were particularly important in the formation and development of the Døle Trotter. These were called Veikle Balder, Toftebrun and Dovre. Dovre, registered in the breed records as G 130, is the true foundation sire of this small trotting horse. The Døle Trotter (also known as the Norwegian Trotter), which has been developed by a more persistent introduction of trotting blood, has certainly made great progress and in fact lowered its own record to below 1'22" per kilometer. However, from a purely competitive point of view it is certainly no match for the true racing trotters and is consequently limited to amateur events. In its native Norway the Døle Gudbrandsdal is still used in some areas for transporting timber, and for general farm work.

Breed: Døle Gudbrandsdal
Place of origin: Norway
Height at withers: 14.2–15.2 hands
Weight: 1,190–1,390 lb (540–630 kg)
Structure: meso-brachymorphic
Colour: bay—brown—black; grey and dun (rare)
Temperament: energetic and patient
Aptitude: heavy draught work—farm work—trotting races—riding horse
Qualities: strong, with good endurance
Head: heavy—rather square—profile straight—ears long—eyes small—full forelock
Neck: quite short—muscular—mane full and flowing
Body: withers broad and quite pronounced—back long and straight—loins strong—croup broad, muscular and quite sloping—tail set-on low, full and flowing—chest broad and deep
Legs: short and sturdy—well muscled—feathered below the cannons—shoulder strong and muscular, nicely sloping—joints broad and firm—cannons short—foot broad with tough horn

HERDING

For centuries, man has relied on the strength and endurance of the horse to help him round up and control vast herds of livestock—a partnership that still exists today in some parts of the world. The all too familiar North American cowboy sitting astride a Quarter Horse or a Canadian Cutting Horse is by no means the sole example of the mounted herdsman. Varying in appearance from region to region, mounted herdsmen are found wherever there are extensive plains, or alternatively wherever the geographical conditions of a particularly harsh and inaccessible region do not permit the building of a highway network (for example, the Bogotà cordillera in Colombia). The Brazilian *vaqueros*, with their traditional buckskins and distinctive open sandals fitted with spurs (the climate in these parts is too hot to wear high boots) had their heyday in the seventeenth century. However, even nowadays, in certain northeastern and central parts of the country, and in the Rio Grande do Norte and western Bahia areas, they still play an important role, and techniques such as the use of the lasso, have changed little over three centuries. In Argentina the cowboy is called a *gaucho*, and in Colombia and Venezuela a *llanero*. In Australia horse breeders in the Red Center region of the Northern Territory catch and tame horses called Brumbies, which have proved to be good and hardworking in those parched desert regions, as yet untouched by proper highways and where living conditions are far from easy.

The use of large, articulated trucks and trailers for transporting livestock has greatly reduced the role of the herding horse, whose task it was at one time to steer herds of cattle across boundless areas, keeping on the move from dawn until dusk. However, there are still old tracks in use leading to Darwin, from where livestock is shipped to various markets, and to Alice Springs, where it is loaded on to cattle trains. In parts of Europe, too, horses have been used for herding since ancient times. In Italy the *buttero* looked after livestock in the Maremma region of Tuscany and Latium for hundreds of years, wearing a rather forbidding black outfit and carrying a characteristic metal-tipped stick.

Nowadays, most of these figures have already faded into the past, or are being threatened by changes in livestock-rearing techniques and new technology. The horse, however, will always have its uses, even if, like the Quarter Horse, these are not the same as they once were.

CRIOLLO

The Criollo is bred and reared throughout South America and in each country it differs slightly in size and name. Nevertheless, in all the different countries concerned it is easy to detect the mark of the Barb and the Andalusian. The Criollo is in fact a direct descendant of the horses brought across to South America by Christopher Colombus and the Spanish *conquistadores* during the late fifteenth and early sixteenth century. After being hunted by local Indians, many of these horses regained their freedom and for a long time lived in the wild state. This in turn enabled them to develop outstanding qualities, including resistance to disease, sickness, adverse environmental conditions and a frugal nature. The almost invariably small size and the usually dark grey colouring of the coat indicate this animal's ability to tolerate extremely tough living conditions that made life something of a struggle for survival. In Argentina, where the physical characteristics are more in accordance with the requirements of the breed, the Criollo has been the typical horse used by the *gauchos* for as long as anyone can remember. Argentine breeders are proud of their results and organize endurance trials over extremely long distances of up to 400 miles (600 km) to be covered in just a fortnight, with heavy loads and without any reserve of water or fodder. This type of competitive event enables the horse to demonstrate its capacity to survive, relying entirely on what it finds en route. After the introduction, about a century ago, of stallions imported from Europe and the United States, the breed started to deteriorate, losing both its original resistance to disease and its sober habits. As a result of strict selection procedures begun in the twentieth century,

Breed: Criollo
Place of origin: South America
Height at withers: 14–15 hands
Structure: mesomorphic
Colour: chestnut—grey—black—bay—roan—dun—mouse dun—part colours; frequent white markings and a possible eel stripe in some coats
Temperament: willing and persevering
Aptitude: riding horse
Qualities: resistant to disease—good endurance—speed—ability to carry weight
Head: of average size—profile straight or slightly convex—face broad—ears small and pointed—eyes lively—muzzle short and tapered
Neck: muscular and arched—of average length
Body: withers pronounced—back straight and broad—loins powerful—flanks rounded—croup well muscled and rounded—tail well set-on—chest broad and deep—ribs well rounded
Legs: quite short—solidly built and muscular—joints well developed with plenty of bone—shoulder long and sloping—pasterns short—hoof small but well shaped and hard

Breed: Mangalarga
Place of origin: Brazil
Height at withers: 14–15 hands
Structure: mesomorphic
Colour: bay—chestnut—grey—roan
Temperament: docile but energetic
Aptitude: riding horse
Qualities: resistant
Head: quite long—profile straight—forehead broad—ears long—eyes bright
Neck: quite long and muscular—full mane
Body: withers pronounced—back short and straight—loins strong—croup rounded—tail full and flowing—chest wide
Legs: solid—muscular, with good bone—shoulder sloping and well muscled—joints and tendons strong—pasterns long—hoof well shaped and sturdy

however, this situation has been brought under control, and from 1918 onwards the breed has had its own Stud Book. The Chilean Criollo, called the Caballo Chileno, derives from the Argentine type and is a sturdier horse with better endurance and resistance. In Colombia the breed is known as the Guajira, so-named after the region in the northwest of the country where the *indios* breed and rear this horse. In Venezuela the Criollo is called the Llanero: it is less solidly built and lighter than the Argentine version, and in addition it often has a slightly convex profile along the forehead and muzzle that most resembles that of the Andalusian and the Barb.

In Peru this breed is called the Salteno; it is not so tall and comes in three different types: the Costeño, also known as the Peruvian Paso or Peruvian Stepping Horse, because of its distinctive high-stepping gait called the "paso llano;" the Morochuco, which is most common in the Andean region, characterized by an occasionally protruding forehead and by smaller eyes; and the Chola, whose build makes it better suited to farm work. In Brazil there are three distinct breeds: the Crioulo of the Rio Grande do Sul, which has a distinctly Barb-like look to it and is also used in equestrian sporting events; the Mangalarga, which differs most markedly from the others, and has been obtained by crosses with the Andalusian and the Altér-Real; and the Campolino (named after the breeder who produced it, Cassiano Campolino), which resembles the Mangalarga and is used both as a draught horse and for riding.

Canadian Cutting Horse

MAREMMANA

This horse is the classic mount used by cattle herdsmen, the *butteri*, in the Maremma region of Tuscany and Latium in Italy. Rather common looking, it is a sturdy animal with a solidly-built body and stands up well to bad weather conditions and awkward terrain due to having been traditionally bred in the wild state. However, with increased mechanization in the agricultural sector, changes in crops and the introduction of new techniques in livestock rearing and farming, the importance and potential uses of the Maremmana have been reappraised. In recent times English Thoroughbred blood was introduced into the breed with the obvious aim of improving the general appearance and increasing the stature, but to the detriment of the breed's original hardiness and exceptional stamina. In addition to this modern version (the "improved" Maremmana) that has gradually become more refined and elegant in appearance as a result of

Maremmana

CANADIAN CUTTING HORSE

This horse is derived from the Quarter Horse, which it resembles both in physical appearance and in temperament. It is extremely skilled at working with large herds of freely-roaming cattle and consequently proves indispensable to cowboys. However, the Cutting Horse also competes with the Quarter Horse in a sporting event that is becoming increasingly popular in Canada —the rodeo.

careful breeding, there are other varieties of Maremmana: the Maremmana-Tolfetano, which is reared in the wild state in the Tolfa mountains, and the Monterufolino Horse, which is on the verge of becoming extinct. Both these breeds are small. There is also the Catria Horse, which is bred in the province of Pesaro, and has been developed from the Maremmana by crossing with Franches-Montagnes stallions. The Monterufolino Horse was characterized by an invariably uniform black coat. In the past it was bred in the hilly region situated between the provinces of Grosseto, Sienna and Pisa.

Breed: Maremmana
Place of origin: Italy
Height at withers: 15–15.3 hands
Structure: meso-dolichomorphic
Colour: bay—brown—burnt chestnut—black
Temperament: well balanced—energetic—enduring
Aptitude: riding horse—light draught work—farm work
Qualities: hardy—frugal—resistant—good jumper
Head: long and slightly heavy—ewe-like profile
Neck: a good length and muscular, with a fairly broad base
Body: withers high and well muscled—back short and straight—loins short—croup sloping—chest full
Legs: solid and sturdy—good joints—shoulder good and sloping—hooves well shaped and proportioned, with strong horn—regular natural stance

Breed: Canadian Cutting Horse
Place of origin: Canada
Height at withers: 15.2–16.1 hands
Structure: meso-dolichomorphic
Colour: bay—brown—black—chestnut—grey
Temperament: active—well balanced
Aptitude: cattle horse—riding horse—rodeo
Qualities: agile—swift—quick off the mark
Head: well proportioned with a straight or slightly convex profie
Neck: well set-on and well proportioned
Body: withers fairly pronounced—back straight—croup broad and sloping—chest broad and well developed
Legs: shoulder broad and sloping—joints clean—tendons firm—foot well shaped with strong horn—good natural stance

LIGHT DRAUGHT AND FARM WORK

With the rapid spread of mechanization during this century the horse's role as a light draught animal and saddle horse has been increasingly reduced. Many tasks once carried out by this noble creature on farms all over the world, such as carrying people, light farm work and drawing light carts, can now be completed using tractors, cars, or other types of machinery.

The horses used for jobs like these were generally of the mesomorphic type (medium build) or, at most, of the meso-brachymorphic type (medium-heavy build), and were extremely versatile since they could be used for riding as well as for light draught work. In addition to their harmonious lines, all these horses had a noticeably solid, sturdy build; a well-muscled neck of medium length; high, broad withers; shoulders nicely sloping, not too long and fairly muscular; the chest, muscular and deep; the back of medium length; the loins short and strong; the croup broad and well muscled; the legs strong with large hocks and knees; and the feet of average size.

The mesomorphic type is halfway between the brachymorphic (with short lines) in which the crosswise diameters are greater and the dolichomorphic (with long lines) in which, on the contrary, height and length are most prominent. Even though nowadays in most developed countries it is relatively uncommon to see farmers setting out to work their fields either on horseback or in horse-drawn carts, in some more inaccessible parts of the world the use of horses has not been totally dispensed with. It should not be forgotten that, in the future, limited resources may well give man no option but to use horses much more widely once again and, in fact, as recently as the Second World War, horses were reintroduced to pull trams through the major cities of various countries. In relation to machinery, moreover, the horse offers various advantages, both ecological, in that a horse does not pollute the air, and economical, since horses produce manure which can be used as organic fertilizer. In support of machines, however, it should be said that unlike animals these only consume fuel when they are actually working, and need less looking after in other respects, consequently making them cheaper to run.

FINNISH HORSE

This breed descends from native ponies, which have been crossed with other breeds of varying type and origin. The Finnish horse is a versatile animal, nowadays used in harnessed trotting events that are very popular in Finland. It seems to be the fastest of all the northern trotting horses.

In the past two different versions were bred: a light horse, the Finnish Universal, which is similar to the present-day type, and a heavier type, the Finnish Draught, used for more demanding tasks. The present-day Finnish horse tends to be too light to be considered a real draught horse, and too heavy to be considered a good saddle horse.

Breed: Finnish horse
Place of origin: Finland
Height at withers: up to 15.2 hands
Weight: 1,100–1,280 lb (500–580 kg)
Structure: mesomorphic
Colour: chestnut—bay—grey—black and brown (rare)
Temperament: docile and good-natured
Aptitude: medium-light draught work—light draught—trotting races—farm-work—riding horse
Qualities: willing and courageous
Head: not too large but quite heavy—squared—profile straight—ears small and pointed—eyes gentle
Neck: strong, of average length—not well set-on
Body: withers quite pronounced—back quite short—croup sloping—tail set-on low—chest high and deep—abdomen drawn in
Legs: not very long but strong—shoulder muscular, fairly sloping—joints large and clean—pasterns short—foot well shaped

FRANCHES-MONTAGNES

The origins of this breed date back to the end of the last century and its development has been greatly influenced by blood from the English Thoroughbred and the Anglo-Norman, both of which breeds have had their particular effect on the original Swiss horse from the Bernese Jura region. Some authorities contend that contributions were also made by the Ardennes and the Arab, the latter blood coming from the Babolna Stud in Hungary. Although not a particular common breed in terms of numbers, the Franches-Montagnes is a remarkably versatile agricultural horse. Within the breed itself it is possible to isolate two individual strains: one tends to have a greater girth and presents a greater development of the muscles; the other is lighter, and more suited to cross-country riding. These strains may from time to time be crossed with each other to produce horses with specific requirements.

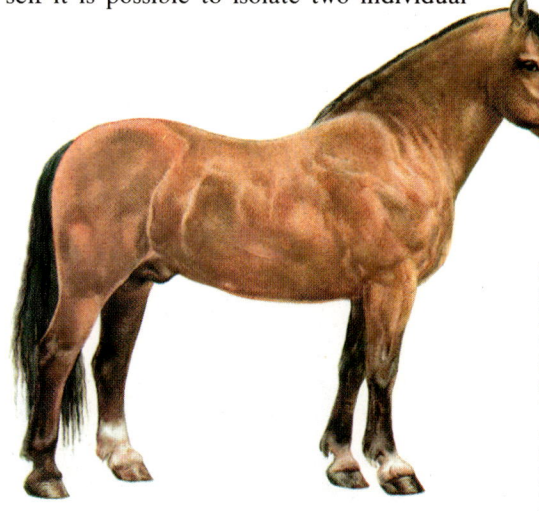

Breed: Franches-Montagnes
Place of origin: Switzerland (Swiss Jura)
Height at withers: up to 15.2 hands
weight: 1,210–1,430 lb (550–650 kg)
Structure: mesomorphic
Colour: bay—chestnut
Temperament: well balanced—active—docile
Aptitude: light draught—farm work—riding horse
Qualities: matures early—undemanding—versatile
Head: quite heavy with prominent jawbones—profile straight—ears small—full forelock
Neck: muscular, with a broad base—arched
Body: withers broad and quite pronounced—back straight—loins strong—croup slightly sloping—chest full and deep—abdomen well rounded
Legs: short and clean—shoulder nicely sloping—joints good—hoof tough

CLEVELAND BAY

This breed, which claims to be one of the oldest in Britain, comes originally from the Cleveland district of North Yorkshire, from which it takes its name. In the past it was used by travelling merchants, known as "chapmen," which is why it was also popularly called the "Chapman Horse." However, the Cleveland Bay also had ample opportunity to show its great versatility in a wide range of other tasks, such as agricultural work, transporting heavy loads of coal from the mines, and even hunting. During the second half of the eighteenth century, due to the infusion of blood from the English Thoroughbred and the Arab, it became a highly-prized coach horse, and was used in particular for ceremonial occasions and state visits, with the result that today it is still well represented in the stables of the English royal family. Since crosses between the Cleveland Bay and lighter animals, in particular the English Thoroughbred, invariably produce taller horses with excellent bone and displaying all the Cleveland Bay's specific qualities of hardiness and endurance, this horse has frequently been used to improve the quality of other breeds. However, this crossing reached a point where it was threatening the continuity and purity of the breed. As a result, in 1884, the Cleveland Bay Horse Society was established, and this organization imposed various limits on which horses could and could not be entered in the Stud Book. Animals that did not display the required degree of purity were generally excluded. However, in 1950, because the number of entries had dwindled quite dramatically, the Society finally acknowledged that the production of cross-breeds was the principal function of the breed. Nowadays, crosses between the Cleveland Bay and the English Thoroughbred produce the English hunter, an excellent hunting breed and a fine show jumper. In the past, similar crosses between the same two breeds had been used to produce the Yorkshire Coach Horse, a much sought-after carriage horse.

Breed: Cleveland Bay
Place of origin: Great Britain
Height at withers: 16–16.2 hands (measurements outside these limits should not disqualify what is otherwise a good sort)
Structure: mesomorphic
Colour: bay—dark bay (white markings apart from a very small star are not admissible)
Temperament: docile
Aptitude: saddle horse—light draught—medium-light draught—farm work
Qualities: resistant—longevity—good hunter in the field
Head: quite large—profile slightly convex—ears large—eyes gentle and expressive—jaws pronounced
Neck: long and well muscled
Body: withers not very pronounced—back not too long and straight—croup long and slightly sloping—tail well set-on—chest deep
Legs: quite short, well muscled and strong—shoulder sloping and muscular—knee and hock large and clean—cannons long—pasterns not too long—foot broad but well proportioned with tough horn blue in colour

Murgese

Karabair

MURGESE

The origins of this breed date back to the days of Spanish rule in Italy, and its development was decisively influenced by both Barb and Arab Stallions imported by the Count of Conversano. In 1874 the Austrian Emperor acquired some stallions from the Count, and these contributed to one of the bloodlines of the famous Lipizzaner horses which are still in existence today. After a period of decline the selection of the present-day Murgese horse was undertaken in 1926, under the initiative of a regional stud farm in Foggia. The Murgese is bred and reared in the wild state in a fairly tough environment consisting of scrubby grazing land, oak and mixed woodland in hilly areas with low rainfall. Only during critical periods is the grazing fodder supplemented by extra rations of oats or barley. In general, this is a well-built horse in which the dual early influence of the Barb and the Arab is evident from the alternating existence of certain features including the shape of the croup, which may be sloping (as in the Barb) or flat (as in the Arab). Because of its docile nature the Murgese is well suited to cross-country riding and trekking. In 1948 the Murgese Breeders Association was established.

Breed: Murgese
Place of origin: Italy (Puglia)
Height at withers: 15–16 hands
Structure: mesomorphic
Colour: black—grey with a black head—bay—chestnut
Temperament: lively—docile
Aptitude: farm work—medium–light draught—saddle horse
Qualities: hardy
Head: light, sometimes with prominent jawline—profile straight or slightly ewe-like—forehead broad—ears small and mobile—full forelock
Neck: sturdy with broad base—mane full
Body: withers quite pronounced—back straight, occasionally slightly concave—loins broad and short—croup long and broad, tending to be flat or sloping—chest full and well developed
Legs: hard with large, strong joints—shoulder nicely sloping—forearm of medium length—thigh a good length—cannons and pasterns short—hooves regular and hard—good natural stance

KARABAIR

This Russian mountain breed goes back a very long way and its appearance would suggest that it almost certainly descends from the Arab. A tough, and stocky animal, it shows exceptional resistance both to cold and exhaustion, and is bred in three distinct types, all similar in size: a heavier saddle and light draught horse, a lighter saddle horse, and a third type with longer lines which is used only for draught. The Karabair is well suited to mountainous regions, and is able to negotiate steep and demanding tracks with great agility. Its wide range of useful qualities have led to its being used to improve other breeds, and in fact it has contributed to the evolution of the Don.

Breed: Karabair
Place of origin: USSR (Uzbekskaya)
Height at withers: 15–15.3 hands
Structure: mesomorphic
Colour: chestnut—bay—grey—brown and black (relatively rare)
Temperament: calm and patient—energetic
Aptitude: saddle and pack horse—light draught
Qualities: strong, agile and enduring
Head: small with rather prominent jawline—profile straight—ears long and set well apart—eyes large and bright
Neck: a good length—muscular
Body: withers high and pronounced—back straight and not too long—croup muscular and sloping—chest full and deep
Legs: solid—muscular with good bone—shoulder sloping and muscular—joints large—tendons hard—foot small with tough horn

KARABAKH

The origins of this breed go back a very long way, and its present-day appearance clearly betrays a strong Oriental influence. The Karabakh appears, in fact, to have been considerably influenced by blood from Arab, Turkmene and Persian horses. It lives in the mountains which separate Azerbaijan in the USSR from northwest Iran and, helped by its small size, it has adapted very impressively to the harsh conditions of this region which is generally regarded as the birthplace of the breed. The Karabakh has a distinctive and handsome bearing, and on account of its qualities, it has been used in the development of other breeds, one of the most important of which has been the Don.

Karabakh

Breed: Karabakh
Place of origin: USSR (Azerbaijan)
Height at withers: approx. 14.1 hands
Structure: mesomorphic
Colour: golden dun (with eel stripe)—chestnut (sorrel)—bay—grey—with possible white markings—darker mane and tail
Temperament: quiet but energetic
Aptitude: saddle and pack horse
Qualities: strong, with good endurance
Head: small—well set-on—profile straight—eyes expressive—nostrils wide—muzzle narrow
Neck: long and well shaped
Body: withers pronounced—back long and straight—flanks well formed—croup sloping—tail set-on a little low—chest deep
Legs: hard—muscular with good bone—shoulder sloping but a little flat—joints clean—tendons set well apart—foot well shaped with tough horn, blue in colour

KABARDIN

This breed, which originated in the Caucasus in Russia, can probably be traced back to the Arab and the Turkmene, as can be seen from its typically Oriental features. Its origins in extremely mountainous areas have equipped this horse with the special qualities that make it particularly well suited to negotiating steep, rugged tracks and coping with considerable differences in altitude. As well as being a good-natured animal, the Kabardin displays both strength and endurance. It is sure-footed and agile and has an uncommonly developed sense of direction, two qualities which make it an ideal mountain horse. In 1936 it was put through various endurance trials in which, during the winter and in mountainous terrain, it is said that it covered some 2,000 miles (3,000 km) in just 47 days. When it is moved away from its customary surroundings it also displays excellent suitability as a riding horse and can even be used to good effect in equestrian events. Because of its aesthetic and other fine qualities it has, in the past, been used to improve other breeds such as the Tersky.

Breed: Kabardin
Place of origin: USSR (Caucasus)
Height at withers: 14.2–15 hands
Structure: mesomorphic
Colour: bay—dark bay—black—grey
Temperament: quiet and sensitive—energetic
Aptitude: riding horse—pack animal
Qualities: longevity—frugal—agile—strong—good endurance
Head: well proportioned—slightly elongated—profile straight or sometimes slightly convex—ears long with the tips pointed inwards—jaws pronounced
Neck: quite long and muscular—mane flowing
Body: withers not very high but long—back short and straight—loins short—croup sloping—tail set quite low and full—chest full and deep
Legs: solid—good bone and muscular—shoulder fairly straight and well muscled—joints clean—tendons well detached—hooves well shaped with hard horn

Kabardin

LOKAI

The Lokai originates in the USSR, in the mountainous region of Tadzhikistan, where it performs a dual role as a saddle horse and a pack horse. It is a relatively old breed, dating back to the sixteenth century, with a fairly varied ancestry, including contributions from the Iomud, the Karabair and the Arab. The generally good conformation and the proud bearing of this horse clearly reveal its noble origins. It is a small but sturdy horse. The most common coat colours are grey, bay and chestnut, typically presenting dazzling golden highlights. If removed from its native environment the Lokai shows itself to be particularly well suited to equestrian sporting events.

Breed: Lokai
Place of origin: USSR (Tadzhikistan)
Height at withers: up to 14.3 hands
Structure: mesomorphic
Colour: chestnut—bay—grey; black and dun (rare)
Temperament: docile and willing
Aptitude: saddle and pack horse
Qualities: agile, with good endurance—bold
Head: well proportioned and well set-on—profile straight or slightly convex—ears small—eyes lively
Neck: quite long and well shaped
Body: withers quite prominent—back short and straight—croup sloping—tail set-on low—chest full and deep
Legs: solid—muscular with good bone—shoulder sloping and well muscled—joints clean—tendons clearly defined—pasterns a good length and sloping nicely—foot well shaped with hard horn

Lokai

TORIC

The Toric has only developed as a breed since the last century. Its origins are somewhat mixed, with blood from the Arab, the Ardennais, the Hackney, the East Friesian, the Hanoverian, the Orlov, the Norfolk Roadster, the English Thoroughbred and the Trakehner all making a contribution. All these horses were crossed with the Klepper, an old indigenous draught horse descending from the Arab and the Ardennais. For this reason the Toric was also known as the Estonian Klepper or Double Klepper. This horse is well suited to light agricultural work, even though its physical appearance clearly reveals its noble origins, making it look more like a very heavy saddle horse than a draught horse.

Breed: Toric
Place of origin: USSR (Estonia)
Height at withers: 15–15.2 hands
Structure: mesomorphic
Colour: chestnut—bay—dark bay—grey; with white markings
Temperament: quiet and patient
Aptitude: farm work—light draught
Qualities: good endurance and willing
Head: of medium size and well set-on—profile straight—ears long—jaws pronounced
Neck: quite long and muscular
Body: withers low—back slightly hollow, short, broad and muscular—loins strong—croup slightly sloping—tail well set-on—chest full and deep—ribs well rounded
Legs: short and solid—shoulder sloping and very muscular, quite massive—joints large and clean—cannons and pasterns short—tendons strong—foot of average size with white horn

Latvian

Toric

LATVIAN

The origins of this particularly versatile horse date back to prehistoric times and it probably descends from the primitive forest horses of northern Europe. The Latvian bears a marked resemblance to the North Swedish Horse and the Døle Gudbrandsdal, suggesting that all these breeds derive from the same ancient stock as has produced all northern European heavy draught breeds. Since the seventeenth century the breed has received infusions of blood from various German saddle and carriage horses, as well as from the Arab and the English Thoroughbred, this latter more recently than the others. The breed is now considered to have been firmly established since 1952. In addition to the Harness Horse there is a lighter version, sometimes known as the Latvian Riding Horse, and a heavier version, better suited to draught work. In general this is a strong, well-built horse, although a little on the massive side.

Breed: Latvian (Latvian Harness Horse)
Place of origin: USSR (Latvia)
Height at withers: 15.2–16 hands
Structure: mesomorphic
Colour: black—grey—chestnut—bay—brown
Temperament: docile, quiet and steady
Aptitude: saddle horse—farm work—light and heavy draught
Qualities: strong and with good endurance
Head: quite large—profile straight—ears small—eyes gentle—full forelock
Neck: long and muscular—mane flowing
Body: withers quite pronounced—back straight—croup long and slightly sloping—tail full and long—chest high and deep
Legs: quite short—well muscled and solid—some feather on rear of cannons and fetlocks—joints large and strong—feet well shaped

HEAVY DRAUGHT WORK AND AGRICULTURE

There was a time when all the most arduous agricultural tasks and the transportation of heavy loads, in both town and country, fell exclusively to the horse. Man, therefore, had to select individual horses, capable of developing considerable work potential (horsepower) by transforming the chemical energy contained in their feed into mechanical energy. These horses, all of them of the heavy, brachymorphic or at the very least, the slightly lighter meso-brachymorphic type, were characterized by the following features: a heavy head; a short, muscular neck; broad withers; the shoulder not too sloping, or tending to be straight; back and loins short, straight and wide, and powerful; a sloping croup with well-developed muscles; short legs and large feet. These characteristics were necessary to make these animals powerful "machines" capable of producing a considerable amount of energy which could be used for a wide range of tasks. The sight of horses harnessed to ploughs or to carts laden with corn or other products of the land was once common in country areas, as was the sight of the tram horse or horses drawing heavy carts in towns and cities. Nowadays, however, with the progress of technology and mechanization, such sights have become something of a rarity, although in some countries, for example in eastern Europe the horse still remains an active part of the agricultural economy, to which it continues to make a valuable contribution.

IRISH DRAUGHT

The origins of this breed are uncertain, although they can in part be traced back to the Connemara. It is a valuable and tireless horse when it comes to farm work and also proves a swift coach horse, with good endurance and a supple, easy action. The Stud Book for the breed, which dates back to 1917, maintains very strict standards, and currently lists about 7,000 mares and 600 stallions. The Irish Draught is a natural jumper, a particular quality that it invariably transmits to its offspring, especially when crossed with the English Thoroughbred, to produce the hunter. The hunter is the pride of Irish horse breeding, and in order to protect it the government has adopted restrictive measures, more or less prohibiting the export of members of the breed. With its quiet but dynamic temperament, this is a well-built animal, with a fairly massive physique, and distinctive and very well-developed hindquarters.

Breed: Irish Draught
Place of origin: Ireland
Height at withers: 15–17 hands
Structure: meso-brachymorphic
Colour: bay—brown—grey—chestnut
Temperament: quiet and dynamic
Aptitude: medium-heavy draught—farm work—riding horse
Qualities: a good jumper
Head: well proportioned—profile straight—forehead wide—ears straight
Neck: of average length and strong
Body: withers prominent—back long and straight—croup quite sloping—tail well set-on, full and flowing—chest full and deep—abdomen drawn in
Legs: solid and muscular—not much feather—shoulder nicely sloping, massive and powerful—joints large and strong—cannons and pasterns solid—hoof broad and rounded

JUTLAND

The origins of this breed go back over 1,000 years and in fact the ancient Romans were almost certainly familiar with the Jutland as the steed used by the Vikings. In the Middle Ages it was used as a charger in tourneys. During the nineteenth century it was improved by Suffolk Punch and Cleveland Bay blood, and somewhat more recently by Ardennais blood. A major contribution was made by a Suffolk Punch stallion called Oppenheim LXII, which was imported into Denmark in 1860. This stallion also made a decisive contribution to the development of the Schleswig, the origins of which are quite similar to those of the Jutland and this helps explain the similarity between these two breeds. The overall appearance of the Jutland is a massive but compactly built horse with harmonious lines. The most common colour is chestnut with the mane and tail long and full, and somewhat lighter in colour.

Breed: Jutland
Place of origin: Denmark (Jutland)
Height at withers: 15.2–16 hands
Weight: 1,430–1,760 lb (650–800 kg)
Structure: brachymorphic
Colour: chestnut—bay—grey—roan; often with white markings
Temperament: docile but energetic
Aptitude: heavy draught—farm work
Qualities: good endurance and eager
Head: well proportioned—profile slightly convex—eyes small
Neck: short—muscular—arched
Body: withers low and broad—back short and strong but often slightly hollow—loins broad and muscular—croup wide and quite sloping—chest full and deep
Legs: quite short and muscular—feathered—fairly solid—shoulder straight and muscular—hoof large and round

SHIRE

This breed is probably descended from the famous charger used in the Middle Ages for jousts and tourneys, the Great Horse. Originally created in the Netherlands for military purposes, by crossing the largest and most powerful breeds of draught horses in northern Europe, this medieval horse also received a clear input of Oriental blood, for which, it would seem, the Romans were responsible. In absolute terms this is the tallest horse of all and in its category it comes equal first, in terms of stature, with the Belgian Heavy Draught although it is, in fact, generally more massive than its Belgian counterpart. Some individuals can reach a height of over 19 hands at the withers and weigh as much as 2,650 lb (1,200 kg). The Shire Horse Society was established in 1878, and has been in charge of breed records and registration ever since. To begin with the Shire was used as a cart horse, but over the subsequent years it has been used for general agricultural work, particularly for transporting timber, as well as for hauling omnibuses in cities.

In the twenty year period from 1950 to 1970 the breed went into a decline, simply due to its having been substituted by mechanization. However, in recent years there has been a clear revival of interest and in some parts of Great Britain in particular, the Shire can once again be seen drawing beer carts through city streets. The Shire is characterized by full feathering on the legs and its hindquarters, which are relatively lightly developed in relation to the bulk of the animal.

Breed: Shire
Place of origin: England
Height at withers: 16.2–17.3 hands
Weight: 1,760–2,650 lb (800–1,200 kg)
Structure: brachymorphic
Colour: bay—brown—black—grey (often dappled)—chestnut; frequent white markings
Temperament: docile and good-natured
Aptitude: heavy draught—farm work
Qualities: strong, with good endurance
Head: lean in relation to the rest of the body—profile slightly convex—forehead broad—ears long—eyes large and prominent—jawbone prominent
Neck: fairly long—muscular—slightly arched
Body: withers form an extension of the neck-line and are quite broad—back short—croup not too powerful and sloping—chest broad and muscular—ribs rounded
Legs: quite short and carrying much feather below the knee and hock to the hoof—well muscled—shoulder long, sloping and muscular—joints large and sturdy—cannons quite long—pasterns short—good feet

BELGIAN HEAVY DRAUGHT

According to fossils, unearthed in the region between Dinant and Liège, which extends along the right bank of the river Meuse, the origins of this breed would seem to date back to a type of prehistoric horse that was in existence during the alluvial period of the Quaternary. In this breed it is possible to single out three distinct morphological types: the Heavy Draught or Brabant, the Medium Draught or Condroz and the Belgian Ardennes. The Belgian Heavy Draught has a sluggish constitution, which is noticeable in its docile but possibly too impassive temperament. It is a strong and willing horse, and in addition it develops early and lives to a good age. At work it performs with a slow but extremely powerful action. The most common colours are roan and chestnut, the latter combined with a considerably lighter tail and mane. In the past it was exported to many European countries as well as to the United States. In Italy, towards the end of the last century it was used to improve the old Cremonese, which it eventually replaced, and it has also had a decisive influence on the development of the Italian Heavy Draught. In the United States it has produced the American Belgian Horse, which is distinctively taller, ranging from 17 to 19 hands. The Belgian Medium Draught is smaller and less heavy, but it still has the typical build of a brachymorphic horse; the Belgian Ardennes, on the contrary, has a livelier temperament and is more suited to fast, heavy draught work due to its comparatively nimble and brisk action. The Belgian Ardennes is the outcome of crosses between the Belgian Heavy Draught and the French Ardennais blood. The Stud Book for this breed dates back to 1885, and is put out by the Société Royale pour le Cheval de Trait Belge.

Breed: Belgian Medium Draught (Condroz)
Place of origin: Belgium (Condroz)
Height at withers: 15.3–16 hands
Weight: 1,320–1,760 lb (600–800 kg)
Structure: brachymorphic
Colour: bay—roan—chestnut
Temperament: quiet
Aptitude: heavy draught—farm work
Qualities: willing

Breed: Belgian Ardennes
Place of origin: Belgium (northwest)
Height at withers: 14.3–15.3 hands
Weight: 1,100–1,320 lb (500–600 kg)
Structure: brachymorphic
Colour: bay—roan—chestnut
Temperament: lively
Aptitude: fast heavy draught—farm work
Qualities: good endurance

Breed: Belgian Heavy Draught (Brabant)
Place of origin: Belgium (Brabant)
Height at withers: 16.1–17 hands
Weight: 1,760–2,200 lb (800–1,000 kg)
Structure: brachymorphic
Colour: chestnut—bay—red-roan—grey—roan
Temperament: docile and impassive
Aptitude: slow, heavy draught-work
Qualities: strong and willing
Head: small in proportion to body—square—profile straight or slightly snub—ears small—eyes small—full forelock—jawbone prominent
Neck: short and muscular, with a very broad base—arched—well set-on
Body: withers muscular, broad and low—back broad and muscular (sometimes slightly hollow)—loins broad and short—flanks well developed—croup muscular and double, rounded—chest broad, muscular, full and deep—ribs very well rounded—abdomen well developed
Legs: short and sturdy—shoulder long and sloping, very muscular—joints large and solid—cannons have a good circumference—pasterns short and feathered—hooves broad but flat, with soft horn

SCHLESWIG HEAVY DRAUGHT

This breed can be traced back to Denmark's Jutland horse and, like the Jutland, was undoubtedly improved by the influence of the Suffolk Punch through the stallion Oppenheim LXII. Throughout the nineteenth century the Schleswig was not only a valuable and useful animal for a wide range of farm tasks, but also proved particularly well suited to drawing omnibuses and carts carrying freight in towns and cities. The Stud Book for the breed dates back to 1891. However, with the advent of mechanization, like so many other breeds of heavy draught horses, the Schleswig has gone into steady decline.

Breed: Schleswig Heavy Draught
Place of origin: West Germany (Schleswig Holstein)
Height at withers: 15.2–16 hands
Weight: 1,430–1,760 lb (650–800 kg)
Structure: brachymorphic
Colour: chestnut—bay—grey; frequent white markings
Temperament: docile but energetic
Aptitude: heavy draught—farm work
Qualities: good endurance and willing
Head: well proportioned—profile slightly convex—eyes small
Neck: short—muscular—arched
Body: withers low and broad—back strong but often slightly hollow—loins broad and muscular—croup wide and rounded—chest deep
Legs: quite short and muscular—moderately feathered—quite solid—shoulder quite straight and muscular—hoof large and round

Schleswig

Dutch Draught

DUTCH DRAUGHT

The origins of this breed only go back as far as 1918, when Zeeland-type mares were crossed first with Belgian Heavy Draught and then with Belgian Ardennes stallions. This explains its close resemblance to the Belgian Heavy draught. Its impressive and massive physical structure does not prevent this horse from displaying an easy and relatively nimble action. The Dutch Draught spread quite rapidly at first, but the arrival of mechanized farm machinery has considerably limited its potential uses.

Breed: Dutch Draught
Place of origin: Holland
Height at withers: 16.3 hands
Structure: brachymorphic
Colour: chestnut—bay—grey—black (rare)
Temperament: quiet—active—lively—willing
Aptitude: heavy draught
Qualities: strong, with good endurance
Head: well shaped and square—profile straight—forehead broad—ears short and straight—eyes not large but intelligent—jaws clearly defined
Neck: short and powerful—well set—on
Body: withers low and broad—back short and straight—loins muscular—croup sloping—tail set-on low—chest broad and muscular, roomy
Legs: strong and muscular—quite well feathered—shoulder long and nicely sloping—joints large—foot solid

RHINELAND HEAVY DRAUGHT

The Stud Book of this breed was established in 1876. Originally used for heavy draught work in transport and agriculture, the Rhineland is descended from the Ardennais with probable blood contributions from the Belgian Heavy Draught. In the days when heavy draught horses were in great demand this breed was widespread in Germany, and was often given different names depending on the region in which it was reared, such as the Niedersachsen Heavy Draught from Lower Saxony, which even now goes by this different name although it still has the same original features of the Rhineland.

Breed: Rhineland Heavy Draught (Rhenish)
Place of origin: West Germany
Height at withers: 16–17 hands
Weight: approx. 1 tonne
Structure: brachymorphic
Colour: chestnut—red roan (with black or flaxen mane and tail)—bay
Temperament: quiet and docile
Aptitude: heavy draught—farm work
Qualities: strong, with good endurance
Head: small but rather heavy-jawed—profile straight—eyes small—full forelock
Neck: quite short—broad—muscular—full mane
Body: withers low and broad—back broad and short, often slightly hollow—loins broad and muscular—flanks muscular and rounded—croup broad and muscular, quite sloping—chest full—abdomen rounded and bulky
Legs: short and feathered—shoulder powerful and muscular and quite straight—joints large—very well developed muscles—cannons short—hoof broad and strong

ARDENNAIS

This ancient breed is thought to be a descendant of the draught horses that Julius Caesar so admired in Gaul and which he described in his *De Bello Gallico*. In times gone by it was popular with the military as a war horse and Napoleon himself made wide use of it in his Russian campaign. In fact the Russian Ardennes probably derives from horses left behind by the French emperor as his armies retreated. The Ardennais has also produced the Swedish Ardennes and the Belgian Ardennes. All these breeds are very similar both in terms of physical appearance and in their extraordinary strength and endurance, which put them among the most powerful of all the heavy draught horses. Of all these breeds the one that most markedly differs from the others is the Belgian Ardennes, which has been influenced by the Belgian Heavy Draught, to such an extent that it is generally regarded as a lighter variety of this breed. The Swedish Ardennes, likewise, has been strongly marked by the consistent input of Belgian Heavy Draught blood, with the result that the stature of this horse tends to be rather higher, ranging from 15.2–16 hands.

In its country of origin and in all those countries where it has been introduced, the Ardennais is used in transport and agriculture, carrying out a variety of heavy draught duties, although sadly, it has now been largely replaced by mechanization.

Breed: Ardennais (or French Ardennais)
Place of origin: France (Ardennes region)
Height at withers: 15–15.3 hands
Weight: 1,100–1,320 lb (500–600 kg)
Structure: brachymorphic
Colour: bay—chestnut—roan; dark bay and dark chestnut (permissible); black is not permitted
Temperament: quiet but energetic
Aptitude: heavy draught—farm work
Qualities: strong, with good endurance
Head: slightly on the heavy side—profile straight—face broad—ears small and pointed—eyes large—nostrils wide—jaws heavy
Neck: short and muscular—broad at the base—mane full and flowing
Body: withers rather low, broad and muscular—back broad, short and straight—loins broad—croup rounded and very muscular—chest broad and roomy—abdomen rather pendulous
Legs: short and muscular—strong—carrying moderate feather—shoulder sloping and muscular—joints solid—foot broad

POITEVIN

This horse is little known outside France and descends from horses imported by the Dutch from the Netherlands, Norway and Denmark, to be used in land reclamation projects in the region around Poitiers. Here, on the marshy terrain, its unusually large feet gave it a distinct advantage over other breeds. More than anything else this breed owes its reputation to the fact that the mares are used to produce mules by being mated with the unusually large Poitevin jackass. For this reason the Poitevin horse is known also as "Mulassier" meaning "mule breeder."

Boulonnais

Poitevin

Breed: Poitevin (Cheval du Poitou)
Place of origin: France (Poitou)
Height at withers: 15.2–17 hands
Weight: 1,540–1,980 lb (700–900 kg)
Structure: brachymorphic
Colour: bay—grey—dun
Temperament: lazy—well balanced—not very lively
Aptitude: heavy draught—farm work
Qualities: no outstanding quality
Head: heavy—profile straight or convex—ears large and thick—eyes small and not very expressive—full forelock
Neck: short and broad—muscular—mane full
Body: withers broad and muscular, reasonably well defined—back straight, wide and long—loins broad—croup quite long and sloping—tail full and flowing—chest deep—abdomen quite well developed
Legs: short and feathered—quite large—shoulder slightly sloping but not well formed—joints large—cannons long—foot large

BOULONNAIS

Controversy surrounds the origins of this breed. According to some authorities it goes back to before the Romans invaded Great Britain, and is descended from the horses of the Numidian cavalry, stationed in France on the Boulogne coast. Others maintain that it derives from Hun steeds that had probably been abandoned by Attila as he fled from western Europe, whilst others still, claim that the Boulonnais is a descendant of the old Flemish horse. However, despite these conflicting opinions, there is no doubt that the breed has benefited from a consistent input of Eastern blood, introduced by way of animals brought back by the Crusaders on their return home from foreign parts. It also seems certain that at some stage it was crossed with Mecklenburg stallions, with the aim of making it sturdier, and increasing its size so that it could more easily withstand the weight of its rider and his heavy armour. In 1066 William the Conqueror introduced it into Great Britain where it contributed towards the formation and development of the Old Norfolk Horse.

The Boulonnais is bred and reared in northwest France and, with its elegant and distinguished appearance, the only heavy draught horse with which it can be likened is the Percheron. This similarity is undoubtedly the result of refinements brought to both breeds by infusions of Eastern blood. Since the seventeenth century, it has been possible to distinguish two clearly distinct types of differing sizes: a small Boulonnais used for rapid transport, and another larger version suitable for heavy draught. The Petit Boulonnais or Small Boulonnais is now becoming extinct, but in the last century it was used to transport fish from the north coast of France to Paris, becoming popularly known as the "Maréyeur," a French word used to describe wholesale fishmongers. The breed's Stud Book dates back to 1886.

Breed: Boulonnais
Place of origin: France (northwest)
Height at withers: 15.1–15.3 hands (small); 15.3–16.3 hands (large)
Weight: 1,210–1,430 lb (550–650 kg) small; 1,430–1,650 lb (650–750 kg) large
Structure: brachymorphic
Colour: grey (usually dappled)—chestnut—bay
Temperament: energetic and lively
Aptitude: heavy draught—farm work—fast heavy draught (small type)
Qualities: strong, with good endurance
Geographical distribution: northern Europe—United States—South America
Head: small and squared—profile straight—forehead broad—ears well proportioned—eyes large and lively—nostrils wide
Neck: short and muscular—broad and arched
Body: withers broad and muscular, low and clearly defined—back short and straight—flanks well developed—croup slightly sloping and often double—chest full with well-rounded ribs—abdomen well shaped
Legs: strong—quite short—shoulder sloping and muscular—joints large—thigh muscular and very well developed—hoof well formed and sturdy

PERCHERON

This breed comes originally from Le Perche, a region to the south of Normandy spanning the four departments of Orne, Sarthe, Loiret-Cher and Eure-et-Loir, and is probably descended from an ancient indigenous breed deriving from *Equus caballus sequanus*. During the course of its development, the Percheron has certainly profited greatly from infusions of Eastern blood, as is clearly shown by the elegant shape of its head and its velvety coat. The first of these contributions was probably made in the eighth century A.D, using horses captured from the Saracens after the defeat inflicted upon them at the Battle of Poitiers by Charles Martel, and the second in the Middle Ages by Arab stallions imported by the Comte de Perche when he returned from the Crusades and from travels in Spanish territory. Within the breed it is possible to distinguish two types of differing sizes: the small version, also known as the Percheron Postier, which is lighter but now on the decline, and the larger version used in the nineteenth century, for drawing omnibuses in towns and cities.

In France the Percheron has produced a whole series of local breeds, each one of which has its own Stud Book: these include the Trait Augeron (*trait* means draught), the Trait de la Loire, the Berichon from the Berry province, the Trait du Maine, the Gros Trait Nivernais, and the Trait du Saône-et-Loire. The breed's Stud Book, based in Nogent-le-Rotrou, was established in 1883, and since 1911 it has been restricted exclusively to individuals that have both mare and sire registered. The Percheron is the most common heavy draught horse in the world. In the United States it has given rise to a new variety, but it does not have the same elegant proportions as the original type. It was introduced into Great Britain during the First World War, and its Stud Book has been strictly maintained since 1919. However, members of the breed coming from the United States had already been introduced into England even before this, and in fact in the latter years of the nineteenth century and the early years of this century 90 per cent of the horses used to draw the London omnibuses appear to have been Percherons. The breed is very popular and nowadays is highly prized not only by the English, but also in Canada, South America, Australia and South Africa, where it was used in the Boer War. Despite its considerable size the Percheron is so well proportioned, combining power and endurance with an elegant and graceful action, that it does not look as heavy as it actually is.

Breed: Percheron (Trait Percheron)
Place of origin: France (Le Perche region)
Height at withers: 14.3–17.3 hands (smallest and largest of both sizes)
Weight: 1,320–2,200 lb (600–1,000 kg)
Structure: meso-brachymorphic
Colour: grey (distinctively dappled)—black—roan (rare)
Temperament: very quiet, sensitive and energetic
Aptitude: heavy draught—farm work—fast heavy draught (small type)
Qualities: strong, with good endurance
Geographical distribution: France—Great Britain—United States—Canada—Argentina—South Africa—Australia
Head: long, handsome and harmonious—small in relation to the size of the body—profile straight—ears well proportioned—eyes large with an expressive look—jaws strong
Neck: short and broad—well shaped—muscular—quite arched—full, flowing mane
Body: withers quite pronounced—back broad, short and sometimes slightly hollow—loins full and rounded—flanks well proportioned—croup broad and muscular (sometimes double), rounded—chest broad and muscular—girth generous and deep—abdomen rounded
Legs: quite short—sturdy—shoulder sloping and muscular—joints large—thigh muscular and long—pasterns short—foot large and solid with dark horn—natural stance almost always good

AUXOIS

This breed dates back at least as far as the Middle Ages and in its original form was somewhat smaller than its modern counterpart. It probably derives from the old Burgundian heavy, and in the past it was used for drawing coaches, carriages and carts. During the nineteenth century the breed was markedly influenced by both the Percheron and the Boulonnais, while, in more recent times, there has been a greater tendency to cross with the Ardennais. Nowadays strict regulations and selective breeding ensure the maintenance of type and coat colour.

Breed: Auxois
Place of origin: France
Height at withers: 15.2–16 hands
Structure: brachymorphic
Colour: bay—roan
Temperament: quiet—good-natured—willing
Aptitude: heavy draught—farm work
Qualities: very strong, with excellent endurance
Head: light—profile straight—forehead broad—ears long—eyes with a gentle expression
Neck: short and muscular—quite broad
Body: withers not very prominent—back straight—croup sloping—tail set-on low—chest broad—girth deep
Legs: slender in relation to the size of the body, but strong—shoulder long and sloping

Comtois

COMTOIS

This very old breed has probably been bred in the Franche Comté region since as early as the sixth century A.D. and is directly descended from the Germanic horses imported by the Burgundians, a people coming from northern Germany who, in 411 A.D. founded the kingdom of Burgundy. In the late Middle Ages it was used as a war horse or charger. The Comtois is bred on the borders of France and Switzerland in a rugged and mountainous region that covers the departments of Doubs, Haute-Saône and the Jura and has a quick, lively action which is quite unusual for such a heavy horse. Like all mountain breeds, the Comtois is active and sure-footed, this latter quality being crucial in hilly areas where the roads and tracks are of poor quality and often very steep. The Comtois is a well-built horse, with well-developed hindquarters.

Breed: Comtois
Place of origin: France (Franche Comté)
Height at withers: 14.3–15.3 hands
Weight: 1,100–1,320 lb (500–600 kg); adult stallions up to 1,590 lb (770 kg)
Structure: brachymorphic
Colour: chestnut—bay
Temperament: active—willing—docile
Aptitude: heavy draught—farm work
Qualities: strong and hardy with good endurance—well suited to mountainous regions
Head: square—profile straight—forehead broad—full forelock
Neck: short and muscular—full mane
Body: withers moderately well defined, broad and muscular—back straight—croup wide and sloping—tail set-on low—girth generous and deep
Legs: light, in relation to the size of the body, but strong—shoulder quite long and sloping—tendency to sickle hocks—lowest parts feathered—foot strong and sure

Auxois

TRAIT DU NORD

This breed descends from the Ardennais, the Belgian Heavy Draught and the Boulonnais, from which it inherits its heavy build and calm temperament. However, as well as inheriting the characteristics peculiar to these three breeds, the Trait du Nord is also noted for its exceptional hardiness. This horse is extremely resistant to bad weather conditions and cold climates, enabling it to spend the harsh winters of northern France out of doors, unless truly exceptional weather conditions occur. It is remarkably strong, and capable of drawing heavy carts over hilly terrain. The Trait du Nord is bred and reared primarily in the area around Lille, near the Belgian border, as well as in the Calais, Aisne and Somme regions and the department of Seine et Marne.

The breed's Stud Book only dates back as far as 1919. During the Second World War the Trait du Nord suffered a considerable decline in numbers but concerted efforts are currently being made to restore it to its former glory.

Breed: Trait du Nord
Place of origin: France
Height at withers: approx. 16 hands
Weight: 1,320–1,760 lb (600–800 kg)
Structure: brachymorphic
Colour: bay—roan—red roan—chestnut
Temperament: energetic but quiet
Aptitude: heavy draught—farm work
Qualities: strong and hardy
Head: heavy—profile straight—ears small—eyes small—jaws clearly defined
Neck: short and broad—muscular
Body: withers broad and not very well defined—back short and straight—loins broad—croup wide and muscular, and quite sloping—chest broad—girth deep—abdomen well developed
Legs: short and strong—well muscled—moderately feathered—shoulder muscular and nicely sloping—joints large—foot well shaped—good natural stance

Trait du Nord

NORIKER

This breed dates back to Roman times and takes its name from the ancient Roman province of Noricum, which corresponds roughly to modern Austria. The breed was improved during the Renaissance as a result of the introduction of Andalusian and Neapolitan blood. Even though the breed was actually established, standardized and registered as far back as 1884, it did not have its own Stud Book until 1903. This listed 450 stallions and over 1,000 mares. This same year also saw an updating of basic breeding and rearing techniques, which became more methodical and rational as a result. In the past, because of its origins, the Noriker was also known as the "Styrian and Carinthian Horse," while nowadays it is still known in some places as the "South German Cold Blood." In Austria a spotted version, known as the Pinzgauer, is bred in the vicinity of Salzburg, throughout the Tyrol and into the north Italian region of Alto Adige where it is still used for heavy draught duties in mountainous areas, inaccessible to machines. In Germany a lighter variant called the Oberlander is bred in Bavaria: the height of this variety ranges from 15.1–15.3 hands and its weight from 1,430–1,510 lb (650–680 kg).

Noriker

Breed: Noriker (Pinzgauer, Oberlander, South German Cold Blood)
Place of origin: ancient Roman province of Noricum, corresponding roughly to modern Austria
Height at withers: 15.3–16.2 hands
Weight: 1,540–1,980 lb (700–900 kg)
Structure: meso-brachymorphic
Colour: bay—chestnut (sometimes roan)—brown—black—spotted (Pinzgauer)—patched and grey (rare)
Temperament: docile and quiet
Aptitude: heavy draught—farm work
Qualities: strong and undemanding
Geographical distribution: alpine regions of Italy, Austria and Germany
Head: quite heavy—profile straight or slightly convex
Neck: short, thick and muscular
Body: withers broad and not very prominent—back long and slightly hollow—croup full and sloping—tail set-on quite low down, long and full—chest broad and muscular—girth deep
Legs: well muscled—shoulder quite straight and muscular—knee and hock large and solid—pasterns short and feathered—foot broad with well shaped hoof, quite flat

ITALIAN HEAVY DRAUGHT

The Italian Heavy Draught dates back to 1860, when the Stud Farm at Ferrara first began breeding native stallions from the Po Delta, subsequently introducing English Thoroughbred, Hackney and Oriental blood. Towards the turn of the century efforts were made to increase the weight of the breed, using Boulonnais, Ardennais and Norfolk-Breton stallions. Horse breeding, particularly in the north Italian Veneto region, was seriously affected by the First World War, and rigorous steps had to be taken to remedy the situation once hostilities were over. As a result the Italian Heavy Draught was crossed with Ardennais and Percheron stallions. The greatest contribution, however, was made by the Breton, and following a long and patient programme of selective crossbreeding the distinctive characteristics of the modern breed were eventually established.

The Stud Book dates back to 1961 and horses entered in it bear a double brand, the first placed on the left-hand side of the thigh at the age of six months, and the second applied to the left-hand side of the neck at the age of 30 months. The brand consists of a shield 4½ in (11 cm) high and 3½ in (9 cm) wide, in the center of which is a five-runged ladder.

Breed: Italian Heavy Draught
Place of origin: Italy
Height at withers: 14.2–15.2 hands (mares); 15–16 hands (stallions)
Weight: 1,320–1,540 lb (600–700 kg)
Structure: brachymorphic
Colour: dark liver chestnut with light mane and tail—chestnut—red roan—bay—socks and other specific markings may be present—other coats are also permissible
Temperament: good-natured—active—reasonably highly-strung
Aptitude: heavy draught—farm work
Qualities: willing—hardy—nimble in relation to its size
Head: quite light, square—profile straight or sometimes slightly convex—forehead broad and flat—ears quite small—eyes large and lively—nostrils wide—full forelock—jaws well defined
Neck: short and muscular with a very broad base—full mane
Body: withers quite prominent and muscular—back short and straight—loins strong—flanks short and rounded—croup (preferably double) rounded and quite sloping—tail well set-on—chest broad and muscular—girth generous and deep—ribs well rounded—abdomen well held
Legs: short, some feather at the bottom—shoulder moderately sloping, a good length and set close to the body—cannon short—pastern short and quite sloping—knee and hock large tending to be rounded—hoof not large but well proportioned and nicely shaped—good natural stance

SOVIET HEAVY DRAUGHT

This breed first developed towards the end of the last century when indigenous draught mares were crossed with Belgian, and probably also Percheron, stallions and the resultant progeny then interbred. This is the commonest and most widespread breed in the Soviet Union, and is frequently used to improve other heavy draught breeds both on state-managed farms and on the collective farms known as kolkhozes. Despite its heavy build, this compact little horse has a steady and supple gait, both at the walk and at the trot. It is a valuable, good-natured animal well equipped to meet the many and varied requirements of heavy farm work.

Breed: Soviet Heavy Draught
Place of origin: USSR
Height at withers: 15.2 hands
Weight: 1,430–1,720 lb (650–780 kg)
Structure: brachymorphic
Colour: chestnut—bay—roan
Temperament: energetic, quiet and kind
Aptitude: heavy draught—farm work
Qualities: hardy and strong
Head: well proportioned, but with pronounced jaws—profile straight or slightly convex—ears nicely proportioned and pointed—eyes have a gentle expression—full forelock
Neck: short and muscular—with full mane
Body: withers low and broad—back short, straight and strong—loins full and strong—croup sloping and muscular—tail flowing—chest and girth generous and deep—abdomen rounded
Legs: strong and sturdy—shoulder quite straight and muscular—knee and hock solid—forearm and legs short—hoof broad and roundish

VLADIMIR HEAVY DRAUGHT

The development of the Vladimir breed began in the latter half of the nineteenth century, when local mares were crossed with a variety of heavy draught breeds, including the Ardennais, the Percheron, the Suffolk Punch, the Cleveland Bay, the Clydesdale and the Shire. After the Russian Revolution the best examples of the resultant progeny were interbred to establish a fixed breed type, which was achieved in 1946, when the breed received its official name. Registration and selection is strictly controlled by means of arduous practical trials involving drawing exceptionally heavy loads. The breed is reared principally in the regions of Vladimir and Ivanovo where it in fact originates. This is a well-built, powerful horse, but in spite of its massive size, it is generally well-proportioned.

Breed: Vladimir Heavy Draught
Place of origin: USSR (Vladimir)
Height at withers: 15.1–16 hands
Weight: 1,500–1,675 lb (680–760 kg)
Structure: brachymorphic
Colour: chestnut—bay—brown—black; frequent white markings
Temperament: energetic—willing—quiet
Aptitude: heavy draught—farm work
Qualities: very strong
Head: of average size but rather heavy-jawed—profile often slightly convex—ears good and straight
Neck: of medium length and muscular—broad at the base—arched
Body: withers quite high and long—back straight and short—loins muscular—croup wide and sloping—chest and girth wide and deep—abdomen drawn in
Legs: short and solid—quite well feathered—shoulder sloping and powerful—thigh muscular—hoof broad and roundish

RUSSIAN HEAVY DRAUGHT

This breed has been gradually developing over the past hundred years and originated from local mares who were crossed with various other heavy draught horses such as the Swedish Ardennes, the Belgian Heavy Draught and the Percheron, also receiving an interesting contribution from the Orlov. As a result of successive interbreeding it was soon possible to establish a fixed breed type. This breed was specifically created to meet the requirements of farmers, and therefore had to be able to carry out a wide variety of tasks and duties in agriculture, which represents the backbone of the Ukrainian economy. It is a small, compact horse, reaching an average height of only 14.2 hands, and has a well-proportioned and powerful build, with very well-developed hindquarters and a supple and easy action.

Breed: Russian Heavy Draught
Place of origin: USSR (Ukraine)
Height at withers: approx. 14.2 hands
Structure: brachymorphic
Colour: chestnut—roan—bay
Temperament: quiet but energetic
Aptitude: heavy draught—farm work
Qualities: strong and hardy
Head: of medium size—profile straight or slightly convex—forehead wide—ears pointed—eyes have a lively expression—full forelock
Neck: of average length and muscular—arched—with a full and flowing mane
Body: withers low and broad—back short and straight—loins wide and muscular—flanks powerful—croup broad and slightly sloping—tail long and full—chest and girth deep with well-rounded ribs—abdomen drawn up
Legs: short, with not much feather—shoulder sloping and powerful—hooves strong

SOKOLSKY

The development of this breed, over the last hundred years, has been greatly influenced by the Norfolk, the Belgian Heavy Draught, the Belgian Ardennes and the Anglo-Norman. Used solely for farm work it is an economical animal, showing willing and excellent endurance.

Breed: Sokolsky
Place of origin: Poland and the USSR
Height at withers: 15–16 hands
Structure: meso-brachymorphic
Colour: chestnut (most common)—bay—brown
Temperament: docile and quiet
Aptitude: heavy draught—farm work
Qualities: strong, with good endurance
Head: slightly on the heavy side—profile straight—ears straight—eyes expressive
Neck: quite long and muscular
Body: withers prominent—back straight—croup sloping—chest and girth deep
Legs: strong and well muscled—shoulder nicely sloping—cannons short—tendons strong—hoof broad and rounded

LITHUANIAN HEAVY DRAUGHT

This breed began to be developed towards the end of the nineteenth century, and derives from local Zhmud horses which were crossed first with the Finnish horse and later with the Swedish Ardennes. As a result of selective breeding of this progeny the determining features of the breed type finally became firmly established and were officially registered in 1963. Since then strict control has been exercised over which stallions should be used at stud. In both appearance and development the Lithuanian Heavy Draught bears a close resemblance to the Latvian Harness Horse. Both these breeds still play an important role in the agricultural economy of the areas in which they are reared, successfully proving that it is possible to reconcile the use of horses with the modern requirements of mechanized farming techniques. Both the Lithuanian and Latvian breeds display an attractive action at the walk and at the trot.

Breed: Lithuanian Heavy Draught
Place of origin: USSR (Lithuania)
Height at withers: 15–16 hands
Structure: brachymorphic
Colour: chestnut (with flaxen mane and tail)—bay—black—grey—roan
Temperament: quiet
Aptitude: farm work—heavy draught
Qualities: strong, with good endurance
Head: well proportioned—profile straight—ears large—full forelock—jaws
Neck: quite short—muscular—arched—full mane
Body: withers wide and fairly pronounced—back straight—croup rounded—tail well set-on, full and flowing—chest broad and muscular—girth deep
Legs: short and muscular—solid—shoulder sloping and muscular, quite massive—knee and hock large and strong—cannons long—hoof broad

Lithuanian

MURAKOZ

This breed, only developed during this century, originates from the region surrounding the river Mura in Hungary. The horse was produced from a nucleus of local mares crossed with Belgian Ardennes, Percheron and Noriker stallions as well as with indigenous Hungarian stock. The Murakoz is well suited to heavy farm work, and is also bred and reared in Poland and Yugoslavia. During the Second World War the breed suffered such heavy losses that it was necessary to introduce new blood, by once again crossing the mares with Belgian Ardennes stallions. At the present time two different versions are being reared, one lighter and shorter in stature, the other taller and heavier. This horse is vigorous and fairly agile when it moves, despite its impressive size. It has a compact, powerful build and is sturdy and robust.

Murakoz

Breed: Murakoz
Place of origin: Hungary
Height at withers: approx. 16 hands
Structure: brachymorphic
Colour: chestnut (mane, tail and feather on the legs tending to flaxen)—bay—brown—black—grey
Temperament: docile and energetic
Aptitude: heavy draught—farm work
Qualities: strong and undemanding
Head: quite long and heavy—profile slightly convex—ears long—eyes with a gentle expression
Neck: short and muscular
Body: withers low and broad—back short—croup sloping—tail set-on low—chest broad and deep—abdomen drawn up
Legs: short and solid—well muscled—good bone—knee and hock well developed—shoulder sloping and powerful—cannons and pasterns feathered—hoof well proportioned and round

PONIES

ORIGINS AND GEOGRAPHICAL DISTRIBUTION
USES AND USEFULNESS

Ponies are small horses measuring less than 14.2 hands at the withers. It is difficult to establish with any certainty the original derivation of these small horses, but it is known that during the evolution of the horse smaller forms have emerged every so often, examples being *Archaeohippus* in the Miocene and *Hipparion* in the Pliocene. Whereas the first of these appears to have died out rather rapidly, the second produced a number of fertile branches and extensively colonized Europe, Asia and Africa. Following the discovery of important American fossils it seems most likely that ponies have the same origins as other horses and consequently descend directly from the famous *Equus przewalskii przewalskii Poliakov*, the size and stature of which is not particularly striking, reaching a maximum of only 14 hands at the withers. There can be no doubt that small stature is generally advantageous to the survival of a species, whereas an unduly large size can be a hindrance. Small animals tend to be lighter and therefore faster, and do not have to rely so heavily on a regular supply of food. In addition, the small size regulates the ratio of volume to body surface area, and this in itself makes for a more balanced metabolism. In effect, when an animal grows in terms of volume, the surface area of its body will also increase but to a lesser extent (this is known as the quadratic variation of surface area with the cubic variation of volume). This creates major problems in dissipating the internal heat produced by the oxidation processes of the cells. It also explains why, not only for the horse, but for all land-dwelling animals, including *Homo sapiens*, it is a disadvantage to be too large. Today the largest living animal is the elephant, the sole survivor of a considerable number of giant animal forms now extinct, ranging from the familiar dinosaurs of the Tertiary period to the giant armadillo, discovered in fossil form by Charles Darwin in the *pampas* of Argentina, and, even to *Australopithecus robustus*, which lived more than two million years ago and was discovered by Richard Leakey in Kenya in the East Rudolph basin. A small animal also has an advantage in other ways: it will be more tolerant to extremes in temperature and adverse climate, given that its small body offers less resistance to wind and other weather conditions; it is less conspicuous and therefore finds it easier to hide; and it tends to be tougher and able to move much more easily over uneven terrain and amid shrubby vegetation.

The term "pony" is in fact fairly aspecific, being used correctly to describe actual breeds, either natural or produced by man by means of artificial selection and cross-breeding, as well as incorrectly, as a synonym for "small horse." So-called polo ponies, for example, are not actually ponies at all and do not form a breed, since they are the result of various combinations that have led to the formation and development of small, light-boned horses, which are both nimble and strong, and whose characteristics are not defined by any standards. With the exception of the American, Mongolian and Indian ponies, all other ponies can be traced back to one common ancestor, the Celtic pony, which is now extinct. According to fossil remains this animal reached a height of between 12.2 and 13.3 hands at the withers and in general physical bearing and stance was very similar to the horse. The head, however, was smaller with a shorter muzzle, and more akin to that of present-day ponies. It probably developed from crosses between a variety of Eurasian wild horses, and then spread rapidly throughout Europe, giving rise to a wide range of breeds, some of which have retained their original features in a fairly distinctive way. Of these, the breed that most closely resembles the Celtic pony is undoubtedly the Icelandic. Other breeds, on the contrary, have become conspicuously removed from it, taking on a physical appearance that tends more and more towards that of the horse, especially when the influence of blood from other sources has been decisive. Such is the case with the Welsh pony, which has benefited from an important contribution from the English Thoroughbred, the Hackney pony, the Greek Pindos, and, in Asia, the Manipuri. In addition to the Icelandic, Europe also boasts another pony with primitive characteristics. This is the Skyros, which hails from the Aegean island of the same name. It is rather unrefined in appearance, hardy rather than attractive to look at, and to some extent brings to mind the Tarpan. The Skyros is possibly one of the few original breeds still living today. Because of its striking resemblance to *Equus przewalskii przewalskii Poliakov* and more especially to the Tarpan, from which it inherits its incredible hardiness, the Spanish Sorraia should also be included in this group of original breeds. The Sorraia is a relatively awkward breed to tame and train, and its overall appearance is primitive and poorly proportioned.

The ponies of Asia, on the other hand, have a well-defined point of reference in the form of the Mongolian pony, which descends directly from the Asiatic wild horse, is strong and hardy, and also resembles the Tarpan. In physical build the Tibetan, Spiti and Bhutia ponies all have many points in common with the Mongolian pony. Other ponies display their ancient origins through particular characteristics. The Indonesian Bali pony, for example, has an upright, bristly mane reminiscent of the ancient Asiatic wild horse of Mongolia.

The original American pony breeds descend from the Spanish jennet, which, although now extinct, was an extremely important factor in the development of all American horse breeds. Formed as a result of crosses between Arab and Barb horses, and cold-blood horses from the Pyrenees, the jennet was in fact the first horse to be shipped to the Americas by early Spanish explorers. However, nowadays not all American ponies have this same root, since some of them are merely a local version of imported European breeds, while others, such as the Pony of the Americas, are produced by crossbreeding. This latter breed was obtained out of a Shetland stallion and an Appaloosa mare.

Ponies share many common features besides size, including a plentiful supply of energy and good endurance when working. In relation to its size, the Shetland, which is the smallest of the European ponies, is regarded as the strongest horse of all. A Shetland pony is capable of drawing loads weighing up to about 1,000 lb (450 kg) and it can carry on its back a load of up to 155 lb (70 kg). Taken as a group, ponies combine these exceptional qualities with a generally well-balanced appearance and elegant movements. They are for the most part easy to domesticate and train and can be put to a wide variety of uses. Some breeds, however, are stubborn and skittish, especially the stallions, and in some instances (such as the Shetland) it may be advisable to resort to castration. Similarly, the Sorraia will not always adapt readily to living with man, due to a strong independent streak.

Ponies occur in most parts of the world, either as an original breed, or as a result of being imported. Great Britain is home to many varied breeds of ponies, including the distinctive and elegant Dartmoor; the ancient Exmoor, which is the oldest native breed; the solidly-built, quiet Dales with its impressive endurance; the New Forest pony, which is descended from wild woodland ponies; the Highland, which is so well suited to hunting over rugged, mountainous terrain; the Hackney pony, which is light and elegant, and an excellent small riding horse; the Shetland, with its distinctive appearance, especially attractive in its long winter coat; the Fell, a small upland horse accustomed to living and working in the hostile environment of the moors and fells in northern England; the Welsh pony, which is unanimously recognized as the most handsome of all the small horses; and the Welsh Mountain pony, slightly smaller than its cousin, but no less attractive.

In Iceland the only truly indigenous breed is the Icelandic pony. In Norway there are the Norwegian Fjord, also known as the Westlands pony, and the Northlands, and in Sweden the Gotland or Skogsruss pony. In France there are the Landais (Barthais), the Ariègeois, sometimes called the Merens, and, from Corsica, the Corsican pony. In the Iberian peninsula there are the Sorraia, the Garrano, the Basque pony and the Galician and Asturian pony; in Germany the Senner (which is now sadly extinct) and the Dülmen; in Yugoslavia (Dalmatia and Bosnia-Herzegovina) the Dalmatian and the Bosnian. In Greece the Peneia, the Pindos and the Skyros are the only three native breeds of horses; in the Soviet Union the Viatka and the Kazakh, both with their own distinctive characteristics. In Asia, in the Elburz mountains and on the Iranian shores of the Caspian Sea lives the Caspian, a very ancient breed of elegant appearance; in Mongolia there is the Mongolian pony, a direct descendant of the Mongolian wild horse, the founding father of many related breeds; in Assam the Manipuri pony, which is used for polo, the Kathiawari, the Marwari, the Spiti and the Bhutia; in Burma, the Burmese pony, and there are of course many other breeds, all of which are fairly alike, such as the Tibetan, the Chinese and the Hokkaido. Indonesia, too, has many native ponies: the Timor, the Java, the Batak, the Bali, the Sumba and the Sandalwood. In the United States there are the Chincoteague and the Assateague, the Pony of the Americas and the American Shetland, and in Canada there is the Sable Island pony. Argentina boasts the smallest pony in the world called the Falabella, which derives from the Shetland. The Basuto pony of Lesotho and the Malagasy pony of Madagascar are the principal African breeds.

Where work is concerned, ponies are exceptionally versatile due to their physical strength combined with a generally docile nature. They are very widely used for light draught work, and some of them are even named after the loads they draw, like the Indonesian Sandalwood. The various English ponies are all suitable as both riding horses and light draught horses. Some of them, like the Exmoor, the Dartmoor, the Shetland and the Welsh Mountain, are particularly good with children.

In some less industrialized countries ponies are still used for farm work, especially on smallholdings. Other ponies, like the Spiti, the Bhutia and the Tibetan, which live in the Himalayan uplands, still play a vital and irreplaceable role as pack animals, connecting areas which would otherwise be totally cut off. Ponies are also frequently used, nowadays, by tourist agencies all over the world, for pony trekking holidays, which are rapidly increasing in popularity, as a way of visiting the most beautiful and remote regions of a country and escaping from the bustle of the cities.

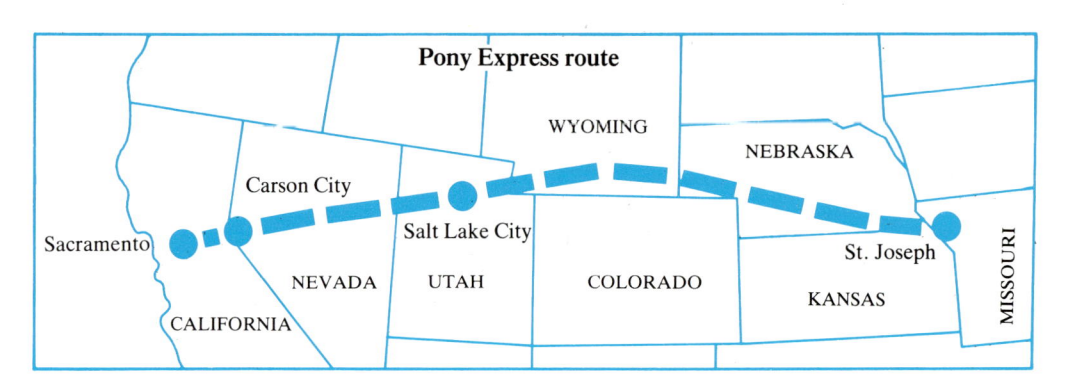

The Pony Express

In the days when railways had not yet been properly developed, and before the invention of the telegraph, Senator William Gwin of California conceived the idea of setting up a postal service, using horses, that would link the western states with the East. The Pony Express, as it came to be called, lasted for about 18 months, running first once, and then twice a week, between 1860 and 1861. The animals used were sturdy Indian ponies, which were descended from the Spanish jennets. By this time there was already a coastal railway that ran south from Oregon and into California, as far as Sacramento. It was from here that the postal service started, ending up in the city of St. Joseph in Missouri, close to the border with Kansas, by way of Nevada, Utah, Wyoming and Nebraska. The route, which covered 2,000 miles (3,200 km) wound its way through the most perilous regions including mountains, plateaus and deserts, rendered even more hazardous and treacherous by the presence of hostile Indian tribes. The brave young riders, usually no more than 18 years old, and armed with pistols and knives to see them through the many dangers that might befall them on their journey, soon became legendary heroes, inspiring many books and films. Despite the enormous problems of this service, which were often worsened by the harsh climate and terrible weather conditions, the Pony Express did manage to function almost without incident, and the mail in its charge was regularly delivered. On every mail run the rider would carry a package weighing not more than 20 lb (8–9 kg) over a stretch of about 75 miles (120 km), after which he would stop at one of the staging-posts scattered along the route and hand the package over to the next rider. The whole route would be covered in eight days, with an average of about 250 miles (400 km) being travelled every day. If one remembers that the Overland Mail, the stagecoach line that carried both passengers and mail, took three weeks to cover the same distance, it is easy to see that the Pony Express provided a truly excellent service in the pioneering days of American history.

FJORD

The physical appearance of this ancient breed still bears a close resemblance to its forbears, the wild horses of the Ice Age. In fact the type of coat itself, dun, with a different coloured mane and tail, the presence of an eel stripe and striped zebra markings on the legs, are all characteristic of its particular ancestry. The Vikings used these ponies as mounts as is proved by various rock and cave paintings in which they are depicted at war. The Fjord is an undemanding pony with good endurance, and as such it is widespread throughout northern Europe, where it is still occasionally used for farm work wherever the terrain is particularly inaccessible. It is also sometimes used as a pack animal due to its considerable strength and is extremely suitable for use with children, and for drawing small, light carriages. It has a distinctive coarse and bristly mane, the particular shape of which calls to mind the type of crested helmet worn by Roman soldiers. Some authorities maintain that all present-day western heavy draught breeds descend from this pony. The Fjord has withstood all attempts to pollute the breed by introducing foreign blood, which is why it is now bred and reared on a thoroughbred basis.

Breed: Fjord (Westlands pony)
Place of origin: Norway

Height at withers: 13–14.2 hands
Structure: mesomorphic
Colour: light dun (with black and silver mane and tail—very extensive eel stripe present—legs sometimes with zebra markings)
Temperament: gentle but stubborn
Aptitude: pack and riding pony—light draught
Qualities: a strong and tireless worker
Head: small, but with prominent jaws—profile straight, sometimes slightly snub—forehead wide—ears small and set well apart—eyes large and expressive—nostrils wide
Neck: short and muscular
Body: withers low—back not too long and often slightly hollow—loins strong—croup quite sloping—tail full and long—chest full and deep
Legs: short and solid—well muscled—shoulder very sloping and muscular—joints large and clean—tendons well separated—light feather behind fetlocks—pasterns long—foot long, with tough horn

Icelandic pony

Fjord

ICELANDIC PONY

This breed owes its presence in Iceland to the Norwegians, who took it there in the ninth century. After Celtic peoples reached Iceland from the Scottish islands, Ireland and the Isle of Man, this pony was almost certainly crossed with other breeds, such as the Shetland, the Highland and the Connemara. The Icelandic pony is extremely versatile and has, in the past, played an important role in the economy of the island. As well as being able to withstand and survive icy winters and natural disasters such as the volcanic eruptions of 1784, it can also cope admirably with hunger, and indeed during the seemingly endless northern winter it often has no option but to search for food beneath the snow, or else to feed on seaweed. It is extremely sure-footed, and thus treads quite fearlessly over even the most treacherous of terrains. Up until the end of the last century these ponies were exported to Europe for use in coal mines, where their small size and hardiness made them very popular. The Icelandic has a very distinctive gait known as the "tølt" which is a fast and comfortable ambling pace, covering a great deal of ground. The pony is also a good, natural pacer. It is a docile, intelligent animal, but with a markedly independent streak.

Breed: Icelandic pony
Place of origin: Iceland

Height at withers: 12–13 hands
Weight: 840–900 lb (380–410 kg)
Structure: mesomorphic
Colour: chestnut—dun (most common)—bay—black—grey—mouse dun—part colours
Temperament: quiet and friendly, but with an independent streak
Aptitude: riding and pack pony—light draught
Qualities: strong—hardy—good pacer
Head: well proportioned and well set-on—profile straight—ears small—eyes lively—full forelock—nostrils wide—jaws a little pronounced
Neck: short and muscular—quite broad at the base—mane full but not soft
Body: withers quite low and broad—back long but sometimes slightly hollow—croup broad and short, muscular and quite sloping—tail long, full and bristly, set-on low—chest deep
Legs: short and strong—shoulder nicely sloping and muscular—joints large and clean—cannons relatively long—pasterns short—hoof tough

Northlands

GOTLAND

This pony which originated on the island of the same name in the Baltic Sea, probably descends from an ancient breed living there since prehistoric times. The fact that it has certain characteristics in common with the Konik and the Hucul would suggest, hypothetically at least, that these three breeds have similar origins. In the nineteenth century the Gotland benefited from contributions of Oriental blood, when two such stallions were introduced into the island. The name Skogsruss, which is sometimes also used to identify this pony, means "little horse of the woods" and indicates the pony's natural habitat. Since 1954 the breed has been protected by the Swedish government, which has determined to ensure that the breed will survive, and as a result these ponies are allowed to live more or less in the wild state in the Lojsta forest. In the past the breed was exported to Belgium and Great Britain for use in the coal mines and to other European countries as a riding pony for children, and as a light draught pony. In Sweden, a small variant of the breed is also used for special pony trotting races. In these events, the Gotland is aided by what is technically a defect in stance, which enables it to pick its way easily over varied terrain, even at an extended trotting pace. The Gotland pony is a hardy and frugal animal, and undoubtedly one of the most attractive of all the ponies.

Breed: Gotland (Skogsruss)
Place of origin: Sweden (Gotland Island)
Height at withers: 12–13.1 hands
Weight: 400–440 lb (180–200 kg)
Structure: mesomorphic
Colour: bay—brown—black—chestnut—grey—dun—mouse dun—palomino
Temperament: intelligent and alert, but often stubborn
Aptitude: riding pony and light draught
Qualities: strong—good trotting horse
Head: small—profile straight—ears small and broad—eyes lively—nostrils wide
Neck: quite short and muscular—full mane
Body: withers prominent—back long, straight and slightly weak—croup sloping—tail full and flowing, but set-on quite low—chest deep
Legs: strong and well muscled—shoulder well muscled and nicely sloping—joints solid—tendons set well apart—cannons long—hoof strong—natural stance not altogether correct (often open at the front and cow-hocked)

NORTHLANDS

The origins of this pony can be traced right back to the northern pony type that was descended from the Mongolian wild horse and the Tarpan, which are also the forbears of the Baltic pony (Konik) and the Celtic ponies (Shetland, Icelandic and Exmoor). This hypothesis is fully backed up by the resemblance in appearance of the Northlands and the Icelandic pony.

Up to the First World War the Northlands was raised traditionally by individual farmers, without following any particular selection criteria. At the end of the war certain breeders made a conspicuous effort to supervise their own activities, and by so doing established a general set of standards. Nevertheless, in spite of initiatives such as these, in 1944 the number of ponies registered had been reduced to just 43. Later that very same year the breed began to recover, and much of the credit for this is due to the stallion Rimfakse, which was widely used to improve the breed. The Northlands pony is an attractive-looking animal, with distinctive, well-developed hindquarters.

Breed: Northlands
Place of origin: Norway
Height at withers: approx. 13 hands
Structure: mesomorphic
Colour: bay—brown—chestnut—grey
Temperament: quiet but energetic
Aptitude: riding pony—light draught
Qualities: strong and frugal
Head: small, light and well proportioned—profile straight—ears small and straight—eyes set well apart—full forelock
Neck: quite short—full mane
Body: withers not too high—back long and straight—croup rounded—chest and girth generous and deep—tail long and full, well set-on
Legs: well muscled and solid—shoulder muscular and nicely sloping—joints large and clean—hoof well proportioned and strong—good natural stance

DARTMOOR

For thousands of years this breed has been living wild on Dartmoor, a rugged moorland area in the southwest part of the county of Devon, the central part of which was probably owned by royalty even before the Norman conquest in the eleventh century. In the past a large number of Shetland stallions was introduced into the region, as a result of which the purebred features of the Dartmoor were affected. Since 1899 this pony has been a registered breed and in order to maintain its purity the Dartmoor Pony Society has imposed strict regulations on the selection of animals to be used at stud. Because of its kind nature, this pony is ideal for young children, and as such it is much sought after. It has a well-balanced appearance with a certain distinguished quality probably deriving from the English Thoroughbred, which has been used on past occasions to improve the breed.

Breed: Dartmoor
Place of origin: Great Britain (Dartmoor, Devon)
Height at withers: 12.2 hands (maximum)
Structure: mesomorphic
Colour: bay—brown—grey—black—chestnut (rare); part colours are not acceptable—extensive white markings are not encouraged
Temperament: quiet and sensitive
Aptitude: riding pony
Qualities: strong, with good endurance
Head: small—profile straight—forehead broad—ears small and straight—eyes quite small—full forelock
Neck: well proportioned and nicely shaped—full mane
Body: withers quite prominent—back generally good—loins broad—croup wide and slightly sloping—tail set-on well, long and full—chest broad and deep—abdomen quite drawn up
Legs: solid and slender—muscular—shoulder long and sloping—joints clean—tendons set well apart—feet well shaped with tough horn

NEW FOREST

This pony lives in the New Forest, an area in the county of Hampshire, reputedly given its name by William the Conqeror who turned it into his private hunting reserve in 1079. Even in those remote times there were ponies roaming freely in these woodlands, although the present-day breed did not really start to be developed until the nineteenth century when, at the request of Queen Victoria, a number of Arab stallions were introduced to the area, to be followed at a later stage by stallions belonging to other pony breeds, such as the Welsh, the Exmoor, the Dartmoor and the Highland. Nowadays, more than a century later, the breed has assumed clearly defined characteristics. These New Forest ponies live in the wild in their surroundings, and their population numbers some two thousand. They are sturdy, well-built animals ideally suited as riding ponies for both children and adults. The mares of this breed are often crossed with horses of normal size to produce animals suitable not only for light draught work or farm duties, but also for equestrian sports.

FELL

This pony takes its name from its place of origin, the fells, or hilly moorland, on the northwestern edge of the Pennines and up into the Lake District. It is similar in appearance to the Dales and both breeds are probably descended from Galloway ponies from the Scottish lowlands, which are now extinct. These ponies were probably crossed with Friesian horses that had been shipped across the English Channel by Roman legionaries. The Fell is extremely resistant to harsh cold weather and strenuous work, and is a frugal and undemanding animal. For centuries it was used for transporting lead from the Pennine mines to the coast where it was loaded on board cargo ships; it has also seen long years of service in the coal mines of Durham and Cumberland and been used for farm work. Nowadays it is used mainly as a riding pony. In 1900 the Fell Pony Society was established and at more or less the same time the National Pony Society began to register the breed in a special section of the Stud Book. These two societies between them have subjected the Fell to close and careful scrutiny, and have managed, during the course of this century, to avoid the contribution of undesirable blood from other breeds wherever this has been possible. The outward appearance of this pony combines strength and sturdiness with a certain elegance of form that prevails despite the heavy feathering on the limbs.

HACKNEY PONY

This breed is a smaller version of the Hackney, from which it derives, and has received contributions from the Fell and the Welsh pony, which have had an influence on its size. The breed was developed in the nineteenth century, becoming permanently established in 1880, although it still does not have its own, separate Stud Book and is still registered in the Hackney's book. Originally created as a light draught pony, it also makes an ideal riding pony, particularly for inexperienced riders.

Breed: New Forest
Place of origin: Great Britain (New Forest, Hampshire)
Height at withers: 12.2–14.2 hands
Structure: mesomorphic
Colour: all varieties—bay and brown are the most frequent—part colours not acceptable—white markings permitted on the head and legs
Temperament: docile
Aptitude: riding pony
Qualities: eager
Head: well proportioned—profile straight—forehead broad—ears quite long—eyes small—nostrils wide—full forelock
Neck: not too long—muscular—mane full and long
Body: withers prominent—back long and straight—croup wide and sloping—tail well set-on, long and full—girth deep—abdomen rounded
Legs: solid and muscular—slender—shoulder quite long, sloping and well shaped—joints clean—tendons set well apart—feet well formed with strong horn

Breed: Fell
Place of origin: Great Britain (Westmorland and Cumberland)
Height at withers: 13–14 hands
Structure: mesomorphic
Colour: bay—brown—black—grey—dun; preferably with no white markings; a small star and small white leg markings are admissible
Temperament: quiet but active
Aptitude: light draught—riding pony
Qualities: strong and frugal
Head: small—profile straight—ears small and pointed—eyes prominent, lively and bright—nostrils wide—"whiskers" on jaws—full forelock
Neck well proportioned—well set-on—well muscled and nicely shaped
Body: withers quite prominent—back long and straight—loins broad and very powerful—croup slightly short and sloping—tail long and full, set-on quite high—chest and girth generous and deep
Legs: long and extremely solid—well muscled—shoulder long, sloping and muscular—cannon has considerable circumference—pasterns not too long—feather on fetlocks—hoof tough, rounded, bluish in colour

Breed: Hackney pony
Place of origin: Great Britain
Height at withers: 12.2–14.2 hands
Structure: mesomorphic
Colour: bay—brown—black—grey—roan; often with white markings
Temperament: dynamic
Aptitude: light draught—riding pony
Qualities: fast—good jumper
Head: light and elongated—profile straight or slightly convex—ears small and pointed—eyes bright
Neck: muscular—arched—well set-on
Body: withers quite pronounced—back short and straight—croup long and rounded—tail set high—chest broad and deep—abdomen drawn in
Legs: slender but strong—shoulder sloping and muscular—knee and hock clean and solid—cannons long—tendons well separated—feet well formed with horn of a good texture—quarters carried somewhat to the rear

DALES

This pony, from the valleys or "dales" on the eastern slopes of the Pennines, has much in common with its neighbour, the Fell pony, in terms of both appearance and origin. The Dales pony, however, is of a heavier build than the Fell due to the decisive contribution made by Comet, a famous Welsh Cob stallion, which was mated with Dales mares in the nineteenth century. All modern Dales can be traced back to this horse. The Dales is a quiet animal and one which, in the past, played an important part in the farming economy of the region, as well as being used in coal mines and as a pack pony. After experiencing a period of decline, coinciding with the advent of mechanization, the breed is currently enjoying a revival due to reviewed interest in horse riding as a hobby and the increasing popularity of pony trekking. The Dales is a solidly built although rather heavy pony with good endurance and a calm, agreeable nature.

Breed: Dales
Place of origin: Great Britain
Height at withers: not more than 14.2 hands
Structure: mesomorphic
Colour: black—bay—brown—grey; white markings rare
Temperament: quiet and sensitive
Aptitude: pack pony—farm work—riding pony
Qualities: strong, with good endurance
Head: small—profile straight—forehead broad—ears small—eyes small—nostrils wide—full forelock
Neck: not too long—muscular—full mane
Body: withers fairly prominent—back not very long and sometimes hollow—loins broad and muscular—croup wide and sloping—tail set quite low down, but long and full—chest deep
Legs: long and well muscled—shoulder nicely sloping—joint large—feather on lower leg—hoof broad, bluish and strong

EXMOOR

This is probably the oldest British pony breed still in existence, although a certain amount of controversy surrounds its origins. The most likely theory is that it descends from the wild indigenous horses of prehistoric times that were subsequently used by the Celts as pack horses, and for pulling war chariots. However, others maintain that it crossed overland into Cornwall from Europe, in the days when Great Britain was still attached to continental Europe. The Exmoor pony is a native of the wild moorland of southwest England from which it takes its name and is well equipped to withstand the harsh winters. This is a solidly built, well-proportioned pony with distinctive mealy markings typical of many primitive pony breeds. It would appear that the Exmoor even played a small part in the creation of the English Thoroughbred, since it features in the most remote genealogy of this breed. The Exmoor is endowed with exceptional strength, making it ideally suited to drawing large, elegant carriages or for use as a riding pony by children and adults alike.

Breed: Exmoor
Place of origin: Great Britain (Devon and Somerset, Exmoor)
Height at withers: 12.2–12.3 hands
Structure: mesomorphic
Coats: bay—brown—mouse dun (invariably with a mealy muzzle and under-belly, extending to between the thighs; white markings are not admitted
Temperament: quiet
Aptitude: riding pony—light draught
Qualities: speed
Head: well proportioned—profile straight—forehead broad—ears small and pointed—eyes expressive and prominent (toad eye)—nostrils wide
Neck: well proportioned and well shaped—full mane
Body: withers prominent, running on from the line of the neck—back long and slightly hollow—loins broad—croup slightly sloping—tail well set-on and full—girth deep—abdomen quite drawn up
Legs: strong and well muscled—shoulder sloping and muscular—forearm long—cannons short—foot small with tough horn

HIGHLAND

The physical features sometimes present in this breed, such as zebra markings and an eel stripe, clearly point to its primitive origins, which may be traced back as far as the Ice Age. However, a certain refinement in appearance also reflects infusions of Arab blood. It is possible to distinguish two varieties of the Highland: the Mainland type and the Western Isles type. Despite the fact that the Mainland type, also known as the Garron, is more recent, and dates back no further than the nineteenth century, it is currently the only variety officially recognized as belonging to the breed. The Western Isles type on the other hand, is smaller and less hardy, but it is also older and in some respects purer. The Highland pony is a strong and sturdy animal, well suited to draught and farm work. It is sure-footed making it particularly suitable for bringing down shot deer from inaccessible mountain regions.

Breed: Highland
Place of origin: Scotland and the Western Isles
Height at withers: 12.2–14.2 hands (Western Isles type); 14.2 hands (Mainland type)
Structure: mesomorphic
Colour: grey—dun—mouse dun—bay—brown—black—liver chestnut (with silver mane and tail); eel stripe common
Temperament: docile and sensitive
Aptitude: riding and pack pony—light draught—farm work
Qualities: strong, with good endurance—excellent mountain horse
Head: well proportioned—profile straight or slightly convex—ears small—eyes gentle and expressive—jaw pronounced—full forelock
Neck: quite long—muscular—quite broad at the base—with long, full mane
Body: withers quite broad and prominent—back short—loins wide and strong—croup muscular, broad and slightly sloping—tail well set-on, very long and full—chest wide—girth deep
Legs: strong and well muscled—shoulder sloping and muscular—joints large and clean—feather at rear of legs below knees and hocks—cannons short—pasterns not too short—feet well proportioned with tough horn

SHETLAND

The earliest remains of the Shetland pony, found on the islands, date back some 2,500 years to the Bronze Age and it is thought that they descended from Scandinavian ponies that crossed into the area at a time when the two lands were joined together. The Shetland is the smallest of all the ponies native to the British Isles. It has good endurance, is undemanding and in relation to its size is undoubtedly the strongest horse in the world. The fierce climate and harsh physical conditions of its natural habitat, where it has survived for thousands of years, have toughened it to a remarkable degree. In the past it was traditionally used for transporting seaweed which, after being burnt, was then used as fertilizer. From the middle of the nineteenth century, because of its remarkable strength and small size, it was exported to various European countries for use in the mines. Nowadays this pony is kept mainly as a pet, being used for drawing light carts or as a mount for children, although uncastrated males do not always make reliable and trustworthy riding ponies. In some parts of Europe it is still employed in agricultural work, particularly horticulture. During the winter months its coat grows longer and thicker, enabling it to protect itself against the bitterly cold weather. The Shetland pony is common in many countries, including the United States, where, because of different breeding conditions, it has undergone modifications that set it apart from the original breed.

Breed: Shetland
Place of origin: Scotland (Orkney and Shetland Islands)
Height at withers: 9–10.2 hands (maximum)
Weight: 330–400 lb (150–180 kg)
Structure: mesomorphic
Colour: bay—black—chestnut—grey—part colours (common)
Temperament: lively—not always docile
Aptitude: riding pony—light draught
Qualities: strong, with good endurance
Head: small—profile straight or snub—forehead broad—ears small—eyes large—nostrils wide—jaws pronounced
Neck: short, but not too short, and muscular—broad at the base—mane full and long
Body: withers broad, not very prominent—back short and often hollow—loins broad and muscular—croup short and rounded—tail set-on high, long and full—girth deep—abdomen rounded
Legs: short and sturdy—shoulder long and sloping—joints large—pasterns of average length—foot round, small and strong
Skin: thin, covered with long thick hair during the winter months

WELSH MOUNTAIN PONY

The Welsh Mountain pony occupies Section A of the Welsh Stud Book, in which only animals that do not exceed a height of 12 hands can be registered. This is therefore the smallest and probably the most elegant of the Welsh ponies, its appearance being somewhat reminiscent of the Arab horse. This similarity is not, however, coincidental since it indicates a certain infusion of Oriental blood in its development. According to some authorities Julius Caesar, himself, encouraged the crossbreeding of local ponies with horses imported from the Orient, at a stud he had formed at Lake Bala. The Welsh Mountain pony has an undeniably pleasing appearance and a distinctive and distinguished bearing that combines well with its free, supple and quick action. It makes an ideal riding pony for beginners and is also good in harness.

Breed: Welsh Mountain pony—Section A
Place of origin: Wales
Height at withers: 12 hands (maximum)
Structure: mesomorphic
Colour: bay—brown—black—grey—chestnut—roan; part colours are not admitted
Temperament: intelligent and lively
Aptitude: riding pony—light draught
Qualities: good endurance—supple, flowing action
Head: handsome and well proportioned—well set-on—profile straight or slightly snub—forehead broad—ears small and pointed—eyes large and expressive—nostrils wide and prominent
Neck: well developed—quite arched—well proportioned—well set-on—flowing mane
Body: withers prominent—back short, straight and sturdy—loins wide and well shaped—croup slightly sloping—tail set high and carried elegantly—chest and girth deep
Legs: strong with good muscular development—shoulder long and sloping, well muscled—joints large and solid—forearm long—foot small and rounded with strong horn

Welsh Mountain pony

Welsh pony

WELSH PONY

This pony is entered under Section B of the Welsh Stud Book, which will only register animals measuring between 12.2 and 13.2 hands. It derives from the Welsh Mountain pony and the Welsh pony of the Cob type both of which it resembles, however, what makes it different from the other two breeds is a greater contribution of Hackney blood. Towards the end of the nineteenth century a small English Thoroughbred by the name of Merlin was introduced into the breeding area. Merlin was descended from the Darley Arabian, and seems to have had a strong effect on the development of this pony. For this reason section B of the Stud Book is also qualified by the heading: "Merlins." The appearance and general characteristics of the breed very much echo those of the Welsh Mountain pony, from which it inherits its gentle and courageous temperament. Like the Welsh Mountain pony its main uses are for light draught work and as a riding pony, in both of which roles it displays an effective flowing and energetic action.

Breed: Welsh pony—Section B
Place of origin: Wales
Height at withers: 12.2–13.2 hands
Structure: mesomorphic
Colour: the same as the Welsh Mountain pony
Temperament: quiet but energetic
Aptitude: riding pony and light draught
Qualities: good endurance—a very handsome action

WELSH PONY OF COB TYPE

This breed occupies Section C in the Welsh Stud Book, which registers animals not exceeding a height of 13.2 hands, but whose physical structure includes them in the "Cob" category. This pony is in fact rather thickset, with shorter legs and a sturdier physique. In addition to light draught work, for which it is ideally suited, it also lends itself very well to use as a riding pony and is particularly suitable for trekking over demanding terrain. It has a brisk, energetic and lively action, which may be explained by the decisive contribution made to its development by the Hackney.

Breed: Welsh pony of Cob Type—Section C
Place of origin: Wales
Height at withers: 13.2 hands (maximum)
Structure: mesomorphic
Colour: same as for Welsh Mountain pony
Temperament: energetic and lively
Aptitude: light draught—riding pony
Qualities: willing, with good endurance
Head: of the pony type—profile straight (a coarse head with a convex profile (Roman nose) is most objectionable)—ears well set-on and neat—eyes set widely apart and prominent, with a bright expression
Neck: long and well carried—moderately lean in mares
Body: withers quite pronounced—back short, slightly depressed towards the withers—back and loins muscular and powerful—croup rounded—tail well set-on—chest wide—girth deep—abdomen well held
Legs: short with some feather—shoulder strong, long and sloping—forearm long—pasterns nicely sloping—foot well shaped with strong horn

Welsh pony of Cob type

RIDING PONY

This breed was created relatively recently and is intended to be a smaller version of the hack. A hack is a type of riding horse that measures up to 15.2 hands, is well built and has an elegant bearing, with a high percentage of English Thoroughbred in its lineage. The Riding Pony has been obtained by crossing English Thoroughbred or Arab horses with native pony mares, particularly Welsh, Dartmoor and Exmoor ponies. Nowadays the breed has its own Stud Book and its own stallions. The main problem with using English Thoroughbred or Arab stallions for crossbreeding with native ponies is that the resultant progeny often bears too close a resemblance to these breeds, and thus no longer corresponds to the type desired. It is therefore important, every now and then, to resort back to original pony blood in order to maintain the required breed characteristics. According to size, this breed is divided into three groups or classes and each individual pony may only compete with members of its own class. The Riding Pony is a graceful animal with excellent conformation. It has an elegant and flowing action and is well balanced and easy to handle, making it particularly well suited to equestrian sporting events, naturally in competitions reserved for children, and horse shows. Another pony, the Working hunter, derives from the Riding Pony, which it resembles quite closely in all but a few details of appearance and conformation that have nevertheless improved its performance. In fact the Working hunter pony is put through trials including jumping—something not required of the Riding Pony. The Working hunter pony is divided into four "classes" for which the height limits are also different: up to 12 hands, 13 hands, 13 to 14 hands, and 14 to 15 hands. Strictly speaking, as far as height is concerned, this latter class lies outside the limits laid down for ponies.

Breed: Riding Pony
Place of origin: Great Britain
Height at withers: up to 12.2 hands (small); 12.3–13.2 hands (medium); 13.3–14.2 hands (large)
Structure: dolichomorphic
Colour: all are admissible; white markings are permitted
Temperament: quiet but energetic
Aptitude: riding pony
Qualities: good jumper
Head: light—profile straight—ears small—eyes large and set well apart
Neck: long and well shaped
Body: withers high and distinct—back straight and of medium length—croup well muscled and rounded—tail well set-on—chest wide—girth deep—abdomen drawn in
Legs: solid and clean—shoulder nicely sloping—joints flat and hard—cannons short—foot a good size and strong

Connemara

Breed: Connemara
Place of origin: Ireland (Connaught)
Height at withers: 13–14.2 hands
Structure: mesomorphic
Colour: grey—bay—brown—black—mouse dun—dun (often with eel stripe)—roan and chestnut (rare)
Temperament: docile
Aptitude: riding pony—farm work
Qualities: strong, with good endurance—good jumper
Head: small—profile straight—ears small—eyes large—nostrils wide—full forelock
Neck: long and well shaped—full mane
Body: withers quite pronounced—back long and straight—croup well muscled and slightly sloping—tail full and long—chest wide—girth deep
Legs: strong and muscular—shoulder long and sloping—joints clean—cannon quite long—tendons set well apart—foot well shaped—good natural stance

CONNEMARA

The earliest origins of this breed are not dissimilar to those of the Highland pony and, like the Highland, it has benefited during its development from infusions of Arab blood. During the Middle Ages the Connemara was also influenced by contributions of Spanish blood, which brought further refinements to the breed. In more recent times this pony seems to have been additionally improved by the English Thoroughbred, and to some extent also by the Norwegian Fjord. The present-day type is becoming further and further removed from the original model, and the sight of a Connemara with its once common mouse dun coat is increasingly rare. In Ireland it is reared in the wild state, but when transferred into areas where the pasture is more lush, it has a tendency to increase in stature and undergo certain structural modifications that set it apart from the standard type. The breed's Stud Book dates back to 1924. In the past this pony was used for farm work, but now it is used as a riding pony and is particularly suitable for young riders. If crossed with horses of a normal size this pony can produce good jumpers that perform well in equestrian events and competitions.

CAMARGUE

This ancient breed possibly dates back as far as the prehistoric horse of Solutré, near Lyons where in the nineteenth century several thousand horse skeletons were unearthed at the foot of a precipice. It seems that primitive man would hunt horses by herding them towards a precipice and sending them hurtling over the edge with no hope of escape. It is said that this pony was much admired by Julius Caesar. More recently the Camargue has undoubtedly benefited from Arab and Barb blood. The breed has been catalogued and registered since 1967. This pony is a native of the Camargue region of southern France in the Rhône delta where grazing is somewhat sparse. It lives in the wild state in herds of up to 40 ponies, and is impervious to the *mistral*, a cold wind that blows down from the north, protecting itself by closing its nostrils and bowing its head in a distinctive way. Because of its light grey or white coat the French also know this pony by the nickname *Crin Blanc*, which literally means "white hair." When domesticated the Camargue is quiet by nature, and used by the *gardiens*, the herdsmen in charge of the famous black Camargue bulls.

Camargue

Breed: Camargue
Place of origin: France (Camargue)
Height at withers: 13.1–15 hands
Weight: 660–880 lb (300–400 kg)
Structure: mesomorphic
Colour: grey (white)—bay and brown (very rare)
Temperament: quiet
Aptitude: riding pony—pack pony
Qualities: hardy, with good endurance
Head: slightly large, with a straight or convex profile—forehead broad—ears short but broad—eyes large and expressive—jaws pronounced
Neck: quite short and muscular—broad at base—full mane
Body: withers fairly prominent—back short and straight—loins quite long—flanks well developed—croup short and slightly sloping—tail full and flowing—girth deep—abdomen rounded
Legs: shoulder straight and quite short—forearm and leg long—joints clean and strong—foot has tough horn

Lucinda Green (née Prior-Palmer) on Be Fair

FRENCH SADDLE PONY

This breed is very recent, and has been created with the same aim and purpose in mind as the English Riding Pony. Its development has involved crossing mares belonging to breeds of native ponies, entered in the French Pony Stud Book, with Arab, New Forest, Connemara and Welsh stallions. Stallions of the resultant progeny were then re-crossed with Connemara, New Forest and Welsh mares, and the female offspring mated with Arab stallions. The norms for the breed have finally been established, and it now has its own section in the French Pony Stud Book. It is a strong animal, with exceptional qualities, and proves a good match for the Riding Pony in both jumping and dressage events, as well as in all-round horse shows where, during the trials, the appearance of the animal is also judged both moving and stationary. Morphologically the French Saddle Pony is most reminiscent of the English Riding Pony which is its closest rival, however, in direct comparison it is slightly more compact and more solidly built.

Breed: French Saddle Pony
Place of origin: France
Height at withers: 12.1–14.2 hands
Structure: dolichomorphic
Colour: all colours
Temperament: quiet but energetic
Aptitude: riding pony
Qualities: good jumper
Head: small—profile straight or slightly convex—ears of medium size
Neck: long and well shaped
Body: withers prominent—back straight—croup sloping—tail well set-on—chest wide—girth deep—abdomen drawn in
Legs: solid—shoulder sloping—joints large and clean—tendons clearly defined and set well apart—foot well proportioned and with tough horn

LANDAIS

This breed is a native of the region around Barthais de l'Adour in southwestern France, where it still lives in a semi-wild state in the forests of the area, which is crossed by the river Adour. It is not a particularly good-looking animal, and its light physical structure probably reflects the conditions under which it has evolved. It seems that in 1900 and again in 1913 it almost certainly benefited from infusions of Arab blood. At this time there were estimated to be some 2,000 members of the breed but today the numbers have dropped considerably, and there are fears that it will become extinct. There are currently only 150 Landais ponies left in existence. The few breeders who are now responsible for this breed have been forced to turn their attention to the use of Arab and Welsh pony stallions, to avoid too much inbreeding.

Breed: Landais (Barthais)
Place of origin: France (Landes)
Height at withers: 11.2–13 hands
Structure: mesomorphic
Colour: bay—brown—grey—chestnut—black
Temperament: quite independent—intelligent
Aptitude: good trotting horse
Qualities: hardy, good endurance in bad weather conditions
Head: small—profile straight—ears small and pointed—eyes large and set well apart
Neck: quite long—broad at the base—full mane
Body: withers prominent—back straight, short and broad—croup short and sloping—tail well set-on—chest not very well developed—abdomen roundish
Legs: sturdy and solid—shoulder nicely sloping—feet with strong hooves

ARIÈGEOIS

It seems very likely that during the course of its development this breed has been influenced by Oriental blood. It lives in a semi-wild state in the mountains and rugged valleys through which the river Ariège flows in southwest France. In appearance it is reminiscent of the Dales pony, although it is smaller and slightly coarser. Perhaps the most outstanding features are its thick mane and tail. The breed's Stud Book was established in 1948.

Breed: Ariègeois (Merens)
Place of origin: France (Ariège)
Height at withers: 13–14.1 hands
Weight: 770–1,100 lb (350–500 kg)
Structure: mesomorphic
Colour: black
Temperament: energetic
Aptitude: farm work
Qualities: strong—well suited to mountainous regions
Head: light—profile straight—forehead flat—ears small—eyes bright—full forelock
Neck: quite short with a broad base—carried well
Body: withers not very pronounced—back straight and long but strong—croup well muscled and sloping—tail long and full—chest wide—girth deep—abdomen drawn up
Legs: short but well proportioned—shoulder quite straight—foot good with strong horn—often cow-hocked

DÜLMEN

This is the only surviving breed of pony in Germany, now that the Senner Pony, once found in the Teutoberg forest of Hanover, appears to have become extinct. The Dülmen, which, together with the Senner Pony, has contributed to the formation of the Hanoverian, has existed since 1316 in a semi-wild state in the Meerfelder Bruch in Westphalia. The breed has now unfortunately lost its purity, which it had maintained for centuries, due to the influence of imported Polish and British ponies. Nowadays, it seems that the numbers of the breed have dwindled, and the largest herd boasts a hundred or so mares. Privately owned by the Duke of Croy, they are rounded up every year and any surplus or less desirable stock is sold.

Breed: Dülmen
Place of origin: West Germany (Westphalia)
Height at withers: approx. 12.2 hands
Structure: mesomorphic
Colour: bay—brown—black—chestnut—dun—roan
Temperament: independent and fairly intractable
Aptitude: none in particular
Qualities: good endurance in bad weather conditions
Head: well proportioned with a straight profile—eyes small—ears a good length—full forelock
Neck: not too long and well shaped—mane full and long
Body: withers quite pronounced—back long and straight—croup wide and slightly sloping—tail long and full, well set-on
Legs: solid and well muscled—shoulder quite long and sloping—tendons clean—joints good—foot well shaped with strong horn

Landais

Ariègeois

Dülmen

SORRAIA

This breed comes from the western part of Spain, and the area north of Lisbon in Portugal, both regions being crossed by the river Sorraia and its various tributaries. It lives in the wild state and is extremely hardy, but if domesticated it will become a good riding and pack pony. The appearance of this pony is most reminiscent of the Tarpan, but its coat with the characteristic zebra markings and eel stripe also resembles the ancient Asiatic wild horse that hails from the steppes of Mongolia, *Equus przewalskii przewalskii Poliakov*. These features are clear indications of its ancient origins, and its direct descent from a very primitive type of horse. Changes in the ecological balance of its natural habitat have had adverse effects on this breed, with the result that the numbers currently in existence have dwindled dramatically. The overall appearance of this pony is not always particularly attractive, but it nevertheless occupies a place of some importance, since it offers tangible evidence of the evolution of the horse as a species.

Breed: Sorraia
Place of origin: Spain and Portugal
Height at withers: approx. 12.2–13 hands
Structure: dolichomorphic
Colour: grey—dun; zebra markings on legs, and eel stripe
Temperament: independent but tractable
Aptitude: riding and pack horse
Qualities: undemanding, with good endurance
Head: quite large—profile straight or slightly convex—ears long with black tips
Neck: long and slender—not well set-on, and not very attractively shaped
Body: withers fairly high—back straight—croup slightly sloping—tail set-on low—chest not well developed
Legs: quite long and solidly built—shoulder not very muscular and quite straight—pasterns long—foot well proportioned

BASQUE PONY

This is a pleasant-looking pony that lives in the wild state, often spending the night out in the open, without shelter, thus showing an uncommon degree of endurance. Better known as a Pottock, which in the Basque language means a "small horse," the breed is a native of the mountainous regions of the Basque Provinces and Navarra, where it has probably lived for thousands of years. Its ancient origins are confirmed by reliable fossil finds that trace it back directly to the horse of Solutré. However, it is clear that, in more recent times, the breed has been positively influenced by Oriental blood. Its distinguished origins are also attested to by the fact that it was crossed with the Anglo-Arab horse, to produce the Tarbais breed in southwest France. In the winter months, when the ground is covered with snow, the Pottock has no option but to feed on spiny plants, which is why, in this season, it develops a handsome set of whiskers on its upper lip as protection. These whiskers disappear again as soon as it changes its diet. Life in the wild is not easy for this creature, and it has to put up with difficult living conditions, including bad weather and poor grazing. The Pottock has recently emerged from a period of relative insignificance in which it was little known, and in the early 1970s the National Pottock Association was established in the northern part of the Basque Provinces (Iparralde), under the supervision of the Haras Nacionales. The scant attention shown to this breed has been an inevitable consequence of agricultural mechanization, which has meant that farmers saw the Pottock mainly as a source of meat, and thus an animal that could be easily reared at very little expense. Nowadays, having proved itself to be a good riding pony for children, as well as having demonstrated the qualities that make it eminently suitable for jumping, dressage and cross-country events in its category, there has been a decisive move towards protecting the breed. It is a strong and sturdy animal that can also be used for trekking in mountains, where it is a good match for many a larger horse.

Breed: Basque pony (Pottock)
Place of origin: Spain (Basque Provinces and Navarra)
Height at withers: 12–13 hands
Structure: mesomorphic
Colour: brown—black; bay—chestnut—part colours (more rare)
Temperament: quiet but energetic
Aptitude: riding pony (trekking)—farm work
Qualities: prolific—strong and sturdy—hardy—good jumper
Head: nicely proportioned and clean—profile slightly concave or sometimes straight—ears not very small—eyes large and expressive—nostrils wide—upper lip pendant, with whiskers (in winter)
Neck: short, ewe-like—well set-on—mane full but bristly
Body: withers high—back long and straight—croup slightly sloping and rounded—tail long and full, set quite low—chest wide with well-rounded ribs—abdomen slightly bulky
Legs: clean and strong—shoulder quite straight—hoof small and strong—good natural stance on forelegs—hind legs often cow-hocked

GALICIAN AND ASTURIAN PONY

This pony, like others living along the Cordillera Cantabrica from Galicia into the Basque Provinces, is closely related to the Celtic pony. In the Quaternary Period, there were three basic types of indigenous pony in Asturia: a small type, known as the Asturçon, with a slightly convex profile and short limbs; a second, larger in size, called the Thieldon, with a straight profile and long limbs; and a third of medium size, the so-called Disex, with a short, erect mane and zebra markings along the body. Of these three types only the first has survived whilst it seems that the second became extinct relatively recently as there is reference to a certain number still in existence in some villages in Asturia at the end of the Spanish Civil War. Its extinction is largely due to lack of attention to breeding and to the presence of stallions from the army, which were intended to step up breeding in the region, but which instead had a negative influence on the conservation of original indigenous breeds. The Disex disappeared, leaving very few traces. It was a typical animal of the woodland, where it lived in the wild state and was frequently hunted by man. The only survivor therefore is the Asturçon, or Asturian pony, which has been used for work and riding for as long as anyone can remember. Today this pony lives high in the Asturian mountains such as the Sierra de Sueve, but the most important group is found in the western part of Asturia. With the difficult living conditions and total lack of human intervention, this breed has run the risk of becoming extinct. However, given its outstanding resistance and ability to search for food in areas inaccessible to larger horses, this no longer seems a danger. In winter its body is covered with a long thick coat of a lighter colour, which gives it a somewhat wild appearance. Recently, with the rediscovery of this pony's importance, associations have been formed to protect and conserve the breed.

Breed: Galician and Asturian pony (Asturçon)
Place of origin: Spain (Galicia and Asturia)
Height at withers: 11.3–13.1 hands
Structure: meso-dolichomorphic
Colour: black—brown; a small star on forehead is admitted
Temperament: tractable—docile
Aptitude: saddle horse—farm work
Qualities: frugal and hardy
Head: large and lean—profile slightly concave (rarely straight)—ears straight and small—forelock thick
Neck: thin with flowing mane
Body: high withers—back straight and muscular—croup narrow and sloping—tail well set-on—chest narrow with flat ribs—abdomen rounded
Legs: slender but tough—straight shoulder—poor natural stance

Galician and Asturian Pony

GARRANO

This pony originates in the Portuguese regions of Minho and Trás os Montes on the borders with Spain, along the valleys of which flows the river Minho and whose mountains are rich in green pastureland. Despite appearances the Garrano has been subject to infusions of Arab blood on more than one occasion. It is a strong pony, used today principally as a pack animal or in light farm work, whilst in the past it was in wide demand as a trotting horse and frequently took part in local trotting competitions. An indication of the age of this breed is given by paintings depicting this type of horse, found in caves that date back to the Paleolithic era. The Garrano seems to have remained virtually unaltered for thousands of years. Perhaps the best examples of the breed can be found at the horse fairs that are held in Vila Real and Famalicão. In the sixteenth century the Garrano gave rise to the Galiceño while even earlier it seems likely that it played a part in the creation of the Andalusian.

Garrano

Breed: Garrano (Minho)
Place of origin: Portugal (Minho—Trás os Montes)
Height at withers: 10.2–12.2 hands
Structure: mesomorphic
Colour: generally chestnut
Temperament: docile and calm
Aptitude: saddle and pack pony—farm work
Qualities: strong and resistant
Head: not large but rather heavy—profile straight—ears small—eyes large and lively
Neck: rather long
Body: withers not too high—back not always straight—croup sloping—tail set-on low—girth deep—abdomen rounded
Legs: strong and tough—shoulder straight—cannons short—joints broad—hoof well proportioned with strong horn

AVELIGNESE

Little is known about the very earliest origins of this ancient breed, but it seems likely that its more recent origins trace back either to a group of horses left behind by the Holy Roman Emperor Louis IV in 1330 on his return to Austria, or to a stallion that he had brought from the Kingdom of Burgundy to be given as a wedding gift to his son Louis V, on the occasion of his marriage, in 1342, to Princess Margaret Maultasch of the Tyrol. Another theory is that it was abandoned in the valleys of the Tyrol in 555 A.D. by the Ostrogoths as they fled from the Byzantine armies. This would help to explain the high percentage of Oriental blood in the breed. Its Arab derivation is also borne out by the shape of its head and profile and it is known positively that the breed benefited from Oriental blood in the mid-nineteenth century. The founding father of the present-day Avelignese breed is Folie (1874), sired by the Arab stallion El Bedavi XXII and out of a local mare. This breed originally comes from Avelengo in Alto Adige, but has now become distributed not only in various parts of Italy, but also in Switzerland, Germany (Bavaria) and especially Austria, where it is bred under the name of Haflinger, the German translation of Avelengo. In Austria a special brand is used for this horse depicting the edelweiss—the national flower—with an "H" in the centre. The Avelignese has a similar brand with the letters "HI." Because of its easy-going nature the Avelignese makes an excellent mount for beginners, and for trekking.

Breed: Avelignese (Haflinger)
Place of origin: Italy (Avelengo—Alto Adige)
Height at withers: 12.2–13.2 hands (mares); 12.3–14.3 hands (horses)
Weight: approx. 990 lb (450 kg)
Structure: mesomorphic
Colour: chestnut (preferably golden); forelock, mane and tail flaxen; blaze common; leg markings usually small
Temperament: docile and quiet
Aptitude: riding pony—medium-heavy draught—farm work
Qualities: good endurance when working, and in uncomfortable conditions—hardy—frugal—excellent in mountainous regions
Geographical distribution: Italy (especially Alto Adige), Austria (Tyrol), Germany (Bavaria)
Head: quite light and clean—very expressive—profile slightly snub—forehead broad—ears small and mobile—eyes bright and lively—groove between jaws open and clean—full forelock
Neck: broad at base and tapering—muscular—well set-on—mane full
Body: withers quite pronounced, broad and clean—back short, broad, muscular and straight—loins broad and short (preferably split)—croup wide and split, very muscular and reasonably sloping—tail well set-on and full—chest full and muscular, high and wide—girth deep with well rounded and arched ribs—abdomen well shaped and drawn up
Legs: short with well-developed muscles—shoulder well formed, muscular—joints large—forearm strong—cannon short and clean—thigh very muscular—hock clean and straight—pastern short—hoof well formed with strong horn—good natural stance

BARDIGIANO

This breed appeared to be descended from a horse that originated in Belgian Gaul, but which was then taken to the Appennine region of Emilia in Italy with the Barbarian hordes, in the wave of invasions that followed the fall of the Western Roman Empire. The breed has been recognized by a ministerial decree that approves the selection criteria and established the Stud Book in 1977, thus guaranteeing the perpetuation of the traditional definition of the Bardigiano (Bardi horse). This breed is particularly well suited to hilly and mountainous regions, and is a useful mount for trekking in areas where the terrain is rugged and demanding. Its appearance is reminiscent of the English Dales pony and the French Ariègeois both of which it closely resembles in terms of size.

Breed: Bardigiano (Bardi horse)
Place of origin: Italy (Bardi)
Height at withers: 13.1–14.2 hands (males less than 13.2 hands are not admitted)
Structure: mesomorphic
Colour: bay—brown—black; chestnut and light bay not admitted; bay with a blaze extending too far to the sides of the face not admitted; small stars and limited leg markings are tolerated
Temperament: quiet but quite highly strung—very docile
Aptitude: riding pony (trekking)—farm work—medium–heavy draught
Qualities: hardy—frugal—good endurance—sturdy and strong
Head: small—profile straight or snub—forehead broad—ears short and straight—forelock thick and full
Neck: a good length—broad at the base—arched—mane full and flowing
Body: withers broad and not very pronounced—back of medium length and straight—loins short, full and straight—croup wide and reasonably sloping—tail long and well set-on, full—chest broad, deep and muscular—girth deep—abdomen clean and well shaped
Legs: shoulder nicely sloping and of good length—well developed and muscular—forearm a good length—thighs muscular and rounded—cannon short—pasterns quite short—joints large and clean—hooves broad preferably with black horn, and solid—good natural stance

SARDINIAN

Little is known about the remote origins of this breed but its appearance suggests a strong Oriental influence. The first reliable historical references date back to 1845. This hardy pony lives in Sardinia in an inhospitable region consisting principally of an upland plateau rising to 2,000 ft (600 m) above sea level. The physical structure of this area, a combination of marble and basalt, certainly does not constitute an ideal habitat for the survival and development of any animal species but the dense, scrub-like vegetation with sparse grazing areas that briefly burst into life at the end of each spring are the surroundings in which the Sardinian pony lives in the wild state.

Breed: Sardinian
Place of origin: Italy (Sardinia)
Height at withers: 12.1–13 hands
Weight: 375–485 lb (170–220 kg)
Structure: mesomorphic
Colour: bay—brown—black—liver chestnut
Temperament: lively—highly-strung—headstrong—difficult to manage
Aptitude: farm work—riding pony
Qualities: hardy, with good endurance—nimble
Head: square—jaws heavy and pronounced—profile straight or slightly convex—full forelock
Neck: strong, with a full mane
Body: low-slung and compact—withers not very pronounced—back slightly hollow—croup sloping—tail set-on low
Legs: slender—shoulder fairly sloping—thighs not very muscular—pasterns long—foot small but neat and sure—natural stance often incorrect (cow-hocked)

Turkish

Bosnian

Sardinian

TURKISH PONY

The precise origins of this breed are obscure, but they are probably similar to those of other breeds that have been developing down the centuries in southern Europe. Because of the geographical situation of its native Turkey the Turkish pony may well have been influenced by Asian breeds and by the Arab horse. It is not a particularly handsome animal: its head is rather ordinary, with long ears; the neck is short and plump, the body thickset and the legs of medium length but with good bone.

Breed: Turkish
Place of origin: Turkey
Height at withers: 14–14.2 hands
Structure: mesomorphic
Colour: bay—brown—grey
Temperament: calm
Aptitude: pack horse—farm work
Qualities: willing—good endurance—energetic

BOSNIAN

It is thought that this pony probably originates from the Tarpan, a theory supported by its similarity to the Polish Hucul. A certain elegance in its appearance also suggests a considerable Oriental influence. Because of its calm temperament and particular aptitudes, the Bosnian pony is in steady demand by farmers. Yugoslavia has hence taken a direct interest in the breed, handling the selection of all stallions and supervising mating, while private concerns are only authorized to handle mares. This close involvement of the state reflects the importance this breed holds in its native Yugoslavia.

Breed: Bosnian
Place of origin: Yugoslavia (Bosnia—Herzegovina)
Height at withers: 13–14.2 hands
Structure: mesomorphic
Colour: bay—brown—black—grey—chestnut—dun
Temperament: docile
Aptitude: riding pony—farm work—pack horse—light draught
Qualities: determined—undemanding—good endurance
Head: slightly heavy—profile straight—ears small—full forelock
Neck: quite short and muscular—full mane
Body: withers not very pronounced—back straight—croup slightly sloping—chest wide—girth broad and deep
Legs: quite short but well muscled—shoulder long and nicely sloping—joints large and clean—tendons strong—foot well shaped

PINDOS

This very old breed, which has without any doubt benefited from infusions of Oriental blood, is bred in the mountainous regions of Thessaly and Epirus, where it originated. Strong and hardy, this pony is especially well suited to farm work in hilly, upland areas and is also used as a sturdy riding pony. The mares of this breed are frequently used to produce mules. Overall the Pindos is a well-built animal, with a compact, well-proportioned appearance.

Breed: Pindos
Place of origin: Greece (Thessaly and Epirus)
Height at withers: 12–13 hands
Structure: mesomorphic
Colour: bay—black—grey
Temperament: quiet
Aptitude: riding and pack pony—light draught
Qualities: good endurance when under stress
Head: well proportioned and well set-on—profile straight or slightly convex—forehead broad
Neck: quite long and well set-on
Body: withers not very pronounced—back short and straight—croup sloping—girth deep
Legs: long—shoulder very straight and quite muscular—good natural stance

SKYROS

This "primitive" pony, from the island of the same name, bears some resemblance to the Tarpan. In its native surroundings it is used principally for farm work and as a pack pony, while ponies that leave the island can, if they are properly reared and fed, be turned into good riding ponies, particularly suitable for children. It is certainly not an attractive-looking pony, owing to its poorly-shaped shoulders and cow hocks, but it is undoubtedly one of the few breeds still in existence to remain largely uncontaminated by infusions of foreign blood.

Breed: Skyros
Place of origin: Greece (island of Skyros)
Height at withers: 9.1–11 hands
Structure: mesomorphic
Colour: grey—bay—brown—dun
Temperament: quiet
Aptitude: riding and pack pony
Qualities: reliable
Head: small with a straight profile—not well set-on—forehead broad—ears small—eyes small
Neck: short and thick, and not well set-on
Body: withers not very high—back short and straight—croup not well developed and sloping—tail set-on low—chest and girth poorly developed
Legs: slender—shoulder short and straight, poorly shaped—poor natural stance

PENEIA

The pleasing, well-balanced appearance of this pony clearly reveals its Oriental origins. The breed originates from the province of Peneia in the Peloponnese where it is still widely used for farm work, especially as a pack pony. It is a tireless and willing worker, and because of these qualities stallions are used for the production of half-breeds (hinnies), which also have good endurance when under strain.

Breed: Peneia
Place of origin: Greece (province of Peneia in the Peloponnese)
Height at withers: 10.1–14.1 hands
Structure: mesomorphic
Colour: bay—chestnut—black—grey (other varieties are also found)
Temperament: quiet
Aptitude: riding and pack pony—light draught
Qualities: willing—frugal—good endurance when working
Head: well proportioned—profile tending to be convex—ears small
Neck: nicely proportioned and well set-on
Body: withers not very prominent—back short and straight—croup sloping—tail set-on quite low—well-developed haunches—chest wide—girth quite deep
Legs: long—shoulder muscular and nicely sloping—foot small but with strong horn

Pindos

Skyros

Peneia

HUCUL

The origins of this pony are very similar to those of the Konik, to which it bears a close resemblance. In fact, besides being descended from the Tarpan, the Hucul has also benefited from the introduction of Arab blood, especially during the last century. Formal breeding of this pony dates back to the nineteenth century, and has been developing in various centers, one of which is in England. This undemanding animal with excellent endurance, carries out a number of useful tasks, especially in mountainous regions. It has a powerful, but nevertheless attractive appearance.

Breed: Hucul (Carpathian pony)
Place of origin: Poland (Carpathians)
Height at withers: 12.1–13.1 hands
Structure: mesomorphic
Colour: mouse dun—dun—tawny dun—bay—grey (rare)
Temperament: quiet—docile—tolerant
Aptitude: light draught—pack pony—farm work
Qualities: frugal—willing—good endurance
Head: well proportioned—profile slightly snub—ears small and pointed—eyes small—nostrils wide—full forelock
Neck: well shaped and a nice length—mane long and full
Body: withers quite pronounced—back long and straight—flanks well formed—croup sloping—tail set-on low, but full and flowing—chest and girth wide and deep
Legs: well muscled with solid joints—shoulder quite sloping—cannon long—foot small with tough horn

KONIK

In Polish the name of this sturdy pony means simply "little horse." The Konik is undoubtedly the closest living descendant of the Tarpan, even though its outward appearance is considerably more refined, probably as a result of infusions of Arab blood. However, if physically it is some way removed from its progenitor from the steppes, as far as its endurance and its undemanding nature are concerned it is virtually the same animal. Because of its many qualities the Konik has played an important part in the formation of numerous other breeds of Polish and Russian horses and ponies.

Breed: Konik
Place of origin: Poland
Height at withers: 12.3–13.3 hands
Structure: mesomorphic
Colour: mouse dun and dun (with eel stripe—mane and tail darker coloured or black—lower limbs dark or black, sometimes with zebra markings)—grey—bay (with bluish highlights)
Temperament: quiet and willing, but independent and fond of its freedom—sometimes quite stubborn
Aptitude: farm work
Qualities: frugal and long-lived
Head: slightly heavy—profile slightly convex—ears small and pointed—nostrils wide—forelock full—quite well set-on
Neck: quite long but broad and muscular—mane full and long
Body: withers quite pronounced—back short—loins well set-on—back straight—croup sloping—tail set-on quite low, but full and flowing—chest wide—girth deep
Legs: solid, with large, clean joints—shoulder very sloping—tendons strong—foot small and well shaped

VIATKA

A descendant of the old Klepper and the Konik, this breed has good conformation and is small but solidly built, making it particularly suitable for light farm work, as well as for drawing troikas. It has a brisk trot, and although its action does not cover much ground, this gives it an advantage particularly in deep, heavy snow. Because of its various useful features and good qualities, the breeding of this pony is closely supervised by the state.

Breed: Viatka
Place of origin: USSR (Baltic States)
Height at withers: 13–14 hands
Structure: mesomorphic
Colour: bay—grey—roan—mouse dun—dun (possibly with eel stripe and zebra markings on the legs, with black mane and tail)
Temperament: quiet—energetic—willing
Aptitude: farm work—light draught
Qualities: lively and fast
Head: not large but quite long, with heavy jaws—profile slightly snub—ears of medium length, set well apart—eyes bright and lively—nostrils wide—full forelock—quite well set-on
Neck: of medium length but broad and muscular—mane long and full
Body: withers quite pronounced and broad—back long and straight—loins broad and powerful—croup quite sloping and muscular—tail set-on quite low but full and flowing—chest wide—girth deep—abdomen drawn in
Legs: solid—good muscular development—shoulder sloping and muscular—joints large and clean—cannons quite short—tendons strong—pasterns long—hooves well formed

Konik

Hucul

Viatka

KAZAKH

This pony bears a certain resemblance to the Asiatic wild horse, even though it is relatively more refined in appearance as a result of a consistent input of Don blood. The Kazakh is capable of finding sufficient food for itself even in the most arid of places on the edge of the desert or during the winter months when the ground is covered with snow. In addition it has very good resistance to both cold and fatigue. Two different versions are bred and reared: the Dzhabe and the Adaev. The Dzhabe has a rather coarse head, a short, muscular neck and is usually bay or liver chestnut in colour, although brown, black, grey or mouse dun are also found. The Adaev has a distinctive light head, a small, compact body, straight back and prominent withers and is usually grey, bay, chestnut or dun. The Adaev type has been influenced by the Akhal-Teké, the Iomud and the Karabair, which have given it a gentler appearance, but have also made it less suited to the type of living conditions in which the Dzhabe usually has to survive. In more recent years a third type of Kazakh has been gradually developing, issuing from crosses between mares of this breed and Don, English Thoroughbred, Russian Trotter and Orlov stallions. Similarly, the Deliboz, which boasts Arab, Persian and Turkmene blood in its ancestry, has also been influenced by the Kazakh, which has recently been introduced to the breed, along with the Karabakh. The Deliboz, which as a rule has a grey or bay coat, is a riding and pack pony, which is reared in Azerbaijan and used for long distance rides.

Breed: Kazakh
Place of origin: USSR (Kazakhstan)
Height at withers: 12.2–13.2
Structure: mesomorphic
Colour: bay—brown—black—chestnut—dun—mouse dun—grey
Temperament: willing—quiet
Aptitude: riding pony
Qualities: undemanding—good endurance, especially over long distances

Zemaituka

Bashkir

Kazakh

ZEMAITUKA

The characteristic eel stripe, present on the coat of this pony, gives a clear indication of its prehistoric origins. It probably descends from the Asiatic wild horse and, despite its appearance, there is no evidence of Arab blood flowing in its veins. The Zemaituka is certainly not a particularly attractive pony, but it is strong and frugal, and capable of surviving on very poor quality food that would be refused by most other horses. In addition, it has good resistance to cold and fatigue and can cover more than 40 miles (60 km) a day.

Breed: Zemaituka
Place of origin: USSR (Lithuania)
Height at withers: 13–13.2 hands
Structure: mesomorphic
Colour: bay—brown—black—mouse dun—dun—yellow dun; eel stripe present
Temperament: energetic—quiet—willing
Aptitude: farm work—light draught
Qualities: very resistant to fatigue—frugal
Head: of average size and quite coarse—profile straight—forehead wide—ears small—eyes expressive—fairly well set-on
Neck: of medium length and broad—muscular
Body: withers low and of medium length—back short and straight—croup sloping—tail set-on low—girth deep
Legs: short—fairly good muscular development—shoulder straight but well muscled—joints (especially the hocks) rather poor—pasterns a good length and nicely sloping—foot well formed with tough horn

BASHKIR

This is a sturdy pony with a fairly attractive appearance. There are, in fact, two distinct types of pony, one of which inhabits the steppes and the other, which is smaller and lighter, the mountains. Both types make good riding and light draught horses, with the heavier, "steppe" type being used for drawing troikas. Members of the breed have sometimes been improved by crossing with saddle horses such as the Budyonny or the Don, or with draught horses like the Ardennes, or trotting breeds.

Breed: Bashkir (Bashkirsky)
Place of origin: USSR
Height at withers: 13.1–14 hands
Structure: mesomorphic
Colour: bay—chestnut—dun
Temperament: docile and quiet
Aptitude: riding pony—light draught
Qualities: strong, with good endurance
Head: quite heavy—profile straight—ears small—jaws pronounced—full forelock
Neck: short and strong—mane long and handsome
Body: withers quite low—back quite long but sometimes slightly depressed—croup slightly sloping—tail set-on low but full and flowing—chest wide and deep
Legs: short and solid—shoulder nicely sloping—foot small with tough horn

MANIPURI

This ancient breed was probably introduced into India in about 700 A.D. by invading Tartars, who may also have been responsible for introducing the game of polo, although another school of thought maintains that the Chinese were the inventors of this game. Polo, which was already common in Asia, and originated some 2,000 years ago, became very popular with British colonials who saw it being played for the first time in the mid-nineteenth century using ponies of this breed. Even today, in its country of origin, the Manipuri pony is still used for this game, while in Europe and the United States taller and faster horses are now used, especially those breeds that have good acceleration over short distances. The Manipuri has a fairly elegant bearing, combined with well-balanced features that have been handed down from the Arab, from whose influence it has undoubtedly benefited.

Breed: Manipuri
Place of origin: India (Assam—Manipur)
Height at withers: 11–13 hands
Structure: mesomorphic
Colour: bay—brown—grey—chestnut
Temperament: docile but energetic
Aptitude: riding pony
Qualities: fast, with good endurance
Head: light and well proportioned—ears good and straight—eyes almond-shaped—full forelock
Neck: well shaped—full mane
Body: withers fairly pronounced—back straight—croup slightly sloping—tail well set-on—girth deep
Legs: well built and solid—shoulder nicely sloping—foot well proportioned and strong

TIBETAN

This pony is probably descended from the Mongolian and Chinese ponies, although it also has certain features in common with the Spiti and the Bhutia. It is strong and sturdy, with an attractive appearance and its extremely versatile nature makes it suitable for farm work, or as a riding or pack pony.

Breed: Tibetan (Nanfan)
Place of origin: Tibet
Height at withers: approx. 12.2 hands
Structure: mesomorphic
Colour: many varieties (dun is common)
Temperament: docile but energetic—lively
Aptitude: riding pony—pack pony—farm work
Qualities: strong, with good endurance
Head: not too large but with fairly pronounced jaws—profile straight—forehead broad—ears small and pointed—full forelock
Neck: short and muscular—mane very full and long
Body: withers not very high—back short—loins wide and powerful—croup rounded—tail flowing—girth deep
Legs: short and solid—well muscled—good bone, joints sound—shoulder fairly straight—hoof well formed

KATHIAWARI AND MARWARI

These two ponies have many features in common, and can thus be described together. They both descend from native ponies crossed with Arab horses that appear to have swum ashore from a cargo ship wrecked off the west coast of India. Having regained their freedom, these horses joined up with indigenous ponies standing only 13.2 hands high, which were hardy and frugal, but rather coarse in conformation. The influence of Arab blood considerably improved the pony's appearance but did not adversely affect its endurance and frugal nature. These ponies are extremely versatile and can be used for a wide variety of tasks.

Breeds: Kathiawari and Marwari
Place of origin: India (Kathiawar and Marwar)
Height at withers: approx. 14 hands
Structure: meso-dolichomorphic
Colour: bay—brown—grey—chestnut—dun—part colours
Temperament: unpredictable but determined
Aptitude: riding and pack pony—light draught—farm work
Qualities: good endurance—frugal
Head: fairly well proportioned—profile straight—ears pointed with tips turned inwards
Neck: slender and of medium length
Body: withers pronounced—back long and straight—croup sloping—girth deep
Legs: slender and graceful—well structured—shoulder quite straight—foot small and well formed—correct natural stance

Kathiawari

Tibetan

SPITI

The geographical origin of this pony, high in the Himalayas, explains its similarity to the Tibetan pony, from the same region. The Spiti is bred principally for use as a pack animal, a crucial job, which it performs well in this type of rugged terrain. It does not adapt well to living in lowland conditions, since it does not stand up well to humid, suffocating heat; it is a sturdy and vigorous mountain pony with a well-balanced appearance.

Breed: Spiti
Place of origin: India (Himalayas)
Height at withers: approx. 12 hands
Structure: mesomorphic
Colour: grey
Temperament: temperamental
Aptitude: pack pony
Qualities: strong, with good endurance
Head: slightly heavy—profile straight—ears small and pointed—full forelock
Neck: short—mane full and flowing
Body: withers low—back short—loins powerful—croup slightly sloping—tail long and full—girth deep
Legs: short and solid—good bone—well muscled—shoulder sloping and muscular—joints large and strong—foot roundish with strong horn

Spiti

Manipuri

MONGOLIAN

The Mongolian pony descends directly from the Asiatic wild horse, one of the oldest breeds, which has had a great influence on all the Asian breeds. This was made possible by the warmongering and nomadic nature of the various Mongol peoples, who made full use of these animals in their migrations and invasions. The Mongolian pony has many points in common with the Chinese and the Tibetan ponies, and is still bred and reared by nomadic tribes living in Mongolia. It is an extremely versatile animal, and well suited to a wide range of tasks. The breed includes a number of varieties which have developed in relation to the differing environmental conditions existing in the extensive habitat, varying breeding and rearing techniques, and contact with other breeds. The most sought-after variety is the Wuchumutsin, which is reared where the terrain offers better and lusher grazing. Another variety is called the Heilung Chiang, with its distinctive convex profile running from the forehead to the muzzle. There are three more varieties, the Hailar, the Sanho and the Sanpeitze, which are all considerably taller (14–15 hands) and which have been produced by the use of Russian stallions. The Ili, which is reared as a riding and pack pony, has similar origins.

Breed: Mongolian
Place of origin: Mongolia
Height at withers: 12.1–14 hands
Structure: mesomorphic
Colour: bay—brown—black—mouse dun—dun
Temperament: tolerant and active
Aptitude: riding and pack pony—farm work—light draught
Qualities: good endurance—frugal
Head: heavy, with a straight profile—ears short—eyes small—full forelock
Neck: quite short and thickset—mane full and flowing
Body: withers short and low—loins short—back straight, quite short and strong—croup long and sloping—tail full and long—girth deep
Legs: solid with hard, strong bone—well muscled—shoulder quite sloping and muscular—joints large—hoof rounded and hard

BURMESE

Bred by tribes living in Shan State in eastern Burma, this pony has many features in common with the Manipuri pony, even though today it is taller—a distinction that has come about only recently. In addition, when compared with the Manipuri, the Burmese pony is not as quick off the mark, has less speed overall and slower reflexes. In spite of this, and often for want of a better substitute, it was used in the past as a polo pony by British officers stationed in these parts. Compared with the Manipuri it is aesthetically somewhat coarser, with a longer back and a less sloping shoulder, features which suggest that this breed has not been so greatly influenced by Arab blood.

Breed: Burmese (Shan)
Place of origin: Burma
Height at withers: approx. 13 hands
Structure: mesomorphic
Colour: bay—brown—grey—black—chestnut
Temperament: not altogether reliable—often unpredictable—active
Aptitude: pack and riding pony
Qualities: strong, with good endurance
Head: light with a straight profile—eyes almond-shaped
Neck: well proportioned
Body: withers not very pronounced—back straight—croup sloping—girth deep
Legs: slender but strong—shoulder not very sloping—foot small with strong horn

BHUTIA

This breed, from the Indian Himalayas, closely resembles the Spiti and the Tibetan ponies from the same region, in both type and conformation. It is a strong and hardy animal, particularly suited to harsh, rugged terrain.

Breed: Bhutia
Place of origin: India (Himalayas)
Height at withers: 13–13.2 hands
Structure: mesomorphic
Colour: grey
Temperament: unpredictable
Aptitude: pack pony
Qualities: good endurance—frugal—ideal in mountainous regions

CHINESE

There is a very close resemblance between this pony and many other pony breeds scattered throughout the Far East. In fact there are legitimate doubts as to whether the Chinese pony is an actual breed in itself, or whether it merely represents an equine population with features similar to other groups with which it has come into contact in the past. Its similarity to the wild Mongolian pony shows that, like all other Asian breeds, it derives originally from the Asiatic wild horse. The conformation of the Chinese pony is poor, and the presence of certain "primitive" characteristics such as zebra markings and an eel stripe, testify to the limited evolutionary level reached.

Breed: Chinese
Place of origin: China
Height at withers: 12–13.2 hands
Structure: mesomorphic
Colour: all varieties—dun is quite common
Temperament: quite rebellious
Aptitude: riding and pack pony—farm work
Qualities: good endurance—vigorous—suitable for mountainous regions

TIMOR

This small and agile pony, reminiscent of the Greek Skyros pony, also comes from an island and has thus been subject to strict isolation, a factor which has undoubtedly contributed to the conservation of the "primitive" type. It is not particularly handsome, but on the island of Timor it is invaluable to the local population, both as a draught and riding pony, and for lighter forms of farm work.

Breed: Timor
Place of origin: Indonesia (island of Timor)
Height at withers: 9.1–11 hands
Structure: mesomorphic
Colour: bay—brown—black
Temperament: docile and willing
Aptitude: riding pony—light farm work—light draught
Qualities: good endurance—nimble
Head: large and heavy—profile straight—ears short—nostrils wide
Neck: short and muscular—broad at the base
Body: withers quite pronounced—back short—croup slightly sloping—girth deep
Legs: short and solid—shoulders quite straight—foot small with strong horn

BALI

Bred on the Indonesian island of Bali, which has become a thriving tourist resort in recent years, this pony appears to be totally unaffected by everything going on around it, and continues its traditional role as a pack and riding pony both in coastal and inland areas. In fact on the beaches of Bali it can be seen not only giving tourist rides, but also transporting loads of broken coral, which is used in the building industry. Its bristly mane calls to mind that of the original Asiatic wild horse. As a type it is not very far removed from other Indonesian ponies and, in addition, its dun coat with primitive eel stripe attests to its undoubtedly remote origins.

Breed: Bali
Place of origin: Indonesia (island of Bali)
Height at withers: 12–13 hands
Structure: mesomorphic
Coats: dun (eel stripe—mane, tail and extremities dark)
Temperament: docile and quiet
Aptitude: riding and pack pony
Qualities: strong and frugal

Chinese pony

Timor

Bali

SANDALWOOD

Like the Batak, to which it bears a marked resemblance, this pony has probably also been influenced by Arab blood. A native of the Indonesian Sumba and Sumbawa islands, this breed is named after one of their principal exports: sandalwood. The Sandalwood has very good endurance over long distances and is used in local bareback races ranging from 2½–3 miles (4,000–5,000 m) in which it performs well.

Breed: Sandalwood
Place of origin: Indonesia (islands of Sumba and Sumbawa)
Height at withers: 12.1–13.1 hands
Structure: mesomorphic
Colour: many varieties
Temperament: quiet but energetic
Aptitude: riding pony—light draught—pack pony—farm work
Qualities: good endurance—speed

Sandalwood

JAVA

Originally from Java, one of the largest of the Indonesian islands, this pony is quite similar to the Timor, although in comparison it looks somewhat more distinguished and has slightly better conformation. It is also taller and stronger with a more sloping shoulder than that of the Timor and is used principally for pulling the two-wheeled taxis on the island.

Breed: Java
Place of origin: Indonesia (island of Java)
Height at withers: approx. 12 hands
Structure: mesomorphic
Colour: various
Temperament: docile and willing
Aptitude: light draught—pack pony—farm work—riding pony
Qualities: strong, with good endurance

SUMBA AND SUMBAWA

These ponies, from the Indonesian islands of the same names, bear a close resemblance to the Mongolian and Chinese ponies, which would suggest that all three have common origins. It is possible that they were introduced to the islands in very early times by the ancient Chinese. Of the two the Sumbawa is the more docile, and can be ridden bareback without a bit and without reins.

Breed: Sumba and Sumbawa
Place of origin: Indonesia (islands of Sumba and Sumbawa)
Height at withers: approx. 12 hands
Structure: mesomorphic
Colour: dun (eel stripe—mane, tail and extremities dark) and other varieties
Temperament: docile and willing
Aptitude: riding and pack pony
Qualities: good endurance
Head: slightly on the heavy side—profile straight—eyes almond-shaped
Neck: short and broad
Body: withers not very pronounced—back long—croup sloping—girth quite deep
Legs: short and strong—fairly slender—shoulder quite straight—foot well proportioned

BASUTO

This breed is derived from the Cape Horse which was introduced into Basutoland (now Lesotho) probably during the invasion of this territory by the Zulus around 1822. The Cape Horse itself was descended from Barb and Arab horses imported in 1653 by the Dutch East India Company. At the beginning of the nineteenth century, before they were introduced into Basutoland, these horses benefited from further infusions of Arab as well as English Thoroughbred blood. As a breed the Basuto pony dates back to about 1830, but the random way in which it was bred, combined with unfavourable climatic conditions, has gradually transformed both the physique and character of this animal, increasing its courage and endurance, but causing a degeneration in type. It was used in the Boer War and also as a race horse and polo pony, which is somewhat hard to believe in view of its present-day appearance. It is powerful and has good endurance, easily capable of covering 65 miles (100 km) a day with a rider weighing over 220 lb (100 kg) in the saddle. This pony manifests a clear tendency to revert to its primitive origins as will any breed that has been carefully created and reared by man if subjected to adverse conditions, or simply left to its own devices. In due course, natural selection will take over and the breed will

BATAK

A native of the island of Sumatra, the largest Indonesian island, this breed represents the most sought-after and valuable pony in the entire archipelago. The Batak is the result of crosses between specially imported Arab stallions and selected mares belonging to different breeds from other islands, and is a sturdy but elegant pony, reasonably tall and with good conformation. The best stallions of this breed are sent to other islands to improve the local breeds. In Sumatra another breed is also reared, called the Gayoe, but this is a heavier animal than the Batak, with a less lively temperament.

Breed: Batak
Place of origin: Indonesia (island of Sumatra)
Height at withers: 12–13 hands
Structure: mesomorphic
Colour: many varieties
Temperament: docile and lively
Aptitude: riding pony
Qualities: frugal
Head: light, with a slightly concave profile—full forelock
Neck: well shaped—arched
Body: withers quite pronounced—back short—croup slightly sloping—tail well set-on—girth deep
Legs: solid and slender—well muscled—shoulder nicely sloping—joints and tendons hard and clean—foot well formed

degenerate to its original form, much better suited to ensuring the survival of the species.

Breed: Basuto
Place of origin: Basutoland (Lesotho)
Height at withers: approx. 14.2 hands
Structure: mesomorphic
Colour: chestnut—bay—brown—grey
Temperament: reliable—brave—tolerant
Aptitude: riding pony
Qualities: good endurance
Head: fairly well proportioned but with slightly heavy jaws—profile straight—eyes expressive
Neck: long and not very muscular
Body: withers quite pronounced—back long and quite straight—croup sloping—tail set-on low—girth deep
Legs: slender but strong—quite short—shoulder quite straight and not very muscular—joints clean—foot has strong horn

CASPIAN

This old breed had probably already been domesticated in 3000 B.C., by the peoples of Mesopotamia who used it for a variety of tasks. It is an attractive looking pony with a superb bearing, possibly suggesting that it may be one of the progenitors of the Arab horse. Until recently this breed was thought to have been extinct since the tenth century, but in 1965 a number of living specimens were discovered in the Elburz mountains and on the shores of the Caspian Sea in northern Iran. There is an important and telling similarity between this pony and the miniature horse of Mesopotamia. Finds unearthed near Kermanshah also clearly show that both the head and the bones are very similar in size and structure to the ancient miniature horse of Mesopotamia.

Breed: Caspian
Place of origin: Iran
Height at withers: 9.2–11.2 hands
Structure: meso-dolichomorphic
Colour: chestnut—bay—grey; white markings on the head and legs in exceptional cases
Temperament: docile and quiet
Aptitude: riding pony
Qualities: strong with good endurance—good jumper
Head: small with tapered muzzle—profile straight—ears short—eyes large—nostrils wide—full forelock
Neck: muscular—slightly arched—long, full mane
Body: withers quite pronounced—back short and straight—croup slightly sloping—tail well set-on and full—girth deep
Legs: well built and solid—good bones and joints—shoulder nicely sloping—tendons set well apart and strong—hoof small and strong

SABLE ISLAND PONY

This pony is bred and reared in the wild state on Sable Island, which lies about 200 miles (300 km) off the coast of Nova Scotia. Its presence on the island is associated with the importation of a group of predominantly French animals which found their way north from New England at the start of the eighteenth century. The breed lives in small herds consisting of between six and eight mares and one stallion. Despite the inhospitable conditions on the island, which has very little natural vegetation, a complete absence of trees and a harsh climate, especially in winter, this pony has managed to survive and, by means of natural selection, become incredibly tough and hardy. The small and wiry appearance generally leaves much to be desired, but of the roughly 300 ponies currently in existence there are one or two good specimens that stand out.

NIGERIAN HORSE

This breed compensates for its lack of aesthetic qualities with its good character and remarkably hardy constitution. It is almost certainly descended from the Barb, which was very probably introduced into Nigeria by nomadic peoples, a hypothesis which is backed up by the markedly sloping conformation of the croup. In appearance it is rather compact with poorly developed hindquarters.

Breed: Nigerian horse
Place of origin: Nigeria
Height at withers: 14–14.2 hands
Structure: mesomorphic
Colour: all types, not clearly defined
Temperament: willing and docile
Aptitude: riding and pack pony—light draught
Qualities: strong in relation to its size
Head: quite flat, with a straight profile—ears small and straight
Neck: short, not striking
Body: withers quite pronounced—back rather short and straight—croup sloping—girth quite deep
Legs: hard, of medium length—shoulder nicely sloping and well shaped—foot has strong horn

AMERICAN WELSH PONY

This breed, which was developed in the United States, is similar in appearance to the original European breed, although there are certain differences, especially with regard to the limits imposed on the height at the withers. A systematic use of original blood, assured by the importation of stallions from Wales, has enabled breeders to remain quite close to the basic type and avoid undesirable degeneration.

Breed: American Welsh Pony
Place of origin: United States
Height at withers: 12.1 (maximum) for section A; 12.2–14 hands for section B
Structure: mesomorphic
Colour: all varieties (except part colours)
Temperament: intelligent—lively—patient—courageous
Aptitude: riding pony—light draught
Qualities: well suited for children to ride

Breed: Sable Island pony
Place of origin: Canada (Sable Island)
Height at withers: approx. 14 hands
Structure: mesomorphic
Colour: bay—brown—grey—black—chestnut
Temperament: quite docile if domesticated and trained young
Aptitude: riding pony—light draught
Qualities: strong—frugal
Head: heavy—profile straight—forehead broad—ears quite large with the tips turned inwards
Neck: quite short—broad at the base
Body: withers quite prominent—back short and straight—croup sloping—tail long but set-on rather low—girth quite full but not too deep—abdomen bulky
Legs: shoulder quite straight—cannons short—hoof small

AMERICAN SHETLAND

Developed in the United States by the selective breeding of high-quality animals imported from Europe, the American Shetland type is taller and lighter than its island-dwelling ancestor, and resembles a miniature Hackney. The American pony displays a marked aptitude for light draught work and is capable of drawing up to twice its own weight, something which is not immediately evident from its actual physical structure. Its gait also calls to mind that of the Hackney, because both have a very high-stepping trot. In North America the breeding and rearing of the American Shetland Pony have achieved very high levels of efficiency and these are reflected by the going prices on the horse market.

Breed: American Shetland
Place of origin: United States
Height at withers: approx. 10 hands (not more than 11.2 hands)
Weight: approx. 330 lb (150 kg)
Structure: mesomorphic
Colour: almost every variety
Temperament: lively and intelligent
Aptitude: riding pony—light draught
Qualities: flowing, elegant action
Head: light—profile straight or slightly snub—ears small—full forelock
Neck: well set-on—well proportioned and elegantly carried—quite arched—full mane
Body: withers quite pronounced—back straight—croup sloping—chest well developed—girth full and deep—abdomen drawn in
Legs: shoulder long and nicely sloping—forearm and thigh quite long—joints clean and solid—tendons set well apart—foot well formed—good natural stance

Pony of the Americas

Assateague

American Shetland

Breed: Pony of the Americas
Place of origin: United States
Height at withers: 11.2–13 hands
Structure: meso-dolichomorphic
Colour: the same as the Appaloosa
Temperament: quiet and docile
Aptitude: riding pony
Qualities: speed—good endurance—an able jumper—versatility
Geographical distribution: USA—Canada
Head: in proportion with the rest of the body—profile slightly dished—ears of medium size, straight and pointed—eyes large and prominent
Neck: well formed—slightly arched
Body: withers prominent—back short and straight—loins broad and well muscled—croup long, muscular and rounded (tendency to be horizontal)—tail well set-on—girth full and deep
Legs: solid and well formed—good bone and joints—well muscled—shoulder nicely sloping—tendons strong—pasterns nicely sloping—foot well proportioned, broad and high at the heel, with the hoof striped vertically

ASSATEAGUE AND CHINCOTEAGUE

According to one theory, these breeds descend from a group of horses that survived shipwrecks at the beginning of the colonial period in America. The island of Assateague, lying off the coast of Virginia and Maryland, is uninhabited by man, providing an ideal environment for these animals to reproduce without interference, although interbreeding has caused a certain degree of regression giving the modern animal a rather stunted appearance. Every year, on the last Thursday and Friday in July a group of ponies is swum across the channel separating the two islands to be sold at an auction held on Chincoteague. These ponies have a rather elongated head which makes them look more like small horses than true ponies.

Breed: Assateague and Chincoteague
Place of origin: United States (Assateague and Chincoteague islands)
Height at withers: approx. 12 hands
Structure: mesomorphic
Colour: all varieties—piebald and skewbald are quite common
Temperament: rebellious and stubborn
Aptitude: light draught—riding pony
Qualities: good endurance in bad weather

PONY OF THE AMERICAS

This breed with its distinctive spotted coat like that of the Appaloosa was founded as recently as 1956. Its progenitor was a horse named Black Hand, foaled out of an Appaloosa mare, crossed with a Shetland stallion and was an exact miniature copy of its mother. The breed is now registered and subjects belonging to it must keep to a very precise set of standards. In practical terms the conformation of the Pony of the Americas should be halfway between the Quarter Horse and the Arab, and must have the typical coat. In Canada and the United States there are now 24 clubs and over 12,000 members of the breed. The Pony of the Americas is an excellent trotting pony and a good jumper, which is why it is used in competitions for young riders; it is also a good trekking mount. Because of its endurance and speed it is often used, again by younger riders, for long distance riding and flat racing. Its head is similar to that of an Arab and it has good conformation and an elegant bearing.

GALICEÑO

This breed is probably descended from the Garrano pony that originated in the Spanish region of Galicia and was taken across the ocean to Mexico in the sixteenth century by the Spanish *conquistadores*. It has a solid, compact build. It is used in Mexico for farm work and as a pack and draught pony. Since 1959 it has spread throughout the United States where it is used as a riding pony for children, and has shown itself to be a good jumper in events reserved for younger competitors.

Breed: Galiceño
Place of origin: Mexico
Height at withers: 12–13.2 hands
Weight: 620–705 lb (280–320 kg)
Structure: meso-dolichomorphic
Colour: bay—black—chestnut—dun; piebald, skewbald and albino coats are not admissible
Temperament: docile and courageous—intelligent—versatile
Aptitude: riding pony—light draught—farm work
Qualities: speed and endurance
Geographical distribution: Mexico—USA
Head: of average size—profile straight—eyes expressive and lively
Neck: quite short and muscular
Body: withers quite pronounced—back short—croup sloping—chest narrow but deep
Legs: strong—shoulder quite straight—leg long—foot small—natural stance not always correct (open at the back and the front)

FALABELLA

The Falabella, which at under 7 hands is the smallest breed in the world, is derived from the Shetland pony. It was developed by the Falabella family at their Recreo de Roca Ranch near Buenos Aires, and is the result of careful selection that concentrated on the elimination of larger animals. Its appearance is more that of a miniature horse than a pony, and this is possibly due to a very small contribution made by the English Thoroughbred. It is a well-proportioned animal with a graceful action making it a popular pet in North America as well.

Breed: Falabella
Place of origin: Argentina
Height at withers: less than 7 hands
Structure: mesomorphic
Colour: very varied (typical Appaloosa coats are sought after)
Temperament: quiet—intelligent
Aptitude: riding pony—light draught
Qualities: very strong for its size
Head: small—profile straight or slightly dished—ears small—eyes large and gentle—nostrils wide
Neck: well formed—mane full
Body: withers quite high—back short and straight—croup slightly sloping—tail well set-on and flowing—girth deep
Legs: quite slender and well built—shoulder sloping and well built—foot well formed

AUSTRALIAN PONY

The head of this pony is similar to that of the Arab horse, which has undoubtedly played a part in the formation of the breed, along with others such as the Welsh Mountain pony, the Exmoor, the Shetland, the Timor pony and the English Thoroughbred. The basic type closely resembles the Welsh Mountain pony. This is a small horse with distinctive rounded and well-muscled hindquarters, and a flowing and attractive action.

Breed: Australian pony
Place of origin: Australia
Height at withers: 12–14 hands
Structure: mesomorphic
Colour: many varieties—grey (most common)—part colours not admitted
Temperament: well balanced
Aptitude: riding pony
Qualities: strong and healthy—elegant movements—well suited for young children
Head: light—profile straight—ears well proportioned and pointed—full forelock
Neck: well formed and well set-on—arched—mane not very full
Body: withers quite high—back short and straight—croup sloping—chest well developed—girth full and deep
Legs: short, with good bone—shoulder long and nicely sloping—joints large—cannons short—pasterns nicely sloping and a good length—tendons clean and strong—foot well formed—good natural stance

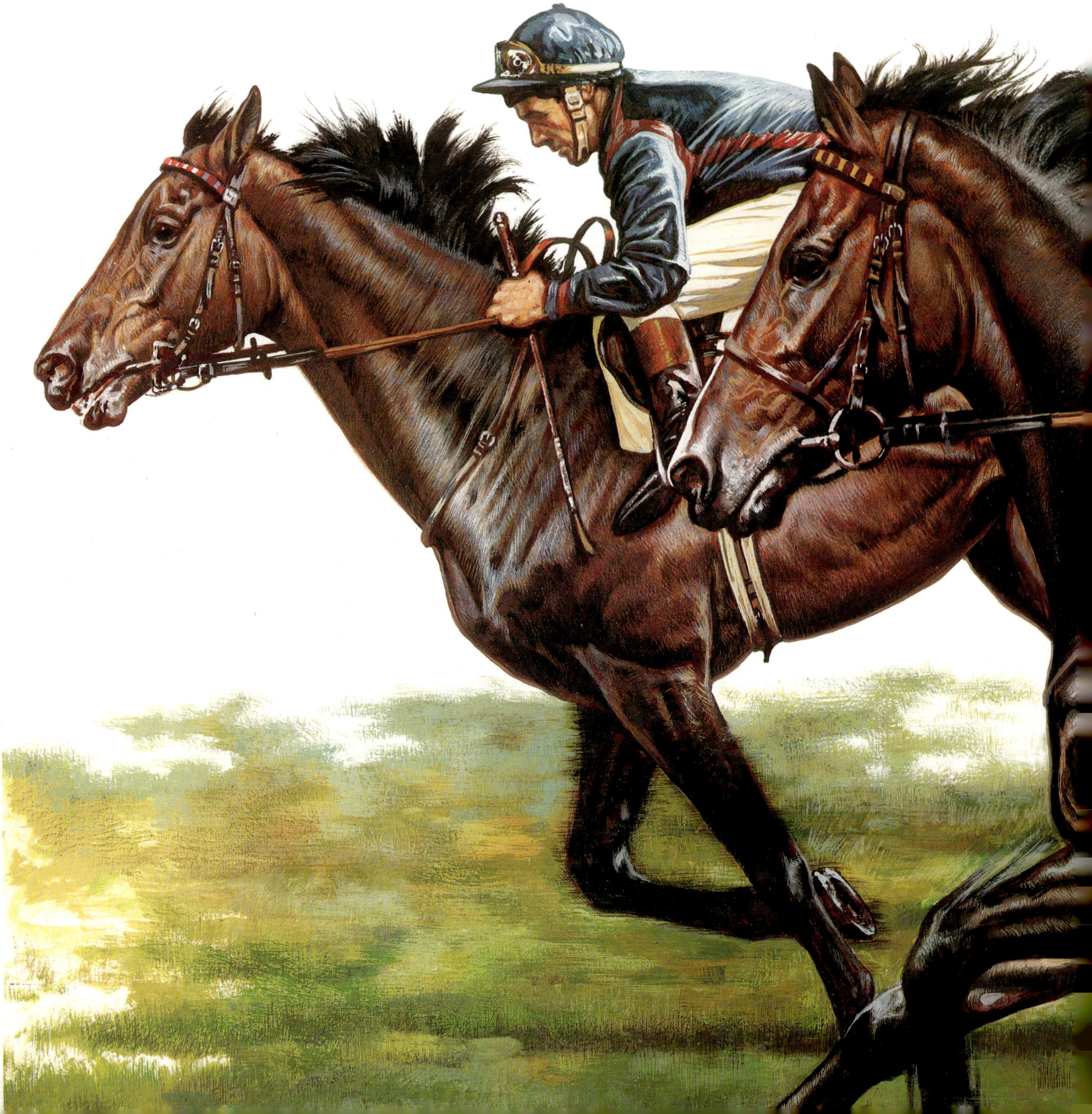

FLAT RACING

The first flat-racing events were held in England in 1074, whereas in France reliable sources refer to similar races being held in Saumur in 1370, and also in Britanny at about the same time, although only during public festivals and similar occasions. In 1465 in Rome Pope Paul II was the patron of the famous Corse dei Berberi (Berber Races) which took place along the Via del Corso and finished in what is now the Piazza Venezia, but in these races the horses were riderless. In England the first flat races on the Epsom Downs took place, using Oriental horses, at the command of Richard the Lion-Hearted (1157–1199), who was also the first patron to award money as a prize to the winner. In 1511, during the reign of Henry VIII, the town of Chester became the home of England's first racecourse. The following year the organizers of Chester Fair awarded the winner of the race being held on that occasion with a decorative wooden ball, which was later replaced by a silver cup. In 1609, not content with the way in which the cup had been cast, the Sheriff of Chester had another made, and then yet another thus ending up with three silver cups, which he decided to award to the first three horses, a tradition which has continued ever since. As early as 1603, again in Chester, the so-called "sweepstake" races had been held, in which the prize or stake consisted of sums of money collected from the entrants. At the beginning of the seventeenth century races were beginning to be held at Newmarket, which is still one of the most important centers in the racing world, but it was not until the reign of Charles II (1660–1685), that horse racing in England really got under way. Meanwhile, in France, from 1651 onwards, "betting races" were held in which the stake was put up by the owners of the horses taking part. The most important promoter of racing in France was the Comte d'Artois, brother of Louis XIV, who ordered the building of the Champ-de-Mars racecourse. The year 1776 saw the start of the regular spring and autumn race meeting at Les Sablons, an area of flat land near Paris on which Longchamp racecourse now stands. Racing in America was greatly influenced by its English counterpart and has echoed developments taking place in England. The first racetrack was built in 1664 at Hempstead and two years later the first so-called official races were held on the land handed over for the purpose by the Governor of New York on Long Island, which today is the site of the Aqueduct racetrack. A milestone in the history of flat racing is represented by the foundation of the Jockey Club in England in 1750. In Italy the development of horse racing was affected by her history of political turmoil although the first race meeting was held at Leghorn in 1739. Racing associations were gradually established in various cities but it was not until 1880 that the Italian Jockey Club was founded. Other countries where flat racing is now an important sport include Germany, where the Stud Book dates back to 1811, and Japan, where the first European-style meetings were held at Yokohama in 1861. Racing (as opposed to trotting) can be divided into flat racing, hurdle racing, steeplechasing and cross-country racing. In a hurdle race the obstacles consist of natural or artificial hedges while in the steeplechase these are accompanied by other obstacles such as ditches, banks, walls and fences. In cross-country events there are also fixed obstacles which imitate the type of natural obstacle found on a country ride. These are set out at regular intervals over the course, which may well follow a different route from the normal racetrack. Horses first enter hurdle races at the age of three, while for the steeplechase and the cross-country event the minimum age is four. Hurdle races are held over demanding distances ranging from 1¾ miles (2,800 m) to 4½ miles (7,200 m), the distance of the Grand National which is held at Aintree, near Liverpool. Flat races, on the other hand, are held over distances of from ½ mile (800 m) to 2½ miles (4,000 m) and more. These distances apply to races reserved for the English Thoroughbred, since races run by the Quarter Horse are shorter, ranging from 300 yards (275 m) to 870 yards (795 m). The classic distance in this type of race is nevertheless still 440 yards (402 m). English Thoroughbred races can be divided into five groups according to the specific distances run and these are: sprints, 5–7 furlongs (1,000–1,400 m); middle distance races, 10 furlongs (2,000 m); classics, 12 furlongs (2,400 m); long distance races, up to 2½ miles (4,000 m); and very long distance races of over 2½ miles (4,000 m).

Races can also be divided according to their nature and importance into Pattern races, Listed races (of national interest only), handicap races, conditions races, weight for age races, newcomers' races, maidens' races (for horses which have not yet been winners), claiming races and selling races. Pattern races are divided, according to their value, into Group I, Group II and Group III races. Apart from professional races there are also both flat and hurdle races for amateurs and ladies.

The whole world of horse racing depends financially on the better or "punter" and the bookmaker, but without owners, trainers, jockeys and the various staff in charge of the actual racecourse (who are also responsible for checking and approving the horses running) racing, and of course its surrounding atmosphere of passionate interest and excitement, would be unable to exist.

ENGLISH THOROUGHBRED

Thoroughbred means "purely bred" and this has been the ambition that has led to the creation of this horse over almost three hundred years. The origins of the English Thoroughbred date back to the early eighteenth century, a time which saw the importation into England of three horses that are the foundation sires of the breed, and the ancestors in the direct male line, of all existing horses belonging to this line. These were the Byerley Turk (a dark bay of Arabian blood), the Darley Arabian (a bay of Arab origin), and the Godolphin Arabian (a brown horse also of Arab origin).

These three stallions came to England somewhere between the late seventeenth and the first quarter of the eighteenth century. They were not the only three stallions originally to contribute towards the foundation of the breed, however, and according to calculations made by Joseph Osborne in 1881 at least 475 other stallions, all of them of Oriental origin, made an initial contribution, although they failed to secure a descendancy in the direct male line capable of continuing down to the present day. Similarly only 40 of the 100 brood mares originally entered in the Stud Book have managed to keep their direct female line alive through their descendants. This initial nucleus of mares was formed by the "Royal Mares," which had been especially selected by the royal family for breeding. These animals represent the results of a careful and closely supervised programme of crossbreeding with the determining contribution of other Oriental blood. Three major bloodlines descend directly from the three foundation sires of the English Thoroughbred. From the Byerley Turk, in the fourth generation, Herod (b. 1758); from the Darley Arabian, also in the fourth generation (ch. 1764); and from the Godolphin Arabian, this time in the second generation, Matchem (b. 1748). In appearance, the English Thoroughbred does not have particularly well-balanced features since selection was made on the basis of the sporting and competitive qualities of the stallions and not on their physical characteristics. Thus there are horses ranging in height from a minimum of 14.3 hands to a maximum of 17 hands. Other features also vary considerably, to the extent that it is possible to categorize the Thoroughbred into three physical types which all have different qualities with regard to their aptitude. The "sprinter" is very swift and tall, with a long back and loins, a deep chest, a sloping croup, and a fairly straight shoulder. The "stayer" has good stamina over distances, and is smaller, with a roomier chest, a shorter back, a flat croup and sloping shoulders. Lastly, there is the "middle-distancer,"

English Thoroughbred

with a sloping croup, sloping shoulder and a rather short back, which shows particular aptitude for steeplechases. The English Thoroughbred's Stud Book dates back to the year 1791 in England, although the Jockey Club had been established in England in 1750, and has been responsible for keeping the Stud Book up to date since then.

Breed: English Thoroughbred
Place of origin: Great Britain
Height at withers: 14.3–17 hands
Weight: 705–990 lb (320–450 kg)
Structure: dolichomorphic
Colour: bay—dark bay—black, chestnut—grey—roan and red roan (rare); frequently with white markings
Temperament: highly strung—energetic
Aptitude: flat racing—saddle horse
Qualities: speed—stamina
Geographical distribution: all over the world
Head: small and well set-on—profile straight—ears well proportioned and very mobile—eyes large and lively—nostrils wide—lips thin
Neck: long and straight (sometimes slightly arched)—well shaped and well set-on
Body: withers prominent and clean—back long (less so in the stayer)—loins well set-on to the croup, which may be sloping (flat in the stayer)—tail set-on high—chest wide (stayer), deep (sprinter), and quite high—abdomen quite drawn up
Legs: long and well formed—shoulder nicely sloping (straighter in the sprinter), long and well muscled—joints large and clean—arm short and muscular—forearm long—thigh and leg long and muscular—cannon short, often a little thin—tendons strong, set well apart and clean—pasterns long—hooves small and strong
Skin: very fine—superficial veins show through

QUARTER HORSE

The Quarter Horse was developed by the first settlers in Virginia and Carolina, who needed a horse with the characteristics and performance to suit their particular requirements. They consequently embarked on a selection process, which involved crossbreeding horses of Andalusian stock with English Thoroughbreds that they had brought over from England. These were English horses that already had the characteristics of the Thoroughbred but could not be defined as such since the breed had not yet been officially recognized. The products of this crossbreeding were used in sprint races over a distance of a quarter of a mile (hence the name of the breed), which were held along the main street of the village. This practical, selective breeding led to the eventual creation of a fast, lively and active horse with very quick reflexes and great agility, making it extremely useful to the cowboys who were quick to recognize this animal's natural ability for this type of work. These qualities make the Quarter Horse still an ideal mount for rodeos today.

Apart from being a sound race horse in its own special area the Quarter Horse is quite widely used for polo, show jumping and hunting and its versatile nature makes it a top class horse for competitive events. The American Quarter Horse Association, established in 1941 at Fort Worth, with its headquarters at Amarillo in Texas, currently lists more than 80,000 regularly registered animals in over 40 countries including the United States. Generally the Quarter Horse is a sturdy, powerfully-built horse with well-developed hindquarters and an exceptionally balanced temperament that clearly distinguishes it from the English Thoroughbred.

Breed: Quarter Horse
Place of origin: United States
Height at withers: 14.1–16 hands
Weight: 940–1,210 lb (425–550 kg)
Structure: dolichomorphic
Colour: chestnut—bay—dark bay—black—liver chestnut—dun—red dun—buckskin—mouse dun—palomino—grey—blue roan—red roan
Temperament: docile—lively and energetic
Aptitude: saddle horse—flat racing
Qualities: nimble and fast—very quick off the mark
Head: short and broad (square)—profile straight—forehead wide—ears of average length and straight, set well apart—eyes large, intelligent, gentle but bright—nostrils wide—jaws slightly prominent
Neck: well formed and muscular—slightly arched
Body: withers fairly pronounced and well defined (clean)—back short and straight—croup long, muscular and rounded, dropping gently to the haunches and the base of the tail—tail set-on low—chest roomy—girth deep
Legs: solid and well muscled—shoulder long and sloping, well muscled—joints broad and clean—thighs muscular—cannons short—tendons clean and set well apart—pasterns of medium length and quite straight—hooves well formed and hard

TROTTING RACING

It is possible that the first trotting races were held in France as early as the fifteenth century, but for more reliable information it is necessary to leap forward almost two centuries to Russia, where it is known for certain that this type of competition was being held in 1775.

In Italy, the first trotting races were held in 1808 in the Prato della Valle in Padua, with money and medals as prizes for the winners. In these races, instead of the present-day sulky, weighing 35–65 lb (15–25 kg) the competitors used another type of small, one-horse carriage, the "Padovanella," which originally weighed 661 lb (300 kg). This weight was reduced to 525 lb (237 kg) in 1842 and further still in 1869, to only 249 lb (113 kg). This same year, in Padua, saw the start of the remarkable career of a horse called Vandalo (ro. 1862). This fantastic animal remained active until he was 20, running in 226 races, and winning 200.

In France the first official trotting races date back to 1836 and were held on the track at Cherbourg racecourse. From that year onwards trotting events have been an important sporting feature in France, due to the breeding and rearing of the French Trotter, the only breed that is any match for the American Standardbred. In the United States, races have taken place along roads since the early nineteenth century, but the first races on proper racetracks were held on Long Island, in New York State. The very first known race was held on June 18, 1806 in New Haven, and was won by Janhey, who trotted the mile in 2′59″. This was, however, an isolated event, as until 1815, horse racing was prohibited in most of the northern States, on grounds of immorality. Only after 1815 did this inflexibly moralistic attitude give way to a more tolerant one, and in 1830 these laws were finally abolished. In 1845 a grey mare by the name of Lady Suffolk set up the first record for the mile with a time of 2′29″½ (1′33″9 km) and in so doing began a history of ever-increasing popularity in trotting events. In fact, from then on numerous successive champions have competed to hold the world record in this event and these include: Lou Dillon (ch.m. 1898—1′58″½), the first horse to break the two-minute record; Uhlan (bl.g. 1904—1′58″); Peter Manning (b.g. 1916 1′56″¾); Greyhound (gr.g. 1953—1′55″¼); Nevele Pride (b.h. 1965—1′54″⅘); Lindy's Crown (b.h. 1976—1′54″⅘); Arndon (b.h. 1979—1′54″); Cornstalk (b.h. 1981—1′53″⅘); and Fancy Crown (b.m. 1981—1′53″⅘). These last two horses trotted the mile at the equivalent per kilometer of 1′10″7, an amazing time, considering it was achieved during a race, and not in a time trial against the clock. Much of the credit for these results is due to certain exceptional stallions used in the United States. The most important of these are Volomite (br.h. 1926), Star's Pride (br.h. 1947—1′57″⅕) and Speedy Scot (b.h. 1960—1′56″⅘).

European breeders have consistently tried to keep pace with their American counterparts, but only the French Trotter has succeeded in competing with the champions from the other side of the Atlantic, with horses such as Jamin (b.h. 1953—1′13″8 km), Roquépine (b.m. 1961—1′15″3 km), Une de Mai (ch.m. 1964—1′13″9 km), Idéal du Gazeau (bl.h. 1974—1′13″2 km), and Jorky (b.h. 1975—1′13″1 km) all of which have made a name for themselves on American turf. Other European countries have also developed their own breeding techniques, often with excellent results. In Italy, there are Mistero (b.h. 1940—1′18″8 km), Tornese (ch.h. 1952—1′15″7 km), Delfo (b.h. 1971—1′13″7 km) and Toujours (b.h. 1976—1′13″7 km); in Germany, Permit (b.h. 1945—1′17″3 km) and Babesia (b.m. 1976—1′13″8 km); in Scandinavia, which, essentially means Sweden, a very important contender in recent years, Ego Boy (b.h. 1967—1′13″8 km), Dartster F (b.h. 1976—1′12″8 km) and The Onion (br.h. 1979—1′12″ km) this latter being the holder of the (absolute) European record since 1983. The enormous progress made by the Swedes is quite evident from the fact that in 1983 they had 40 wins out of as many European Grand Prix meetings. A closer analysis of the times achieved by European trotting horses, however, will show that the Americans were matching them eight years earlier. In fact Lou Dillon's time of 1′58″½ over the mile is equivalent to 1′13″7 km. The only advantage held by European, and particularly French, breeders lies in the greater endurance over distance of their horses, since they are tested over more taxing distances. The exception is Italy which, over the past thirty years, has concentrated increasingly on races held over short and medium distances (1,600–2,000 m).

Trotting races are divided up into classic events for horses of the same age, invitation races, conditions races, class races, and handicap races. In the latter category the more able competitors yield a certain distance at the start to less talented entrants. In addition to races for professionals there are also amateur and ladies' events while in France they hold mounted trotting races in addition to traditional harnessed races. In America, pacer races are very popular. The world record for this event is currently held by Niatross (b.h. 1977—1′49″⅕), and was established in 1980. In non-handicap events a movable starting gate is used. This device lines up all the contestants, each in his own "box," and when the signal is given, all the boxes open simultaneously and the horses head out on to the track. In handicap races, on the other hand, the start is organized with tapes, and the horses make a standing start. Trotting races test the skill and swift reflexes of the driver, who usually trains the horse himself. If a horse "breaks" its pace during a race, and begins to gallop, it is disqualified, unless immediately brought under control and the trot resumed. A horse will also be disqualified if it breaks at the finishing line or if it falls into an unauthorized pace such as the broken trot or the amble.

The trotting horse is usually broken in at about 18 months, and enters its first race or debut at two years. The age limits for horses taking part in trotting races vary all over the world, and some countries do not have any limit at all. A trotter's career tends to be as intense as it is long and may involve participating in several races a week, or even several races in a single day, as in the Grand Prix events, which are divided into a number of different trials.

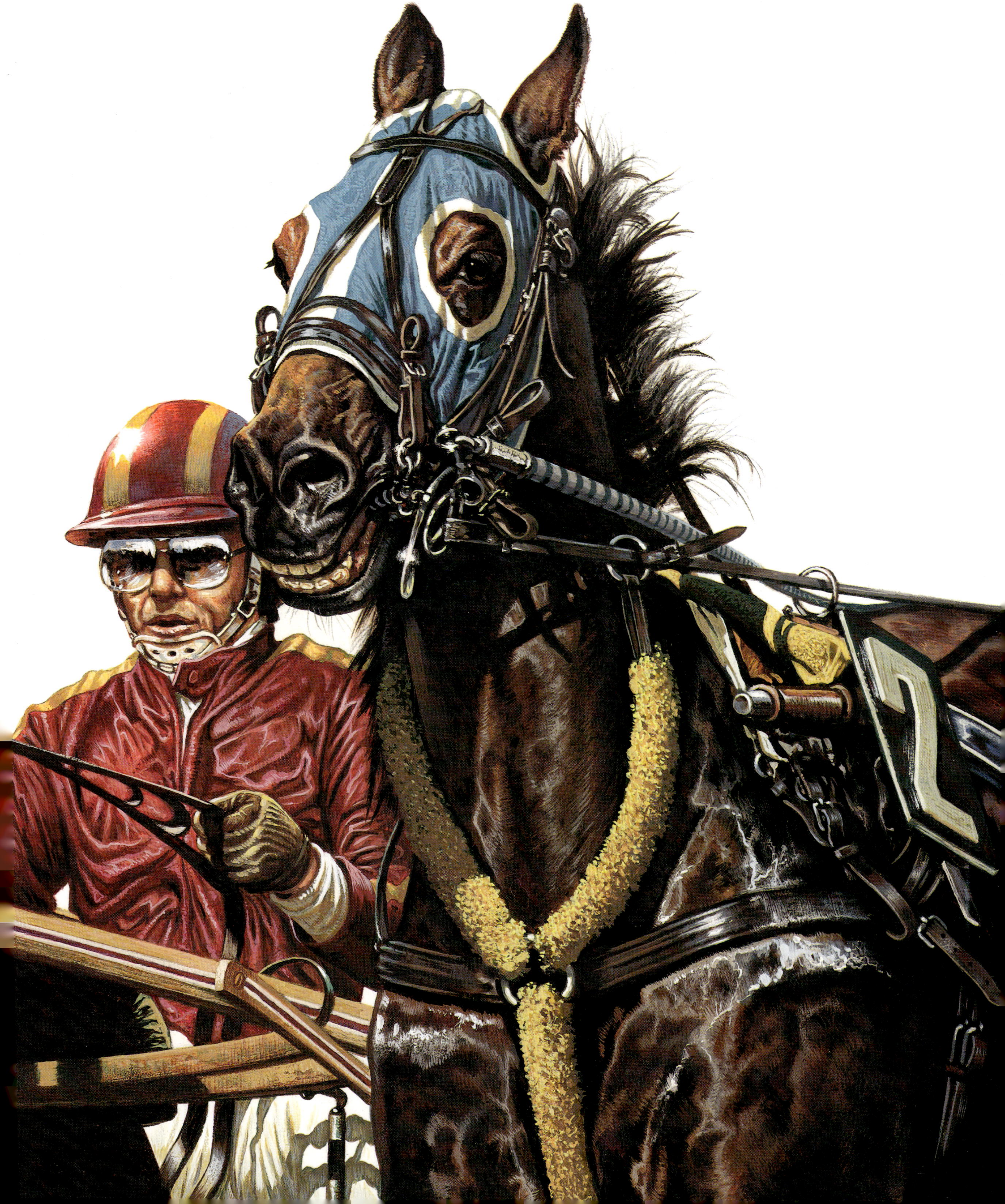

Bellino II

FRENCH TROTTER

This horse is also known as the Norman Trotter, since its earliest origins are closely interrelated with those of the Norman horse. In 1836, at Cherbourg racecourse in France, the first official speed races for trotting horses were held marking the beginning of a very tightly controlled process of practical selection which has brought about the differentiation between the two breeds. The Norfolk (a breed which now no longer exists but gave rise to the Hackney, its modern counterpart) initially played a role in the formation of the French Trotter, as did halfbred English hunters, the Hackney and the English Thoroughbred. A painstaking and severe selection process, carried out over difficult tracks and demanding distances, has resulted in the creation of a sturdy solidly built trotting horse with excellent endurance and stamina over long distances.

At a later stage in its development contributions were made by the Standardbred and Orlov, both trotting breeds with which it has similar, if not actually shared origins, so that ultimately all three can be regarded as varieties of one and the same breed—"the racing trotter." More weight could be added to this theory by the fact that the dividing lines between these breeds are becoming more and more indistinct because of the repeated crossbreeding to which they have been subjected, even though the French Trotter itself does still differ quite markedly from the American Standardbred both in appearance and in its greater endurance over long distances.

The foundation sires of the French Trotter were Conquérant (1858), Lavater (1867), Normand (1869), Niger (1869) and Phaëton (1871). In the early twentieth century 95 per cent of the horses belonging to this breed were descended from these five stallions. Later, selection was directed solely towards the descendants of Conquérant, Phaëton and Normand, particularly the first two. One of Conquérant's descendants was the famous Fuchsia (1883) who, together with Phaëton has impressed his distinctive stamp on the breed. All trotting breeds inherit their aptitude for trotting from Norfolk horses and two English Thoroughbreds: Sampson (1745 out of Blaze) and Orville (b.h. 1799).

The Stud Book for the breed was established in 1922, and since 1941 it has been closed to all animals not possessing the correct qualities. The French Trotter is also used in mounted, as opposed to traditional harnessed, trotting races, a spectacular event which is frequently seen at French racecourses. With regard to the by now frequent crossbreeding between the French Trotter and the Standardbred, it should be said that some authorities have controversially claimed to detect in the subjects obtained, the characteristics of a distinct breed, which they have called the Noram Trotter.

In its model form the French Trotter does not present any uniformity in an absolute sense, because of the selection criteria which, as with other breeds of race horses, are oriented to the perpetuation of practical rather than aesthetic characteristics. The result, nevertheless, is a solidly-built horse that gives the impression of remarkable strength and power. The speed record is currently held by Minou du Donjou (ch.h. 1978 sired by Quioco) established in Stockholm in 1985 with a time of 1'11"5 km.

Breed: French Trotter
Place of origin: France
Height at withers: 15.1–16.2 hands
Structure: dolichomorphic
Colour: bay—black—chestnut
Temperament: quiet
Aptitude: trotting racing (harnessed and mounted)
Qualities: very fast—very good endurance over distance
Geographical distribution: France—Italy—Holland—Sweden—Austria—Denmark—Finland—Malta—Spain
Head: handsome and well set-on—profile straight—forehead broad—ears long and set well apart—eyes bright—nostrils wide
Neck: well formed and muscular—well set-on—broad at the base
Body: withers prominent and clean—back straight—loins well developed—croup long and broad, slightly sloping—tail set-on quite low—chest roomy—girth deep—abdomen drawn in
Legs: slender but sturdy and muscular—shoulder muscular and nicely sloping—joint large and clean—hocks solid and well formed—foot sometimes delicate, better suited to soft tracks
Skin: fine and elastic

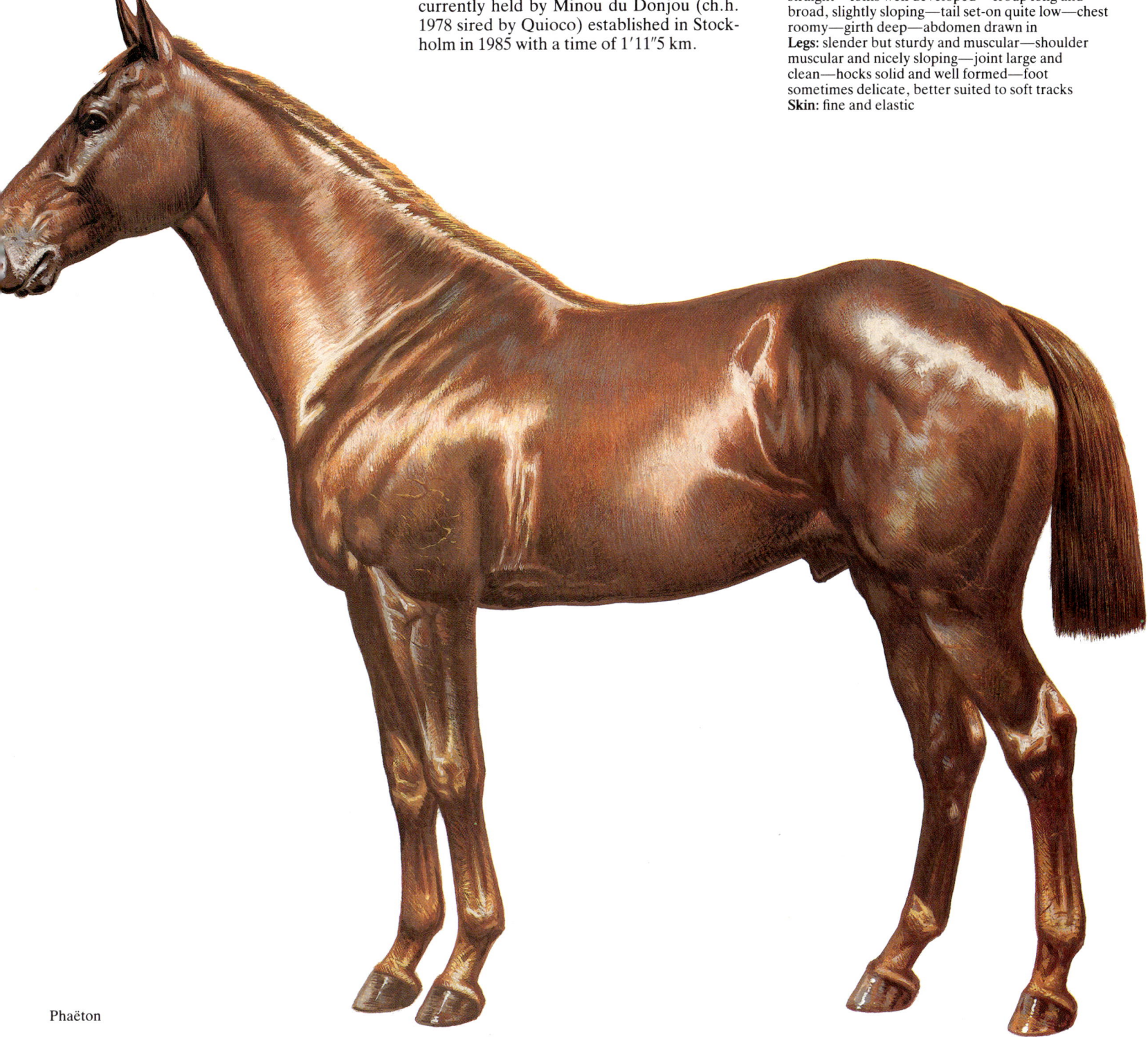

Phaëton

AMERICAN STANDARDBRED

Both pacers and trotters come under the description of Standardbred. Pacing is a gait not normally found in horses and is faster than the trot, which is why it is regarded as inadmissible in trotting races and will result in the disqualification of the offending competitor. In America there are separate events for pacers (using the ambling gait), and for this reason breeders strive to achieve this specific aptitude by crossing horses that display a natural disposition towards this gait. The importance of trotters, however, is far greater than that of pacers, which are really specialized horses within the breed.

The foundation sire of the Standardbred, also known as the American Trotter, is the English Thoroughbred stallion Messenger (gr. 1780), imported to the United States in 1788. Either directly, or through his descendants, this horse has had a determining influence on American breeding, which relied on a nucleus of trotting and pacing mares that had already been carefully selected, even though their origins were somewhat heterogeneous. Another notable contribution to the creation and development of the breed came from a Norfolk stallion, named Bellfounder (1817). He was imported into the United States in 1822, with the aim of introducing a different strain of blood so as to avoid excessive inbreeding.

In the direct male line Messenger was descended from Sampson, who played an extremely prominent role in the formation of trotter breeds, transmitting his particular qualities to his progeny. Hambletonian 10 descends in the third generation and direct male line from Messenger and it is from this famous horse that all present-day American Standardbreds are descended. The other strains that have contributed towards the creation of the breed, such as the Mambrinos (also descended from Messenger), the Clays (which did not have a natural aptitude for trotting), and the Morgans (descended from Justin Morgan) are no longer represented since their direct male line has failed to survive into the present day. On examination of Hambletonian 10's pedigree it is easy to pinpoint the importance of Messenger, who reappears some six times in the first six generations. Among the 1,300 foals sired by Hambletonian 10, three have produced the

Breed: Standardbred
Place of origin: United States
Height at withers: 15.2–16 hands
Weight: 790–1,170 lb (360–530 kg)
Structure: dolichomorphic
Colour: bay—brown—black—chestnut—grey and roan (both rare)
Temperament: willing and competitive
Aptitude: trotting racing—pacing races
Qualities: very fast
Geographical distribution: United States—Canada—Europe—New Zealand—Australia
Head: not too small—profile straight or slightly convex—ears long—eyes lively—jaws slightly prominent
Neck: quite long and muscular—well set-on
Body: withers prominent and muscular—back long and straight—loins short, broad and muscular—croup long, broad and sloping—chest roomy—girth deep—abdomen quite drawn in
Legs: strong—shoulder long and sloping, well muscled—joints broad and clean—forearm long—cannon not too long—tendons set well apart and strong—pasterns long—thighs muscular—foot well developed with strong horn
Skin: fine

Messenger

Hambletonian 10

Mighty Ned

four current blood strains: Happy Medium (from whom the line headed by Peter the Great is descended); Electioneer (from which the now extinct Bingen line was descended); and George Wilkes (from which the Axworthy and McKinney lines descend).

The Standardbred has had a considerable influence on horse breeding in Italy, Germany, Sweden, and the Soviet Union, as well as other countries which have used it to improve and increase their respective stocks. A determining role in the origins of the Standardbred was played by the English Thoroughbred through Sampson, Messenger, Orville and Diomed, who have all passed down their natural trotting ability. Compare these origins with those of the French Trotter and the Orlov, and it is possible to discover similarities that suggest any mating between animals belonging to different "breeds" as true "outcrossing," rather than "crossbreeding," between horses of the same blood (i.e. carriers of the same original blood).

The Standardbred is a good-natured horse. It is willing and competitive, capable of moving at considerable speed, and also of giving impressive bursts of speed, which is the logical outcome of a selection process carried out in trials over short distances such as are popular in the United States. The absolute record is currently shared by Cornstalk (b.h. 1981 out of Lindy's Crown) and Fancy Crown (b.m. 1981 out of Speedy Crown) and was achieved in August 1984 at Springfield with a time of 1'53"⅘ (1'10"7 km). The breed's Stud Book was established in 1871.

ORLOV TROTTER

This horse is named after Count Alexei Orlov, who first championed the breed. In return for helping the Czarina Catherine II succeed to the throne, Orlov was appointed commander of the Russian fleet and following the fleet's victory over the Turkish navy, and as a mark of respect for Orlov's chivalrous conduct, the Turkish admiral presented him with an Oriental stallion by the name of Smetanka. In 1777 Count Orlov had this stallion, which is regarded as the foundation sire of the breed, crossed with various Danish and Dutch Harddraver mares, but after only one season Smetanka died.

However, one of Smetanka's offspring, a stallion called Polkan (out of a Danish mare with a dun coat) was mated with a Dutch mare to produce a phenomenal trotting horse by the name of Bars I (1784): Polkan is regarded as the progenitor of the breed. In due course, as a result of a strict process of selection involving the use of Danish, Dutch, Arab and English mares, together with important contributions from various

Métis Trotter

MÉTIS TROTTER

The Métis Trotter is the result of the introduction of American blood with the express purpose of improving the performance of the Orlov, which had become incapable of competing successfully with the French Trotter and the American Standardbred. This programme, which was begun in the early years of the twentieth century, led to the official recognition of the breed in 1949.

The Métis Trotter is smaller and less solidly built than the Orlov, but it is faster and performs well in competitions. The trotting pace of this docile and energetic animal is distinctive and marked by a flowing, far-reaching action that results in a considerable improvement in speed. The hind foot is often carried in such a way that it makes the horse "dish," that is, as the leg is thrust forward, the foot moves outwards in a circular movement. This defect becomes a distinct advantage in more sustained gaits because it enables a horse to find its way more easily over awkward terrain reduce the likelihood of brushing.

Breed: Métis Trotter
Place of origin: USSR
Height at withers: 15.1–15.3 hands
Structure: dolichomorphic
Colour: bay—brown—black—grey—chestnut
Temperament: docile
Aptitude: trotting racing
Qualities: good speed—fairly good stamina over distance
Head: well proportioned and well set-on—profile straight or slightly convex
Neck: long and muscular—well set-on
Body: withers prominent—back long and straight—croup long and slightly sloping—chest roomy—girth deep—abdomen quite drawn in
Legs: solid—shoulder nicely sloping and muscled, quite long—joints clean—forearm long—cannons short—tendons set well apart—occasionally with sickle hocks

famous English Thoroughbred stallions, and the introduction of horses of Russian and Polish origin, it was possible to establish the distinctive characteristics of this trotting horse. The Stud Book was founded in 1865, and was initially open also to horses that were not purebred but had achieved times of under two minutes over the kilometer. At a later stage this qualification was ruled out and now registration is restricted only to subjects whose sire and dam are entered in the book. The Orlov Trotter has helped to improve other trotting breeds, including the French Trotter, by means of a group of mares imported into France towards the end of the nineteenth century, while numerous horses were also introduced into Italian and German studs. Within the USSR, the contribution made by the Orlov Trotter to the development of other breeds, such as the Don, is remarkable.

The typical Orlov Trotter is a sturdy, solidly-built horse, valuable not only on the racecourse but also for farm work and fast light draught. As a racing trotter, having once swept the field in the early days of French and American trotting events, the Orlov Trotter has now been ousted by these two more recent breeds with which it can no longer compete in terms of speed.

Breed: Orlov Trotter
Place of origin: USSR
Height at withers: 15.1–17 hands
Structure: meso-dolichomorphic
Colour: grey (often dappled)—bay—black; chestnut (rare)
Temperament: very docile
Aptitude: trotting racing—fast light draught—farm work
Qualities: strong, with good endurance—very good stamina over distance
Head: well proportioned and well set-on—profile straight—forehead broad—eyes lively
Neck: long and muscular—slightly arched and well set-on
Body: withers quite pronounced—back long and straight—loins powerful—croup broad, slightly elongated and slightly sloping—tail well set-on—chest roomy—girth deep
Legs: sturdy and strong—well muscled—shoulder good, straight and muscular, quite long—joints solid and clean—tendons set well apart—arm and forearm long—cannons long with good circumference—hoof well formed

Orlov Trotter

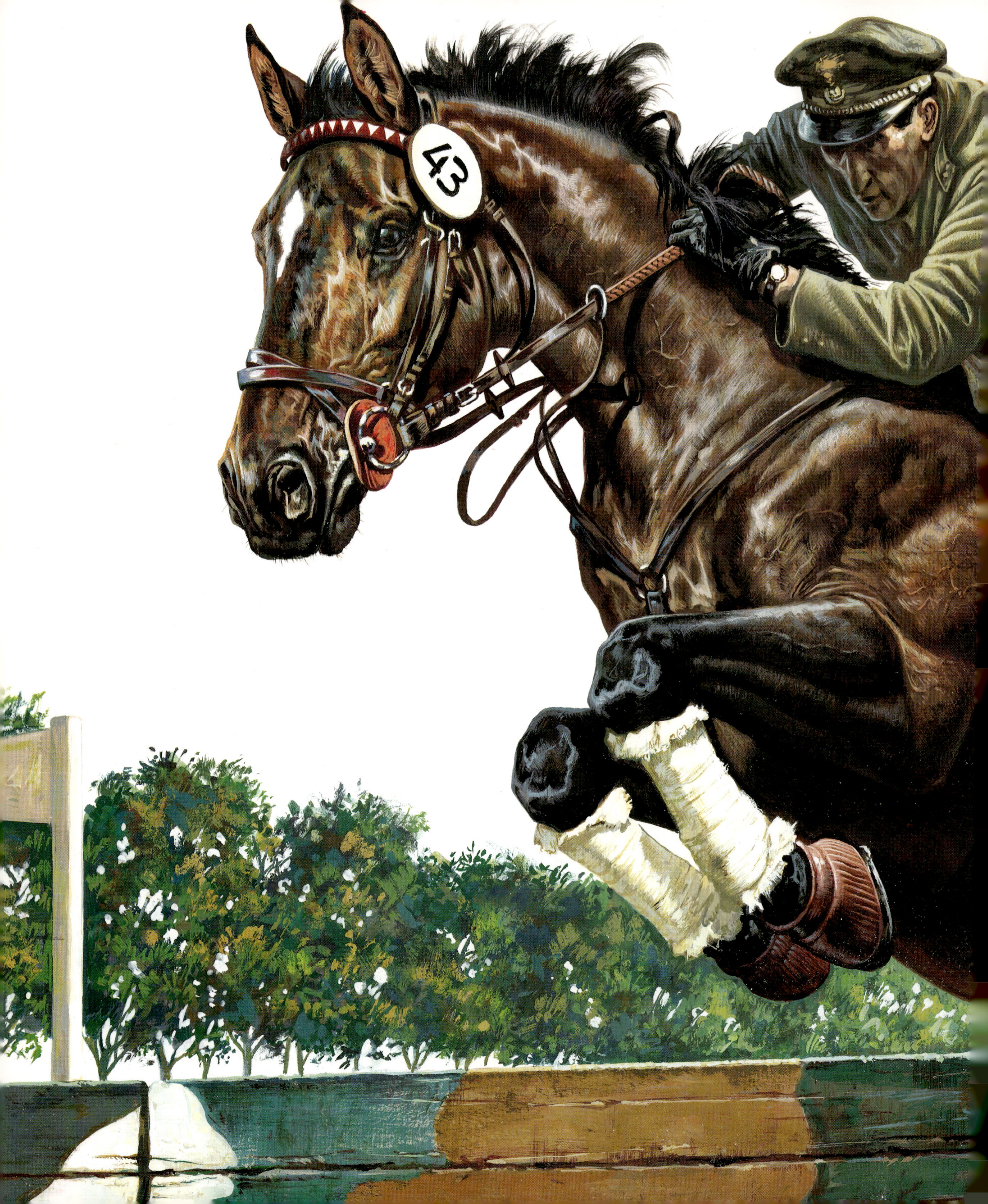
43

HORSEMANSHIP

The elegance, agility and speed of horses have all encouraged man to see them no longer purely as draught animals, but as valuable mounts for riding. Although nowadays riding is essentially a sporting or tourist activity, in some parts of the world it is still very much an everyday practice. In the steppes of Central Asia, the people of Mongolia are excellent and often acrobatic horsemen, learning to ride at a very young age, and in the Sahara there are the proud nomadic tribes of "blue men," the Tuareg of the North African desert, on their steeds descended from the famous Barb horses.

One logical consequence of the art of horsemanship combined with man's natural love for competitive games is horse racing, and, in fact, the first races with mounted riders would seem to date back to as early as 648 B.C. in Greece, during the 33rd Olympic Games. The oldest information on the many techniques of horsemanship to have survived until the present day, is Xenophon's *Hippike*, which dates back to 365 B.C. This is a collection of semi-technical essays dealing with the various aspects of horse breeding and rearing, domestication, training and riding techniques. Xenophon was in fact more interested in the use of horses for battle and war than for sporting and competitive events, and his writings give advice on how the horseman should conduct himself on the battlefield.

In another text, the authorship of which cannot be attributed with any certainty to Xenophon, there is a eulogy on hunting, not as an end in itself, but rather as an excellent training for preparing the horseman in the arts of war. The famous Roman cavalry was organized along the lines of Xenophon's writings, achieving very high levels of efficiency and acting as a model for other contemporary peoples. With the decline and eventual fall of the Roman Empire, and the ensuing social upheaval, skilled horsemanship went into a decline which lasted until the Middle Ages. This period saw a renewal of interest and opened up a new and glorious era in which the cavalry was to triumph until the nineteenth century.

During the Renaissance, especially in Italy, a new type of horsemanship began to develop, which was no longer concerned with war. Riding schools were established in Naples, Mantua and Padua and their extremely high standards of instruction and training for riders were soon emulated in other parts of Europe. This was the beginning of what has come to be called "classical equitation" or haute école, the rules and regulations of which are to be found in many writings of the day, describing how, in these schools, due consideration was given not only to the most rational way of riding and controlling a horse, persuading it to perform impressive and often very difficult exercises and acrobatic feats, but also to the scientific study of the physical structures of the horse and its movements.

For a long time therefore, Italy, which had been greatly influenced by both Greek and Roman culture, led the field in the art of horsemanship, but was overshadowed between 1600 and the end of the nineteenth century, first by France and England and later by various other European countries. Riding schools boasting very high standards sprang up everywhere and Italy's importance became secondary since, as a result of political unrest, there were no longer any courts sufficiently wealthy and well established to absorb the high running costs.

It was not until 1823 that Carlo Felice founded a school of horsemanship in Italy at the royal castle of Venaria, with a large schooling area (manège) and a parade ground. The school was not particularly distinguished since it trained officers from all the services, as well as those in the royal division, but when it moved to Pinerolo, after 1849, it became a fully-fledged cavalry school necessitating the employment of two instructors from the School of Vienna—Wagner and Paderni—who, although responsible for the revival of dressage, were unfortunately unable to adapt to the different and specific requirements of the Italian

135

cavalry. After a period of relative inactivity, Italian horsemanship once again became the focus of world attention thanks to new techniques evolved by a young officer at the School of Pinerolo, a certain Federico Caprilli (1868–1908). The Caprilli method, which was bound up with the Graeco-Roman school, caused radical upheavals in the old school of classical equitation, which was traditionally based on stylized, aristocratic models, invariably forcing the horse to adapt to its rider who would often expect it to perform unnatural movements and paces that hampered its freedom of action. Caprilli eliminated these rigid and formal elements from horse riding and after making a close study of the horse and its movements he concluded that, if the animal were to perform well, it was necessary to allow it a certain amount of freedom so that it could maintain its balance, in both racing and jumping. The position of the saddle was moved forward, so that the weight of the rider was no longer resting on the hindquarters of the horse, thus enabling it to use its powerful hind legs to maximum advantage.

In addition, the head and the neck were left freer, by carefully slackening the tension of the reins. This is particularly important in jumping, when the horse stretches its neck and thrusts the weight of its own body forwards. If the rider hampers this stretching movement the horse then has no option but to make a "vertical" jump from all four feet, and if it gets too close to the obstacle to be negotiated it will not be able to see it properly, and possibly stumble, since horses have a blind spot below their heads. The rider's attitude to his horse must be one of constant attention and he should not expect too much of the animal too soon, but proceed patiently by degrees, taking into account the particular temperament and aptitudes of the animal. It is important to give the horse a certain degree of independence, therefore it is a mistake to help when there is no need, or alarm it by preventing it from doing anything on its own initiative.

The most important thing in good horsemanship is for the rider to keep the horse under control at all times, avoiding conflicts between his authority and the inclinations of the animal, which will, as a rule, willingly accept the feeling of being ridden, but does not like to feel it is being badly ridden or forced to do certain things. A disobedient horse displaying peculiar behaviour is often merely the outcome of an inexperienced rider whose erratic movements, often caused by fear, upset the animal's physical equilibrium. The result is that the horse is forced to make abrupt movements that in some circumstances may even unseat the unskilled rider. Similarly, too much pressure on the mouth, a typical fault committed by novices whose attempts to control the horse are often violent, will frequently cause the animal to try bolting to protect itself from the pain being caused by the bit. Finally, the weight of the rider should not always be placed in the same spot; rather, the rider should shift his weight by moving in time with the animal's movements. The position in the saddle should always be as light as possible, and the rider's upper body should move forwards or backwards, as well as sideways, so that the center of gravity of the horse remains constant.

The new technique proposed by Caprilli, of working with, rather than against the horse, was based on the fundamental consideration that the horse is not a machine to be maneuvered and programmed at man's will, but a living being, with all its inherent problems and a considerable degree of both intelligence and will-power. This approach was criticized by many of his contemporaries as being provocative and complicated. However, violent opposition to the new system of horsemanship soon disappeared after the spectacular successes scored by the Italian team at the 1908 Olympic Games in London. The method devised by Caprilli, was subsequently adopted and polished first by Piero Santini, one of his pupils, and then by Wilhelm Museler. It spread rapidly, first throughout Europe, and then to the United States, producing many teams of outstanding horsemen and women.

Raimondo d'Inzeo on Fiorello II

Good horsemanship naturally depends on the selection of a sound animal and this requires an ability to assess the particular suitability and qualities of a horse such as stature, girth and the proportions between the various parts of its body. The horse must be closely examined, both when standing still and moving, and on different types of terrain. The prospective rider must check its different paces, its speed, its stamina and endurance, its lightness and its docility. Once the suitability of a horse has been established, the rider must then be properly trained. He must learn not only the techniques of good horsemanship, but also how to communicate with the horse by the touch of hand and legs, tone of voice and use of the whip and spurs if and when necessary. A good horseman feels and looks confident and is capable of handling the horse with skill and deftness, without having to use force.

CLASSICAL EQUITATION

The art of classical equitation, or haute école riding, uses very different techniques from those described by Xenophon in his treatise on horsemanship, which have more in common with methods used today. Accessible only to the wealthy aristocracy, it was developed and closely guarded in the exclusive European riding schools of the Renaissance period and aimed at the technical and stylistic perfection of advanced movements performed by horse and rider. The apparent ease with which these undeniably elegant and spectacular haute école exercises are accomplished, in fact conceals years of intensive training, and often suffering, in which the unnatural is made to appear natural. This makes it extremely difficult for the admiring onlooker to appreciate their complexity and to determine how this transformation is possible. Is it the horse's willingness to follow his master's commands or the rider's ability to impose his will on the horse—or even a combination of the two, both man and animal working together towards a common goal? Whatever the answer, it is the perfect training and physical and mental harmony of both horse and rider that form the basis of a school of equitation which has survived even through the darkest periods in our history.

Haute école originated in France, largely as a result of the efforts of François de la Guérinière, who lived from 1687 to 1751. This man was responsible not only for establishing rules of horsemanship that are still valid today, but he also considered the welfare of the horse itself, which in those days was often burdened down with painful harnesses and bits and schooled by brutal and inhumane methods. The teaching and instructions of this man who is rightly called the "Father of Classical Equitation" subsequently spread beyond France into many other European countries, eventually being accepted by the famous Viennese School. The methods used for teaching haute école, which is far more complex than ordinary dressage, involve a series of figures of varying degrees of difficulty carried out with the horse's feet on the ground; then the feet slightly elevated; and then raised up high —the so-called airs above the ground. The first group of exercises includes all the specific paces: the *pas d'Aure*, invented by the Comte d'Aure (1799–1863), which involves making the horse move forward by collecting the hind legs right beneath the body and greatly extending the forelegs; the *piaffe*, which is a *passage*, similar to a trot, carried out on the spot; the *trot rassemblé* or collected trot, which is a shortened, rhythmic trot, with the feet raised as high as possible above the ground; the Spanish trot (*trot espagnol*), which is like the collected trot, but with the front feet thrust further forward; the flying change in which the horse changes leading leg, at the canter, during the moment of suspension (*changement du pied au temps*); the *terre à terre*, a sort of canter in two beats consisting of a series of small jumps carried out by raising and simultaneously lowering first the two front feet and then the two hind feet; and the *reculer* or reverse step. The low elevation group of exercises include: the *appuyer à gauche ou à droite au galop* (work on two tracks at the canter, involving flexion to the right or left);

Correct position of the saddle and stirrups when the horse is at rest

the *pirouette à droite ou à gauche* (right or left pirouette), which is a full turn on the spot to right or left carried out with the horse pivoting on its haunches, either both standing still, at the walk or canter; the *levade*, in which the horse rears up on its deeply bent haunches drawing its forefeet in under its chest; the *courbette*, in which, starting from the *appuyer* position, the horse extends its forelegs upwards, and on its hind legs, leaps forwards several times—but although spectacular this is a very demanding exercise, and only a few horses are capable of performing it. The *capriole*, together with the *courbette*, is the hardest of the airs above the ground and consists of a vertical leap during which the horse unleashes two energetic kicks with its front feet, its hind feet momentarily remaining suspended almost horizontally in the air.

FRENCH SCHOOLS

The oldest school of classical equitation is the School of Versailles, which was founded by Louis XIV in 1680. Although it no longer exists, it has passed on its tradition to the School of Saumur, where one of the most notable leading horsemen was the Comte d'Aure, who, in about 1850, introduced racing and cross-country riding. The officers and non-commissioned officers of the school, who are known collectively as the *Cadre Noir* because of their formal black uniform with gold buttons, gold épaulettes and bicorne hat, still have a reputation for being a highly trained cavalry corps, as they demonstrate in their annual "Carousels." The main object of this school of equitation is to produce highly skilled and versatile horsemen capable of using the horse for considerably more than show purposes.

GERMAN AND SPANISH SCHOOLS

In the wake of the French schools came the German school, first in Hanover (in 1734) and today, after various ups and downs, at Warendorf in Westphalia. The German school is based essentially on outdoor work and much importance is attached to hunting, racing (steeplechase and cross-country), horse shows, eventing, and some dressage. The school of horsemanship at Zarzuela, near Madrid, which derived from the old Valladolid school in 1802, is also based on the principles of French equitation. Here, too, the accent is on outdoor work. The cross-country training course at Zarzuela is regarded as particularly difficult, and includes a sheer drop of some 50 feet (15 m). In 1910 traditional methods were replaced by the Caprilli system following the outcome of a series of trials contested by teams trained in the two different methods.

THE SPANISH SCHOOL OF VIENNA

Founded by Charles VI in 1729, and still functioning today, this school, more than any other, has succeeded in carrying its original character down into the present day. It is based on the principles laid down by François de la Guérinière and is extremely strict in applying them. Initially entrance was exclusively restricted to officers of the court and imperial dignitaries, but was in due course relaxed to include the wealthy middle classes, and respected officers and similar figures from abroad. The horses used at the Spanish Riding School are Lipizzaners, descended from six stallions: Pluto, Conversano, Napolitano, Favory, Maestoso, and Siglavy. Training starts early with foals, which are worked free for at least two years before being mounted. Instruction is rigidly disciplined and traditional, closely following the tenets of classical equitation and its typical range of figures.

LIPIZZANER

This horse is named after the Yugoslavian village of Lipizza, which, at the time when the breed was being created, was in what was then Austria. For this reason Austria is now commonly regarded as the birthplace of this horse. Its origins in fact date back to the sixteenth century when Archduke Charles of Styria founded a stud here, starting out with a nucleus of mares of Italian origin, which were brought in from Verona, the Po Valley and Aquileia, and two Andalusian stallions brought north from Spain. The breed flourished and soon became famous when it began to supply the Spanish Riding School in Vienna with horses. This school was founded in 1729 by Charles VI and given its name in an attempt to emphasize the high percentage of Andalusian blood in the horses there. From the year 1717 onwards, however, the Andalusian stallions were superseded by Neapolitan, Kladruber and Frederiksborg stallions, and in time their role was taken over by Arab stallions. With the fall of the Austro-Hungarian Empire, the stud farm was moved to Piber, but the Lipizza farm, which was now in Italy, was able to continue its activities, due to favourable agreements made around the peace treaty table. At the end of the Second World War the stud farm at Lipizza was annexed to Yugoslavia, while the Piber farm was dismantled and evacuated by the Americans for fear that its contents might fall into the hands of the Russians who were advancing on the eastern front. The Lipizzaner is currently bred and reared not only at Piber (in Austria) and Lipizza, but in Italy at Monterotondo near Rome, and in Hungary, at Babolna. Within the Lipizzaner breed there are six distinct families descending from the same number of stallions: two Andalusian, the grey Maestoso and the red roan Favory; two Neapolitan, the brown Conversano and the bay Napolitano; one Frederiksborg, the grey Pluto; and one Arab, the grey Siglavy. The predominance in these progenitors of the grey coat, is just as usual and widespread among their descendants. Other coats which can occur are black, bay and roan. It is worth noting that grey animals are born black and only develop their permanent coat as they grow older. The Lipizzaner has retained the stamp of the Andalusian and the Neapolitan (itself derived from the Andalusian) which gives it a balanced and well-structured appearance. It is a sturdy horse with a long life expectancy, although it does not develop particularly early. It is docile but energetic, and has a keen intelligence.

Breed: Lipizzaner
Place of origin: Austria
Height at withers: 15–15.2 hands
Structure: meso-dolichomorphic
Colour: grey (predominantly)—black—bay—roan—white
Temperament: docile but lively and energetic
Aptitude: saddle horse—light draught—fast heavy draught—farm work
Qualities: undemanding—intelligent—willing—good endurance and stamina
Geographical distribution: Austria—Yugoslavia—Hungary—Italy
Head: long—profile straight or slightly convex—ears small—eyes large and expressive—nostrils wide—jaws pronounced
Neck: sturdy, arched and well set-on—mane silky
Body: withers not very prominent, broad and muscular—back long, sometimes slightly hollow—loins broad and muscular—croup short, broad, muscular and well rounded—tail well set-on, with long, fine hair—girth broad and deep
Legs: strong and hard—well muscled—shoulder sloping and muscular—joints broad and clean—tendons set well apart—foot small with strong horn—correct natural stance

ALTÉR-REAL

This breed owes its origins to 300 mares selected and imported in 1747 by the House of Braganza with a view to establishing a national stud at Vila de Portel in the province of Alentejo in southern Portugal. Later in the eighteenth century the Altér-Real was used for the performance of haute école exercises in the then famous royal manége. The breed was seriously contaminated at the time of the Napoleonic invasion when not only Arab blood, but English Thoroughbred, Norman and Hanoverian blood was introduced indiscriminately. The patient task of reforming the breed by the use of Andalusian horses was subsequently undertaken, and this project has seen important developments in the twentieth century, thanks to government intervention encouraging strict selection procedures, which have ensured the continuity of the breed down to the present day. The Altér-Real is a well-built, elegant horse with a supple and versatile action particularly well suited to haute école and dressage.

Breed: Altér-Real
Place of origin: Portugal
Height at withers: 15.1–16.1 hands
Structure: meso-dolichomorphic
Colour: bay—brown—grey—chestnut (rare)
Temperament: quiet and intelligent
Aptitude: saddle horse
Qualities: an ability to learn the haute école exercises and movements
Head: of average proportions—profile straight or more frequently convex—eyes expressive—jaws pronounced—full forelock
Neck: quite short—well muscled—arched—full, flowing mane
Body: withers pronounced—back short—loins powerful—croup muscular and rounded—tail well set-on, long and full—chest roomy—girth deep
Legs: solid and well muscled—good bone and joints—shoulder muscular and nicely sloping—thigh muscular—cannons and pasterns slender but sturdy—tendons clean and strong—foot well formed

DRESSAGE

Dressage is essentially a particular method of training a horse requiring much time and patience, making it advisable to begin when the horse is still young. The first step is to familiarize the horse with a special language consisting of a number of almost imperceptible signs, known as "aids," to which the animal must respond with complete obedience, carrying out whatever is required on each occasion: turning left or right, lengthening or shortening the pace, two-track work, and making smooth transitions from one pace to another. These aids are the means by which the rider is able to control the horse and, depending on the particular circumstances, may be represented by the action of the reins, pressure of the hands or legs, or even a shift in the rider's weight. These instructions are able to produce a deep mental and physical change in the animal often transforming a rebellious horse into one capable of performing complex paces and movements to perfection. This naturally demands a great deal of patient work, based on a strict, graded training programme.

Dressage also serves to some extent to modify the muscular development of the various parts of the horse's body, strengthening the hindquarters, which have to support the rider's weight, and making the forehand lighter. It is important to make sure that the center of gravity of horse and rider combined is kept as low as possible, ensuring a stable equilibrium during the exercises. Dressage, if properly conducted, should never look awkward or unbalanced but should be performed in such a way that the new movements and muscular control acquired by the horse give the impression of being totally natural.

The horse will gradually become accustomed to controlling the use of its muscles, adopting the correct stance, balancing its own weight, coordinating its movements and responding quickly and correctly to the slightest signal from the rider. Training the horse to acquire a measure of self-control is not easy and cannot be taken for granted since it concerns not only the physical appearance, but also the psychology of the animal. The choice of a horse suitable for dressage must therefore be made with extreme care, and animals that are unstable, indecisive, too highly strung or uncooperative should be rejected in favour of a healthy, intelligent horse with good willpower and a natural tendency to obedience. A dressage horse must also be attractive to look at, noble and graceful with a light, well-carried head, narrow ears, large eyes, which express both keenness and concentration, powerful muscles, short loins, healthy legs and a good natural stance.

The training involved in achieving this type of discipline is carried out in a special schooling area, also called a manège. Here, on the track, the horse is made to describe geometric figures, simple to begin with but gradually increasing in difficulty. From the normal rectangular circuit the exercises then advance to increasingly complex figures, squares, and circles of varying sizes, serpentines, diagonals, and combinations of the various geometric figures. All these exercises have to be carried out by the horse, taking care that it not only keeps closely to the prescribed figure, but also maintains its pace, which must be both easy and regular. One basic feature of dressage are the "transitions," which are instant changes from any one of the three natural paces (walk, trot and canter) to another without any loss of control, as occurs under normal circumstances with a horse that has not been trained. The horse must then learn flexion, which is a particular way of carrying the head with the neck arched and the line running from the forehead to the muzzle almost perpendicular; this exercise can be performed with the head straight or flexed to the left or to the right. Then there are the *demi-pirouette* and the *pirouette*, which are half or full turns to the right or left within the horse's length, and there are three types —the turn on the center, the turn on the forehand and the turn on the haunches; the *volte*, which is a full turn on the haunches; *piaffes*, that is, like trotting on the spot; working, extended and collected paces; and work on two tracks. All these exercises should be executed without the slightest trace of effort, almost as if the horse were performing them of its own accord, since the signs made with the hands and legs to which it has become accustomed to respond are extremely light and subtle. The overall result is one of remarkable harmony, elegance and lightness, and a perfect unison between horse and rider, who both move as one. Dressage is one of the sporting events at the Olympic Games and represents numerous competitions on both national and international levels. Created originally in France by a group of cavalry officers (L'Hotte, Montigny, Faverot, Kerbreck and others), who drew up the official rules and regulations, dressage quickly became popular among keen horsemen and women, and spread far and wide.

Dressage events are held in a rectangular arena measuring 60 × 20 m (198 × 66 ft). The exercises must be carried out within a given time and penalty points are incurred if this time is exceeded, or if errors are committed in the sequence. When the allotted time is exceeded before the conclusion of the round, the presentation is not interrupted, but every second marked up incurs half a penalty point. The total number of penalty points is then deducted from the marks awarded to the contestant by each judge (there may be a panel of either three or five judges). When a contestant makes a mistake on the course, notification is given by the chairman of the panel, who rings a bell. This warning is not given in cases where it might needlessly affect the continuation of the presentation. When a contestant makes a mistake in the programme (such as trotting in the raised position rather than seated, or saluting incorrectly), or when, on leaving the arena at the end of the trial, a movement not included in the sequence is carried out, penalty points are also awarded.

Each "error," whether or not it has been signalled by the bell, is penalized in the following way: two points for the first, four for the second, eight for the third, and elimination for the fourth. The penalty points are deducted on each judge's score sheet from the total number of points obtained by the contestant.

If the horse, the rider, or both, should fall, the entrant is not eliminated, but penalized both for the time lost and for the effects which the fall has had on the execution of the movement. The contestant is also penalized on his or her overall score. Use of the voice and sounds, whether isolated or repeated, are considered serious errors and will lower English Thoroughbreds, English halfbreds, which they occur by at least two points. Any contestant who enters the arena before the starting signal or more than 90 seconds after it will be eliminated. It is prohibited to use special reins, any auxiliary equipment, rubber bits and cheekpieces, all types of bandage or leg-guard, and all types of blinkers. The type of bit or mouthpiece to be used is stated for each category of the event and in every category it is strictly forbidden to use whips or crops. The judges' score sheets have six columns: the first for the maximum number of points that can be awarded; the second for the actual points awarded, the third for possible corrections, the fourth for the eventual coefficient to be used, the fifth for the total scored, and the sixth for any observations by the judge regarding reasons for awarding five points or less. Overall marks are awarded after completion of the presentation, particular notice being taken of gaits, eagerness to advance, submission, the position and seat of the rider, and the correct application of the aids. Each figure is

Horst Koehler on Immanuel

marked on a scale from 0 to 10 points based on the following assessment:

10—excellent

9 —very good

8 —good

7 —fairly good

6 —satisfactory

5 —sufficient

4 —insufficient

3 —fairly bad

2 —bad

1 —very bad

0 —not performed

Classification is based on the number of points awarded to the contestant by each judge (the total of the points, which have all previously been multiplied by the corresponding coefficients, plus or minus the penalty points accumulated).

In team events classification is based on the sum total of the points scored by the first three members of each team. If two teams score equal points, the winner is the team in which the member in third place has scored the most points.

Saluting
—Contestants in uniform must give a military salute.
—Lady contestants salute by bowing the head with the right arm held in a natural position close to the body and the reins held in the left hand.
—Civilian (male) contestants salute by raising their hat with the right hand and lowering it with the right arm held close to the body and the left hand holding the reins.

Dress
Military:
—standard uniform
Civilian:
—black or dark jacket, pale beige jodhpurs, hunting cap or bowler, white shirt or sweater with white stock (hunting tie), or a white shirt, collar and tie, black boots, spurs and gloves.
or:
—black jacket, white jodhpurs, hunting cap or top hat, white shirt or sweater with white stock, or white shirt, collar and tie, black boots, spurs and gloves.
or:
—black tail coat, white jodhpurs, top hat, white shirt or sweater with white stock, spurs and gloves.

Crops are not permitted in any category.

SWEDISH WARM BLOOD

The creation of this breed dates back to the seventeenth century and is the result of selective breeding of native animals with blood contributions from very different breeds such as the Arab, the Andalusian, the Friesian, the Hanoverian, the Trakehner and the English Thoroughbred. This is a fine-looking horse, with a solid and well-proportioned physique. It is an intelligent animal with a quiet temperament and was used in the past as a war horse, although nowadays it is exported to many countries as a sporting horse. Besides being a good jumper, it is well suited to dressage, making it ideally suitable for three-day events.

Breed: Swedish Warm Blood
Place of origin: Sweden
Height at withers: 16.2–17 hands
Structure: meso-dolichomorphic
Colour: bay—brown—chestnut—grey
Temperament: quiet and intelligent
Aptitude: saddle horse
Qualities: a good jumper
Geographical distribution: Europe—United States
Head: well proportioned and well set-on—profile straight or convex—ears long—eyes lively
Neck: long and well shaped
Body: withers prominent—back long and straight—croup broad, long and horizontal—tail set-on high—chest roomy—girth deep
Legs: long and strong—well muscled—shoulder nicely sloping and well muscled—joints broad and clean—tendons clean and well defined—hoof well formed and strong—correct natural stance

Swedish Warm Blood

AKHAL-TEKÉ

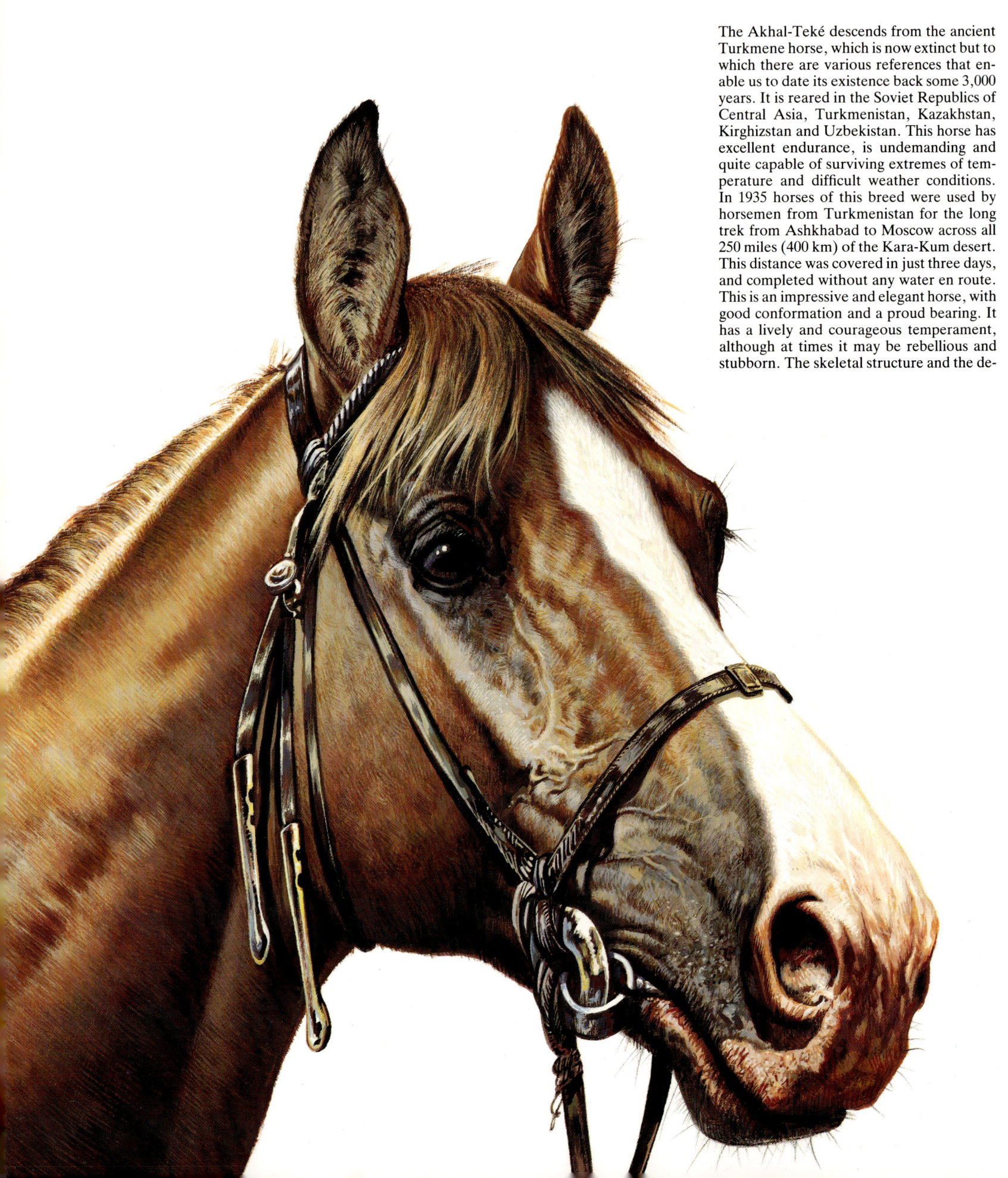

The Akhal-Teké descends from the ancient Turkmene horse, which is now extinct but to which there are various references that enable us to date its existence back some 3,000 years. It is reared in the Soviet Republics of Central Asia, Turkmenistan, Kazakhstan, Kirghizstan and Uzbekistan. This horse has excellent endurance, is undemanding and quite capable of surviving extremes of temperature and difficult weather conditions. In 1935 horses of this breed were used by horsemen from Turkmenistan for the long trek from Ashkhabad to Moscow across all 250 miles (400 km) of the Kara-Kum desert. This distance was covered in just three days, and completed without any water en route. This is an impressive and elegant horse, with good conformation and a proud bearing. It has a lively and courageous temperament, although at times it may be rebellious and stubborn. The skeletal structure and the development of the main musculature clearly indicate its marked aptitude for speed, combined with good stamina, and a full flowing and supple action. It is used with great success in international sporting events, thanks not least to its skill as a jumper and to the ease of its movements. One member of this breed (Absent) won the gold medal in the dressage at the 1960 Olympic Games in Rome.

Breed: Akhal-Teké
Place of origin: USSR (Turkmenistan)
Height at withers: 14.2–15.2 hands
Structure: dolichomorphic
Colour: chestnut—bay—grey—black—dun; often with golden highlights—occasional white markings
Temperament: lively and courageous—sometimes stubborn and rebellious
Aptitude: saddle horse
Qualities: speed—stamina—a good jumper
Head: light and well set-on—profile straight—forehead broad—ears long and mobile—eyes lively and expressive—muzzle tapered—nostrils wide
Neck: long and well formed (sometimes slightly swan-necked)—mane fine
Body: withers clean and high—back straight and long—croup slightly sloping—chest not well developed but in proportion—abdomen drawn in
Legs: long and strong—shoulder sloping and long, well muscled—joints broad and clean—tendons set well apart and clean—pasterns long—hoof well formed
Skin: fine, covered with fine, short silky hairs

EAST BULGARIAN

This breed was developed at the end of the nineteenth century at the Vassil Kolarov stud farm, near Shumen, firstly by crossing English Thoroughbreds, English halfbreds, Arabs and Anglo-Arabs. Once the basic features of the breed had been established only, the English Thoroughbred was used to upgrade its stock.

The East Bulgarian is an excellent saddle horse and a good jumper, with a lively, energetic but quiet temperament and excellent endurance over distances. These diverse qualities make it particularly well suited to competitive sports ranging from dressage to cross-country. It has a solid but elegant appearance giving the impression of power and strength.

Breed: East Bulgarian
Place of origin: Bulgaria
Height at withers: 15–16 hands
Structure: meso-dolichomorphic
Colour: chestnut—black
Temperament: quiet but energetic
Aptitude: saddle horse—light draught
Qualities: a good jumper—remarkable stamina
Head: light and well set-on—profile straight—eyes lively
Neck: quite long—well formed
Body: withers prominent—back long and straight—croup slightly sloping—tail well set-on—chest full and deep
Legs: solid and slender with good muscular development—shoulder nicely sloping and well muscled—tendons clean—foot well shaped

THE THREE-DAY EVENT

The three-day event is a rich, comprehensive and spectacular equestrian competition that requires a great deal of daring and courage from both horse and rider. Along with the Grand Prix for dressage and the Nations Cup for show jumping, the three-day event forms a part of the Olympic Games and is the most demanding of all three equestrian events. As the name suggests it is held over three consecutive days, on each of which the contestants are required to display very different skills and performances.

The first day is the dressage competition, which is held in an arena measuring 60 × 20 m (198 × 66 feet). This consists of the performance of set exercises and is aimed at assessing the horse's balance, obedience and self-control. For each "movement" a score between 0 and 10 points is awarded by the judges; the average of the total number of points awarded is subtracted from the maximum number of points that can be scored (240) and the difference is then multiplied by the coefficient 0.6. This gives a negative score to which the number of penalty points accumulated is then added. The score thus obtained will then be the contestant's final mark. Nowadays the dressage event no longer has to be completed within a set time, as in the past, but any errors made during the programme are liable to be penalized: two points for the first error, four for the second, eight for the third, and elimination if a fourth error is made.

The second day is the speed and endurance test over a course which, in the Olympic Games, measures a maximum of 31.230 km (c.19½ miles) divided into four phases. The first is a road and track test over about 4 miles (6 km) to be covered at a speed of 220 m (240 yards) per minute, with an upper time limit of one fifth of the time allowed. The second phase is a steeplechase of 3,105–3,450 m (c.2 miles) with several fences to be covered at a speed of 690 m (755 yards) per minute, with a time limit of twice that allowed. The third phase, like the first, is another road and track test, of 13,800 m (c.8 miles) to be covered at the same speed as the first. The two road and track tests combined must cover a total distance of 16,060–19,800 m (c.10–12½ miles). The fourth phase is a cross-country event of 7,410–7,980 m (c.4½–5 miles) to be covered at the gallop, at a speed of 570 m (620 yards) per minute, with a time limit calculated on the basis of a speed of 225 m (245 yards) per minute, over a course with a wide variety of natural or fixed obstacles. The fences must be not more than 1.2 m (4 ft) high, not longer than 2.8 m (9 ft 4 in) at the base and 1.8 m (6 ft) at the upper edge; ditches must be not wider than 3.5 m (11 ft 6 in) and banks not more than 4 m (13ft 2 in). Each section of the speed and endurance competition is awarded a certain number of points and penalties based on various formulae. In the road and track phases one penalty point is incurred for every second in excess of the set time limit, but a faster time does not constitute any advantage. Riders compete in these tests one at a time, setting off at five-minute intervals. In the road and track phases each rider is free to choose the gait (unless there are specific rules to the contrary), and can even cover part of the course on foot, leading the horse by the reins. In the steeplechase there are 0.8 penalty or bonus points

Hartwig Steenken on Kosmos

147

for each second of delay or advance, with a maximum of 36 points: in the cross-country event there are 0.4 points for each second over or under the set time, with a maximum of 72 points. As well as the penalty points for the time taken, there are others relative to the fences: a first refusal will incur 20 penalty points, a second refusal at the same obstacle 40, and a third means elimination. If a horse or contestant should fall the penalty is 60 points; the second fall in the steeplechase and the third in the cross-country lead to disqualification. The failure of a contestant to follow the course, and rectify any such error, results in elimination. The obstacles in the steeplechase are of the classic, conventional type (bars, beams, low walls, banks, hedges and fences); those in the cross-country event, on the other hand, can be more varied, as long as they are fixed, keep within the permitted measurements, and resemble as closely as possible the type of natural obstacle that might be encountered on a country trek over varied terrain. After each of the three days a classification is drawn up based on the total number of points scored in the different trials. If there is a tie, the winner is the contestant who has scored the highest number of bonus points in the cross-country event, which is regarded as the hardest event on the second day. Riders who have successfully come through the first two days are then eligible for the show jumping event, which is held on the third day, over a course of 1,000 m (1,080 yards) and includes 12 obstacles with a maximum height of 1.2 m (4 ft) and a maximum width of 3.5 m (11 ft 6 in). The rate at which the course must be covered is 400 m (440 yards) per minute. Each error earns five penalty points, but a first refusal at a jump earns ten penalty points, a second refusal, whether at the same jump or at a different one, earns 20, and the contestant is eliminated at a third refusal, or if he or she fails to follow the course properly, and fails to rectify any error. If the horse or rider fall, 30 penalty points are awarded, and ¼ penalty point is awarded for any second over and above the maximum time allowed. In the event of a tie between two or more contestants, the winner is the rider with the best overall time.

Any horse being entered in the three-day event must be extremely fast, a good jumper, and capable of negotiating very varied and demanding courses. Due to the frequently hazardous nature of the endurance tests the rider must wear a crash helmet to protect his head in the event of a fall, and the horse must be protected by kneecaps, and sometimes bandages according to the horse.

The hardest event of all is undoubtedly the cross-country, which is more gruelling than a normal hurdle race, not only because the obstacles themselves are extremely varied and are thus liable to disorient the horse, but also because of the way they are set out: barriers placed immediately before steep banks, walls followed by water jumps, extremely steep descents over considerable distances that entail negotiating slopes with gradients of 12–16%, and obstacles placed in the middle of ditches. A cross-country course is an intense challenge that sorely tries not only the physical capacities of the rider, but also his courage, tenacity, sporting nature, and desire to win or at least successfully complete the course, simply to prove himself equal to the challenge. The horse, too, must share the rider's will to win and display the same degree of courage and commitment, with an ability to tackle and jump even the most formidable and unfamiliar objects. A horse with these qualities will usually take the initiative, and in such cases the rider must simply give support and encouragement.

It is thus no coincidence that in the event of a tie it is the cross-country event that is the deciding factor in choosing the winner. The trial is so demanding that at the end of the second day many horses are no longer in a fit state to compete; others are so tense that they have to keep on the move for hours to prevent their tendons from swelling. Before being admitted to the show jumping event on the third day all horses must be pronounced fit and sound by a veterinary surgeon. The riders, too, are sorely tried, with some of them incapable of sleeping, despite their state of complete exhaustion.

Getting through all three days is in itself a feat of which any contestant may be justly proud. At the Los Angeles Olympic Games in 1932 only the United States and Dutch teams were placed, while at Mexico City in 1968 only one team—the British entry—managed to complete all the events. Anyone who has ever witnessed a three-day event will know well how emotions run high and will have suffered at every fall, jumped for joy every time an obstacle is cleared, and cheered for the winner, quite regardless of any personal interest in a particular horse, rider, or team. It is the stimulating atmosphere of this type of competition, uniting everyone in a common sporting cause that fired de Coubertin when he came to lay down the foundations of the modern Olympic Games in 1896.

As well as featuring in the Olympic Games the three-day event is the subject of European championships which are held on average every two years, and World championships, which are held every four years, but not in the same years as the Olympic Games.

The three-day equestrian event described here refers, in terms of the distances mentioned, to the Olympic meeting. As a general rule, in this type of competition the endurance test is held over a shorter course, but still somewhere between 12–14 km (8–9 miles) and 30 km (19 miles), and the cross-country event always covers a distance of between 5–8 km (3–5 miles).

HANOVERIAN

The Hanoverian is a very old breed, which has changed radically in appearance during its development from the eighteenth century down to the present day. The beginnings of this process of evolution coincided with the accession to the English throne in 1714 of George Louis, Elector of Hanover, who reigned as George I. Up until this time the local German horse, owing to its physique, had been used exclusively for drawing carts and for general farm work but as a result of the links between Britain and Germany English Thoroughbred blood was introduced into the breed, thus beginning the process of modification. In 1735, in the wake of his father, George II founded the stud at Celle, a town some 25 miles (40 km) from Hanover, where successful attempts were made to obtain a lighter variety, which turned out to be an excellent coach horse and was used for drawing royal carriages until the reign of George V. At the end of the nineteenth century the input of English blood was interrupted to avoid any further modifications to the breed which might decrease its suitability for its, by now, traditional role. Eventually, mechanization both in agriculture and general transport made coach horses redundant and new blood was once again introduced with the aim of obtaining a saddle horse with the present-day features. The English Thoroughbred was used again, and also the Trakehner, which increased the weight, largely as a result of the stallion Semper Idem.

The modern Hanoverian is a quiet, courageous horse and a good jumper, which performs well in the most varied sporting events such as horse shows, dressage, three-day events and hunting. It is a solid, well-built animal with good conformation, often being used to improve other breeds, such as the Oldenburg.

Breed: Hanoverian
Place of origin: West Germany
Height at withers: 16–17 hands
Weight: 1,100–1,300 lb (500–600 kg)
Structure: meso-dolichomorphic
Colour: chestnut—bay—brown—black—grey; frequent white markings
Temperament: courageous and quiet
Aptitude: saddle horse and light draught
Qualities: a good jumper

Head: well proportioned and well set-on—profile straight or convex—jaws well defined
Neck: long and muscular—well set-on
Body: withers pronounced—back long and straight—croup quite long, wide and rounded—tail well set-on and carried with elegance—chest wide—girth deep
Legs: strong and well muscled—shoulder long and sloping—joints broad and clean—tendons set well apart—hoof tough

FURIOSO-NORTH STAR

The origins of this horse can be traced back to crosses between local mares of Nonius derivation, and two stallions imported from England and introduced around the end of the nineteenth century to the famous Mezöhegyes stables in Hungary. These two stallions, the Norfolk Roadster by the name of North Star (1844) and the English Thoroughbred, Furioso (1836), were the foundation sires of two clearly distinct families, although today these have lost their original individuality and the breed is now called by both names. The Furioso-North Star is a very attractive-looking horse, with good stamina and endurance when under stress, and free from any evident defects. Nowadays it makes an excellent saddle horse although in the past it was most prized as a carriage horse. Its numerous qualities make it particularly well-suited to all modern equestrian sports, including dressage, cross-country events and hurdle racing.

Breed: Furioso-North Star
Place of origin: Hungary
Height at withers: 16–16.2 hands
Structure: meso-dolichomorphic
Colour: bay—brown—black
Temperament: quiet but energetic
Aptitude: saddle horse—light draught
Qualities: strong, with good endurance
Geographical distribution: Hungary—Czechoslovakia—Poland—Austria—Romania
Head: well proportioned and well set-on—profile straight
Neck: well shaped—quite long—mane flowing
Body: withers prominent—back long and straight—croup well muscled and slightly sloping—tail well set-on and flowing—chest wide—girth deep
Legs: well muscled—shoulder long and sloping, well muscled—joints solid and clean—tendons set well apart and strong—hoof well shaped, tough—correct natural stance

Furioso—North Star

Graziano Mancinelli on Ambassador

SHOW JUMPING

Show jumping is a particularly spectacular event demanding a high level of skill and commitment from both horse and rider. Since the period immediately preceding the outbreak of the Second World War, from 1938–9, it has gradually increased in popularity and competitions are now held in major cities all over the world; Rome, Paris, Geneva, Dublin, Toronto, Aix-la-Chapelle, and New York among others. At the Olympic Games there is a team event called the Grand Prix des Nations, or Nations Cup, which concludes the equestrian events and the actual Games themselves, in a dazzling spectacle. The widespread enthusiasm that now exists for show jumping, and the competitive spirit which it evokes, are largely a result of the innovations in horse-riding techniques proposed by Federico Caprilli, who showed how, with practice and experience, it is possible to gain complete control of the horse without causing it pain or discomfort, persuading it to move with ease and agility, negotiating even the most difficult obstacles naturally and smoothly. It is generally accepted that horses do not have a natural ability to jump and under normal circumstances they will do so only when it is absolutely necessary. It is, however, possible to train a horse not to shy from an obstacle but to jump it quickly and easily. Jumping involves a whole series of highly coordinated movements in which the weight of the body is transferred back and forth between the forehand and the hindquarters causing considerable shifts in the center of gravity, for which the horse must compensate with a high degree of muscle control so as not to lose its balance or fall. Not all horses are suitable for training for exercises of this kind. Halfbreds are normally the best types for jumping, although in some countries it is quite usual to find Thoroughbreds being used, even though their particular conformation is more suited to running and they are often highly strung and excitable. It was nevertheless an English Thoroughbred mare called Touch of Class, which, with Joe Fargis (USA) in the saddle, won the individual show jumping event at the Los Angeles Olympic Games in 1984.

As well as having the right physical aptitude, a horse that is to be used for show jumping must be endowed with courage, intelligence, powerful muscles (especially in the hindquarters), and a long, free neck. It should also have perfect control over all its muscles and be capable of making rapid changes in direction within very restricted areas; it must be able to change pace and gait very quickly and be ready to respond to the slightest sign from the rider, and it has to be very quick off the mark. A good show jumper will also share the competitive spirit that fires the rider and must therefore have an instinctive ability to cooperate. Training a show horse requires a great deal of time, dedication and patience on the part of the rider, who should aim to achieve a personal understanding with the horse based on mutual trust. Eventually the rider should be able to think in the same way as the horse to anticipate and interpret its reactions. Without this type of relationship many of the most amazing performances in international show jumping would have been impossible. These include victories such as those of the Italians, Piero and Raimondo d'Inzeo and Graziano Mancinelli, the Frenchman D'Oriola and the Brazilian Nelson Pessoa, on their no less famous mounts The Rock, Posillipo, Rockette, Lutteur and Grand Geste. Victory in a show jumping event is invariably the result of a whole series of factors which, in addition to the horse having been trained to perfection, also include the rider's great horsemanship, a keen sense of timing and perfect control on the part of both horse and rider. Also of great importance are the rider's personality and individual capacities, which may in some cases make up for any shortcomings in schooling programmes and even run counter to some of the basic tenets of perfect horsemanship.

Show jumping is organized into a series of competitions in which penalty points are given for every infraction committed. Faults may be concerned with obstacles (which may be knocked down or, in the case of a bank, wrongly negotiated) or the circuit (such as straying from the track). Instances of disobedience on the part of the horse include having to rectify errors of sequence, veering off to the side of the jump, stopping in front of the fence, napping (rearing, going backwards, turning) or refusing to approach the jump.

A horse that repeatedly refuses a jump will be eliminated if the time exceeds 60 seconds. It will also be eliminated if it does not cross the starting line within this time or if, after jumping the final obstacle, it fails to reach the finishing line. The same time is also allowed, again with the penalty being elimination for the contestant to resume his round after a fall.

In all jumping competitions it is forbidden to allow the horse to wear any kind of blinkers, fixed martingale, particularly restrictive or painful mouthpieces or bits, checkreins, rubber straps and head-lowering devices.

Penalty points are set out according to one of three different tables. In table A, four penalty points are given for each obstacle knocked down and for each wrongly negotiated bank, three points for a first refusal, six for a second, and elimination from the

Nelson Pessoa of Brazil

Hans Günter on Halla

competition for a third. If the horse or rider, or both fall, eight penalty points are incurred, and a quarter of a point is given for each second taken over and above the time allowed for the entire course. A contestant will be eliminated if the horse and rider, or one of the two, fall for a second time. Table B lists faults according to time rather than points and a penalty of ten seconds will be incurred for every obstacle displaced or knocked down. Similarly refusals or falls are automatically penalized for the loss of time they involve and lastly, two penalty seconds are given for each second or fraction of a second over and above the maximum time allowed. Table C is also based on time penalties, but this time they are calculated according to the length and difficulty of the course. This table also awards a penalty of one second for each second commenced over and above the time allowed. The penalty if the horse or rider, or both, fall for a second time is elimination.

The term "course" means the circuit which the contestant must follow within the boundaries of the competition area to carry out a specific test or trial, from the starting line in the direction indicated by flags, to the finish. The total length of the course must not be more than the total distance in meters obtained by multiplying the number of obstacles for a given category by 60. The start must be not less than 6 m (20 ft) and not more than 25 m (85 ft) from the first obstacle. The finishing post must be not less than 15 m (50 ft) and not more than 25 m (80 ft) from the last obstacle. The start and the finish must be marked, like the outer limits of the various obstacles and compulsory passages, by flags, the one on the left being white, and the one on the right, red. Knocking down a flag does not incur any penalty unless it is caused by a refusal or by the horse veering off to the side in which case the round must be stopped and taken up again from the same spot after the flag has been replaced. In such cases the contestant is given a penalty of six seconds if the flag marks the finish, any single obstacle, or the first jump of a combination, eight seconds if it marks the second part of a combination jump and ten seconds if it marks the third or any further part of a combination jump.

In enclosed or in small open-air arenas, the finish may be as close as 6 m (20 ft) to the last obstacle. Some classes have the so-called "jump-offs," which entail a second or third round under precisely the same conditions and rules as govern the initial round. These events take place over the same obstacles and are used to decide the winner of the competition from competitors who have tied for first place in the previous round. Depending on the programme the jump-off may be contested with all or some of the jumps raised and widened, and over a complete or shorter course. In this latter case, however, there must always be at least six obstacles, with the exception of the six-jump trials. In a jump-off the start and finish lines must be repositioned in accordance with the distance of the course when there are changes such as the removal of a jump, or a change in the sequence of jumps. This latter is only possible when the number of obstacles has been reduced. The fences in the jump-off event may not be raised or widened if the contestants who have tied in the preceding course have scored any penalties. In jumping classes where time is the principal criterion, in addition to the time allowed, which is based on the length of the course itself and a potential speed of 350–400 m (375–440 yards) per minute, there is an actual time limit of twice the maximum time. If this limit is exceeded the contestant is eliminated. In tests where the competitor has to jump the largest number of obstacles in a given time, this time must never be longer than 90 seconds.

Show jumping events thus differ from each other in the type of round involved, the way in which they are carried out and the type of penalty system used. The most common classes are the following:

1) Precision classes. Table A applies. The time taken to cover the course is not a factor in working out the final classification, as long as the contestant does not exceed the maximum time allowed. There is usually just one round, possibly followed by one or two jump-offs.

2) Jump-offs—Table A applies. If, after the first round, several contestants have scored equal marks, a second round is held, sometimes with fewer obstacles. If there is still a tie, the classification is based on time taken.

3) Against the clock competitions. These differ from the above in as far as there is only one round, after which, in the event of equality of faults the competitors are classified according to the time taken.

4) Parcours de chasse or hunt course. Tables B or C may apply. The course is not set but the rider must jump all the obstacles once.

5) American classes. The competitor is eliminated as soon as an error is committed. The winner is the rider who manages to negotiate the highest number of obstacles, but if there is a tie the fastest time will win.

6) American relay classes. This involves two-man teams. The second rider starts at the point where the first has made an error.

7) Puissance or power competitions. Table A applies. All the obstacles, except the first, which can be 1.3 m (4 ft 4 in) high must be more than 1.4 m (4 ft 8 in) in height. If there is a tie, a series of jump-offs is held over obstacles, which may be raised and widened, going down to just two in number.

8) Single high-jump. This involves just one

Eddie Macken on Boomerang

Dress
The following forms of dress are compulsory for competitors during the events, during the course inspection and during the prize-giving ceremony.

Military:
—standard uniform

Amateurs, juniors and professionals
—club uniform, approved by the FEI (Fédération Equestre Internationale)
or:
—pink, which includes a black or dark-blue hunting cap, a red or "pink" jacket, white or off-white jodhpurs, white shirt, collar and tie, or white shirt or sweater with white stock (hunting tie), black boots with or without brown trimmings;
or:
—black (or blue for ladies) which includes: black hunting cap, black jacket (or blue for ladies), white or pale beige jodhpurs, white shirt, collar and tie, or white shirt or sweater with white stock, black boots with or without brown trimmings.

Michael Matz on Jet Run

jump, the height of which is increased jump by jump. Riders may have three attempts at each height.
9) Single long-jump. This involves a single water jump, the length of which is extended after each series of jumps. There are three attempts at each distance.
10) Six-bar competition. Table A applies. This consists of a multiple jump with six upright fences set at the same height or at increasing heights. Successive jump-offs are held with all the jumps raised (only in the event of clear rounds); from the second jump-off onwards it is possible to reduce the number of obstacles. A maximum of four jump-offs is permitted.

In the high- and long-jump classes the following system of penalties is applied:
—two points for knocking over an obstacle (or setting a foot in the water);
—three points for a refusal, or veering to the side;
—elimination for the third error committed at the same height or distance.

In these competitions the winner is the rider who clears the greatest height or distance, whatever the number of errors committed at previous heights or distances. Only if there is a tie at the greatest height or distance will the errors that have been committed in the previous test or tests be taken into account.

Pierre Jonquères D'Oriola on Charleston

DUTCH WARM-BLOOD

This horse traces back to two much older Dutch breeds, the Groningen and the Gelderland, with important infusions of blood from the English Thoroughbred and stallions belonging to the principle breeds of riding horse in France and Germany. The Stud Book of this breed dates back to 1958 and the Dutch Warm-blood Society keeps a watchful eye on the breeding programme and its development. As well as being used for light draught work, this horse gives outstanding performances in sporting events and has distinguished itself both in jumping and dressage. Members of the breed that have become internationally famous include Calypso, ridden by Melanie Smith (USA), winner of the Volvo World Cup, and Dutch Courage, ridden by Jennie Loriston-Clarke (GB), who won the bronze medal at the Dressage World Championships in 1978.

This horse has a particularly flowing and supple action, which only highlights its attractive appearance.

Breed: Dutch Warm-blood
Place of origin: Holland
Height at withers: approx. 16.2 hands
Structure: meso-dolichomorphic
Colour: bay—brown—chestnut—black—grey
Temperament: quiet—willing
Aptitude: saddle-horse and light draught
Qualities: a good jumper
Head: well proportioned—profile straight or slightly convex—forehead wide—ears mobile and a nice size—eyes expressive—nostrils wide
Neck: a good length and well muscled—well set-on
Body: withers prominent—back straight—loins powerful—croup slightly sloping—tail well set-on—chest broad and muscular—girth deep
Legs: strong and well muscled—shoulder long and sloping—forearm long—joints broad and clean—tendons strong—foot well proportioned with solid horn

GELDERLAND

The origins of this breed can be traced back to mares native to the Gelderland province, which benefited from being crossed with Neapolitan, Norman and Norfolk Roadster stallions. More recently, during the course of the nineteenth century, additional blood from the Anglo-Norman, Oldenburg and Hackney was introduced.

This horse is distinctive for its elegant bearing as well as its flowing action and rather high-stepping, eye-catching trot. It is often likened to the Groningen, which it is in fact replacing in response to modern demands. As well as being suitable for fast, light draught work it makes a useful riding horse and is a reasonably good jumper. The present trend is to use it for crossing with other saddle horses, particularly the English Thoroughbred, with the aim of enhancing this natural ability. Although the Gelderland is a generally useful and versatile horse, aesthetically it reveals more than a few irregularities giving it a rather unbalanced appearance.

Breed: Gelderland
Place of origin: Holland (Gelderland)
Height at withers: 15.2–16 hands
Structure: mesomorphic
Colour: chestnut—grey—bay—black; frequently with white markings
Temperament: docile
Aptitude: light draught—saddle horse—farm work
Qualities: a good jumper
Head: rather flat and long—profile straight or slightly convex—full forelock
Neck: well proportioned—arched—muscular—not well set-on, but with a full mane
Body: withers fairly prominent and broad, merging with the line of the neck—back long and straight—croup short, broad and horizontal—tail set high—chest full and deep
Legs: well muscled—shoulder long and sloping, well muscled—forearm and leg quite long—foot broad—reasonable natural stance

FRENCH ANGLO-ARAB

The English Thoroughbred and the Arab have long been crossed all over the world in attempts to obtain a good riding horse possessing the combined qualities, but none of the defects, of these two outstanding breeds. It is, however, to the French, that the development of the finest example is due. The French Anglo-Arab was first selected at the studs of Tarbes and Pau in the Pyrenean region of southwest France, which were originally founded by Napoleon. It was then further developed at the Pompadour Stud Farm, by crossing with broodmares of Oriental origin, undoubtedly descended from horses abandoned by the Moors after their defeat at Poitiers in 732 A.D., during their retreat southwards over the Pyrenees. These very horses had a marked effect on the local horse population and were the progenitors of the Tarbes or Pyrenean breed as well as the Limousin (from Limoges). The French Anglo-Arab has received important contributions from highly prized stallions such as Massoud (1814–1843), regarded by Morris as the ideal model for his studies, which led to his theory dealing with the angle of the various joints. The French Anglo-Arab is a solidly built animal with good conformation, an energetic but quiet temperament and a distinguished bearing, making it one of the most popular breeds of saddle horse. Because of its notable aptitude for jumping it is used with great success in show jumping. A prerequisite of the Stud Book is that all animals to be included must have at least 25 per cent Arab blood.

Breed: French Anglo-Arab
Place of origin: France (Pyrenees)
Height at withers: 16–16.3 hands
Structure: meso-dolichomorphic
Colour: bay—brown—chestnut—grey (rare); with frequent white markings
Temperament: energetic but quiet
Aptitude: saddle horse
Qualities: an excellent jumper
Head: small and well set-on—profile straight—forehead broad—eyes large
Neck: well proportioned—muscular—well set-on
Body: withers high and well defined—back straight—loins short and broad—croup long and flat—tail well set-on—chest wide—girth deep
Legs: robust and strong—shoulder long and sloping—joints clean—tendons set well apart—forearm and leg long and well muscled—foot solid—good natural stance

TRAKEHNER

This breed was developed principally for the army at the Stud of Trakehnen, founded in 1732 by Friedrich Wilhelm I of Prussia. Initially, contributions were made by stallions of various breeds and above all by "Schweiken" horses—a local breed with remote origins that had been present in the region since the Middle Ages, and which had benefited from infusions of Oriental blood as far back as the sixteenth century. The present-day breed is the result of a series of crosses predominantly with the Arab and the English Thoroughbred. At the end of the Second World War, in the winter of 1944–5, the local people took flight before the advancing Russian troops, moving more than 650 miles (1,000 km) to the west and taking with them as many of their horses as possible. The extremely harsh weather conditions made their trek even more of an ordeal, and demanded great powers of endurance; nevertheless over 1,000 horses reached West Germany (a mere handful when compared with the 25,000 mares registered in 1939), where new stud farms were set up. The horses left behind in East Prussia gave rise to the Masuren.

The Trakehner is a solidly built horse, showing great freedom of movement at all paces, especially at the gallop. It is a natural jumper, and is often used for show jumping. Its numerous qualities have made it particularly suitable for improving other European breeds (including the Holstein), as well as some American breeds.

Trakehner

Norman

NORMAN

At the end of the eighteenth century the precise origins of the horse population in Normandy were uncertain although it had undoubtedly been influenced by Arab horses brought to France after the Crusades. The stock was further influenced by the importation of Young Rattler, a Norfolk stallion foaled in England in 1811 out of a daughter of the English Thoroughbred mare Snap, and sired by the Thoroughbred Rattler, a direct male descendant of the great Godolphin Arabian. Young Rattler, who is now considered to be the foundation sire of the Norman, also had a great influence on the forbears of the French Trotter. The Norman is a good jumper and is successfully used now in show jumping competitions. A cob type is also bred for farm work. The breed's Stud Book was established in 1950, under the title of Selle Français and admits selected, but not necessarily purebred, mares, English Thoroughbred stallions, Arabs and French Trotters, all of which breeds have contributed to the development of the present-day type. Of the animals belonging to this "new" breed 45 per cent are sired by a Selle Français, 33 per cent by an English Thoroughbred, 20 per cent by an Arab, and 2 per cent by a French Trotter. Crosses between English Thoroughbreds and French Trotters, Anglo-Arabs or Arabs and French Trotters, and English Thoroughbreds and Anglo-Arabs (on condition that the Arab blood accounts for at least 25 per cent) are also permitted.

There are five different types of Selle Français—three of medium weight and two of the heavy type. The medium weight type includes the small group (up to 15.3 hands), the medium group (15.3–16.2 hands) and the large group (over 16.2 hands). The heavy type is divided into the small group (up to 16.2 hands) and the large group (over 16.2 hands). The distinction between the medium-weight type and the heavy type is based on the horse's ability to carry riders of a certain weight.

This is a well-built animal, with a graceful and balanced appearance that reflects the influence of Arab and English Thoroughbred blood in particular.

Breed: Norman—Selle Français—French Saddle-horse
Place of origin: France (Normandy)
Height at withers: 15.2–16.3 hands
Structure: meso-dolichomorphic
Colour: bay—chestnut—grey (rare)
Temperament: quiet but energetic
Aptitude: saddle horse
Qualities: a good jumper
Head: small and well set-on—profile straight or convex—ears long—eyes deep-set—jaws pronounced
Neck: long and well muscled—well set-on
Body: withers long and prominent—back straight—croup long and muscular, slightly sloping—chest wide and deep
Legs: not very long but solid and well muscled—shoulder long and nicely sloping—joints clean—tendons set well apart—cannons short and thin—foot with tough horn

Trakehner

Breed: Trakehner (East Prussian)
Place of origin: West Germany
Height at withers: 16–16.2 hands
Structure: meso-dolichomorphic
Colour: chestnut—bay—brown—black—grey (rare)
Temperament: quiet but dynamic
Aptitude: saddle horse—light draught
Qualities: a good jumper
Head: well proportioned and well set-on—profile straight—forehead broad—eyes lively
Neck: long and well set-on—well formed
Body: withers quite pronounced—back straight—croup well muscled and slightly sloping—tail well set-on—girth deep
Legs: strong and well muscled—shoulder long and sloping, well muscled—joints broad and clean—tendons set well apart—hoof solid—good natural stance

HOLSTEIN

This is one of Germany's oldest breeds, and there is evidence that it dates back to the fourteenth century from a stable owned by the monastery of Uetersen, in the marshlands to the northeast of the Elbe estuary. During the Middle Ages the Holstein was simply a heavy war horse of the same type as the Great Horse, but it also retained its importance for the military in later periods when it was used not just as a cavalry horse, but as a gun horse, for pulling artillery.

The first regulations about the breed did not come into being until 1680 but these were subsequently modified in 1719 and again in 1782. Contributions to the development of the Holstein have been made over the centuries first by horses of Oriental origin, Spanish and Neapolitan horses, and then by the English Thoroughbred, the Cleveland Bay and the Trakehner. Recently frequent and systematic use has been made of the English Thoroughbred, with the aim of enhancing the particular qualities that make this horse well suited to show jumping and three-day events. The present-day Holstein is distinguished by its free and flowing action at the gallop, and for its supple and elegant trot; it is also a good jumper.

Breed: Holstein
Place of origin: West Germany
Height at withers: 16.1–16.2 hands
Structure: meso-dolichomorphic
Colour: bay—brown—black—grey—chestnut
Temperament: docile—quiet—energetic
Aptitude: saddle horse
Qualities: a good jumper
Head: long and well set-on—profile straight or slightly convex—ears rather long—eyes lively and expressive—nostrils wide
Neck: long and well shaped—muscular—carried elegantly
Body: withers prominent—back straight and often long—loins robust—croup full and muscular, slightly sloping—tail well set-on and carried elegantly—chest full and deep
Legs: strong and well muscled—shoulder sloping, long and muscular—joints broad and clean—cannons fairly long—tendons set well apart—hoof tough

MECKLENBURG

Although smaller in build, in many ways the Mecklenburg resembles the Hanoverian. After the Second World War the breed was revived in East Germany, where the State directly controls the mating of its stallions in its own studs, while the mares are usually privately owned. This animal has a fairly compact physical structure marked by well-developed hindquarters.

Breed: Mecklenburg
Place of origin: East Germany
Height at withers: 15.3–16.2
Structure: meso-dolichomorphic
Colour: bay—brown—black—chestnut (sorrel)
Temperament: docile and quiet
Aptitude: saddle horse
Qualities: strong and courageous
Head: of average proportions
Neck: sturdy
Body: withers pronounced—back straight—loins broad and powerful—croup sloping—chest full and deep
Legs: strong—solid bone structure—shoulder nicely sloping—joints clean—hoof rounded and strong

EINSIEDLER

This breed is named after a town called Einsiedeln in the Swiss Canton of Schwyz. Here, in a Benedictine monastery there is evidence of the existence of a stud dating back to 1064. This breed therefore, like many others, has been developed by monks undergoing a series of modifications over the years with the introduction of Hackney and Norman blood. Modern breeding of the Einsiedler is based principally on the Norman, which is why it is sometimes also known as the Swiss Norman. This horse serves many purposes, and is also used by the Swiss army, which uses the breed's skill at jumping to its full advantage in horse trials and show jumping. It resembles the modern Selle Français, both in conformation and structure, though not achieving this breed's harmony of form, much less its performance.

Breed: Einsiedler (Swiss Norman)
Place of origin: Switzerland
Height at withers: 15.3–16.2 hands
Structure: mesomorphic
Colour: bay—chestnut
Temperament: docile
Aptitude: saddle horse and light draught
Qualities: a good jumper

Einsiedler

SPANISH ANGLO-ARAB

This horse is the result of crosses between Arab-Spanish mares and English Thoroughbred stallions, which is why the breed displays all the features of the Anglo-Arab. It is a fine and versatile saddle horse and a good jumper, making it particularly well suited to a wide variety of equestrian sports, from show jumping to dressage. It has a quiet but energetic temperament and shows considerable courage; for both these reasons it is used in Spain to test the fighting spirit and stamina of young bulls destined for the bullring.

Breed: Spanish Anglo-Arab (Hispano)
Place of origin: Spain
Height at withers: 15.1–16 hands
Structure: meso-dolichomorphic
Colour: bay—chestnut—grey
Temperament: quiet but energetic
Aptitude: saddle horse
Qualities: a good jumper

Spanish Anglo-Arab

SARDINIAN ANGLO-ARAB

It is easy to distinguish the Oriental origins of this breed. Arab horses were introduced into Sardinia around the tenth century, at a time when the Saracens dominated the island. As a result of crosses with the native horse, which was smallish in stature, and later with Andalusian stallions, imported by Ferdinand the Catholic in the early sixteenth century, it became possible to establish the basic characteristics of the breed. With the arrival in Sardinia of the Savoys in 1720, horse breeding suffered a marked period of decline, and only began to recover at the start of the twentieth century when important contributions were made by Arab stallions. The subsequent and repeated use of English Thoroughbred stallions has led to the formation of the Sardinian Anglo-Arab as it is known today. In some individual cases the breed achieves a truly impressive physical appearance and size—far larger than in the past, when it generally measured only about 14.2 hands.

Breed: Sardinian Anglo-Arab
Place of origin: Italy (Sardinia)
Height at withers: under 16 hands (small); 16–16.3 hands (medium); over 16.3 hands (large)
Weight: 880–1,210 lb (400–550 kg)
Structure: dolichomorphic
Colour: bay—chestnut—grey (dappled)
Temperament: well balanced
Aptitude: saddle horse
Qualities: hardy—strong—swift—a good jumper—excellent staying power
Head: light, square, with a straight profile—well set-on—ears small and mobile—eyes large and lively—nostrils wide and mobile
Neck: light—muscular—well set-on and carried well
Body: withers full and pronounced—back straight or slightly hollow—loins short and muscular—croup nicely sloping and well proportioned—tail well set-on and well carried, with plenty of hair—chest broad—girth full and deep with well arched ribs—abdomen quite drawn in
Legs: solid with broad joints—shoulder long and sloping—cannons thin but strong—tendons set well apart and clean—pasterns nicely sloping and a good length—foot has strong horn and well proportioned hoof—regular natural stance
Skin: thin and elastic

SALERNO

The Salerno descends from the Neapolitan, a breed that was very popular during the Middle Ages, and received repeated infusions of Oriental and Spanish blood. Selection of the breed, also known as the Persano, dates back to the Bourbon period under the reign of Charles III, king of Naples and then of Spain, who was the promoter of this horse from 1763 onwards. The breeding programme suffered greatly with the unification of Italy, and was finally suppressed altogether in 1874 by a ministerial decree. In the twentieth century, however, a revival movement got under way, and the breed was slowly but enthusiastically restored, first as a carriage horse but later as a saddle horse. In order to upgrade its riding qualities, English Thoroughbred blood was introduced into the breed (replacing the Arab which was used in the past) with particular emphasis on animals with notable "staying power." The most conspicuous results of this change in direction have been the increase in stature (from between 15.2 and 16 hands to between 16 and 17 hands), and the increasingly rare occurrence of the once common grey coat.

Recently a group of 40 selected mares has been moved to Grosseto in Italy, near the Army Animal Training Centre which is responsible for supplying the Italian mounted police and cavalry with animals for both service and sport.

Breed: Salerno (Persano)
Place of origin: Italy (Salerno)
Height at withers: 16.1–17 hands
Weight: 880–1,100 lb (400–500 kg)
Structure: meso-dolichomorphic
Colour: bay—chestnut—black—grey
Temperament: quiet—balanced—energetic
Aptitude: saddle horse
Qualities: a good jumper
Head: light and well set-on—profile straight—forehead wide and square—eyes lively—nostrils wide
Neck: long and well set-on
Body: withers quite pronounced and muscular—back well proportioned—loins short—croup muscular—girth deep
Legs: shoulder long and nicely sloping—cannons sometimes slender but strong—hoof has strong horn—good natural stance
Skin: thin

PLEVEN

This recently developed breed has been undergoing selection since the end of the nineteenth and the early twentieth centuries in the Georgi Dimitrov state-owned agricultural establishment near Pleven, from which it takes its name. Its handsome appearance is unmistakably that of an Anglo-Arab and its development has been influenced by crosses between Russian Anglo-Arab stallions and local Arab and crossbred mares. Later, over a period of some 25 years Arab and Gidran stallions have been used. By 1938 the permanent features of the breed had been fixed and since then English Thoroughbred blood has also been introduced.

Breed: Pleven
Place of origin: Bulgaria
Height at withers: approx. 15.2 hands
Structure: dolichomorphic
Colour: chestnut
Temperament: intelligent—good-natured—lively
Aptitude: saddle horse—farm work
Qualities: a good jumper
Head: well proportioned—profile straight
Neck: quite long and well muscled
Body: withers high—back long and straight—croup slightly sloping—chest well developed—girth full and deep—abdomen drawn in
Legs: shoulder long and nicely sloping—forearm and leg long and well muscled—joints broad and clean—cannons long—tendons set well apart and strong—foot well formed—good natural stance

GIDRAN ARABIAN

The progenitor of this breed was Gidran, an Arab stallion of the Siglavy strain, bred and reared at the Babolna stud in Hungary and descended from another stallion which bore the same name and which had been imported to Hungary in 1816. The present-day breed was formed by means of a series of crosses with the English Thoroughbred, and Gidran stallions are now exported throughout eastern Europe to be crossed with local mares. This extremely fiery horse has a most distinguished bearing and balanced appearance. It is well suited to light draught work but is most prized as a saddle horse.

Breed: Gidran
Place of origin: Hungary
Height at withers: 16.1–17 hands
Structure: dolichomorphic
Colour: chestnut
Temperament: lively—not always docile
Aptitude: saddle horse and light draught
Qualities: a good jumper
Head: small and well set-on—profile straight—ears small—eyes large and lively
Neck: quite long—well shaped
Body: withers pronounced—back straight and long—croup well muscled, wide and usually short—tail well set-on—chest full and deep
Legs: well muscled—shoulder sloping and well muscled—thigh well developed and muscular—cannons quite short—tendons set well apart and clean—foot well formed with strong horn—good natural stance

165

MALAPOLSKI

This recently developed breed is similar in appearance to the Wielkopolski, although there is still a good deal of variation in type according to the region in which the horses are bred. It is a light horse and of greater quality than the Wielkopolski, having been influenced by Oriental and a certain amount of English Thoroughbred blood. There are two principal types of Malapolski: the larger Sadecki, used for draught work and greatly influenced by the Furioso, and the Darbowsko-Tarnowski, which has much Gidran blood.

Breed: Malapolski (Polish Anglo-Arab)
Place of origin: Poland
Height at withers: 15.3–16.2 hands
Structure: dolichomorphic
Colour: bay—brown—chestnut—grey—roan—black
Temperament: calm—balanced
Qualities: excellent stamina—good jumper

UKRAINIAN RIDING HORSE

This breed was created shortly after the end of the Second World War by crossing German Trakehner and Hanoverian, as well as English Thoroughbred stallions with local Hungarian Nonius, Gidran and Furioso-North Star mares. Selection was continued by again using English Thoroughbred stallions and English halfbreds (English Thoroughbred X Hanoverian). The yearlings are broken in at 18 months and training is begun. The foals are consequently selected according to practical trials involving either flat racing or other competitions such as cross-country, hurdle racing or dressage. The best animals are admitted to the breed and reared on state horse farms. Although some members of this breed do not display exceptionally well-developed hindquarters, the overall appearance is generally desirable. The good bone and well-developed muscles make this horse suitable not only for equestrian sports but for light draught and farm work. The Ukraine was once Europe's major grain supplier, and although today things have changed, agriculture still plays an important part in the economy of the region. Because of its qualities as a good saddle horse and jumper, and the way in which it is selected and reared, the Ukrainian Riding Horse undoubtedly deserves recognition as a sporting horse.

Breed: Ukrainian Riding Horse
Place of origin: Soviet Union (Ukraine)
Height at withers: 15.3 hands (females); 16.3 hands (males)
Structure: meso-dolichomorphic
Colour: bay—chestnut—black
Temperament: balanced
Aptitude: good jumper
Head: quite large—profile straight—ears not too long and upright—eyes lively
Neck: long and well-muscled
Body: withers high—back slightly hollow towards the withers—croup long and slightly sloping—chest deep
Legs: tough—shoulder long and sloping—joints broad—forearm long—foot well proportioned

Malapolski

Budyonny

Ukrainian Riding Horse

BUDYONNY

This horse is named after the man who created it, Marshal Budyonny (or Budenny), a hero of the Russian Revolution and a leading figure in the Second World War. In the years immediately following the fall of the Tsar, the Marshal undertook the task of selecting horses at the military stud farm at Rostov, with the aim of producing a horse for military use. This breed has been obtained by crossing the Don horse with the English Thoroughbred, and it was first officially recognized in 1948. The Budyonny is a healthy, sturdy horse with a graceful and balanced appearance and displays great freedom of movement at all paces, but especially at the gallop. It has a docile but energetic temperament, a natural talent for jumping and, in fact, meets all the requirements for modern sporting events.

Breed: Budyonny
Place of origin: USSR (Rostov)
Height at withers: 15.2–16 hands
Structure: meso-doliochomorphic
Colour: chestnut (predominantly)—bay—grey—brown—black (rare)
Temperament: docile but energetic
Aptitude: saddle horse and light draught
Qualities: a good jumper
Head: well proportioned—profile straight or slightly concave—well set-on
Neck: long and well formed
Body: withers prominent—back straight and long—croup slightly sloping—tail well set-on—chest wide and deep
Legs: long—good bone and muscular development—shoulders sloping and well muscled—tendons well defined and set well apart—hooves well formed and strong

TERSKY

The origins of this breed can be traced back to an early breed that was used by the Cossacks and which was significantly improved during the nineteenth century by Count Strovanov with the introduction of Kabardin blood. It was further perfected, after the Revolution, by Marshal Budyonny, who introduced blood not only from the Kabardin, but also from the Don, the Arab and the English Thoroughbred. The breed, which was officially recognized in 1948, was originally developed for military use, but with the sudden changes that came about in battlefield strategy and in the modern army, its importance was redirected towards equestrian competitions. Because of its natural aptitude for jumping, and its freedom of movement it is particularly well suited to a wide variety of sporting events including show jumping, cross-country and dressage. It is a docile and intelligent animal, and is currently bred at the state studs of Stavropol and Tersk.

Breed: Tersky (Tersk-Terskij-Terek)
Place of origin: USSR (Stavropol)
Height at withers: 15–15.2 hands (mares also 14.3 hands)
Structure: meso-dolichomorphic
Colour: grey
Temperament: docile and intelligent
Aptitude: saddle horse—light draught
Qualities: a good jumper
Head: well proportioned—profile straight or slightly snub—ears pointed and of medium length, mobile—eyes large and lively
Neck: well formed and of average length
Body: withers prominent—back straight and not too long—croup quite flat—tail set-on high—girth full and deep
Legs: well structured and well muscled—shoulder long and sloping—joints and tendons clean—foot well formed

Tersky

WALER

This horse is named after New South Wales, the region in which the breed originated as a result of crosses between Arab, English Thoroughbred and Anglo-Arab stallions with mares of various strains and stock including some belonging to the Cape breed (the first breed to be introduced into Australia from South Africa). Since the start of the twentieth century use has been made of the Anglo-Arab alone, resulting in a horse that was particularly well suited to the military, and is used by the Australian cavalry and the Indian army. In Sydney, because of its good reputation in times of war, a monument was erected in its honour. From 1932 onwards the Waler has gone into a steady decline and consequently it has altered in many respects. The present-day breed is now far removed from the original. In 1971 a special society was set up to register and control the selection of the few true members still existing, with the aim of increasing the numbers and reviving the breeding of this type of horse.

It is a docile and courageous horse, with a good aptitude for jumping, often being used in hurdle races and other similar events, as well as for polo.

Breed: Waler (Australian Stock Horse)
Place of origin: Australia
Height at withers: 15–16 hands
Structure: meso-dolichomorphic
Colour: bay—brown—black—grey—chestnut
Temperament: docile and courageous
Aptitude: saddle horse and light draught
Qualities: a good jumper
Head: well proportioned—profile straight—ears long—nostrils wide
Neck: long and well formed
Body: withers prominent—back long and straight—croup slightly sloping—girth full and deep
Legs: solid and well muscled—shoulder quite straight but well muscled—joints strong (specially the hocks)—tendons clean and set well apart—foot well shaped

Waler

FOX HUNTING

It is impossible to establish exactly how and when man became a hunter, and it may have been pure chance that first led him to sample meat and thus become an omnivore. Although this modification to man's feeding habits may seem of little importance, it proved crucial to his survival, because the meat-based diet, which is richer in higher proteins, gave him increased physical strength and contributed to the development of his brain, and consequently his intelligence. Man had no option but to organize some sort of system between himself and others, to devise forms of communication, study methods of attack and design increasingly effective weaponry, such as the type of propelled harpoon used by the Magdalenian people in the Upper Palaeolithic, at the end of the Pleistocene era. When an animal was slain, a use was found for every part of it: the flesh for eating, the hide for making clothing and forms of shelter, the bones for fashioning utensils or handles, the ivory and horn for carving ornamental objects, the fat for heating and lighting and the tendons for making ropes and nets. These activities of prehistoric man are well documented in many caves such as Ambona, Terra Amata, La Madeleine, Lascaux, Le Mustier, Altamira and La Quina, in which tools and the remains of slain animals have been discovered, together with marvellous ceiling and wall paintings, depicting hunting scenes with wounded animals. One very beautiful example is the black and yellow horse in a cave at Lascaux in the Dordogne region of France, which dates back to approximately 12,000 B.C. Hunting therefore developed out of a basic need for food and a less rigorous way of life. As time passed, and man's habits and requirements changed, so hunting gradually, through increasingly elaborate techniques and instruments, assumed a new significance as a sport. Today man practises many forms of hunting but the most well known is probably fox hunting, which involves the use of horses.

Fox hunting is a typically English sport, although it is also popular in France, Italy, and many other countries. Before they discovered the pleasures of fox hunting the English were keen deer and stag hunters, for which they relied on the help of a dog called the staghound. As the number of deer decreased over the years, and with the consequent movement towards fox hunting, it became necessary to develop a type of dog that would be better suited to the new form of hunting. Consequently, after a careful and patient process of selective breeding, a new type of hound emerged called the foxhound. This dog was extremely fast, lively, intelligent, and well suited to working in large packs. Hunting scenes with packs of hounds have been depicted by many famous artists. One particularly well-known painting is by Paolo Uccello, commissioned for the hunt held by Charles V in honour of the Duke of Saxony (Ashmolean Museum, Oxford).

Considerable importance is naturally attached to the choice of horse and the way it is trained for the sport. Once again the English and the Irish have proved themselves masters in the art of selecting a particular type of horse known as a hunter which is the best suited to this purpose.

For the most part these horses are half-breds obtained by crossing specific breeds and they must have certain common characteristics, such as good endurance at a sustained and extended gait; they must be easy to handle, and capable of negotiating ditches and fences in their path; they must not be easily frightened or alarmed, and they must be docile, sociable and good-natured. Fox hunting meets, organized by associations that establish regulations and dates, involve a quite complicated ceremonial procedure, in which each participant has a special role to play. At the top of the pyramid is the Master of Foxhounds who is responsible for the general organization of the hunt and its staff and will know the hunting area well. Then there is the huntsman in charge of the hounds, whose job is to lead the hounds to the scent of the fox. The whippers-in are there to ensure that the pack stays together and does not become dispersed; lastly, the grooms have the job of tending to the horses and are responsible for their physical fitness.

All these different roles involve a precise hierarchical interdependence, and this hierarchy must be closely adhered to. It is seriously frowned upon if the hunt staff and officials impede one another in an attempt to get to the fore, or if they take on roles which are outside their particular brief. It is absolutely forbidden to obstruct the Master in the performance of his duties. He must always be ahead of the other participants to play his leading role in the hunt: it is his task to give the signal which permits the field to close in and kill the fox and it is the Master alone who may acknowledge the skills of the other huntsmen and award the honours. The size of the pack of hounds is calculated in relation to the area of the land over which the hunt will take place. It is important that there are neither too few hounds nor too many. If the pack is too large there is a risk that the hounds will get in each other's way, and compete too fiercely with one another.

Dress for the hunt also follows a strict set of rules, and contributes to the visual spectacle of this sport. The most elegant dress, which was once reserved for the stag or deer hunt but is now also used for competitors for dressage events, consists of a red (known as pink) or black double-breasted and cutaway riding coat with swallow tails, worn over white or beige jodhpurs. A top hat and heavy black leather riding boots with tan tops finish off the outfit. The most commonly worn dress, for both gentlemen and lady subscribers consists of a black jacket worn with the hunting cap (a hard hat with peak) or a bowler, pale jodhpurs and black boots. Gentlemen alone may wear a long single-breasted jacket, either all red or red with black velvet cuffs and collar. At the neck all hunt members wear a wide knotted tie or cravate known as a hunting stock, which is held in place with a pin. The tie is the only item of clothing where personal preference is permitted. All the other items of clothing must abide by the regulations. Although there are now fox hunting societies in many parts of the world this sport is still most popular in England where, according to estimates made by the British Field Sports Society, there are more than 230 hunts. The diffusion of this sport is, however, seriously hampered by many problems. Aside from the increasing shortage of open spaces unencumbered by buildings, the fact is that fox hunting is seen as an essentially élitist pursuit, both because of its origins as an aristocratic pastime, and also because it tends to be an expensive sport for those taking part. Nowadays, moreover, this sport is more and more widely viewed as an anachronism, and a symbol of class distinctions that are gradually losing their significance. It is also seen by animal lovers as a pastime that attracts individuals who derive pleasure from killing an animal whose chances of defending itself are extremely slender.

IRISH HUNTER

This horse cannot be regarded as a breed in the true sense of the word, since it represents the issue of a particularly successful crossing between the Irish Draught Horse and the English Thoroughbred. As a result it is technically a half-breed even though its morphological features generally remain constant from generation to generation.

It is famous as a hunter since it is endowed with great stamina and staying power over all kinds of terrain. Today it is principally recognized and sought after as an exceptional jumper. It is sure-footed and courageous, and because of these varied qualities is widely used as a competition horse at trials and shows. Depending on the weight of the rider which the horse is capable of supporting, there are three distinct categories: light —up to 170 lb (75 kg), medium—up to 185 lb (82 kg) and heavy—up to 215 lb (95 kg). The English also have horses of this type, replacing the Irish Draught Horse by the Cleveland Bay (in most cases) or the Suffolk Punch, but they have as yet failed to match the results achieved by the Irish. The hunter is a well-built horse, with a balanced, solid appearance and good endurance.

Breed: Irish hunter
Place of origin: Ireland
Height at withers: 16.2–17.1 hands
Structure: mesomorphic
Colour: bay—brown—black—grey—chestnut
Temperament: quiet and docile
Aptitude: saddle horse
Qualities: a very good jumper with good stamina
Head: nicely proportioned—profile straight or slightly convex—eyes lively—jaws well delineated—well set-on
Neck: long and well muscled—slightly arched—well set-on
Body: withers clean and prominent—back short—croup broad, muscular and slightly sloping—chest full and deep
Legs: solid and well muscled—shoulder sloping and well muscled—joints broad and clean—tendons set well apart—hoof well formed with tough horn

POLO

Even though the game of polo has conspicuously British connotations, its remotest origins can be traced back to Asia. It probably originated in what was formerly Persia (now Iran), and then spread swiftly to other parts of Asia, such as Tibet, China, Japan and India, where it was adopted by British army officers during the long period of the Raj. Naturally the game of polo has changed much over the years and the rules of the modern game are different, both with regard to the number of players making up a team (there were often a great many), and with regard to the types of horse used. In Mongolia, for example, mules were the most usual mounts. In India polo was played essentially with Manipuri ponies from Assam—small, slender and elegant horses which are fast, tough, easy to handle and have good endurance. Nowadays, besides ponies, many other types of horse are used, which, although they do not form a specific breed, must nevertheless comply with a very precise set of requirements dictated by the nature of the game.

As a general rule horses used for playing polo are not very large, to make the game more agile and fast, and they are often produced by crossing English Thoroughbred stallions with local ponies (as occurs in the United States), with the Criollo (in Argentina), and with the Welsh pony (in Europe). Although the horse itself plays an important part in polo, the role played by the rider is no less demanding. He must be highly trained in a specific method of horsemanship, which will ensure that he can stay firmly in the saddle using only the strength of his buttocks and thighs so that his upper body and arms remain unencumbered and free to move in order to strike the ball with the special flexible mallet. A good polo player must be able to guide the horse more with his legs and body than with his hands and must have an excellent sense of balance which will prevent him from falling during clashes on the field, or when he has to lean outwards to hit the ball. Polo is a sporting event which, in the past, was included in the Olympic Games (Paris 1924 and Berlin 1936). Its subsequent exclusion may possibly be because there are very few countries able to present a sufficiently good team, as this is still not a very widespread sport. This is principally because polo is still a game for the élite, reserved for a small social class once represented by the aristocracy but today determined purely by financial means. Despite this, in countries where polo is played quite widely, such as Great Britain, Argentina and the United States, people from all walks of life come and watch, attracted by its intrinsically spectacular nature. As a spectator sport polo is a varied and exciting game, involving speed, skill and suspense, which thrill and delight the onlookers. A major attraction is the Cup of the Americas, which is held periodically between the United States and Argentina, both countries where this game is extremely popular. In the United States, as far back as 1960, there were no fewer than 80 polo clubs, scattered all over the country. In its modern form polo dates back to 1860, and is now supervised by the regulations laid down by the Hurlingham Polo Club in London. Every other participating country now accepts this authority.

Polo is played on a standard ground of 300 × 160 yards (274 × 146 m), using a ball with a maximum diameter of 3¼ inches (8.25 cm) made of willow or bamboo root. A flexible polo stick or mallet made of cane is used to strike the ball. There are four players in each team and the game essentially involves striking the ball into the opponent's goal which is 8 yards (7.3 m) wide. The ball must be struck in accordance with precise rules. A match is divided up into six periods called chukkas, each of which lasts for 7½ minutes. Referees, also on horseback, immediately stop play at the end of each chukka and are also responsible for penalizing any foul play, such as cutting across an opponent, not striking the ball from the left shoulder or riding dangerously. It is also their decision to allow goals and award penalties. In New York, Chicago and Australia a variety of indoor polo is played, with three-man teams, on smaller grounds and with a different set of rules from outdoor polo.

RODEOS

The traditional American rodeo is a competitive event in which cowboys have the opportunity to display both their skill and courage. The spirit and atmosphere that surround these occasions can be compared with the medieval tournament, despite the difference in social class of the respective participants. The Texan cowboy, who first appeared in the United States between 1820 and 1830, along with his *gaucho* counterpart from the South American pampas, instantly represent a life of adventure, coupled with a style of behaviour and dress that originated as a result of practical necessities, but have ended up by creating fashions still in circulation today. The wide-brimmed hat (stetson) helped to keep off the burning rays of the sun, and had to be properly worn to stay on in high winds; the bandanna knotted at the back of the neck protected the throat and was drawn up over the mouth to keep out desert dust; the heavy boots had high heels to give a better hold on the stirrups; the leather legging or chaps offered good protection against spiny bushes, rocks and the horns of animals. To all this was added the tall, lean, bow-legged figure of the cowboy himself, with the typical rolling gait of one used to spending long hours in the saddle, and with all the courage and hardiness which, in the early years of the nineteenth century, made them the only men who dared to make inroads into the arid deserts of Arizona and New Mexico, and into the Rocky Mountains, above latitude 92°. Originating, therefore, as a nomadic horseman, highly skilled but often coarse, brash and tough, and frequently without education, the cowboy was gradually immortalized, veiled by an aura of legend, becoming the focus of popular dances, songs and folk-tales which play such an important part in American folklore.

All that was needed to become a cowboy was proven skill in the saddle and an ability to steer and round up livestock and handle the lasso and a six-shooter. Cowboys are still very much a part of the North American tradition, even though they may have lost their aura of heroism and hard-living. Today the cowboy no longer leads such a free-roaming independent life and, with the industrialization of livestock farming, he has become an ordinary farm hand. However, the legacy of his forbears still survives in his outstanding skill as a horseman and in the style of his clothing. The horse most widely used by cowboys is the Quarter Horse. With its quick reflexes, good speed over short distances and strong sense of cooperation, this horse is the best suited to the everyday work of herding cattle and consequently adapting well to the spectacular thrills of the rodeo. Like the medieval tournament, the rodeo is also governed by rules and regulations, which eventually decide the winners. A rodeo takes place in several phases called events which essentially echo the cowboy's daily tasks. For example, in "saddle bronc-riding" the contestant must mount a wild horse and remain in the saddle for at least ten seconds, holding the reins with just one hand, with the other free and held up in the air. In the "calf-roping" event he must chase and catch a calf with the lasso, then dismount from his horse and tie any three of the calf's legs together in the shortest possible time; in the "bareback" bronc-riding event the contestant must display extraordinary skill by mounting a wild, unbroken horse which has only a girth around it instead of a saddle. Other events have also been added to these classic exercises, but they are outside the cowboy's professional activities. These modifications have been introduced both to satisfy the demands of the cowboys themselves, always keen to try their hand at increasingly difficult events, and to provide the crowds of spectators always present at these meetings, with more excitement and variety. Some of the more popular additional events are "bull-dogging," in which the cowboy has an assistant whose task is to ride alongside a young bull, thus forcing it to run fast and straight; at this point the cowboy draws alongside the young bull, leaps on to its back, and starts to twist its neck by gripping its horns, until the animal is on the ground with all its legs extended. Another is called "Brahma bull-riding" which involves riding particularly lively young local bulls or Indian Brahma bulls (with humped necks). This is the most dangerous event, because if the cowboy falls he may well be charged by the bull. There are of course other events resulting from specific local demand, the most exciting of which are "barrel racing" and "pale-bending" (a kind of slalom between posts).

Besides the Quarter Horse, the Mustang and Palomino are also frequently used at rodeos.

CIRCUS HORSES

Horses are an important feature of any circus. The circus as we know it today is the result of a long period of historical and cultural development which has, over the years, introduced new forms of attraction to stimulate public interest with a varied and eye-catching programme in which striking displays of skill are performed by man and animal alike. In ancient Rome, however, the circus was a place designed for horse and chariot races rather like the Greek hippodrome, except that tests of skill were also carried out there, such as standing on the back of a galloping horse or jumping from one horse to another while on the move. The track was oval, surrounded by tiers for the public, between which there were gates (vomitories) giving access to the arena. At one end of the oval stood the Porta Pompae, through which the opening procession made its entrance, led by the magistrate in charge of the games, together with the priests and all those participating in the different contests. At the opposite end stood the Porta Triumphalis, through which the winners would enter to make their lap of honour and receive the applause of the crowd. In Rome this type of spectacle became so popular that the Roman emperors built larger and larger circuses to accommodate the huge crowds. The Circus Maximus, the remains of which can still be seen between the Aventine and the Palatine, underwent a series of extensions and could eventually hold 150,000 spectators in the reign of Julius Caesar, increasing to over 380,000 under Nero and Trajan. The track measured about 2,150 × 420 feet (650 × 125 m). A great many other circuses were then built, both in Rome and in the imperial provinces, thus creating widespread enthusiasm for this form of spectacle which in time also included hunting events, gladiator combats and fights between wild animals.

The present-day circus began to take shape towards the end of the eighteenth century, but because the programme was no longer dictated by a fixed structure, the horse was no longer used for races, since it was impractical to have tracks the size of those in Greek and Roman circuses. Attention was therefore focused not on the speed of the horse but rather on its qualities of intelligence, memory and sensitivity and it was thus expected to perform a wide range of exercises, many of which were quite spectacular. A circus horse can count, beating out the numbers with its hoof, solve problems, walk upright on its hind legs, perform dance steps, gallop around the track and carry out complicated figures, lie down and pretend to sleep, and sometimes even cover itself with a blanket. The most brilliant performance by the horse in the circus ring is the so-called "liberty" act, performed by many horses together decorated with splendid trappings. The word "liberty" here means simply that the horses are riderless, and not attached to each other, but their route around the track is precisely marked out by marching music and the crack of the trainer's whip. Each horse knows its place, and its radius of action, and can thus move in a synchronized way with all the other horses (there are usually a dozen), without overlapping or colliding. The result is an agile, swift, elegant and harmonious spectacle which ends with the "courbette," when all the horses stand upright on their hind legs in front of their trainer as a sign of obedience, and in recognition of the public's applause. In another type of performance ballerinas and acrobats rely on the perfect timing of the horse to carry out dance routines or complicated exercises on its back, while it is galloping around the ring.

In American circuses in the early years of the nineteenth century there was a particularly fashionable type of spectacle known as the "Wild West," which involved performing breathtaking stunts on horseback, mock fights between cowboys and Indians and branding. The best-known Wild West showman was William F. Cody, better known as Buffalo Bill who, mounted on his famous Appaloosa, worked as a pair with Annie Oakley, known popularly as Little Sure Shot, who, while riding at the gallop would shoot and shatter glass balls and extinguish

173

the glowing butt-ends of some of the more courageous spectators' cigars.

Obviously a circus horse could not be expected to perform these types of exercise without training. Each movement and each gait are the result of a long period of instruction, directed with patience, love and dedication by the circus people, to which the horse readily submits, and thus achieves a perfect understanding with its trainer. One particular horse, the famous Clever Hans, was able to perceive the slightest muscular twitch, and the slightest variations in the psychological tension of his trainer, gleaning instructions which he then used to solve complex arithmetical problems, announcing the results by beating out the numbers with his front hooves. The types of horse used in circuses vary, depending on the task they are being expected to perform. Arab, Lipizzaner and fierce Cossack stallions are most ideally suited to "liberty" acts. Powerful horses, with a wide croup and calm obedient nature, such as the large Norman horses, are best for acrobatic and ballerina acts. Ponies are widely used in circuses both for "liberty" acts and for exercises with young artists.

RIDING SCHOOLS

With the increase in the general level of affluence and amount of leisure time available, the horse, once a status symbol reserved for the upper classes has today been rediscovered and reevaluated. A growing number of people now take up riding, which combines the advantages of a sport with the pleasure of living in touch with a sensitive, intelligent animal, trained to tolerate even the complete beginner.

Riding schools are extremely popular nowadays, and have specially designed tracks with floors which, whether indoors or outdoors, are both hard-wearing and soft enough to cushion any fall. Apart from the characteristics of the floor, indoor riding facilities have to meet certain specific structural requirements: the height of the building must be between 7.5 and 10 m (24 ft 8 in–32 ft 1 in); the roof must be provided with skylights for illumination; the doors through which the horses pass must be at least 2m (6 ft 6 in) wide and 4 m (13 ft) high; and the walls must be lined with wood (kneeboard) and slope outwards. Military riding schools normally have two tracks, a large one for the troops and a small one for the officers, plus an open-air track.

In recent years, some riding schools have practised a new form of motor rehabilitation for spastics and disabled people, as a useful accompaniment to exercises in the gymnasium and swimming pool. Hippotherapy, as it is called, is officially recognised by medical science. Docile, well-trained, particularly responsive horses are used, able to cooperate actively with the riders, enabling them to perform series of movements which help them recover the use of specific groups of muscles. Once again, the horse has proved its value to man, in the important field of health.

RIDING HOLIDAYS

The pace of modern-day life is such that many people, overwhelmed by the stress of day-to-day living, wish to find a more humane alternative. They are learning to appreciate nature, aware that their biological rhythms cannot be suppressed without giving rise to neuroses, trying to forget their troubles temporarily, and free their minds of the burden of an existence which is becoming increasingly difficult, in spite of modern labour-saving devices. Special types of holiday have been devised to cater for this need: farming holidays, where one can till the land as in times past; craft holidays where one can rediscover the pleasure of creating something with one's own hands, and riding holidays, providing physical contact with an animal. Horse riding, and pony trekking holidays began in Great Britain, where the love of horses is part of the cultural tradition, but they have now spread to virtually all countries. Many more places now provide organized holidays on horseback, often accompanied by an expert. The horses are docile and well-trained, able to tolerate inexpert riders or children, and travel for many hours. They enable their riders to exchange the pressures of modern urban life for the peace of the countryside where they can learn again to delight in the colour of a flower or the shade of the woods, and look upon animals with a friendly eye. Fishing holidays on horseback are also popular in America, the fish being caught in shallow streams or pools, whilst in Ireland, as an alternative to trekking holidays, one can rent brightly-coloured "gypsy caravans" looking very much like the old tinkers' carts and drawn by strong, patient horses.

PARADES

Military parades on horseback are a major tourist attraction even today, as now that their original purpose as a display of martial power has been lost, the emphasis is increasingly on pageantry. Divisions of mounted troops do, of course, still exist, but for ceremonial rather than military purposes. This is the case with the Italian Presidential Guard, a special squadron of the Carabinieri, established in 1842. The "Corazzieri" (Cuirassiers), a select group clad in breastplates and helmets with long horse tails, forms the Guard of Honour inside the Quirinale (Presidential Palace) in Rome and escorts visiting foreign dignitaries. The Italian Carabinieri are also world-famous for the display known as the "Carosello dei Carabinieri" (Tournament of the Carabinieri) in which the soldiers, in full military regalia and mounted on white horses, perform complex maneuvers in close formation. The most spectacular part is when two squadrons charge each other head on, with swords unsheathed, stopping short when they are only a few inches apart. Obviously the horses have to be particularly well-trained to do this. Similar tournaments are held in other parts of the world, that of the Republican Guard in Paris being a notable example, as well as those held in Germany and Switzerland. In Canada, the Royal Canadian Mounted Police, dating from 1873 but organized in its present form since 1920, once played a major part in maintaining law and order in the northwestern regions, but nowadays, the "Mounties" serve a representative purpose, their displays with the red-uniformed lancers being known and admired throughout North America.

One cannot mention parades without paying due homage to Great Britain. The spectacle of the Queen's Horse Guards with their red and blue uniforms, cuirasses and helmets, accompanying the royal coach to Westminster for the annual opening of Parliament is unique. Equally spectacular is the grand parade for the ceremony of Trooping the Colour, which takes place on the Queen's official birthday, and the parades in honour of visiting Heads of State. Everything is studied down to the last detail: the soldiers' uniforms are a play of colour; the helmets, swords and brasses, flashes of light; the horses have the dignity and composure of equestrian monuments and move solemnly in unison, aware of the importance of the occasion. These magnificent spectacles, of which the horse is the protagonist, attract a wide audience not just on account of their undoubted beauty, but because of the human propensity for romanticism and nostalgia.

HORSE SHOWS

The first competitive horse show probably took place in the eighth century B.C. and they have continued in some shape or form to the present day. To start with, they were chiefly concerned with the skills of working horses, but now that the horse is rarely needed for this purpose, the shows are mainly devoted to saddle and harness animals. In England, the Horse of the Year Show takes place at Wembley stadium each year. It is dedicated to all types of horse and is a typically English celebration of an animal that has become an integral part of British culture. The show is open to all categories of horse, provided they have distinguished themselves in their specific field during the year. It is a lively, spectacular occasion. The Queen's Horse Guards open the show with a solemn roll on the drums, then each horse does a turn of the stadium with its rider and is applauded by the crowd. There are prizes for each category. In America, horse shows were at first confined to the Atlantic Coast region, but have gradually spread to all areas, including Canada, and they have tremendous public appeal. The American Horse Shows Association organizes most of them and sets standard rules and regulations. The shows are arranged in a number of ways: some are gymkhanas lasting half a day; others last for more than a week and include various types of performance at different levels. They normally take two to three days, starting with a careful examination of the horse, of its physical conformation, stance, muscle power, colour, and state of health; then it is put through its paces—its gait is examined, along with its speed, brilliance of action and readiness of response.

WELSH COB

Section D of the Welsh Stud Book is devoted to this horse, which is a larger version of the Welsh pony of the Cob type. It is similar in conformation to the Welsh Mountain pony. However, its precise origins are not clear and Arab and Spanish horses may have contributed to its development, as well as the Hackney. Its ancestor is the Welsh Mountain pony, which accounts for it being included in the same Stud Book. It is the typical cob shape, of strong constitution but agile, spirited and courageous.

These qualities made it a good light draught horse in the past, and it was occasionally used for drawing carriages although nowadays it is mainly used for riding. It is at home on difficult terrain and is also a fairly good jumper making it suitable for trekking and also for show jumping.

Breed: Welsh Cob—Section D
Place of origin: Great Britain (Wales)
Height at withers: 14.2–15.2 hands
Structure: mesomorphic
Colour: bay—brown—black—chestnut—roan—grey; except part colours
Temperament: courageous but gentle
Aptitude: light draught and saddle horse
Qualities: endurance—good jumper—good bearing
Head: small but well proportioned (pony type)—profile straight—ears small and pointed—eyes prominent and set well apart
Neck: long and well built—arched—muscular
Body: withers quite pronounced—back quite short—croup long, broad and rounded—tail set-on high and carried well—chest broad and deep
Legs: short and sturdy—muscular—shoulders sloping and muscular—fore and hind legs long—joints broad and clean—pasterns of the correct length and angle—feet well proportioned with a strong hoof—slight feather permitted, provided it is silky

IRISH COB

This was produced by crossing the Connemara, Irish Draught and English Thoroughbred. Like the other cobs, which all have a height of between 14.2 and 15.2 hands, the Irish is stocky, with short limbs, and a well-developed musculature. It is lively and agile, and often a good jumper. Although it has been bred since the eighteenth century, it cannot be considered an established breed, as it sometimes exceeds the height limits for its category, and must therefore be regarded as a strong type of horse with good stamina, developed for light draught work and riding. Mechanization has restricted the uses of the Irish cob, but it is nonetheless an excellent saddle horse, its sturdy frame making it suitable for use both by beginners and experienced riders.

Breed: Irish cob
Place of origin: Ireland
Height at withers: 15–15.2 hands
Structure: mesomorphic
Colour: bay—brown—black—grey—chestnut
Temperament: sensitive and dynamic
Aptitude: saddle—light draught
Qualities: strong—a good jumper
Head: distinguished—profile convex—ears small
Neck: quite short and muscular
Body: withers quite pronounced—back short and straight—croup rounded and muscular—tail well set-on—chest broad
Legs: short and sturdy—shoulder powerful and sloping—foot rounded with a strong hoof

BEBERBECK

Development of this breed started near Kassel in 1720. The original aim appears to have been quite different from the end result, in that the intention was to produce a Palomino. Local brood mares were crossed first with the Arab and subsequently, with the English Thoroughbred. The stud was closed in 1930 and the numbers of this breed have since fallen. It has excellent bone and in appearance it is rather like a heavier version of the Thoroughbred.

Breed: Beberbeck
Place of origin: West Germany
Height at withers: over 16 hands
Structure: meso-dolichomorphic
Colour: bay and chestnut are most common
Temperament: quite courageous—steady—patient
Aptitude: saddle horse—farm work
Qualities: willing

WÜRTTEMBERG

Development of this breed began at the Marbach stud at the end of the sixteenth century by crossing local indigenous mares with Arab, Suffolk Punch and Caucasian stallions. Later, contributions were also made by the Trakehner, Norman and Anglo-Norman. The Württemberg is a strong horse with good conformation and an even temperament. The Stud Book goes back to 1895.

Breed: Württemberg
Place of origin: West Germany
Height at withers: approx. 16 hands
Structure: mesomorphic
Colour: bay—brown—black—chestnut; with white markings
Temperament: steady and docile
Aptitude: saddle and light draught horse—farm work
Qualities: strong and hardy
Head: square, of average size—profile straight—ears straight
Neck: well shaped
Body: withers prominent—back long and straight—loins strong—croup slightly sloping—tail well set-on—chest deep
Legs: strong and muscular—shoulder nicely sloping and muscular—hooves tough and well formed

SHAGYA ARABIAN

This horse originated from the Babolna state stud, founded back in 1789, where in 1816, under military orders all the available mares were crossed with Oriental stallions. Fresh Arab blood was later introduced over the ten-year period from 1830 to 1840 following the importation of brood mares and stallions directly from the Orient. Of these stallions, one in particular, the grey Shagya, proved an excellent stud, giving rise to homogeneous progeny the majority of which inherited his colour. The Shagya Arabian became widely distributed not just in Europe, particularly Eastern Europe, but also in the United States. Numerous studs are still to be found in the Old World, in Austria, Germany, Romania, Czechoslovakia, Poland and Yugoslavia, apart, of course, from Hungary. In build and appearance this horse has virtually all the characteristics of the Arab. Whilst essentially a saddle horse, it is also suitable for use as a harness horse.

Breed: Shagya Arabian
Place of origin: Hungary
Height at withers: approx. 15 hands
Structure: mesomorphic
Colour: grey (most common)—black (extremely rare)
Temperament: lively and energetic
Aptitude: saddle—harness
Qualities: speed and endurance
Distribution: Europe—United States

EAST FRIESIAN

Until the Second World War, this breed developed in tandem with the Oldenburg, which was of similar origin, and exchanges and crosses between the two breeds were frequent until the division of Germany prevented this from continuing. Since then, the two breeds have developed along different lines. The East Friesian has benefited from the contributions made by Arab stallions from the Marbach stud and Hungarian stallions from Babolna. The grey stallion Gazal has been the most notable contributor. The influence of Arab blood greatly refined the East Friesian, but more recently the Hanoverian has been used, to produce a type of horse more in keeping with modern demands.

Breed: East Friesian
Place of origin: East Germany (Thuringia)
Height at withers: 15.2–16.1 hands
Structure: meso-dolichomorphic
Colour: bay—brown—chestnut—grey—black
Temperament: spirited and courageous
Aptitude: saddle horse—light draught
Qualities: elegant, free movement
Head: well proportioned—profile straight—eyes lively—nostrils wide
Neck: long and arched
Body: withers quite pronounced—back long and straight—croup slightly slanting—tail well set-on—chest broad and deep
Legs: shoulder long and sloping—forearm and leg long and muscular—thigh muscular—joints broad and clean—tendons well defined and strong—good natural stance

East Friesian

Shagya Arabian

WIELKOPOLSKI

A recently-developed breed descending from what used to be two separate breeds, the Poznan and the Masuren as well as other formerly distinct regional types. All these horses had similar qualities and were characterized by the influence of varying amounts of Arab, Hanoverian, East Prussian and English Thoroughbred blood. Although no longer officially recognized, certain distinct regional types are to be found living alongside the Wielkopolski. This is an animal of good conformation, with powerful hindquarters, a strong constitution, maturing relatively early, and a good mover. Oriental and Trakehner stallions have contributed a great deal to its development. The Wielkopolski is suitable for riding and light draught work.

Breed: Wielkopolski
Place of origin: Poland
Height at withers: 15.1–16.1 hands
Structure: mesomorphic
Colour: bay—brown—chestnut—grey—black
Temperament: calm—steady—courageous
Aptitude: saddle and light draught horse
Qualities: sturdy conformation
Head: well formed—profile straight—ears straight—eyes lively—nostrils wide
Neck: correctly proportioned—slightly arched—well set-on
Body: withers quite pronounced—back quite long and straight—croup slightly sloping—chest high and deep—abdomen drawn in
Legs: shoulder long, muscular and sloping—forearm and leg long and muscular—joints broad and clean—cannons quite long—tendons neat and well defined—pasterns nicely sloping—foot well formed

NONIUS

This breed descends from a French stallion called Nonius, out of a Norman mare and an English half-bred stallion, which had been captured by the Austrians after their victory over Napoleon at the Battle of Leipzig. Whilst not aesthetically outstanding, this stallion sired a number of excellent sons at the Mezöhegyes stud in Hungary where he was crossed with Andalusian, Lipizzaner, Kladruber, Arab, Norman and English half-bred mares. Besides being very prolific, he left his unmistakable stamp on his progeny, the result being a fairly late-developing horse that does not reach maturity until it is six years old, but which, on the other hand, is quite long-lived. This breed is in great demand nowadays and there are two distinct varieties: the small Nonius, which is versatile but not very pleasing in appearance, despite being derived from the English Thoroughbred, and the large Nonius, which is produced by crossing with the Anglo-Norman, and which is valued as a carriage horse.

Breed: Nonius
Place of origin: Hungary
Height at withers: 14.2–15.2 hands (small) 15.2–16.2 hands (large)
Structure: mesomorphic
Colour: brown—black
Temperament: calm and willing—lively
Aptitude: saddle horse—light and medium-light draught
Qualities: strong and resistant
Distribution: Hungary—Czechoslovakia—Romania—Yugoslavia—Bulgaria
Head: rather long but light and well set-on—profile straight or slightly convex—forehead broad—ears long—nostrils wide
Neck: long and muscular—well set-on
Body: withers clean and quite prominent—back long but sometimes slightly hollow—croup rounded, not very broad—tail well set-on—chest broad and deep
Legs: solid and muscular—shoulder long and nicely sloping—joints clean—tendons set well apart—pasterns short—hoof well formed and quite tough

DANUBIAN

This breed was developed around the start of the twentieth century at the Pleven state stud by crossing Nonius stallions with Gidran mares. The result was as might be expected—quite a powerful light draught horse, which is also sometimes used under saddle. The Danubian is not particularly pleasing to look at, various parts of its body being clearly out of proportion; the powerful trunk, shoulders, hindquarters and neck frequently look as though they do not belong to the same horse as the more delicate head and comparatively slender legs. Good jumpers can be produced by crossing mares of this breed with the English Thoroughbred.

Breed: Danubian
Place of origin: Bulgaria
Height at withers: approx. 15.2 hands
Structure: meso-dolichomorphic
Colour: dark chestnut—black
Temperament: steady but active
Aptitude: light draught and saddle horse
Qualities: strong and enduring
Head: well proportioned—profile straight
Neck: of average length—strong—broad-based
Body: withers prominent—back quite long and straight—croup slightly sloping—tail well set-on—chest wide and deep
Legs: long and slender—shoulder slightly sloping but powerful—forearm quite long—cannons and pasterns short—hooves well formed

PERSIAN ARAB

It would be more logical to consider this horse as a type of Arab rather than a breed in its own right, both because of the considerable resemblance between them and because they presumably have common origins. The Persians have moreover always insisted on importing Arabs from the Negev Desert to supplement and improve their breeding. The resulting progeny are called Hoor if both parents are Arabs; Beradi if only the mother is Arab and Hedijn if only the father is Arab. From this one can see the close connection between the two breeds, which would more than justify their being considered together. The Persian Arab is, however, of a slightly different build from the Arab and is considerably larger, probably a result of the different environment in which it is raised.

Apart from the Persian Arab, two other highly-prized breeds of horse are produced in Iran—both saddle horses and probably derived from the Persian, therefore of Arab type: the Darashouri, a strong, elegant horse originating from the Fars region of southern Iran, north of the Persian Gulf, and the Jaf, a native of Kurdistan and therefore used to the harsh life of the desert. Great importance is attached in Iran to a halfbred known as the Tchenarani, which has been produced since 1700 by crossing Persian stallions with Turkmene brood mares. This horse is produced for its own particular qualities, and therefore it is not usually interbred since this causes the progeny to deteriorate. It is an elegant animal with powerful hindquarters, much prized as a saddle horse. Crossing Turkmene stallions with Persian brood mares did not give such satisfactory results, and is not therefore practised.

Breed: Tchenarani
Place of origin: Iran
Height at withers: over 15 hands
Structure: meso-dolichomorphic
Colour: bay—chestnut—black—grey
Temperament: gentle—spirited—willing
Aptitude: saddle horse
Qualities: strong with good endurance
Head: small and well formed—profile straight—eyes large and clear—forelock thick
Neck: long and arched
Body: withers prominent—back short and straight—croup sloping—tail flowing and well set-on—chest broad and deep—abdomen drawn in
Legs: sturdy and muscular—shoulder sloping—joints and tendons clean—foot strong

Breed: Persian Arab
Place of origin: Iran
Height at withers: 14.2–15.1 hands
Structure: mesomorphic
Colour: bay—chestnut—grey—black (rare)
Temperament: spirited and energetic
Aptitude: saddle horse
Qualities: fast and with good stamina

Breed: Darashouri (Shirazi)
Place of origin: Iran (Fars region)
Height at withers: approx. 15 hands
Structure: meso-dolichomorphic
Colour: chestnut—bay—grey—black (rare)
Temperament: docile—spirited
Aptitude: saddle horse
Qualities: tenacious

Breed: Jaf
Place of origin: Iran (Kurdistan)
Height at withers: approx. 15 hands
Structure: meso-dolichomorphic
Colour: chestnut—bay—grey—black (rare)
Temperament: gentle but spirited—courageous—highly strung
Aptitude: saddle horse
Qualities: resistant

KARACABEY

This horse originated from crosses between local brood mares and imported Nonius stallions, whose influence is still quite evident. The Karacabey has good conformation and is versatile and enduring, besides being the only Turkish horse to display uniformity of type and constant transmission of characteristics.

Breed: Karacabey
Place of origin: Turkey
Height at withers: 15.2–16.1 hands
Structure: mesomorphic
Colour: bay—brown—chestnut—grey—black—roan
Temperament: willing—balanced
Aptitude: saddle and medium-light draught horse—pack horse—farm work
Qualities: enduring and versatile

SYRIAN

This horse probably derives from the Arab, which it resembles in a number of features. According to some sources, its performance is even better, particularly with horses originating from the Anazeh strain. It is a strong animal with good endurance, well able to withstand the rigours of life in the desert, where it lives with the Bedouins. It has an elegant bearing, the principle differences from the Arab being that it is larger, with a rather untamed expression and a less balanced conformation being somewhat angular in appearance. The Syrian Government, aware of the value of this breed, has taken the necessary steps to protect its integrity, including arrangements for publication of the first volume of a Stud Book.

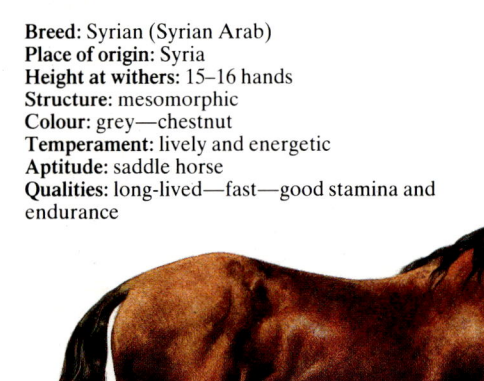

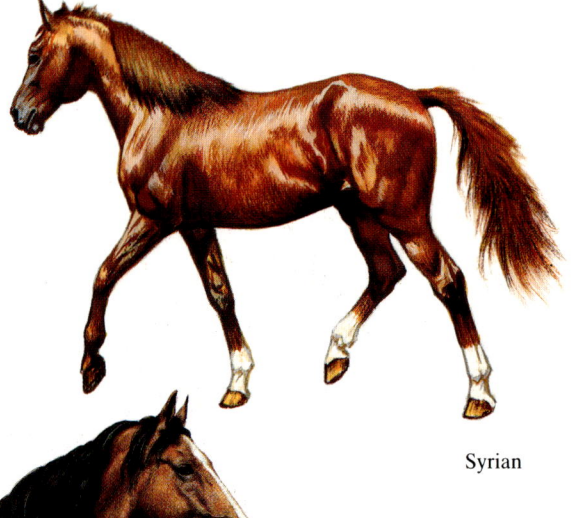

Breed: Syrian (Syrian Arab)
Place of origin: Syria
Height at withers: 15–16 hands
Structure: mesomorphic
Colour: grey—chestnut
Temperament: lively and energetic
Aptitude: saddle horse
Qualities: long-lived—fast—good stamina and endurance

Karacabey

Iomud

Syrian

Don

IOMUD

A descendant of the ancient Turkmene horse, the Iomud shows exceptional resistance to fatigue and to the arid heat of the desert, being able to survive without water for long periods rather like a camel. It is a solidly-built horse, even if it is more compact and less rangy than other breeds such as the Turkoman and Akhal-Teké, which are of similar origin. The commonest colour is grey. Because of its qualities, it is well suited to cross-country races.

Breed: Iomud (Jomud—Yomud)
Place of origin: Soviet Union (Turkmenistan)
Height at withers: 14.2–15 hands
Structure: meso-dolichomorphic
Colour: grey—chestnut—bay—black
Temperament: patient but energetic
Aptitude: saddle and light draught horse
Qualities: strong with good endurance—a good jumper
Head: light and well formed—profile straight or slightly convex—ears pointed—eyes large
Neck: well shaped but rather thick—of average length
Body: withers fairly prominent—back long and straight, slightly depressed towards the withers—croup slightly sloping—chest deep—abdomen drawn in
Legs: solid and muscular—shoulder sloping—joints broad and clean—tendons well defined—hoof well formed

DON

This breed can be traced back to the old Don horse, small of stature but energetic and sturdy, which was improved in the eighteenth century by crossing with Karabakh, Turkmene and Karabair stallions. Subsequently, at the beginning of the last century, the Orlov was introduced, followed by the English Thoroughbred towards the end of the century. The Don is a tough but attractive-looking horse with a solid, sturdy build making it particularly suited to life on the steppes crossed by the river from which it takes its name. It is one of the basic Soviet breeds of horse and is used to improve many other breeds or even in the creation of new ones, such as the Budyonny.

Breed: Don
Place of origin: Soviet Union
Height at withers: 15.1–15.3 hands
Structure: meso-dolichomorphic
Colour: bay—brown—black—grey—chestnut
Temperament: steady but energetic
Aptitude: saddle and light draught horse
Qualities: strong and hardy
Head: of average proportions and well set-on—profile straight—eyes large and expressive
Neck: of average length—well formed
Body: withers prominent—back long and straight—croup long and slightly sloping—chest broad and deep
Legs: long and muscular—shoulder generally sloping and well formed—joints broad and clean—tendons strong—foot broad with tough horn

NOVOKIRGHIZ

This breed, which was officially recognized in 1954, is so named to distinguish it from the old Kirghiz horse of the nomadic tribes, from which it is derived. The Novokirghiz was in fact produced in the 1930s by crossing first with the English Thoroughbred and later with the Don, followed by inbreeding and the more recent addition of halfbred Anglo-Don blood. In a short time the characteristic features of the breed were thus firmly established. It is a well-built horse with a balanced appearance, tough and sufficiently versatile to be equally useful as a saddle, pack or light draught horse. It is also well suited to mountain areas like the one from which it originated, between Soviet Asia and China.

Breed: Novokirghiz (Kirghiz)
Place of origin: Soviet Union (Kirghiz)
Height at withers: 14.2–15 hands
Structure: mesomorphic
Colour: bay—brown—grey—chestnut
Temperament: docile but energetic
Aptitude: saddle horse—light draught—pack horse
Qualities: strong with good endurance
Head: small and well formed—profile straight—ears pointed
Neck: long and well formed
Body: withers pronounced—back straight and long—croup slightly sloping—chest well developed
Legs: rather short but stocky and muscular—shoulder correctly sloping—joints and tendons clean—hoof hard and well formed

TURKOMAN

This breed is closely related to the Akhal-Teké and the Iomud, being like them a descendant of the ancient Turkmene, which is now extinct. It has a number of features in common with the Akhal-Teké, both breeds being used for racing in their country of origin as they combine speed with exceptional endurance. However it is more docile and tractable than the Akhal-Teké and is an elegant horse of proud bearing that combines an aristocratic appearance with a solid frame and good conformation. It is a good, free mover able to gallop at considerable speed.

Breed: Turkoman (Turkmene)
Place of origin: Soviet Union (Turkmenistan)
Height at withers: approx. 15.2 hands
Structure: dolichomorphic
Colour: grey—bay—brown—black—chestnut; white markings frequent
Temperament: docile and courageous
Aptitude: saddle horse
Qualities: speed and endurance
Head: well proportioned and well set-on—profile straight—forehead broad—ears long
Neck: long but sometimes rather muscular
Body: withers high and well defined—back long and straight—croup long and sloping—chest deep
Legs: long and thin but strong—muscular—shoulder sloping, long and muscular—pasterns long—hoof small and hard
Skin: fine

KUSTANAIR

The Kustanair is a well-established, ancient Oriental breed, originating from the city of the same name in Kazakhstan. Two distinct types are now produced: a more solid version obtained by the use of Orlov and Don blood, and a lighter, more elegant version, which has been improved with the aid of the English Thoroughbred. The Kustanair is mainly used for riding but is also suitable for light draught work, being strong and hardy, as well as extremely frugal. It is a typical product of its native environment.

Breed: Kustanair
Place of origin: Soviet Union (Kazakhstan)
Height at withers: 15–15.2 hands
Structure: mesomorphic
Colour: bay—brown—black—grey—chestnut—roan
Temperament: calm but energetic
Aptitude: saddle horse—light draught
Qualities: versatile—strong with good endurance
Head: rather light—profile straight—forehead broad—eyes small—lower jaw well defined
Neck: of average length and muscular
Body: withers quite pronounced and muscular—back long and straight—croup sloping—chest broad and deep
Legs: long and muscular—shoulder long and sloping—good bone structure—joints clean—hoof well formed

Novokirghiz

Turkoman

Kustanair

LUSITANO

The precise origins of the Lusitano are uncertain but are probably similar to those of the Andalusian, which it resembles in some respects. This horse was used in the past for military purposes and is still used today for light farm work, but it is most famous for its role in Portuguese bullfights, in which the *rejoneador* confronts the bull on horseback. Part of the skill of this *torero* is in avoiding any injury to his mount, which must leave the arena uninjured. The Lusitano is now clearly on the decline, although it is still the top Portuguese breed. It is a horse of good conformation, but its role has been strictly limited since the advent of mechanization by the virtual demise of the cavalry and the disappearance of horse-drawn carriages.

Breed: Lusitano
Place of origin: Portugal
Height at withers: 15–16 hands
Structure: mesomorphic
Colour: grey—chestnut—brown
Temperament: docile
Aptitude: saddle horse—light draught
Qualities: agile and easy to handle—very frugal
Head: small with straight profile—ears small—eyes lively—jaw not pronounced
Neck: short and rather thick—slightly arched—well set-on
Body: withers clearly visible but not prominent—back short and straight—croup rounded—tail set-on low—chest broad
Legs: shoulder muscular and correctly sloping—forearm and thigh long—joints solid—good natural stance

CARTHUSIAN

The Carthusian monks of Jérez de la Frontera devoted themselves to the selective breeding of Andalusian horses as long ago as 1476. The Carthusian horse originated from the studs founded by these monks in Seville and other parts of Andalucía. The horse is more Oriental in appearance than the Andalusian, as both the Arab and the Barb were used systematically in its development, and all pressures from the reigning monarchs of the time to introduce different types of blood were resisted. Most of today's Carthusians are descended from the famous stallion Esclavo and are reared in state-owned studs near Cordoba, Jérez de la Frontera and Badaioz. The Carthusian is a docile, intelligent and friendly horse. It has good conformation and a well-balanced appearance. The most common coat is grey, due to the influence of two stallions of this colour in the first half of the twentieth century.

Breed: Carthusian
Place of origin: Spain
Height at withers: approx. 15.2 hands
Structure: mesomorphic
Colour: grey (predominant)—chestnut—black
Temperament: docile and quiet
Aptitude: saddle horse—light draught
Head: light and well set-on—profile slightly convex—forehead broad—ears small—eyes large and lively
Neck: correctly proportioned and arched—well set-on
Body: withers not too prominent—back straight—croup muscular and rounded—tail well set-on—chest broad
Legs: sturdy—shoulder fairly sloping—joints broad and clean—good natural stance

Carthusian

Lusitano

CALABRESE

Originally of Arab derivation, during the Bourbon period, this horse was crossed with the Andalusian, which gave it particular elegance of movement. Its size has been increased by a careful process of selection, and the more recent use of English Thoroughbred stallions has greatly improved its performance. Oriental blood has however been reintroduced from time to time to maintain its distinctive characteristics, which are a dependable nature, balanced appearance and good endurance.

SICILIAN

The Sicilian is an equine population of clear Anglo-Oriental derivation, forming distinct native groups, rather than a breed as such. Those in the eastern provinces of Sicily (Catania, Syracuse, and Ragusa) are more elegant in appearance with pronounced dolichomorphic features, whereas those further inland are more compact and nearer to the mesomorphic type, although there is much variation.

Breed: Sicilian
Place of origin: Italy (Sicily)
Height at withers: 15.1–15.3 hands
Structure: meso-dolichomorphic
Colour: bay—chestnut—black—grey (dappled)
Temperament: spirited and highly strung
Aptitude: saddle and light draught horse
Qualities: resistance to fatigue—excellent stamina
Head: light—profile straight or slightly convex—ears small—eyes lively—nostrils wide
Neck: of a good length—muscular—well set-on
Body: withers high—back short—back and loins strong—croup angular and tending towards horizontal—tail well set-on and flowing—chest broad and deep
Legs: long and muscular—shoulder sloping—joints clean—tendons strong and well defined—foot well formed and in proportion

SAN FRATELLO

This horse is reared in the wild state in Sicily, in the oak and beech woods of the Nebrodi mountains in the province of Messina, where the high ground is characterized by hard winters and hot summers. These climatic factors, together with the meager pastureland and the rigorous selection process exercised in their breeding, have combined to make the San Fratello a strong horse with a powerful body and outstanding resistance. Despite the introduction of Spanish Anglo-Arab, Anglo-Arab, Salerno and more recently, Nonius blood, the San Fratello has resisted all attempts at improvement, the only horse to which it has shown any affinity being the Maremma, with which it has been successfully crossed. Hence it has remained fairly pure. The San Fratello is particularly useful for trekking holidays on account of its strength and exceptional docility. The colts are trained as pack horses at the age of about 30 months, while the fillies are put to stud at the five centers set up by the Istituto di Incremento Ippico di Catania (Catania Horse Breeding Institute). The San Fratello breed numbers about 2,000. It is a well-proportioned horse with an elegant bearing, combining appreciable aesthetic qualities with exceptional strength.

Breed: San Fratello (Sanfratellano)
Place of origin: Italy (Sicily)
Height at withers: 15.2–16 hands
Weight: 1,100–1,300 lb (500–580 kg)
Structure: meso-dolichomorphic
Colour: black—bay—brown
Temperament: lively
Aptitude: saddle and pack horse—light draught
Qualities: hardy and frugal
Head: slightly heavy—profile straight or occasionally convex—ears straight—eyes expressive
Neck: correctly proportioned
Body: withers quite prominent—back straight—loins short and strong—flank well formed—croup wide and muscular, slightly sloping—tail well set-on—chest wide and deep
Legs: well formed and in proportion—shoulder nicely sloping—joints tough—good bone and muscular development—tendons strong—pasterns correctly sloping—hoof solid

Calabrese

Breed: Calabrese
Place of origin: Italy (Calabria)
Height at withers: 16–16.2 hands
Structure: meso-dolichomorphic
Colour: bay—brown—chestnut—grey—black
Temperament: active—lively—docile
Aptitude: saddle horse
Qualities: tireless—dependable
Head: well formed—profile straight or slightly convex—forehead broad
Neck: correctly proportioned
Body: withers prominent—back straight—loins short—croup slanting—chest broad and deep
Legs: shoulder long and sloping—tendons strong—hoof with strong horn good natural stance

Sicilian

MORGAN

A small bay horse called Figure of barely 14 hands was born in Massachusetts in about 1790, probably sired by an English Thoroughbred stallion out of a mare of mixed Arab, Welsh Cob, Harddraver and Fjord blood. Given in payment of a debt to an innkeeper in Vermont by the name of Thomas Justin Morgan, when the latter died, this animal, which everyone now called Justin Morgan's Horse, after changing owners several times, ended up in the hands of a farmer who put it to a wide range of uses, as well as entering it for various types of race, in which it earned a reputation for being unbeatable. However, the horse was outstanding above all as a stallion at stud, passing on its characteristic appearance and exceptional speed and versatility to all its progeny, thus producing a new breed that took the second half of its name.

Justin Morgan's horse lived to be over 30 and eventually died in 1821. The Morgan is mainly found in the United States, where it is still used in amateur trotting races, its place on the racecourse having been taken by the American Saddle Horse, to the development of which it in fact contributed. Time has not altered the original characteristics given to this breed by its founder, but its shape and stature have been improved. A handsome creature overall, sturdy and compact, but elegant, it is also used for riding and makes a good jumper.

Breed: Morgan
Place of origin: United States
Height at withers: 14.2–15.3 hands
Weight: 880–1,100 lb (400–500 kg)
Structure: mesomorphic
Colour: bay—chestnut—black; white markings common
Temperament: docile but energetic
Aptitude: harness and saddle horse
Qualities: fast and with good stamina—versatile
Head: of average size and slightly tapering from the jaw to the muzzle—profile straight—ears small and pointed—eyes set well apart and expressive—nostrils broad
Neck: of average length and muscular—arched—mane thick
Body: withers well defined but not too high—back short and wide—loins strong—croup rather long and rounded—tail well set-on and full—chest broad and muscular—girth deep
Legs: sturdy and muscular—shoulder long, sloping and muscular—well-developed bone structure and joints—forearm long and muscular—cannons short—tendons well defined—pasterns of medium length and not too sloping—hoof well formed, of average size and good thickness

PINTO

The Pinto was officially recognized in 1963 with the institution of a Stud Book by the American Paint Horse Association. To be registered, a horse must have both parents already listed or if only one is present, then the other must be a certified Quarter Horse or English Thoroughbred. The Pinto was apparently developed by the American Indians, who captured many horses brought to the New World by the Spanish *conquistadores*; a few of these had broken coat patterns (two of the ones which came over with Cortez had coats of this type). The Pinto was much appreciated by the American Indians partly because of the camouflage it offered, and this preference is amply documented by cowboy films. The Arabs, on the other hand, had no regard for part-coloured horses, to which they referred disparagingly as "the cow's brother." Even today the Pinto is often held in low esteem by horse lovers on account of its dubious pedigree, but the fact that it has now been recognized for over 20 years should undoubtedly help overcome this prejudice. Two stallions are regarded as having founded the breed: Sheik and Sun Cloud. There are two basic types of pattern: the Overo, with white patches on a coloured ground, and the Tobiano with coloured patches on a white ground. Of the two types, the Tobiano would seem to be the dominant gene and the Overo recessive. The Pinto is an extremely docile animal, which is equally good as a saddle or harness horse. It is particularly suitable for inexperienced riders. The characteristics of the breed are not yet clearly defined or constant, as breeders have concentrated hitherto on the type of coat. It tends, however, to be a sturdy, fairly compact horse with an elegant bearing.

Breed: Pinto (Paint Horse)
Place of origin: United States
Height at withers: 14.3–15.3 hands
Structure: mesomorphic
Colour: piebald or skewbald
Temperament: docile and calm
Aptitude: saddle—light draught
Qualities: sturdy
Head: well proportioned—profile straight—face broad—ears quite large but straight
Neck: well formed and muscular
Body: withers fairly pronounced—back short—croup rounded—tail well set-on—chest broad and deep
Legs: sturdy and muscular—quite short—shoulder long and sloping—joints and tendons strong—hoof rounded and in proportion

APPALOOSA

The distant origins of the Appaloosa are similar to those of other American breeds and can be traced back to the horses brought over to America by the *conquistadores* in the sixteenth century. Some of these animals were abandoned and captured by the Indians, or reverted to the wild, for example, the Mustang in the United States and the Criollo in South America. The Appaloosa owes its development to the Nez Percés—a tribe of Indians which occupied the region crossed by the Palouse river from which the breed takes its name. They fixed the characteristics of this horse by appropriate crossing, the selection process later being continued by white Americans, and in 1938 the breed was officially recognized. The distinctive feature of the Appaloosa is its colouring, which is the same as that found in Chinese art of the T'ang dynasty (618–907 A.D.), Persian art and even the cave drawings at Peche-Merle in France from the Upper Paleolithic era. These ancient examples raise questions concerning not only the true origins of the breed, but also whether this particular colouration occurred randomly at different, isolated periods in history or whether it has persisted constantly through the ages. There is therefore some controversy as to whether it should be considered a true breed or simply a particular type of coat or if indeed it is necessary to make a distinction between the two. To complicate matters still further, the foals of the Appaloosa are born with coats of a uniform colour, the characteristic markings only appearing later and invariably being of a different colour from those of the parents. This breed is still used by cowboys and in circus acts, but the Appaloosa undoubtedly deserves better treatment. This fairly compact horse with good conformation, a noble head and elegant bearing, is in fact a very fine galloper and a good jumper and the colour of its coat has done it some disservice in the past, by masking its true qualities.

Breed: Appaloosa
Place of origin: United States
Height at withers: 14.2–15.2 hands
Weight: 880–1,280 lbs (400–580 kg)
Structure: mesomorphic
Colour: distinctive, six types: snowflake—leopard—frost—marble—spotted blanket—white blanket
Temperament: steady and docile—athletic
Aptitude: saddle horse
Qualities: agile and with good endurance
Head: small and well set-on—profile straight—ears pointed—eyes large with obvious sclera
Neck: long and muscular—mane short and sparse
Body: withers quite pronounced—back short and straight—croup rounded and muscular—tail short with sparse hairs of varying length—chest deep
Legs: sturdy and muscular—shoulder long and sloping—good bone structure and joints—hoof with vertical black and white stripes
Skin: with areas of grey-pink mottling

PALOMINO

The Palomino cannot yet be regarded as an established breed, as its characteristics are far from uniform, both in terms of height and conformation. The one feature all Palominos have in common is in fact the distinctive coat, the colour of "a newly-minted gold coin," which can theoretically be produced in any other breed. Strangely enough, it is not possible to transmit this colour reliably and breeders have so far failed successfully to solve this problem. The origins of the Palomino are equally mysterious and according to some authorities, it goes back to the time of Homer. A preliminary attempt at registering this horse was made in the United States in 1932, but the two societies established in California in 1941 and Texas in 1946 failed to achieve recognition. It is much appreciated as a saddle horse in America, whilst the pony version is reared in Britain and provides an ideal mount for children, on account of its docility.

Palomino

Breed: Palomino
Place of origin: United States
Height at withers: 14–16 hands
Weight: 1,100–1,145 lb (500–520 kg)
Structure: mesomorphic
Colour: distinctive: the colour of "a newly-minted gold coin;" white markings permitted on the face only (not exceeding a star, stripe or extended stripe) and on the lower limbs (below the knees and hocks)—forelock, mane and tail lighter or darker than the coat (ivory—silver—flaxen) with not more than 15% dark hairs.
Temperament: docile and quiet
Aptitude: saddle horse
Qualities: easily managed and a good jumper
Head: small and well set-on—profile straight—ears small—eyes dark or hazel, both of the same colour
Neck: well formed and quite long—mane resplendent
Body: withers quite pronounced—back straight—croup rounded—tail flowing and well set-on—chest deep and quite broad
Legs: muscular—shoulder long and sloping—good skeleton and joints—tendons clearly defined—hoof well formed
Skin: fine and dark

Missouri Fox Trotting Horse

Albino

MISSOURI FOX TROTTING HORSE

Although this horse has been bred in Missouri and Arkansas since the beginning of the nineteenth century, it still does not have clearly defined, constant characteristics. Its most salient feature is the distinctive four-beat gait, appropriately named the "fox-trot," in which the animal canters with its forelegs and trots or walks with its hind legs. The motion of the limbs is accompanied by a rhythmic movement of the head, producing a clearly audible beat, which is the noise of the hooves often accompanied by that of the top and bottom rows of teeth chattering together. This animal has well-developed hindquarters and is widely used by cowboys, as it makes an ideal mount, being reliable and enduring in action, and capable of travelling long distances at an average speed of 5–10 mph (8–16 kmh).

Breed: Missouri Fox Trotting Horse (Missouri Fox Trotter)
Place of origin: United States (Missouri and Arkansas)
Height at withers: 14–16 hands
Structure: mesomorphic
Colour: chestnut—bay—black—grey—piebald or skewbald
Temperament: calm but energetic
Aptitude: saddle horse
Qualities: characteristic gait
Head: well proportioned—profile straight—ears pointed and of a good shape—eyes large and expressive
Neck: in proportion and well formed
Body: withers prominent—back short and straight—flanks full—croup muscular and rounded—tail well set-on—pectoral region broad and muscular—chest broad and deep
Legs: sturdy—shoulder muscular and well sloping—hoof well formed and in proportion to the size of the horse—good natural stance

ALBINO

The Albino originated in Nebraska in 1937, the foundation sire being Old King, from an Arab stallion and a Morgan mare. Despite attempts to fix its physical characteristics, the Albino has not yet achieved recognition as a true breed, although it is a sound animal, light but with good bone structure, long-lived, intelligent and docile. It is used as a leisure horse for riding, in circus acts and films.

Albinism is in fact an anomaly consisting of the partial or total absence of pigmentation, the result being a coat composed partly or wholly of white hairs on a pink skin, and blue eyes, both skin and eyes being sensitive to the sun. Thus an albino can be of any breed, rather than constituting a breed in itself. The factor for albinism is apparently dominant with the result that if an Albino stallion is crossed with a pony brood mare, albino ponies will constantly be obtained.

The American Albino Horse Club which sets the standards for this variety has created a distinction between the true albino (white) and the cream, changing its name in 1970 to the American White Horse Club. This was regarded as necessary because all Albinos were not pure white. The American Cream, as the new type of horse is now called, can be one of several combinations of colours:
1) ivory-white body, with white mane (lighter than body), blue eyes and pink skin;
2) cream body, mane darker than body, cinnamon-coloured skin and dark eyes;
3) body and mane of the same pale cream colour, with blue eyes and pink skin;
4) body and mane of the same cream colour, with blue eyes and pink skin.

The American Cream can vary in conformation, resembling, for instance, the Morgan, the Quarter Horse, the English Thoroughbred or the Arab.

Breed: Albino
Place of origin: United States
Height at withers: ideally 15.2 hands
Weight: 1,100–1,145 lb (500–520 kg)
Structure: mesomorphic
Colour: creamish-white
Temperament: very docile
Aptitude: saddle
Qualities: natural aptitude for learning exercises

AMERICAN SADDLE HORSE

This horse originated in Kentucky and was therefore first known as the Kentucky Saddlebred or Kentucky Saddle Horse. It was created by the colonists as a dual-purpose saddle and light draught horse for use on their vast plantations in that state. The English Thoroughbred, the Morgan, the Narragansett Pacer and probably also the Hackney, contributed to its development. The most outstanding feature of this breed is its repertoire of three or five different gaits, depending on its training. Three-gaited saddle horses perform the three basic gaits: the walk, trot and canter, whilst five-gaited animals can perform two additional, wholly artificial gaits: the "slow gait" or four-beat "stepping pace" and the "rack" which is a faster version of the other. Three-gaited saddle horses are displayed with the mane and tail almost completely clipped, while five-gaited animals have a long mane and the tail is decorated in various ways. The American Saddle Horse Breeders Society, which was founded in 1891 and is based at Louisville in Kentucky, now has over 140,000 members. It is a horse of good general conformation, imposing stature and elegant stance: the head is carried erect, which gives it a bold, proud bearing. However, this breed is the subject of some controversy, since although some experts value its artificial features, others regard them as unnatural and therefore ugly.

Breed: American Saddle Horse (Kentucky Saddlebred—American Saddlebred)
Place of origin: United States
Height at withers: 15–16 hands
Weight: 1,340–1,190 lb (450–540 kg
Structure: meso-dolichomorphic
Colour: bay—black—chestnut—grey—roan (rare); white markings frequent
Temperament: docile but energetic
Aptitude: saddle—light draught
Qualities: strong with good endurance
Head: small—profile straight or slightly ewe-like—ears pointed—eyes large and expressive—nostrils wide
Neck: long and arched—muscular
Body: withers prominent—back straight and quite long—croup horizontal—tail well set-on and carried erect due to nicking of the muscles or nerves (myotomy or neurotomy)—chest broad and deep
Legs: long and slender—muscular—shoulder long and sloping, muscular—good skeletal development—good joints—tendons clearly defined—pasterns long and sloping—hoof small and strong with heels open—front legs thrown forwards, back legs straight on hocks

TENNESSEE WALKING HORSE

There are more than three thousand members in the Stud Book for this breed, which was registered only in 1935. The foundation sire was the stallion Black Allan (1886) of Morgan and Hambletonian blood. Through the descendants of his son, Roan Allan, this stallion gave rise to a progeny which was later strongly influenced by the English Thoroughbred, American Trotting Horse and American Saddle Horse, as well as Canadian and American pacers such as the Narragansett of Rhode Island. The Tennessee Walking Horse is characterized by a peculiar four-beat "running walk" which is very comfortable for the rider. The movements of this gait are so long and rhythmic that the imprint of the hind feet extends beyond that of the forefeet. This horse has a docile, friendly nature, which makes it ideal as a leisure horse, especially for beginners and elderly riders. It has a smooth, easy gallop, which is why it was originally used by the owners of cotton plantations who spent many hours each day in the saddle: hence the alternative name of Plantation Walking Horse. It is perhaps the only horse for which a saying, sounding like an advertising slogan has been invented: "Ride one today and tomorrow you won't be able to do without it." It is typically a strong and solidly-built horse with good conformation.

Paso Fino

Native Mexican

Tennessee Walking Horse

Breed: Tennessee Walking Horse (Tennessee Walker)
Place of origin: United States
Height at withers: 15–16 hands
Structure: mesomorphic
Colour: black—chestnut—bay—brown—roan—grey
Temperament: steady and docile—lively
Aptitude: saddle horse
Qualities: impressive, comfortable gait
Head: rather large—profile straight—ears pointed—eyes gentle—nostrils wide
Neck: arched and muscular—broad-based
Body: withers fairly pronounced but not prominent—back straight, quite short and strong—loins powerful—croup muscular and tending to be horizontal—tail set-on high and held erect due to nicking—chest wide and muscular
Legs: sturdy and muscular—shoulder long, muscular and sloping—well-developed skeleton and good joints—tendons clearly defined—hoof strong and in proportion

PASO FINO

This is a descendant of the Spanish horses taken to American by the *conquistadores* in the sixteenth century, the difference in build between it and its ancestors being the result of adaptation to its new environment. It is characterized by three natural, lateral, four-beat gaits: the *paso fino*, which is the slowest, the *paso corto*, which is the smoothest and most sustained, suitable for travelling long distances, and the *paso largo*, which is the quickest. The Paso Fino horse is bred in Puerto Rico, Colombia and Peru. Certain differences do exist between the horses from these three countries, but these are becoming less marked in the American Paso Fino reared in the United States. It is a compact horse with powerful hindquarters.

Breed: Paso Fino
Place of origin: Caribbean and Equatorial South America
Height at withers: 14–15 hands
Structure: mesomorphic
Colour: all varieties
Temperament: lively but steady
Aptitude: saddle horse
Qualities: strong and willing
Head: correctly proportioned—profile straight or snub—ears small and pointed—eyes lively—nostrils wide
Neck: well formed—strong and muscular
Body: withers quite pronounced—back short and straight—loins strong—croup rounded—tail well set-on—chest wide and deep
Legs: strong and well-built—shoulder correctly sloping—cannons short—hoof strong

NATIVE MEXICAN

Like the other South American breeds, this horse originated from animals introduced by the *conquistadores* in the sixteenth century, which reverted to the wild and were later recaptured after having bred freely without interference from man. They are thus predominantly Andalusian, with some Arab and Criollo blood.

Breed: Native Mexican
Place of origin: Mexico
Height at withers: approx. 15 hands
Structure: mesomorphic
Colour: all colours
Temperament: lively—tenacious—intelligent
Aptitude: saddle horse
Qualities: agile and versatile

BREEDS THAT HAVE REVERTED TO THE WILD

Some horses have, for various reasons, escaped from human control, resulting in those breeds which are generally regarded as being wild or semi-wild, but which are more accurately described as having "reverted" to the wild. There are not many of them, and they all developed in comparatively recent times in areas that were favourable both for their vast expanse and for their ecological system which allowed these horses to find their own biological "niche" without unduly upsetting the delicate equilibrium that exists between all living creatures. If not subjected to outside interference (above all by man) this ecological system permits a balanced exploitation of natural resources and harmonious development of all elements of that system. Obviously, however, even the formation of these newly-wild breeds can be traced back to man, and his custom of taking his domestic animals with him to the countries he conquered. It is not coincidence that they are found in North America, from which the horse had disappeared about 10,000 years ago, and in Australia, where it had never existed. When a new arrival invades an area of land which already supports numerous forms of life, a new ecological balance has to be established. If this does not happen, the environment will inevitably deteriorate, given that the complex relationships between the different animal species will be altered, both in relation to each other and to the other multiple environmental factors which allow the energy necessary to life to be distributed among them in the most economical manner. This is expressed in terms of two fundamental conditions: first, the vegetation of the earth's surface must not be destroyed by an excessive number of consumers; secondly, the ratio of prey to predators must remain balanced. Then, the situation varies according to whether the establishment of a new species takes place in wild territory or in areas which are at least partially cultivated. The Australian Brumby is an important case in point. It reverted to the wild when large numbers of horses were abandoned during the Gold Rush in the second half of the nineteenth century. Australia is one of the most uniform parts of the world in terms of its physical features and there are in fact no natural boundaries to act as obstacles to the spread of animals, and her fauna mainly consists of small herbivores. The largest animal is of course the kangaroo. The only carnivore lives in Tasmania. This is the thylacine, also known as the Tasmanian wolf, owing to a certain resemblance to that animal, although it is in fact a marsupial which has developed the dentition typical of carnivores. An environment such as the one described is thus ideal for a large herbivore like the horse: the natural features of the land, the absence of predators and the existence of vegetation, above all in the cultivated areas, enabled the Brumby to readapt extremely well to life in the wild and multiply in an uncontrolled fashion, to the point of posing a serious problem for the Australians, who on a number of occasions have been forced to trap and kill it. But this is not the only case of ecological disturbance in Australia as a result of the thoughtless introduction of animals not included in the local fauna. The destruction caused to crops by escaped rabbits and subsequently to the fauna by the foxes, which were introduced to Australia in an effort to control them, are all too familiar. The foxes, in fact, found it more convenient to hunt the wombat and other small indigenous marsupials which were slower and easier to catch than rabbits, to the extent that these animals risked extinction. In

Wyoming, on the other hand, wild horses have not created such serious problems, as they established themselves in a more balanced environment which was inhabited not just by small herbivores and predators, but by large, fleet-footed herds of bighorn sheep and elks, while the northeastern regions of Yellowstone Park were grazed by herds of American bison up until the final decades of the nineteenth century. All these animals were capable of actively competing with the new arrivals for use of the pastures, and the result was a reciprocal control of the numbers of the various herds; furthermore, the geographical situation of the territory, enclosed between mountain ranges, prevented these horses from spreading into the great central plains and damaging the crops. Similarly, the Mustang, which takes its name from the Spanish word *mesteño* (wild), was restricted to the west coast, particularly California and Mexico, unable to expand eastwards because of the Rocky Mountains. All the breeds which have reverted to the wild are tough, strong, fast, resistant to the elements and capable of feeding themselves on a few blades of grass when times are hard. In physical appearance, they have "gone backwards in time," as they have, to some extent at least, regained their former characteristics, with a progressive loss of the modifications induced by man by artificial selection. To human eyes, these horses "lack beauty," but the concept of beauty is, as we all know, highly subjective and changeable. Furthermore, when applied to members of species other than our own, it is very often confused with those of utility and expedience, without regard for whether or not our aesthetic ideal conflicts with the biological needs of the animal concerned. The colours of the coats of wild horses are not clearly defined and can vary a great deal; simple, compound and part coloured varieties are common, and "primitive" colours (such as dun and palomino) which are so difficult to produce on stud farms, are frequently to be found. These horses live in small communities of between five and six to about 30 individuals, led by a stallion which will not tolerate the presence of other males capable of copulating. When the young colts reach sexual maturity, they are expelled from the herd and forced to live at some distance from it, except for the occasional attempt to re-enter it or win a female. When the leader grows old or falls ill, furious battles break out between the young stallions to assume control of the herd; the strongest will prevail, and it will be the characteristics of this horse that are transmitted to his numerous progeny.

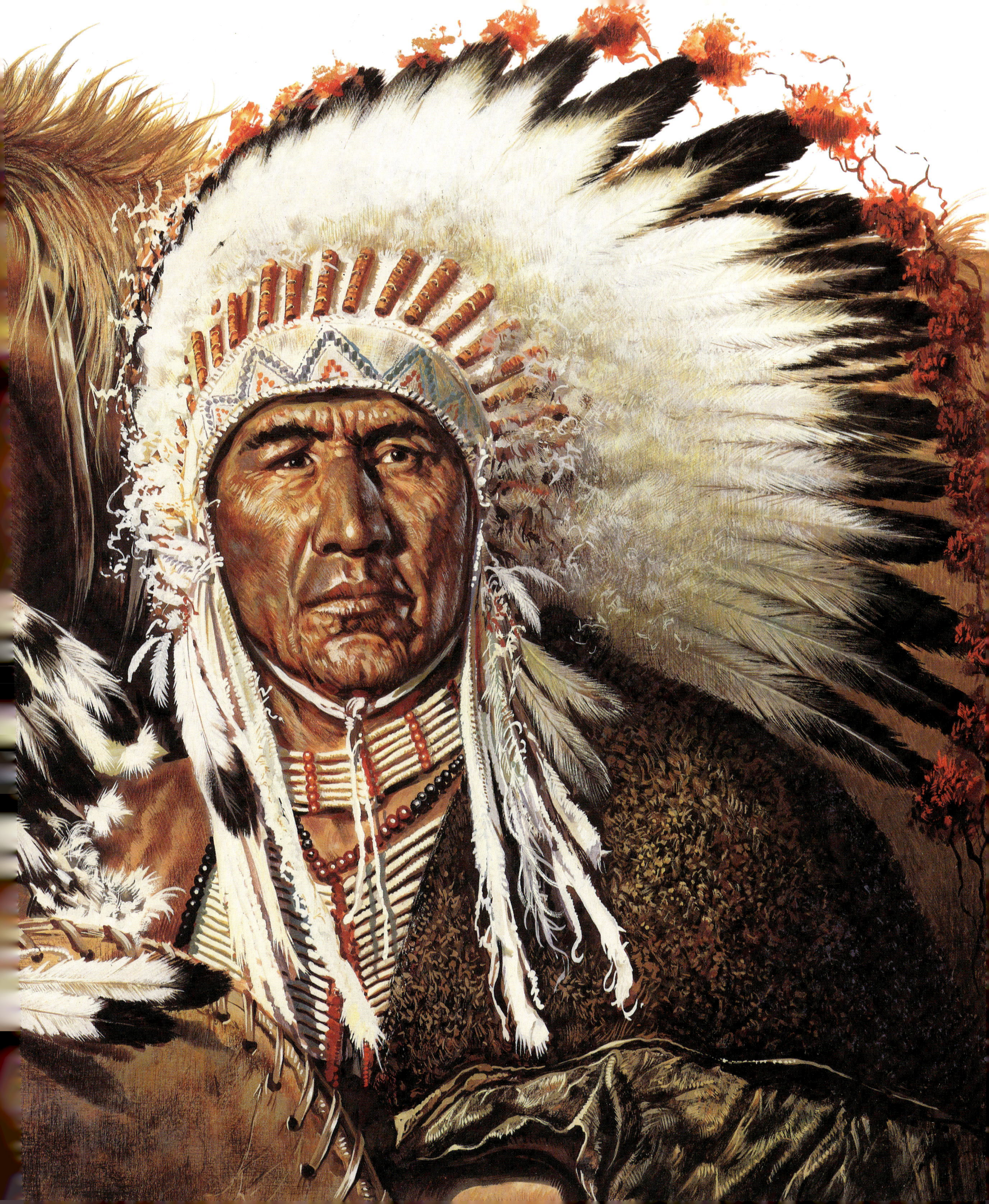

MUSTANG

The Mustang is the most typical example of a horse that has reverted to the wild. It used to live in herds along the coasts of California and Mexico, but now its numbers have been greatly reduced by merciless hunting. Of the more than two million animals in existence at the beginning of the twentieth century, only a few thousand are left, enclosed in ranches, and in fact they have been subject to registration and control since 1957. The Mustang originated from horses brought over to the American continent by the Spanish *conquistadores*; some of these animals managed to escape while others were captured by the Indians, subsequently regaining their freedom. As a result, herds of animals were formed which reproduced according to the laws of natural selection, or the survival, of the fittest. The Mustang is not an attractive-looking animal and also shows considerable deformity within its own type, but it has extraordinary resistance and is characterized by sturdy limbs and strong feet. Physically, these horses have regressed, as is clearly shown by the reappearance of the primitive dun colours. The rebellious nature of the Mustang is exhibited to great effect in the rodeo.

Breed: Mustang (Spanish Mustang)
Place of origin: United States
Height at withers: 14–15 hands
Structure: mesomorphic
Colour: very varied, often dun, palomino or mouse-coloured
Temperament: courageous but independent and intractable
Aptitude: saddle horse
Qualities: strong and resistant

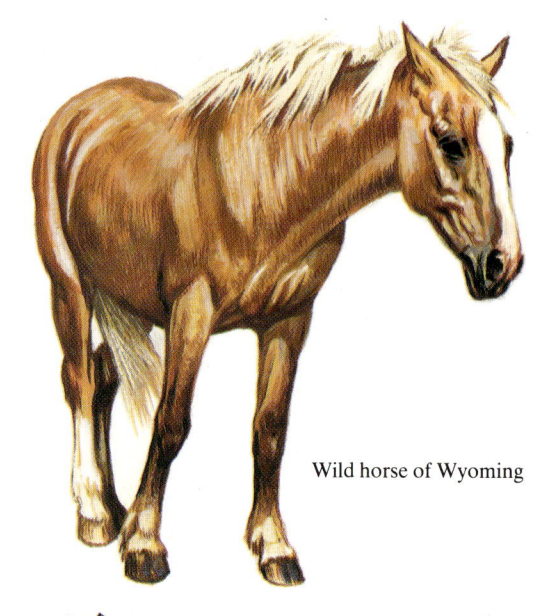

Wild horse of Wyoming

Brumby

Mustang

WILD HORSE OF WYOMING

This horse, which is established in the Wyoming Desert, is also erroneously called wild, whereas it is really a breed that has reverted to the wild. Its origins are quite similar to those of the Mustang, and it descends from horses imported first by Cortez and later by European colonists who came to settle in America. The original stock thus consisted of Spanish, Arab, Berber and Turkmene horses. The wild horses of Wyoming have been systematically captured in large numbers, thus contributing to the formation of other American breeds, such as the Pinto and the Palomino.

Breed: Wild horse of Wyoming
Place of origin: United States (Wyoming Desert)
Height at withers: 15–16 hands
Structure: mesomorphic
Colour: very varied, mainly palomino
Temperament: independent
Aptitude: life in the wild
Qualities: resistance

BRUMBY

The Brumby developed around the middle of the nineteenth century when large numbers of horses were abandoned in Australia during the gold rush. These eventually formed herds and reproduced prolifically over wide areas. As in the case of many other breeds which have reverted to the wild, whilst freedom hardened them to all types of physical adversity and heightened their cunning and instinct for survival, it also caused their appearance to degenerate considerably. These horses multiplied to such an extent that a number of them had to be culled, but their cunning meant that such an operation was no easy task, and eventually motor vehicles and even light aircraft had to be used. As a result of this merciless and indiscriminate killing since 1962 the numbers of the Brumby have been so greatly reduced as to make total extinction a distinct possibility.

Breed: Brumby
Place of origin: Australia
Height at withers: very varied—even in excess of 15 hands
Structure: mesomorphic
Colour: very varied
Temperament: wild and intractable
Aptitude: life in the wild state
Qualities: hardy and resistant

SELECT BIBLIOGRAPHY

Bongianni, M. *Guida al Cavallo*, Milan, 1978
   I Grandi Cavalli, Milan, 1983; *Great Horses*, London, 1984; *Champion Horses*, New York, 1984

Dossenbach, M. and H. *The Noble Horse*, Exeter, 1983

Edwards, E. H., and Geddes, C. *The Complete Book of the Horse*, New York, 1974

Foster, C. *The Complete Book of the Horse*, London, 1983

Glyn, R. *The World's Finest Horses and Ponies*, London, 1971

Goodall, D. M. *Horses of the World – An illustrated survey of breeds of horses and ponies*, Newton Abbott, 1973

Goody, P. C. *Horse Anatomy*, London, 1976

Hope, C. E. G., and Jackson, G. N. *The Encyclopedia of the Horse*, London, 1973

Kays, J. M. *The Horse*, New York, 1969

Kidd, J., *et al*. *The Complete Horse Encyclopedia*, London, 1976

Phifer, K. G. *Track Talk*, New York, 1978

Reddick, K. *Horses*, Toronto and New York, 1976

Silver, C. *Guide to the Horses of the World*, Oxford, 1976

Whitlock, R. *Gentle Giants*, Guildford, 1976

INDEX

(Numbers in italic refer to illustrations)

A

Adaev *see* Kazakh
African breeds 39
agriculture, horses in 67, 70–71
    draught work 72, 77
Akhal-Teké 38, 112, 144–5, *144–5*, 181
Albino 38, 188, *188*
Altér Real 38, 71, 139, *139*
American Belgian Horse 79
American Saddle Horse 14, 34, 38, 184, 189, *189*
American Shetland 92, 118, *118*
American Standardbred 36, 38, 64, 126, 128, 129, 130–31, *130–31*, 132
American Trotter 64
American Welsh pony 117, *117*
Andalusian 37, *37*, 39, 42, 43–4, *43–4*, 45, 60, 62, 178, 182, 190
    and draught horse breeds 70, 71, 85
    in classical equitation 138, 139
    and dressage 142
    in show jumping breeds 158, 164
Anglo-Arab 37, 61, 106, 146, 160, 163, 165, 167
Anglo-Norman 37, 44, 61, 139, 174, 177, 178
    and draught horse breeds 72, 88
    in show jumping 158, 160, *160*, 163
Appaloosa 34, 92, 118, 186, *186*
Arab 23, 34, 36, 37–41, *40–41*, 42, 43, 60, 176–81, 184, 188, 190
    and draught horse breeds 72, 73, 74, 75, 76
    and pony breeds 92, 96, 100–102, 104, 107, 111–13, 115–19
    and classical equitation 138, 139
    in show jumping breeds 159, 160, 164, 165 167
    in circus acts 174
Aragonese horse 38
Archaeohippus 31, 90
Ardennais 36, *36*, 38, 52
    and draught horse breeds 68, 79, 80, 81, *81*, 84, 85, 86
Ardennes 72, 112
Ariègeois (Merens) 92, 104, *104*, 108
Asian breeds 38
Asiatic Wild Horse 33, *33*
Assateague 38, 92, 118, *118*
Asturçon *see* Asturian pony
Asturian pony 92, 107, *107*
Australian breeds 39
Australian pony 39, 119, *119*
Australian Stock Horse 39
Austrian breeds 36
Auxois 84, *84*
Avelignese *37*, 108, *108*

B

Bali 38, 91, 92, 115, *115*
Barb (Berber) 36, 39, 41, 42, *42*, 43
    and draught horse breeds 70, 71, 74
    and pony breeds 92, 102, 116, 117
Bardi horse *see* Bardigiano
Bardigiano (Bardi horse) 37, 108, *108*
Barthais *see* Landais
Bashkir (Bashkirsky) 112, *112*
Basque pony (Pottock) 92, 106, *106*
Basuto 39, 92, 116, *116*
Batak 38, 92, 115, 116, *116*
Beberbeck 176, *176*
behaviour, horse 20–22
    vices 22
Belgian Ardennes 35, 79, 80, 81, 88, 89
Belgian Heavy Draught Horse (Brabant), 35, 68, 78, 79, *79*, 80, 81, 85, 88
Belgium, horse breeds in 35
Berber *see* Barb
Berichon 83
Bhutia 91, 92, 113, 114, *114*
body, horse
    qualities 11
    defects 11
Bosnian 37, 92, 109, *109*
Boulonnais 36, 38, 52, 65
    and draught horse breeds 82, *82*, 84, 85, 86
Brabant *see* Belgian Heavy Draught Horse
breed formation 34
Breton 36, 38, 65, 86
Brumby 39, 70, 191, 194, *194*
Budyonny 38, 112, 166, *166*
Bulgarian breeds 36–7
Burguete 38
Burgundian Heavy Horse 84
Burmese 92, 114, *114*

C

Caballo Chileno 71
Calabrese 182–3, *183*
Camargue 36, 102, *102*
Campolino 71
Canadian Cutting Horse 70, 71, *71*
Cape Horse 116
carriages 56–9, *58–9*
Carthusian 182, *182*
Caspian 38, 92, 117, *117*
Catalan 38
Catria 71
Cerdaña 38
Cheval de Corlay 52
Chincoteague 38, 92, 118
Chinese 92, 115, *115*
Chola 71
circus horses 173–4
classical equitation 136–7
    French school 137
    German school 137
    Spanish school of Vienna 137
Cleveland Bay 35, 57, 61, 65, 162, 170
    and draught horse breeds 73, *73*, 77, 88
clipping 26
Clydesdale 34, 35, 63, *63*, 88
coats 23–7
    clipping 26
    markings 27
Comtois 84, *84*
Condroz *see* Medium Belgian
conformation, horse 9
Connemara 35, *35*, 77, 93, 102, *102*, 103, 176
Corlay *see* Cheval de Corlay
Corsican pony 92
Costeño (Peruvian Paso, Peruvian Stepping Horse) 71
Cremonese 79
Criollo 38, *38*, 44, 70–71, *70*, 171
Crioulo 71
Czechoslovakian breeds 36–7

D

Dales 35, 69, 92, 96, 97, *97*, 104, 108
Dalmatian 37, 92
Danubian 37, 178, *178*
Darashouri 179
Darbowsko-Tarnowski 166
Dartmoor 35, 92, 94, *95*, 96, 101
defects 10–11
Deliboz 112
Denmark, horse breeds in 35
Døle Gudbrandsdal 34, 68, 69, *69*, 76
Døle Trotter (Norwegian Trotter) 69
domestication, horse 31
Don 38, 74, 112, 133, 166, 167, 180, *180*, 181
Dongolo 39
Double Klepper *see* Toric
Draught Breton 52, *52*, 65
dressage 140–42, *141*
driving 56–7
Dülmen 92, 104, *104*
Dutch Draught 80, *80*
Dutch Saddle Horse 36
Dutch Warm-blood 158, *158*
Dzhabe *see* Kazakh

E

East Bulgarian 37, *37*, 146, *146*
East Friesian 60, 76, 177, *177*
Einsiedler 36, 163, *163*
English hunter 35
English Thoroughbred 34, 35, *35*, 36, 37, 38, 41, 42, 51, 60, 61, 64, 139, 170, 171, 176, 178, 180, 181, 182, 184, 185, 189, 190
    and draught horse breeding 69, 71, 72, 73, 76, 77, 86
    and pony breeding 91, 94, 98, 100, 101, 102, 112, 119

English Thoroughbred – *cont.*
  in racing 122, 124, *123–4*, 125, 128, 129, 130, 131, 132
  in dressage 142, 146
  and three-day event 148, 150
  and show jumping 152, 158, 159, 160, 162, 164, 165; 166, 167
Eohippus 30, *31*
Epihippus 30
Equus africanus 31
Equus (caballus) gmelini 31, 32, *32*, 91, 94, 105, 109
Equus (caballus) przewalskii (Przewalski's horse) 31, 33, 38, 39, 90, 105
Equus (caballas) sequanus 83
Equus hemionus 31
Equus onager 31
Equus zebra 31
Estonian Klepper *see* Toric
evolution of horse, 30
Exmoor 35, 92, 94, 96, 98, *98*, 101, 119

F

Falabella 38, 92, 119, *119*
Fell 35, 92, 96, *96*, 97
Finland, horse breeds in 35
Finnish Draught 35, 72
Finnish horse 35, *35*, 72, *72*, 89
Finnish Universal 35, 72, 89
Fjord (Westlands pony) 34, *34*, 92, 93, *93*, 102
Flanders horse *see* Belgian Heavy Draught Horse
flat racing 121–2
Flemish 63, 82
forestry, horses used in 67
fox hunting 168–9, *168–9*
France, horse breeds in 36
Franches-Montagnes (Freiberger) 36, *36*, 57, 71, 72, *72*
Frederiksborg 35, 44, 60, *60*, 138
Freiberger 36
French Anglo-Arab 36, 159, *159*
French Ardennais 35, 79
French Saddle Horse *see* Selle Français
French Saddle Pony 103, *103*
French Trotter (Demi-Sang) 36, 64, 126, 128–9, *128*, 130, 131, 132, 160
Friesian 35, *36*, 39, 44, 45, *45*, 60, 61, 63, 96, 132, 142
Furioso-North Star 37, *37*, 150, *150–51*, 166

G

gaits 14
Galiceño 38, *38*, 107, 119, *119*
Galician and Asturian pony 92, 107, *107*
Galloway 96
Garrano (Minho) 92, 107, *107*, 119
Garron *see* Highland
Gayoe *see* Batak
Gelderland 35, *35*, 36, 60, 158, *158*
genetics 39
Germany, horse breeds in 36
Gidran Arabian 37, 165, *165*, 166, 178
Gotland (Skogsruss pony) 34, 92, 94, *94*
Grand Breton 52, *52*
Great Britain, horse breeds in 35
Great Horse 35, 51, 78
Greece, horse breeds in 36–7
Groningen 36, 60, *60*, 158
Gros Trait Nivernais 83
Guajira 71

H

hack 101
Hackney 34, 35, 44, 45, 64, *64*, 65, 76, 128, 176, 189
  and pony breeds 96, 100
  and show jumping 158, 163
Hackney pony 91, 92, 96, *96*, 100, 118
Haflinger *see* Avelignese
Hailar *see* Mongolian
Hanoverian 36, *36*, 61, 76, 104, 139, 142, 148–9, *149*, 162, 166, 177, 178
Harddraver *see* Friesian
harness 67
head, horse 10
Heilung Chiang *see* Mongolian
herding 70
Highland 34, 35, 92, 93, 96, 99, *99*, 102
Hipparion 90
Hispano (Spanish Anglo-Arab) 38, 61, 163, *163*
Hokkaido 92
Holland, horse breeds in 35–6
Holstein 36, 44, 160, 162, *162*
horse show 175
Hucul 37, *37*, 94, 109, 111, *111*
Hungary, horse breeds in 36–7

I

Iceland horse breeds in 34
Icelandic pony 34, *34*, 90, 91, 92, 93, *93*, 94
Ili *see* Mongolian
Iomud 76, 112, 180, *180*, 181
Ireland, horse breeds in 35
Irish cob 35, 176, *176*
Irish Draught 35, 77, *77*, 170, 176
Irish Hunter 35, *35*, 77, 170, *170*
Italian Heavy Draught 79, 86, *86*
Italy, horse breeds in 37

J

Jaf 179
Java 38, 92, 116, *116*
jennets 44, 91, 92
jousts 50
Jutland 35, 77, *77*

K

Kabardin 38, 75, *75*, 167
Karabair 38, 74, *74*, 76, 112
Karabakh 38, 75, *75*, 112
Karacabey 180, *180*
Kathiawari 38, 92, 113, *113*
Kazakh 38, 92, 112, *112*
Kirghiz 38
Kladruber 37, *37*, 44, 62, *62*, 138, 178
Klepper 111
Knabstrup 60
Konik 37, 94, 111, *111*
Kustanair 38, 181, *181*

L

Landais (Barthais) 92, 104, *104*
Latvian 38, 76, *76*
Latvian Harness Horse 89
Latvian Riding Horse 76
Limousin 36, 159

Lipizzaner 36, *36*, 44, 60, 62, 74, 138, *138*, 139, 174
Lithuanian Heavy Draught 38, 89, *89*
Llanero 71
Lokai 38, 76, *76*
Lusitano *37*, 38, 182, *182*

M

Malagasy 39, 92
Malapolski 37, 166, *166*
Mangalarga 71
Manipuri 38, 91, 92, 113, *113*, 114, 171
Maremmana 37, 71, *71*, 183
Maremmana-Tolfetano 71
Maréyeur *see* Petit Boulonnais
Marwari 38, 92, 113
Masuren 160
Mecklenburg 36, 82, 162, *162*
Medium Belgian (Condroz) 35, *35*, 79
Merens *see* Ariègeois
Merychippus 30, *31*
Mesohippus 30, *31*
Métis 38, 132, *132*
military parade 175
Miohippus 30, *31*
Minho *see* Garrano
Missouri Fox Trotting Horse 14, 188, *188*
Mongolia, horse breeds in 33
Mongolian pony 38, *38*, 91, 92, 94, 112, 114, *114*, 115
Monterufolino Horse 71
Morgan 34, 38, *38*, 184, *184*, 188, 189, 190
Morochuco 71
Mulassier *see* Poitevin
Murakoz 37, 89, *89*
Murgese 37, 74, *74*
Mustang 173, 192, 194, *194*

N

Nanfan *see* Tibetan
Native Mexican Horse 190, *190*
Neapolitan 60, 61, 62, 85, 138, 162, 165
New Forest 35, 92, 96, *96*, 103
New Zealand, horse breeds in 39
Niedersachsen Heavy Draught 80
Nigerian Horse 117, *117*
Nonius 37, 150, 166, 178, *178*, 180, 183
Norfolk-Breton 86
Norfolk Cob 51
Norfolk Roadster 64, 76, 150, 158
Norfolk Trotter 51, 65, 69, 128, 130
Noriker 36, 85, *85*, 89
Norman (Selle Français) 36, 44, 61, 72, 88, 139, 160, *160*, 163, 174, 177, 178
North-Hestur *see* North Swedish Trotter
North Swedish Horse 65, 68, *68*, 69, 76
North Swedish Trotter (North-Hestur) 34, 68
Northlands 92, 94, *94*
Norway, horse breeds in 34
Norwegian Døle pony 34
Norwegian Fjord Pony (Westland pony, Swedish Ardennes, North Swedish) 34, *34*, 92, 93, *93*, 102
Norwegian Trotter *see* Døle Trotter
Novokirghiz 181, *181*

O

Oberlander 85
Old Norfolk Horse 82

197

Oldenburg 36, 44, 60, 61, *61*, 148, 158, 177
Orlov 38, *38*, 44, 60, 112, 128, 180, 181
    and draught horse breeds 76, 88
    and racing 131, 132, *132*
Orohippus 30

P

Palio (horse race) 50
Palomino 34, 39, 173, 186–7, *186–7*
Parahippus 30
Paso Fino 38, 190, *190*
Peneia 37, *37*, 92, 110, *110*
Percheron 36, 38, 52, 57, 65
    and draught horse breeds 83, *83*, 84, 86, 87, 88, 89
Percheron Postier 83
Persian Arab 38, 41, 75, 112, 179, *179*
Peruvian Paso *see* Costeño
Peruvian Stepping Horse *see* Costeño
Petit Boulonnais (Small Boulonnais) 82
Phenacodus 30
Pindos 37, 91, 92, 110, *110*
Pinto 38, 185, *185*
Pinzgauer 36, 85
Pleven 37, 165, *165*
Pliohippus 30
Poitevin 57, 83, *83*
Poland, horse breeds in 32, 36–7
polo 171
pony express 92
Pony of the Americas 38, 92, 118, *118*
Portugal, horse breeds in 37–8
Postier-Breton 52, 65, *65*
Pottock *see* Basque
Przewalski's horse 31, 33, 38, 39, 90, 105
psychology, horse 20–22

Q

Quarter Horse 38, 118, 172–3, 185
    and draught horse breeds 70, 71
    in racing 122, 125, *125*

R

Rhineland (Rhenish) 36
Rhineland Heavy Draught 80, *80*
riding holidays 175
Riding Pony 101, *101*, 103
riding school 175
rodeo 172–3, *172–3*
Rottaler 61
Russian Ardennes 81
Russian Heavy Draught 38, 88, *88*
Russian Trotter 112

S

Sable Island 92, 117, *117*
Sadecki 166
Salerno (Persano) 37, 165, *165*
Salteno 71
San Fratello 37, 183, *183*
Sandalwood 38, 92, 115, *115*
Sanho *see* Mongolian
Sanpeitze *see* Mongolian
Sardinian 109, *109*
Sardinian Anglo-Arab 164, *164*
Schleswig 36, 77, 80, *80*
Schleswig Heavy Draught 80, *80*
Selle Français (French Saddle Horse) 36, 44, 61, 139, 174, 177, 178
    and draught horse breeds 72, 88
    in show jumping 158, 160, *160*, 163
Senner 92, 104
senses, horse 18–20
Shagya Arabian 37, 177, *177*
Shetland 34, 35, 92, 93, 94, 99, *99*, 119
Shire 34, 35, 57, 63, 78, *78*, 88
shoeing 15–16
show jumping 152–7, *152–7*
Sicilian (Siciliano) 37, 183, *183*
Skogsruss pony *see* Gotland
Skyros 37, 91, 92, 110, *110*, 115
Sokolsky 37, 88, *88*
Sorraia 91, 92, 105, *105*
South German Cold Blood *see* Noriker
Soviet Heavy Draught 38, 87, *87*
Soviet Union, horse breeds in 38
Spain, horse breeds in 37–8
Spanish Anglo-Arab (Hispano) 38, 61, 163, *163*
Spiti 38, 91, 92, 113, *113*, 114
stagecoach 65
stance 10
Standardbred 34, 36, 38, 64
    in racing 126, 128, 129, 130–31, *130–31*, 132
Suffolk Punch 34, 35, 51, *51*, 57, 170, 177
    and draught horse breeds 77, 80, 88
Sumba 38, 92, 116, *116*
Sumbawa 38, 92, 116
Sweden, horse breeds in 34
Swedish Ardennes 65, 68, *68*, 81, 88, 89
Swedish Warm Blood 34, 142, *142–3*
Switzerland, horse breeds in 36
Syrian 38, 180, *180*

T

Tarbes 36, 106, 159
Tarpan 31, 32, *32*, 91, 94, 105, 109
Tchenarani 179
teeth 16–17
Tennessee Walking Horse 38, 67, 190, *190*
Tersky 38, 75, 167, *167*
Thoroughbred *see* English Thoroughbred
three-day event 146–8, *147*
Tibetan (Nanfan) 38, 91, 92, 113, *113*, 114
Timor 38, 92, 115, *115*, 116, 119
Toric 76, *76*
tourneys 50
Trait Augeron 83
Trait de la Loire 83
Trait du Maine 83
Trait du Nord 85, *85*
Trait du Saône-et-Loire 83
Trakehner (East Prussian) 36, 76, 142, 148, 177, 178
    in show jumping 160–61, *160–61*, 162, 166
transport, horses used in 55–6
trotting races 126
Turkish 109, *109*
Turkmene 38, 75, 112, 144, 180, 181, *181*
Turkoman *see* Turkmene

U

Ukrainian Riding Horse 166, *166*
United States of America, horse breeds in 38

V

Viatka 38, 92, 111, *111*
vices, horse 22
Vladimir Heavy Draught 38, 88, *88*

W

Waler 39, 167, *167*
war, horses and 46–50
Welsh Cob 97, 176, *176*, 184
Welsh Mountain pony 35, 92, 100, *100*, 119, 176
Welsh pony 34, 35, 91, 92, 96, 100, *100*, 101, 103, 104
Welsh pony of the Cob type 100, *100*
Westlands pony *see* Fjord
Wielkopolski 37, 166, 178, *178*
Wild horse of Wyoming 192, 194, *194*
Working hunter 101
Wuchumutsin *see* Mongolian
Württemberg 36, 177, *177*

Y

Yorkshire Coach horse 35, 73
Yugoslavia, horse breeds in 36–7

Z

Zemaituka 38, 89, 92, 112, *112*